Entrepreneurship Education in Tourism and Hospitality Management

Satish Chandra Bagri
Hemvati Nandan Bahuguna Garhwal University, India

R.K. Dhodi
Hemvati Nandan Bahuguna Garhwal University, India

K.C. Junaid
Hemvati Nandan Bahuguna Garhwal University, India

A volume in the Advances in Hospitality, Tourism, and the Services Industry (AHTSI) Book Series

Published in the United States of America by
IGI Global
Business Science Reference (an imprint of IGI Global)
701 E. Chocolate Avenue
Hershey PA, USA 17033
Tel: 717-533-8845
Fax: 717-533-8661
E-mail: cust@igi-global.com
Web site: http://www.igi-global.com

Library of Congress Cataloging-in-Publication Data

Names: Bagri, S. C., editor. | Dhodi, Rakesh Kumar, 1971- editor. | Junaid, K. C., 1992- editor.
Title: Entrepreneurship education in tourism and hospitality management / Satish Chandra Bagri, Rakesh Kumar Dhodi, and K.C. Junaid, editors.
Description: Hershey, PA : Business Science Reference, 2022. | Includes bibliographical references and index. | Summary: "This focus of this book is to highlight various cases of entrepreneurship education in tourism and hospitality across the World and to discuss and analyze the utility of tourism and hospitality entrepreneurship education due to the new digital revolution and global pandemic"-- Provided by publisher.
Identifiers: LCCN 2021059288 (print) | LCCN 2021059289 (ebook) | ISBN 9781799895107 (hardcover) | ISBN 9781799895114 (paperback) | ISBN 9781799895121 (ebook)
Subjects: LCSH: Entrepreneurship--Study and teaching. | Hospitality industry--Study and teaching. | Tourism--Study and teaching.
Classification: LCC HB615 .E634627 2022 (print) | LCC HB615 (ebook) | DDC 338.04--dc23/eng/20220127
LC record available at https://lccn.loc.gov/2021059288
LC ebook record available at https://lccn.loc.gov/2021059289

This book is published in the IGI Global book series Advances in Hospitality, Tourism, and the Services Industry (AHTSI) (ISSN: 2475-6547; eISSN: 2475-6555)

British Cataloguing in Publication Data
A Cataloguing in Publication record for this book is available from the British Library.

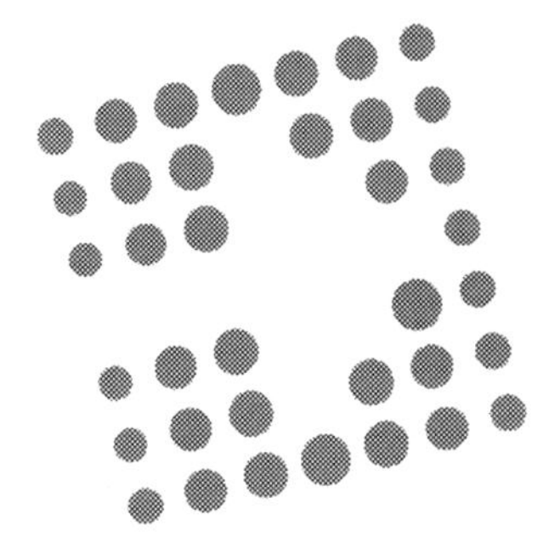

Advances in Hospitality, Tourism, and the Services Industry (AHTSI) Book Series

Maximiliano Korstanje
University of Palermo, Argentina

ISSN:2475-6547
EISSN:2475-6555

MISSION

Globally, the hospitality, travel, tourism, and services industries generate a significant percentage of revenue and represent a large portion of the business world. Even in tough economic times, these industries thrive as individuals continue to spend on leisure and recreation activities as well as services.

The Advances in Hospitality, Tourism, and the Services Industry (AHTSI) book series offers diverse publications relating to the management, promotion, and profitability of the leisure, recreation, and services industries. Highlighting current research pertaining to various topics within the realm of hospitality, travel, tourism, and services management, the titles found within the AHTSI book series are pertinent to the research and professional needs of managers, business practitioners, researchers, and upper-level students studying in the field.

COVERAGE

- Customer Service Issues
- Leisure & Business Travel
- Service Training
- Casino Management
- Service Design
- Tourism and the Environment
- International Tourism
- Hotel Management
- Cruise Marketing and Sales
- Travel Agency Management

IGI Global is currently accepting manuscripts for publication within this series. To submit a proposal for a volume in this series, please contact our Acquisition Editors at Acquisitions@igi-global.com or visit: http://www.igi-global.com/publish/.

The Advances in Hospitality, Tourism, and the Services Industry (AHTSI) Book Series (ISSN 2475-6547) is published by IGI Global, 701 E. Chocolate Avenue, Hershey, PA 17033-1240, USA, www.igi-global.com. This series is composed of titles available for purchase individually; each title is edited to be contextually exclusive from any other title within the series. For pricing and ordering information please visit http://www.igi-global.com/book-series/advances-hospitality-tourism-services-industry/121014. Postmaster: Send all address changes to above address.

Titles in this Series

For a list of additional titles in this series, please visit: http://www.igi-global.com/book-series/

Handbook of Research on Urban Tourism, Viral Society, and the Impact of the COVID-19 Pandemic
Pedro Andrade (University of Minho, Portugal) and Moisés de Lemos Martins (University of Minho, Portugal)
Business Science Reference • © 2022 • 430pp • H/C (ISBN: 9781668433690) • US $315.00

Employability and Skills Development in the Sports, Events, and Hospitality Industry
Vipin Nadda (University of Sunderland in London, UK) Wendy Sealy (University of Chichester, UK) and Emma Delaney (University of Surrey, UK)
Business Science Reference • © 2022 • 260pp • H/C (ISBN: 9781799877813) • US $215.00

Handbook of Research on Sustainable Tourism and Hotel Operations in Global Hypercompetition
Hakan Sezerel (Anadolu University, Turkey) and Bryan Christiansen (Global Research Society, LLC, USA)
Business Science Reference • © 2022 • 430pp • H/C (ISBN: 9781668446454) • US $315.00

Global Perspectives on Strategic Storytelling in Destination Marketing
Ana Cláudia Campos (CinTurs, Universidade do Algarve, Portugal) and Sofia Almeida (Faculty of Tourism and Hospitality, Universidade Europeia, Portugal)
Business Science Reference • © 2022 • 300pp • H/C (ISBN: 9781668434369) • US $240.00

Promoting Social and Cultural Equity in the Tourism Sector
Priscila Cembranel (Universidade Sociedade Educacional de Santa Catarina, Brazil) Jakson Renner Rodrigues Soares (Universidad da Coruña, Spain) and André Riani Costa Perinotto (Parnaíba Delta Federal University, Brazil)
Business Science Reference • © 2022 • 302pp • H/C (ISBN: 9781668441947) • US $240.00

Challenges and Opportunities for Transportation Services in the Post-COVID-19 Era
Giuseppe Catenazzo (ICN Business School, France)
Business Science Reference • © 2022 • 268pp • H/C (ISBN: 9781799888406) • US $250.00

701 East Chocolate Avenue, Hershey, PA 17033, USA
Tel: 717-533-8845 x100 • Fax: 717-533-8661
E-Mail: cust@igi-global.com • www.igi-global.com

Table of Contents

Detailed Table of Contents

Even though there is an increase in tourism research in India during the last 2-3 decades, researchers within the domain of tourism education made an insignificant contribution to entrepreneurship education (henceforth 'EE') programs. The objectives of this research are to study the current status of EE in tourism, to analyse and compare course title, core concepts, major references, and further readings. This study follows a content analysis design, focusing on an in-depth analysis of syllabi of post-graduation tourism programs in Indian higher educational institutions. The syllabi contents were analyzed using the Atlas.ti. The major findings of this study indicate that in India EE in tourism programs is mostly considered as one of the core modules itself than optional/elective modules and part of other courses. Almost all syllabi have included chapters on basic concepts of entrepreneurship, capital financing, business plan, opportunities, innovations, etc. This finding has major implications for designing innovative entrepreneurship courses in tourism programs.

The main aim of the chapter is to describe the professional training of future specialists in tourist and hotel and restaurant service in Ukraine. The object is the training of junior bachelors, bachelors, and masters of services. The subject of the chapter is the conditions of education of future specialists of tourist and hotel and restaurant service in Ukraine. A specialist in the tourism industry and hotel and restaurant business must provide services related to the activities of tourist complexes, restaurants, and hotels to carry out the primary level of management of structural units, operating systems, etc. The novelty of this chapter is to share experiences with colleagues from other countries. Activation of independent cognitive activity of future specialists with the help of project technologies, high level of competence of teachers of higher education institutions, their skill in the implementation of programs, and their harmonious combination in educational and extracurricular activities will contribute to the improvement of entrepreneurship in the field of tourism.

An entrepreneurship is a key factor for any country that aims to become competitive in the knowledge-based global market as it is viewed as a means of promoting economic growth, innovation, and creativity. This opinion has given rise to growing interest in establishing entrepreneurship educational programmes by several countries including Oman. The government of Oman has taken tourism as one of the main economic sectors to diversify its oil-based economy. This chapter focuses on the facilities provided by the government of Sultanate of Oman to encourage and motivate growth of new ventures with context to entrepreneurship education, how the government of Oman is monitoring and assessing its initiatives and strategies, planned and implemented to establish entrepreneurship education in tourism context. The chapter also proposed a conceptual framework on entrepreneurship education in tourism context which can be considered by the policy makers to measure the efficacy and efficiency of the entrepreneurship education strategies and policies.

The present case study brings reflection on the power of pleasure (joy) to better the classic education system. Whilst pleasure was overlooked as an instrument to make positive feedback in students for classic education, PANCOE (and the laboratory of pleasure) goes in the opposite direction. The laboratory of pleasure stimulates students´ skills and performance through the articulation of pleasurable experiences. The results notably show that those students who participated in PANCOE have better degrees than those who did not take part in the experiment. At the same time, the endorphins liberated by positive interactive communication paves the ways for the rise of pleasurable experiences which dispose from better academic performances. Originally PANCOE was designed to standardize the learning process of foreign students. The goal was chiefly oriented to retain the student reducing the academic desertion, which means the rate of students who fail to earn a degree.

Due to the tragic past of South Africa, associated with racial profiling and apartheid, the majority of South Africans who were Black were excluded by repressive policies from active participation in the economy. This led to Black South Africans being underrepresented in tourism. The growth of tourism had not benefited the majority of South Africans who happen to be Black. The lack of participation of the previously disadvantaged groups on the Airbnb platform did not resonate with the principles of Airbnb to achieve shared prosperity. In the Black-owned townships such as Khayelisha in Cape Town, Kayamandi in Stellenbosch, and Soweto in Johannesburg, there had been existing tourism businesses especially in accommodation. These guesthouses and homestays were not attracting enough customers to economically benefit the hosts and make these townships viable tourism destinations. The Airbnb Africa Academy was pioneered to train South African homestay and guesthouse owners to register and become successful hosts on the Airbnb platform.

Service quality is highly related to the quality of training given to the workers and stakeholders. As the requirements of skills are changing in every industry along with the global trends, initiatives like 'Skill India' missions have gone through many changes. This paper analyses the 'Skill India' mission particularly in hospitality and allied sectors. The authors have conducted a broader analysis and critical evaluation of various policies, schemes, initiatives, trends, future perspectives, and challenges in skill training in the hospitality sector. For this purpose, numerous studies, regional study findings, news articles, government reports, official publications, and in-depth interviews with experts have been conducted. The study highlights the existence of a skill gap, major constraints in skilling the youth, quality of skills trained, skilling marginalised, private-public partnership, entrepreneurship initiatives, eSkill opportunities after training, feedback systems, etc. In general, these results suggest that an intensive skill gap exists in many sectors and departments.

Technical and vocational education and training (TVET) is an important contributor to the sustainable economic development to achieve Sustainable Development Goals (SDGs) and Oman Vision 2040. TVET is expected to facilitate the insertion of young people and adults into the labor market and their career progression. The tourism and hospitality sector is a priority sector for a country's Tanfeedh plan for economic diversification. This chapter highlights the historical and existing practices in the Oman's TVET system that can be considered as enterprise-based learning that includes apprenticeship, OJT for students and workers of different ages. This chapter focusses on the practical attempts to incorporate work-based learning leading to identification of the strengths, weakness, and opportunities for all the people concerned. It highlights the present situation and future outlook of technical and vocational education and training in the tourism and hospitality sector in Oman.

Hospitality and tourism requires varying degrees of skills that allow for quick entry into the workforce and business for trainees. It is one of the most diversified industries in the world because of the wide number of different occupations and professions involved in it. With increasing change in both the domestic as well as the global market, technology and customer expectations of the industry itself, the requirements of the hospitality and tourism have also undergone significant transformation. With these ever increasing changes in the industry, graduates are expected to possess more than just specialized knowledge and skills, but also the capacity to be proactive and to see and to respond to problems creatively and autonomously. This chapter critically looks at the place of entrepreneurship education within the hospitality and tourism programs in Ethiopia and Kenya. It adopts a qualitative study by way of unstructured interviews and secondary data analysis. It concludes by proposing various strategies to achieve this, notably an outcome-based system and industry-based learning models.

Foreword

In the modern-day competitive world, the hospitality industry, like other service industries, is growing by leaps and bounds, and is faced with the challenges of ever-growing guest expectations and ever-changing demands. The industry, therefore, has to respond with quality and speed in order to meet these challenges if it has to grow and flourish. Hence, the industry offerings have to be distinct in nature – different from others – and, at the same time, authentic. The key lies in equipping those already in jobs and as well as new entrants with distinctive skills to meet the expectations and requirements of guests. The economic downturn due to the pandemic has forced the hospitality industry to re-visit its entire approach and strategy which has led to technological dependence to a considerable extent, adapt new and innovative ideas, and formulate integrated policies. And, it goes without saying that an all-inclusive and sustainable approach involving all stakeholders, is the need of the hour. In the post-pandemic scenario, travel habits and travel patterns have changed and so have destinations. The supply side, led by service industry, has to change itself so as to strike a fine balance between demand and supply, the latter of which has to be of the highest-possible quality. While many developed countries have taken immediate steps to adopt several new measures to revamp its hospitality industry, developing countries have yet to do so.

The book contains interesting chapters from a wide range of countries by eminent social scientists which provide deep insights on entrepreneurial interests and hospitality education in these countries, particularly rural entrepreneurship, which can provide a good lesson to other developing countries to follow.

I am sure the book would be useful to academics and practitioners alike.

Harsh Varma
United Nations World Tourism Organization (UNWTO), India

Preface

Entrepreneurship education is a rapidly evolving field that is critical to the development of well-equipped and competent business leaders. The importance of training the future generation of managers and leaders cannot be overlooked as they play a vital role in ensuring the survival of various industries and companies. And its popularity among business management programs and skill-based courses has seen a huge increase in recent times (Fayolle, 2018). Recently the same trend has been reflected in tourism and hospitality education as a new entrepreneurship ecosystem and entrepreneurs played an important role in the sector's success even during its hardest times. Entrepreneurial education is the process of equipping students/trainees with the ability to identify new business opportunities along with grooming their knowledge and skills to mobilise resources, commercialise an idea, face risks and provide solutions for problems through entrepreneurship initiatives (Jones et al., 2014). As the future of the industry demands people with critical thinking, creativity, and innovative skills, the development of a comprehensive tourism and hospitality curriculum including topics of entrepreneurship education is critical (Ahmad, 2015). The book provides an in-depth look at various cases of entrepreneurship education in tourism and hospitality industries across the world as well as their recent changes and developments. This book connects industry and academia by providing more practical insights on the theme. The publication aims and features research exploring the trends, challenges, and future perspectives of entrepreneurship education in tourism and hospitality programs around the world through different case studies. It also features cutting-edge research on a wide range of topics, including teaching pedagogy, curriculum design, government policies & initiatives, students' motivation & attitude, creation of incubation centres and knowledge parks, academia-industry interface, and successful regional skill development models. To contribute to this topic, this book contains 10 chapters authored by experts globally which highlight different theoretical and practical insights around the world. Each chapter includes a broad understanding of entrepreneurship education in the region, extensive case evaluation, and future insights based on it.

The first chapter, "An Analysis of Entrepreneurial Intention of Tourism and Hospitality Undergraduates in Sri Lanka," reveals tourism undergraduates' entrepreneurial intentions and the challenges faced by them in Sri Lanka. The authors adopted both quantitative and qualitative approaches to analyse the situation. Furthermore, the study highlighted that tourism undergraduates have a moderate level of intention for their entrepreneurship, but face the difficulty to pool funds for the venture comes as a major challenge. The chapter results ensure further implications for educators and governmental bodies to initiate new entrepreneurship supporting projects in the country.

The second chapter, "Entrepreneurship Education in Postgraduate Tourism Programs: A Content Analysis of Syllabi from Indian Universities," presents an overall account of and current status of entrepreneurship education in Indian tourism academic programs. The chapter analyses and compares course title, core concepts, highlighted contents, major references and further readings in syllabi of post-graduation tourism programs in Indian higher educational institutions. This study follows a content analysis design and presents the results with the help of word cloud analysis and network analysis by using the software Atlas.ti. The major findings of this study indicate that the entrepreneurship education module in tourism programs is considered one of the core modules and is mostly taught in the final year or semester. The chapter further enlightens the status, scope and need of entrepreneurship education in tourism programs. Research results also suggest implications for designing innovative entrepreneurship courses in tourism programs to ensure quality education and training for future tourism graduates.

The third chapter, "Education of Tourism and Hotel-and-Restaurant Specialists in Ukraine," discusses the professional training of future specialists in tourist and hotel and restaurant service in Ukraine. The authors examine the conditions of education/training in Ukraine, especially in the tourist and hotel and restaurant services. The chapter further recommends the activation of independent cognitive activity of tourism and hospitality professionals with the help of technologies, a high level of competence of teachers, and skill implementation in educational and extracurricular activities for the improvement of entrepreneurship in the field of tourism.

The fourth chapter, "Entrepreneurship Education Development in the Context of Tourism in Oman," provides insights on a growing interest in establishing entrepreneurship educational programmes in Oman. The authors describe how the Oman government has made tourism one of the major industries for diversifying its oil-based economy, facilities provided by the government of Sultanate of Oman to encourage entrepreneurship education, and how the government of Oman is monitoring and assessing its initiatives and strategies planned and implemented to establish tourism entrepreneurship education. In addition, this chapter proposes a conceptual framework for entrepreneurship education in tourism. This can be taken into account by policymakers to measure entrepreneurship education strategies and the effectiveness and efficiency of their policies.

The fifth chapter, "Joy Labs: Discussing the Advantages and Disadvantages of PANCOE – University of Palermo, Argentina," analyzes alternative education systems or methods to ensure better academic performance. This chapter includes a case study that reflects on the power of pleasure (joy) to improve the mainstream education system. The author researched PANCOE (and the laboratory of pleasure) and its impacts on students' performance-based learning. PANCOE is a successful experiment based on Joy Labs (University of Palermo, Argentina) that combines pleasurable techniques and applications to stimulate student performance. The chapter findings have implementations for planning entrepreneurship educational activities for students interested in different dimensions and stages of the entrepreneurship journey. The authors have tried to explain the importance of the same with the help of a successful case study.

The sixth chapter, "Teaching South Africans How to Become Successful Hosts on Airbnb: The Case of the Airbnb Africa Academy," explores why south African marginalised communities have not yet actively participated in the tourism business, and how Airbnb Africa Academy making a revolution by providing proper training to homestay and guesthouse owners to register and become successful hosts on the Airbnb platform. The authors have applied various research methods to analyse the activities of Airbnb Africa Academy in regional tourism entrepreneurship training and the responses of locals getting benefits from the initiatives. The chapter findings can be adapted for planning and practising homestay and guesthouse entrepreneurship training in any region in the world.

The seventh chapter, "Skill India Mission Programme in the Hospitality Management for Quality Products and Services," proposes new dimensions for reducing the skill gap in India, by studying the 'Skill India Mission' and its various initiatives. The authors analysed the 'Skill India' mission, related policies, and sub initiatives, particularly in hospitality and allied sectors to understand the current status, recent trends, future perspectives, and challenges in skill training. Numerous literatures, local study results, newspaper articles, government reports, official publications, and in-depth expert interviews have been conducted for developing the findings. This study confirms the importance and scope of the "Skills India" initiative in hospitality management to ensure high-quality products and services. Moreover, the chapter also enhances theoretical knowledge on skilling the hospitality sector in the new era of digitalisation in the service sector.

The eighth chapter, "Entrepreneurial Tourism Education in TVET System in Oman: Present and Future Outlook," evaluates historical and existing practices in the Technical and Vocational Education and Training (TVET) system to encourage entrepreneurship in the sultanate of Oman and initiatives Oman Vision 2040. The authors tried to highlight the current status and prospects of entrepreneurial learning in technical and vocational education and training in the tourism and hospitality sector of Oman. For understanding the same, new educational and training models like enterprise-based learning, including hands-on and other forms of on-the-job training, and learning for students and workers of all ages have been analysed. The highlight of the chapter is the findings on the practical attempt to incorporate entrepreneurial learning to identify the strengths, weaknesses, and opportunities of all stakeholders.

The ninth chapter, "Entrepreneurship in Tourism Education: The Case of Ethiopia and Kenya," explores how the Ethiopian government planned entrepreneurship educational activities and courses in tourism programs and its results in graduates. The chapter considered both public and private institutions which offered tourism and hospitality courses with entrepreneurship modules. Further, it also studies the learning process, training facilities available, kinds of skills trained, training the trainers, upcoming initiatives, private-public participation in training and local community participation in entrepreneurship education.

The tenth chapter, "Rural Entrepreneurship Skill Development Through Regenerative Tourism in Channapatna, Karnataka," presents an idea on regenerative tourism and rural entrepreneurship training. The chapter discusses the importance of skill development in rural tourism destinations and how concepts of regenerative tourism support the promotion of entrepreneurship education. Regenerative tourism is designed to recognize the coexistence of the natural and social environment and to regain what nation and local people have invested in tourism development. The authors have taken the case of Channapatna, ("the land of toys", Karnataka) for establishing the idea of regenerative tourism for skill development of rural entrepreneurship opportunities.

In view of all the case studies that have been included in the present publication we are confident that the research findings will advance the literature in the field of entrepreneurship education in tourism and hospitality by broadening the discussion on the recent trends, ongoing challenges, interdisciplinary approaches, role of stakeholders, innovative teaching pedagogy, and future perspectives in creating next-generation tourism and hospitality entrepreneurs, educators and researchers more skilled. This book is intended for all stakeholders of the tourism and hospitality sector, especially educators, policymakers, university administrators, entrepreneurs, teacher educators, entrepreneurship trainers, program planners, educational leaders, researchers, and students who are interested in entrepreneurship education in tourism and hospitality. In summary, this book combines different perspectives from researchers with multiple backgrounds and regions to enlighten entrepreneurship education in tourism and hospitality management.

Satish Chandra Bagri
Hemvati Nandan Bahuguna Garhwal University, India

R. K. Dhodi
Hemvati Nandan Bahuguna Garhwal University, India

K. C. Junaid
Hemvati Nandan Bahuguna Garhwal University, India

Chapter 1
An Analysis of Entrepreneurial Intention of Tourism and Hospitality Undergraduates in Sri Lanka

Edina Wiligas Biyiri
Rajarata University of Sri Lanka, Sri Lanka

D. M. M. I. Dissanayake
Rajarata University of Sri Lanka, Sri Lanka

ABSTRACT

Entrepreneurship development is one of the most significant factors in the economic development of a country. However, when compared to other countries in Asia, Sri Lanka reports a low entrepreneurial rate. Thus, this study's primary focus is to analyze the tourism undergraduates' entrepreneurial intention and the challenges faced by the undergraduates to start a business. To achieve the objectives, both quantitative and qualitative approaches have been adapted. The population of the study comprises all the tourism undergraduates in state universities of Sri Lanka. A sample of 166 tourism undergraduates has been surveyed. The findings indicate that the tourism undergraduates have a moderate level of intention to start their own business and perceived feasibility and perceived desirability significantly influence their entrepreneurial intention. Tourism undergraduates perceive financial difficulty as the major challenge to start a business. Implications for educators and governmental bodies and future research directions are highlighted.

DOI: 10.4018/978-1-7998-9510-7.ch001

INTRODUCTION

Entrepreneurship can be identified as a vital factor in the economic growth of a country and it plays a major role in national development as it creates new job opportunities for a skilled workforce, increases the demand in the market, brings product innovations to create competition in the market to produce quality products and it generates a source of income to the government by maintaining the structure of the economy (Holmgren & From, 2005).

The tourism industry is regarded as a driver of economic and social change. Tourism entrepreneurship not only solves societal issues but also boosts a country's economic growth and development, resulting in an increase in GDP. Employment has always been a major topic in development. Tourism is one of the largest and fastest-growing industries in the world. Tourism entrepreneurship has can be regarded as a critical component of strategic support for business development. The industry offers numerous opportunities for small business development.

The importance of entrepreneurship has been recognized in developing countries like Sri Lanka as a tool to solve the problem of unemployment and achieve economic growth and development (Gamage, 2003). Thus, encouraging entrepreneurship has paramount importance in this context.

In developing entrepreneurship in a country, education plays a major role. The higher education institutes should deliver tertiary education, ongoing skills training, and a research environment that encourage innovations with commercial applications. Universities enhance the entrepreneurial potential of potential entrepreneurs (Van Burg et al., 2008).

The universities have an inevitable responsibility to produce qualified graduates, who contribute to the national economy. Nevertheless, the graduate un-employability rate of Sri Lanka is very high compared to other developing countries such as Malaysia and Singapore (Wickramasinghe, 2010). According to the tracer study of graduates carried out by the University Grant Commission, Sri Lanka in 2018 indicates that the overall un-employability rate of graduates of the state universities is 32.2%.

Entrepreneurship in the tourism sector is promising for businesses in the area of tourist destinations (Kuratko, 2009). In the Sri Lankan context tourism is one of the major sectors that contributes to the national economy. Therefore, entrepreneurship can be promoted in remedying the un-employability among the graduates in Sri Lanka. In this scenario, identifying the entrepreneurial intention of the undergraduates is vital particularly in countries like Sri Lanka to mitigate the negative social and economic impacts of the unemployment issues.

Therefore this study mainly focuses on identifying the entrepreneurial intention of the undergraduates, determinants of the entrepreneurial intention, and their perceived challenges to becoming an entrepreneur.

BACKGROUND

In the Sri Lankan economy, the tourism and hospitality industry is one of the key industries and major foreign exchange generating industries in the national economy. Many scholars have highlighted that tourism entrepreneurship is vital to ensure the tourists' experience and satisfaction in a destination or a country (Bardolet & Sheldon, 2008; Blake et al., 2006; Getz & Carlsen, 2005).

Considering the requirements of the industry, many higher educational institutes in Sri Lanka including state universities offer degree programs related to the tourism field (Dahanayake, et al., 2019; Samarathunga & Dissanayake, 2018). Approximately, 200 fresh graduates join the industry annually from government universities (Wijesundara, 2015). Currently, four state universities in Sri Lanka offer tourism degree programs. University of Sabaragamuwa and Uva Wellassa University of Sri Lanka produce about 50-150 tourism graduates per annum (Ranasinghe, 2019), while Rajarata University of Sri Lanka and the University of Kelaniya. produce about 50-120 tourism graduates per annum.

Since the tourism and hospitality industry offers multiple opportunities for small business development (Ciochina, et al., 2016), it is vital to investigate whether the undergraduates are willing to become an entrepreneur in the tourism sector after their graduation and what challenges they face in starting a business. Based on this background this study is aimed to analyze the level of the entrepreneurial intention of the tourism and hospitality undergraduates and the challenges of tourism and hospitality undergraduates to become an entrepreneur.

According to the 2018 annual report of the Finance Ministry, there is only 2.8 percent of the entrepreneurs are recorded from the total workforce operating in Sri Lanka (Liyanage, 2020). This is a very low rate compared with the other countries in the region such as Bangladesh (11.6), and Thailand (27.5). On the other hand, Sri Lanka has a very high graduate un-employability rate compared with other developing countries in the region. The average overall graduate employability ratio in Sri Lanka is 54% (Nawaratne, 2012).

The fewer entrepreneurs in the country and the high graduate un-employability rate indicate that many graduates are reluctant to start their own business in Sri Lanka. This questionable background should attract the scholar's attention immediately and suitable recommendations must be made in order to develop the Sri Lankan economy through the contribution of entrepreneurs by fully incorporating the skilled and knowledgable graduates pass out from universities.

Thus, the study mainly attempts to examine,

1.) the entrepreneurial intention of the undergraduates who follow Tourism and Hospitality Management Degrees in state universities in Sri Lanka

2.) the determinants of the entrepreneurial intention of tourism undergraduates in Sri Lanka, and
3) the challenges they encounter in becoming entrepreneurs.

LITERATURE REVIEW

Entrepreneurship is derived from the French term "entreprende," which means "to undertake" (Carton, Hofer & Meeks, 1998). Entrepreneurship has been defined by many scholars. Onuoha (2007) defines entrepreneurship as " the practice of starting new organizations or revitalizing mature organizations, particularly new businesses generally in response to identified opportunities". According to Hisrich et al., (2013) Entrepreneurship refers to the recognition and exploitation of opportunities, which lead to the creation of new ventures.

Schumpeter (1965) defined entrepreneurs as "the individuals who exploit market opportunity through technical and/or organizational innovation". According to Bolton and Thompson (2004) entrepreneur is "a person who habitually creates and innovates to build something of recognized value around perceived opportunities". Hisrich (1990) characterizes an entrepreneur as "someone who demonstrates initiative and creative thinking, is able to organize social and economic mechanisms to turn resources and situations to practical account, and accepts risk and failure".

As an important study topic, previous studies focused on explaining and predicting the choice of an entrepreneurial career (self-employment) (Kuratko et al., 1997). Recently, many studies (Autio et al., 2001; Tkachev and Kolvereid, 1999; Veciana et al., 2005; Esfandiar et al., 2019; Ahmad et al., 2019; Luong and Lee.,2021) have been conducted focusing on the undergraduates' entrepreneurial intention.

Entrepreneurial intention refers to the intention of an individual to start a new business and it is regarded as the immediate determinant of entrepreneurial behavior. Bird (1988) defined entrepreneurial intention as "a state of mind that directs attention, experience, and action towards a business concept".

Many countries have taken initiatives to invest in developing entrepreneurship education (Altinay et al., 2012) since entrepreneurship is one of the major engines which drive both social and economic growth of their countries (Keat et al. 2011). On the other hand, education plays a crucial role in cultivating the entrepreneurial intention of students (Gurel et al., 2010). The synergy between higher education, the economy, and policies is crucial in creating a country's entrepreneurial basis (Stipanović et al., 2021).

Consequently, entrepreneurship education is rapidly been developed recently in Sri Lankan higher education sector. Entrepreneurship education is defined as "the whole set of education and training activities - within the educational system or not – that try to develop in the participants' intention to perform entrepreneurial behaviors, or some of the elements that affect that intention, such as entrepreneurial knowledge, the desirability of the entrepreneurial activity, or its feasibility" (Lin ˜a´n, 2004). University undergraduates have advanced human capital and higher potential and the possibility to become entrepreneurs (Rauch & Rijsdijk, 2013). Thus, advancing and developing human capital for the business world is becoming more challenging and critical for universities (Scarpetta et al., 2012).

The tourism and hospitality industry is believed to be highly competitive contributing to the national and regional economy extensively as the industry has spread across several sectors such as accommodation, catering, transportation, sightseeing, shopping, entertainment, and other numerous aspects (Fong et al., 2018). Therefore, encouraging and motivating tourism and hospitality undergraduates to become entrepreneurs leads to creating more job opportunities and triggering the economy of a country (Altinay et al., 2012).

Tourism entrepreneurship can be defined as various activities related to tourism, hospitality, and leisure sectors by creating and operating a legal tourist's enterprise (Bagherifard, et al., 2013). Preceding literature examining the differences between tourism entrepreneurship and other types of entrepreneurship claimed that tourism entrepreneurs are motivated to achieve a higher quality of living since there are more opportunities and earnings in the tourism industry (Solvoll et al., 2015). Tourism businesses are typically viewed as small to medium-sized businesses that provide tourists with leisure and recreational possibilities.

However, some scholars argue about the extent of preparing tourism and hospitality undergraduates to become entrepreneurs since tourism and hospitality education is still considered highly vocational and action-oriented and therefore students are not much skilled at critical thinking and working outside existing procedures (Airey & Tribe, 2000; Echtner, 1995) which is crucial for fostering entrepreneurship (Kirby, 2005). However, tourism and hospitality education is developed rapidly during the last decade (Hsu et al., 2017). However, few studies have confirmed that tourism and hospitality education can influence the entrepreneurial intention of the students effectively (Zhang et al., 2020; Gurel et al., 2010).

Previous scholars have explored the entrepreneurial intention of tourism undergraduates using different theoretical frameworks. Esfandiar et al. (2019) developed an integrated model to explain individuals' intentions for entrepreneurial activities of tourism students in Iran. The study reported that desirability is the main determinant of entrepreneurial goal intention, followed by self-efficacy, feasibility, opportunity, attitude, and collective efficacy.

The study carried out by Ahmad et al. (2019) to predict entrepreneurial intention among tourism students in Bangladesh by applying the theory of planned behavior and the entrepreneurial event model suggests that attitude and subjective norms significantly influence perceived desirability, and perceived desirability and perceived feasibility predict entrepreneurial intention.

Luong and Lee (2021) have investigated the motivational effects of entrepreneurial desires and entrepreneurial self-efficacy drivers of entrepreneurial intentions in tourism and hospitality students in New Zealand. The results indicate that entrepreneurial self-efficacy and entrepreneurial desires directly influenced entrepreneurial intention.

Phuc et al. (2020) conducted a study to explore the importance of factors, which impact on tourism undergraduate students' entrepreneurial intention in Vietnam. The findings indicate that subjective norms, attitudes toward entrepreneurship, perceived behavioral control, and entrepreneurship education had direct effects on entrepreneurial intention.

Another study conducted by Lakshitha and Biyiri (2021) explored the tourism and hospitality undergraduates' entrepreneurial intention in Sri Lanka by applying the Theory of Planned Behavior. According to the results, personal attitude, subjective norms, and perceived behavioral control significantly affect the undergraduates' entrepreneurial intention

Despite many Sri Lankan higher education institutes offering entrepreneurship courses, little is known about tourism and hospitality management undergraduates' intention to become an entrepreneur. In this climate, the present study aimed to explore the entrepreneurial intention of the tourism and hospitality management undergraduates of three state universities that offer tourism and hospitality management degrees. Perceived desirability, perceived feasibility, and social norm, as antecedents of their intentions to become entrepreneurs and the challenges they encounter when becoming entrepreneurs will be examined.

THEORETICAL FRAMEWORK

According to the literature related to the entrepreneurial intention, some researchers have analyzed the entrepreneurial intention, as an interest, or propensity of students (Ang and Hong, 2000; Autio, et al., 1997; Begley, et al.,1997; Scott and Twomey, 1988; Vecianaet al., 2005; Wang and Wong, 2004). Some studies have focused on personality characteristics or respondents' personal background while other studies focused on the contextual factors of entrepreneurial intention. Scott and Twomey (1988) investigated the ambitions of university students and the results indicate that parental influence and work experience as significant factors. Begleyet al.(1997) compared the role of socio-cultural factors.

Accordingly, most of the entrepreneurial intentions models which describe the relationship between personal characteristics and the entrepreneurial intention of individuals (Ajzen, 1987; Bird, 1988; Krueger & Brazeal, 1994), are particularly based on two models; the Entrepreneurial Event Model (Shapero, 1982) and the Theory of Planned Behaviour (Ajzen, 1991). It's proven that both these models strongly predict entrepreneurial intention (Krueger et al., 2000).

The Entrepreneurial Event Model suggests that an individual's intention to start a new business depends on three factors: 1.) perceptions of desirability, 2.) propensity to act, and 3.) perception of feasibility while the Theory of Planned Behaviour suggests that there are three key factors which influence the behavioral intention of an individual namely: 1.) attitudes towards the act, 2.) social norms, and 3.) perceived behavioral control.

However, Brannback et al. (2006) state that entrepreneurial models are primarily being determined by perceived desirability and perceived feasibility. Few scholars (Krueger et al., 2000; Li, 2007) have identified that the social norm factor is also influencing the entrepreneurial intentions of individuals. Thus, in this study Perceived desirability, perceived feasibility, and the social norm will be aligned to explore the predicting power towards entrepreneurial intentions.

Perceived Desirability

Perceived desirability is defined as "the degree to which one finds the prospect of starting a business to be attractive; in essence, it reflects one's affect towards entrepreneurship" (Krueger, 1993)

Entrepreneurial motivation and entrepreneurial intention are greatly influenced by the desirability of an individual (Achchuthan & Nimalathasan, 2012). Further, few studies have identified that there is a positive relationship between the desirability and entrepreneurial intention of students in many countries (Segal et al., 2002; Veciana et al, 2005; Fitzsimmons & Douglas, 2011; Esfandiar et al, 2019; Ahmad et al,2019; Luong and Lee, 2021). Based on the above empirical findings, the following hypothesis was developed.

Hypothesis One: The perceived desirability of tourism undergraduates in Sri Lanka has a significant impact on their entrepreneurial intention.

Perceived Feasibility

Lu et al, (2011) refer to perceived feasibility as self-efficacy and it has been used in many prior studies related to entrepreneurial intentions (Krueger & Brazeal, 1994; Krueger et al., 2000). Basu and Virick (2001) identified that entrepreneurial education influence the students' entrepreneurial self-efficacy. A study conducted by Venkatapathy and Pretheeba (2014) using postgraduate students, identified that education level and the business experience of the family have a significant impact on the entrepreneurial intention of individuals. Another study (Peterman & Kennedy, 2003) suggests that entrepreneurial education greatly enhances the desirability of students in starting new businesses.

Moreover, previous studies (Guerrero et al, 2006; Singh et al.,2012; Esfandiar et al., 2019; Ahmad et al, 2019) also have identified that perceived feasibility has a significant influence on university students' entrepreneurial intention. However, little is known about the influence of the perceived feasibility on the entrepreneurial intention of the tourism and hospitality management undergraduates in the Sri Lankan context.

Thus, the second hypothesis of the study was developed;

Hypothesis Two: The perceived feasibility of tourism undergraduates in Sri Lanka has a significant impact on their entrepreneurial intention

Social Norm

The behavioral intention of the individual is a function of subjective norms. The perception of parents, friends, and community on entrepreneurial behaviors of individuals is referred to as social norms in this study. However, there are some contradictions in the findings of the studies on the relationship between social norms and entrepreneurial intention. This inconsistency occurs mainly due to the different attitudes, beliefs, values, cultures, and traditions of the society and individuals (Reihana et al., 2007).

Reitan (1996) suggests that subjective social norms have high predicting power in determining behavioral intention. Further, Diochon et al. (2002) and Kolvereid (1996) also found that there is a strong relationship between social norms and entrepreneurial intention. On the other hand, Krueger et al. (2000) state that social norms have no significant impact on entrepreneurial intention.

Thus, the third hypothesis of the study was developed;

Hypothesis Three: Social norms have a significant impact on the entrepreneurial intention of tourism undergraduates in Sri Lanka

METHODOLOGY

This survey employed both qualitative and quantitative methods and involved the distribution of questionnaires to tourism and hospitality management undergraduates to collect the primary data. SPSS and N-Vivo software are used to analyze the data in order to achieve the research objective. Further, the reliability and validity of the study will ascertain in order to ensure consistency. Figure 1 depicts the conceptual framework for the study.

Figure 1. Conceptual framework

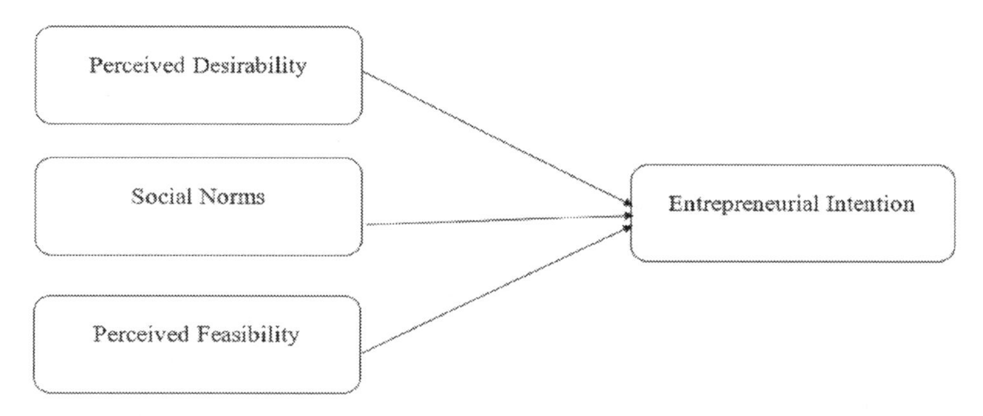

The primary data for the study were collected using a structured questionnaire and it was distributed through online channels. 166 responses were received for the final analysis. The instruments of the questionnaire were adapted from existing measures (Linen & Chen 2009; Saadin & Daskin 2015). The first part of the questionnaire included questions on demographic information of students. The second part of the questionnaire consists of the instruments created for perceived desirability, social norms and perceived feasibility, and entrepreneurial intention. The third part of the questionnaire consists of an open-ended question inquire of the challenges faced by the undergraduates to become an entrepreneur. A five-point Likert scale ranging from 1 as strongly disagree to 5 as strongly agree, is used for the measurement. Descriptive and inferential tools were used for analyzing the primary data. Accordingly, regression analysis was employed to explore the influence of perceived desirability, social norms, and perceived feasibility on entrepreneurial intention. The responses related to the challenges faced by the undergraduates to become an entrepreneur were analyzed through content analysis using the Nvivo 12 plus software.

FINDINGS OF THE STUDY

According to the demographic analysis, the sample consists of 118 female undergraduates and 48 male undergraduates. According to the age distribution, 80.1% of respondents belong to the 22-24 age category, 13.3% of respondents belong to the 20-21 age category and 6.6% of respondents belong to the 25-29 age category. The respondents are from different universities as 47% represent the Rajarata University of Sri Lanka, 24.7% represent Uva Wellassa University, 22.9% represent the Sabaragamuwa University of Sri Lanka and 5.4% represent the University of Kelaniya. 22. Undergraduates have stated that any of their close family members have a business and the majority (77.7%) have claimed that any of their close family members do not have a business.

Table 1. Measures of the variables

Variable	Measures
Perceived Desirability	Prefer own business than a promising career. Future success lies in starting own business. Friends like to see me start business. Relatives like to see me start a business Family like to see me start business.
Perceived Feasibility	I can manage staff. My skills and abilities help me to start business. I am confident to start business. I have access to information to become entrepreneur. I have good social network to become entrepreneur. I have access to capital to become entrepreneur. Easy to start business.
Social Norms	Owning business is respected by community. Owning business is respected by family. Owning business is respected by relatives. Owning business is respected by friends.
Entrepreneurial Intention	I am ready to do anything to be an entrepreneur. My professional goal is to become an entrepreneur. I will make every effort to start and run my own firm. I am determined to create a firm in the future. I have very seriously thought of starting a firm. I have the firm intention to start a firm someday.

Table 2. Demographic analysis

Variable		Frequency	Percentage
Gender	Male	48	28.9
	Female	118	71.1
Age	20-21 years	22	13.3
	22-24 years	133	80.1
	25-29 years	11	6.6
University	Rajarata University of Sri Lanka	78	47.0
	University of Kelaniya	9	5.4
	Sabaragamuwa University of Sri Lanka	38	22.9
	Uva Wellassa University of Sri Lanka	41	24.7
Any of close family members have a business	Yes	37	22.3
	No	129	77.7

Analysis of the Study

The research used Cronbach's alpha value to assess the internal consistency of the items within a scale. Alpha values were calculated for each multi-item scale. All the calculated alpha values are found to be above 0.70 indicating the fact that all scales are reliable. The relationship between perceived desirability, social norms, perceived feasibility, and entrepreneurial intention has been examined using the Pearson correlation analysis. The results are depicted in table 3.

Table 3. Correlation analysis

		Perceived Desirability	Perceived Feasibility	Social Norm	Entrepreneurial Intention
Entrepreneurial Intention	Pearson Correlation	.653**	.419**	.744**	1
	Sig. (2-tailed)	.000	.000	.000	
	N	166	166	166	166

According to the correlation analysis, all the P- values are 0.000. These values are less than 0.01, therefore the result is highly significant. All the coefficients of correlations are positive. This indicates that perceived desirability, social norms, and perceived feasibility have a positive significant relationship with undergraduates' entrepreneurial intention. Perceived feasibility has the strongest relationship with undergraduates' entrepreneurial intention while social norms have the weakest relationship.

TOURISM UNDERGRADUATES' ENTREPRENEURIAL INTENTION

Tourism undergraduates' entrepreneurial intention was analyzed using descriptive analysis. The findings of the descriptive analysis depict in table 4.

Table 4. Tourism Undergraduates' Entrepreneurial Intention

	Minimum	Maximum	Mean	Std. Deviation
	Statistic	Statistic	Statistic	Statistic
I am ready to do anything to be an entrepreneur	1.0	5.0	3.524	1.0369
My professional goal is to become an entrepreneur	1.0	5.0	3.705	.9925
I will make every effort to start and run my own firm	1.0	5.0	3.892	.9849
I am determined to create a firm in the future	1.0	5.0	3.952	.9459
I have very seriously thought of starting a firm	1.0	5.0	3.807	1.0145
I have the firm intention to start a firm someday	1.0	5.0	3.729	.9810

According to the table, all the mean values range from 3.5 – to 3.9 indicating that the tourism undergraduates have a moderate level of intention to become an entrepreneur.

HYPOTHESIS TESTING

Regression analysis was performed to predict the influence of perceived desirability, social norms, and perceived feasibility on undergraduates' entrepreneurial intention. Table 5 shows the summary of the regression model.

According to table 5, multiple correlations "R" is 0.768, which indicates that there is a strong joint association between perceived desirability, social norms, and perceived feasibility and undergraduates' entrepreneurial intention. R-square is 0.590. This indicates that 59% of student undergraduates' entrepreneurial intention n has been covered by the model. Adjusted R-square is also representing that 58.3% of the dependent variable has been covered by the model. Durbin-Watson test statistic is 1.889, which is very close to 2 and between 1.5 and 2.5. Therefore, residuals are independent and the model is valid. Regression ANOVA is given in table 6.

The probability of F test statistics of the regression ANOVA is highly significant as the P-value is 0.000. This indicates that the model is jointly significant and independent factors jointly undergraduates' entrepreneurial intention. The individual effect has been analyzed in table 7.

Table 5. Summary of the Regression Model

Model	R	R Square	Adjusted R Square	Std. Error of the Estimate	Durbin-Watson
1	.768[a]	.590	.583	.53284	1.889

Table 6. Regression ANOVA

Model	Sum of Squares	df	Mean Square	F	Sig.
Regression	66.270	3	22.090	77.803	.000b
Residual	45.995	162	.284		
Total	112.265	165			

The probability of perceived desirability is highly significant with positive beta values. Which is less than 0.05 indicating that perceived desirability significantly influences positively on undergraduates' entrepreneurial intention. Perceived feasibility significantly influences positively on undergraduates' entrepreneurial intention, since the probability of the variable is less than 0.01 with positive beta values. The probability of social norm is higher than 0.05, which indicates that social norm has no significant individual effect on undergraduates' entrepreneurial intention.

Table 7. Individual effect

Model	Unstandardized Coefficients		Standardized Coefficients	t	Sig.	Collinearity Statistics	
	B	Std. Error	Beta			Tolerance	VIF
(Constant)	.303	.255		1.189	.236		
Perceived Desirability	.283	.088	.256	3.215	.002	.397	2.516
Perceived Feasibility	.649	.081	.560	8.053	.000	.523	1.912
Social Norm	.016	.067	.015	.240	.810	.614	1.627

Based on these findings, H1 and H2, have supported that perceived desirability and perceived feasibility significantly influence undergraduates' entrepreneurial intention. However, the findings show that the social norm does not have a significant influence on undergraduates' entrepreneurial intention therefore H3 is not supported. As the diagnostic tests for regression results, the researcher tested several assumptions. In the model summary, the Durbin- Watson test is at the accepted level and residuals are independent. All the Variance Inflation Factors (VIF) are less than 10 and the Tolerance value is>0.1, which indicates that independent factors are not highly or perfectly correlated. Therefore, no multicollinearity problem was found in the regression model. Accordingly, the regression model is highly valid.

PERCEIVED CHALLENGES FOR ENTREPRENEURSHIP

Undergraduates were inquired about the barriers or challenges they face in order to start their own business. The responses were analyzed using the thematic analysis the findings are shown in figure 2.

According to the analysis, the majority of the respondents have claimed that finding the initial investment or finding the capital for the business is the most challenging aspect to becoming an entrepreneur. 53% of the respondents' opinion includes that the most challenging factor in starting a business is the financial challenge.

Lack of knowledge regarding the businesses is the second most challenging factor perceived by the tourism undergraduates to start a business. About 8% of the respondents' opinion claim that lack of knowledge is a barrier to starting a business.

Further, 6% of the respondents' opinions indicate that external factors are another barriers for the undergraduates to succeed in business. According to the undergraduates' view, external factors such as the unfavorable political situation in the country, economic challenges that the country is facing, the Covid 19 pandemic, and also the family background (financial difficulties, lack of encouragement, lack of entrepreneurial knowledge and experience of the family) are the challenges of the external environment for undergraduates to prosper as an entrepreneur.

Identifying the ideal market segment is another challenge perceived by the undergraduates to start their own business. About 4% of the respondents' opinions indicate that it is difficult for them to identify the ideal market segment. Additionally, business competition, finding human capital, and not having proper guidance are the other challenges perceived by the tourism undergraduates to become an entrepreneur.

Figure 2. Perceived Challenges

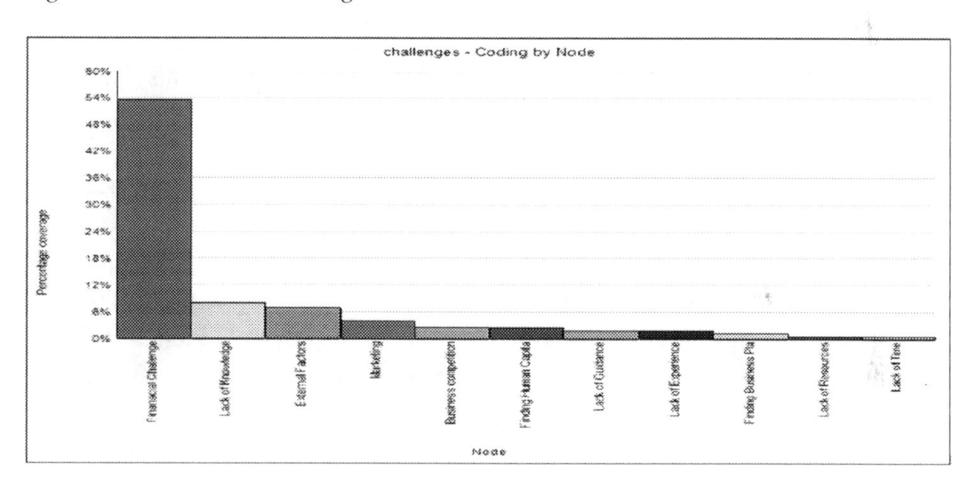

DISCUSSION AND RECOMMENDATIONS

Entrepreneurship development is important for economic progress, and tourism is seen as an appealing sector for aspiring entrepreneurs in this regard. Many scholars have looked at the factors that influence an individual's decision to become an entrepreneur.

The findings indicate that the tourism undergraduates have a moderate level of intention to start their own business. It is necessary to ascertain the causes for the lack of entrepreneurial intention among the graduates. According to the previous studies, it is consistently indicated that Sri Lankans, in general, are not favorable towards business as an occupation (Weeratunge, 2010) Another reason for lack of entrepreneurial intention is the clear preference amongst graduates towards government jobs followed by the private sector (Miriza, 2017). Further, In the Sri Lanka Youth Entrepreneurship Roadmap (2004), has identified that lack of access to finance, lack of access to business support, and the outdated policy and regulatory environment are the major economic factors that restrict the potential youth entrepreneurs in Sri Lanka.

In many Entrepreneurship is now identified as a core area of study in both graduate and undergraduate levels in many local universities. The Sri Jayewardenepura University has established a Small and Medium Enterprise Development Support Unit (SMEDSU) under the Entrepreneurship Department to provide academic programs to develop the entrepreneurial knowledge, skills, and attitudes of potential entrepreneurs.

According to the study's findings, the perceived feasibility and perceived desirability significantly influence on tourism undergraduates' entrepreneurial intention. When starting a business the feasibility of starting a business plays a significant role. The finding reflects that the perceived feasibility is the most influencing factor on undergraduates' entrepreneurial intention. This finding is similar to the studies (Guerrero et al., 2006; Singh et al., 2012; Esfandiar et al., 2019; Ahmad et al.,2019)

The influence of desirability is another significant factor on undergraduates' entrepreneurial intention according to the findings. Similar findings have been also reported in some studies (Segal et al., 2002; Veciana et al, 2005; Fitzsimmons & Douglas, 201; Esfandiar et al., 2019; Ahmad et al.,2019; Luong and Lee, 2021).

Different findings have been reported in the context of related literature related to the influence of social norms on entrepreneurial intention. In this study, it was found that the social norms do not have a significant individual influence on undergraduates' entrepreneurial intention. This finding is similar to the findings of Krueger et al. (2000).

The findings provide several implications. The findings indicate that perceived desirability is an important predictor of undergraduates' entrepreneurial intention. Further, the moderate intention of undergraduate tourism students in Sri Lanka to start up their businesses emphasizes the importance of raising proper awareness among the undergraduates concerning the opportunities and potential of the tourism industry for starting a business.

It was found that perceived feasibility is the most influencing factor. Further, their perception of lack of financial ability has been identified as the most challenging factor for tourism undergraduates to start their own businesses. It is recommended to the government, universities policymakers, and financial institutes to introduce and implement favorable financial policies, which encourage undergraduates to start businesses at an early stage.

The second most challenging factor for undergraduates to start a business is the lack of knowledge. This shows the importance of providing undergraduates with proper entrepreneurial education that involves management, marketing, finance, and accounting. Currently, most of the tourism degree programs in Sri Lanka have only one course unit for entrepreneurship and some do not have a course unit for entrepreneurship. Thus, it is highly recommended to include the entrepreneurship-related subject into the curriculum of the tourism degree programs. Further, involving students in developing business plans, and analyzing case studies are some methods that the educators may use apart from teaching the theories.

Networking is also critical for entrepreneurs to obtain access to resources, business ideas, financing, and knowledge. Therefore, creating networking opportunities with successful entrepreneurs in the tourism industry is an important implication for inspiring and acquiring knowledge.

Moreover, the universities should take a more proactive approach by developing a strategy to support students who are interested in starting a business. Universities may create forums such as business development centers to assist and guide the students, who have entrepreneurial intentions. It is suggested for policymakers of the universities to allocate an annual budget for entrepreneurship programs.

On the other hand, it is important to encourage the young graduates to start their own businesses by providing incentives and removing the barriers to registering their business and continuing their business. In Budget 2019, Sri Lanka announced an earmark of 10% of all government procurement to be reserved for small entrepreneurs. This is a good initiative by the government to encourage entrepreneurs. Thus an appealing policy framework with proper implementation is necessary for creating an environment for business start-ups.

FUTURE RESEARCH DIRECTIONS

Entrepreneurship plays an important role in creating and introducing innovation to the tourism sector, and this the tourism industry is even more important in developing countries heavily depending on the tourism industry. This implies that more research is necessary to have a better understanding of developing entrepreneurship.

The current analysis was limited to state universities, which offer tourism and Hospitality Management Degree programs. Thus, it is suggested a survey with a larger sample size should be conducted including students from other hotel schools and other private institutes across the country. Future research, when examining tourism students' entrepreneurial intention, is recommended to include more variables and examine whether the tourism students' entrepreneurial intention varies based on the demographic factors.

CONCLUSION

The main objective of this study was to analyze the tourism and hospitality undergraduates' entrepreneurial intention, the determinants of the undergraduates' entrepreneurial intention, and the challenges faced by the undergraduates to start a business. According to the results of the study tourism undergraduates have a moderate level of intention to start their own business. Further, the perceived feasibility and perceived desirability significantly influence tourism undergraduates' entrepreneurial intention, and the financial difficulty is the major challenge perceived by the tourism undergraduates to start a business. Based on the results of the analysis, managerial and practical implications are provided.

REFERENCES

Achchuthan, S., & Nimalathasan, B. (2020). scholars and undergraduates perspective regarding level of entrepreneurial intention of the management undergraduates in the university of Jaffna, Sri Lanka. *Academicia: An International Multidisciplinary Research Journal, 10*(6), 1118. doi:10.5958/2249-7137.2020.00718.1

Ahmad, N. H., Ramayah, T., Mahmud, I., Musa, M., & Anika, J. J. (2019). Entrepreneurship as a preferred career option. *Education + Training, 61*(9), 1151–1169. doi:10.1108/ET-12-2018-0269

Airey, D. (2001). Education for hospitality. Search of Hospitality, 276–292. doi:10.1016/B978-0-7506-5431-9.50019-6

Ajzen, I. (1987). Attitudes, traits, and actions: Dispositional prediction of behavior in personality and social psychology. *Advances in Experimental Social Psychology, 20*, 1–63. doi:10.1016/S0065-2601(08)60411-6

Ajzen, I. (1991). The theory of planned behavior. *Organizational Behavior and Human Decision Processes, 50*(2), 179–211. doi:10.1016/0749-5978(91)90020-T

Altinay, L., Madanoglu, M., Daniele, R., & Lashley, C. (2012). The influence of family tradition and psychological traits on entrepreneurial intention. *International Journal of Hospitality Management, 31*(2), 489–499. doi:10.1016/j.ijhm.2011.07.007

Ang, S. H., & Hong, D. G. P. (2000). Entrepreneurial spirit among East Asian Chinese. *Thunderbird International Business Review, 42*(3), 285–309. doi:10.1002/1520-6874(200005/06)42:3<285::AID-TIE2>3.0.CO;2-5

Autio, E., Keeley, R., Klofsten, M., Parker, G., & Hay, M. (2001). Entrepreneurial intent among students in Scandinavia and in the USA. *Enterprise and Innovation Management Studies*, *2*(2), 145–160. doi:10.1080/14632440110094632

Autio, E., Keeley, R. H., Klofsten, M., & Ulfstedt, T. (1997). Entrepreneurial intent among students: testing an intent model in Asia, Scandinavia and USA. *Frontiers of Entrepreneurship Research, Babson Conference Proceedings.*

Bagherifard, S. M., Jalali, M., Jalali, F., Khalili, P., & Sharifi, S. (2013). Tourism entrepreneurship: Challenges and opportunities in Mazandaran. *Journal of Basic and Applied Scientific Research*, *3*(4), 842–846.

Bardolet, E., & Sheldon, P. (2008). Tourism in archipelagos: Hawaii and the Balearics. *Annals of Tourism Research*, *35*(4), 900–923. doi:10.1016/j.annals.2008.07.005

Basu, A., & Virick, M. (2008). Assessing entrepreneurial intentions amongst students: A comparative study. In *VentureWell. Proceedings of Open, the Annual Conference* (p. 79). National Collegiate Inventors & Innovators Alliance.

Begley, T. M., Tan, W. L., Larasati, A. B., Rab, A., & Zamora, E. (1997). The relationship between socio-cultural dimensions and interest in starting a business: a multi-country study. *Frontiers of Entrepreneurship Research, Babson Conference Proceedings.*

Bird, B. (1988). Implementing Entrepreneurial Ideas: The Case for Intention. *Academy of Management Review*, *13*(3), 442–453. doi:10.5465/amr.1988.4306970

Blake, A., Sinclair, M. T., & Soria, J. A. C. (2006). Tourism productivity: Evidence from the United Kingdom. *Annals of Tourism Research*, *33*(4), 1099–1120. doi:10.1016/j.annals.2006.06.001

Bolton, B., & Thompson, J. (2004). Entrepreneurs, Second Edition: Talent, Temperament, Technique (2nd ed.). Butterworth-Heinemann.

Brännback, M., Carsrud, A., Elfving, J., Kickul, J., & Krueger, N. (2006, July). Why replicate entrepreneurial intentionality studies? Prospects, perils, and academic reality. In SMU Edge Conference, Singapore.

Carton, R. B., Hofer, C. W., & Meeks, M. D. (1998). *The Entrepreneur and Entrepreneurship: Operational Definitions of Their Role in Society*. Academic Press.

Ciochina, L., Iordache, C., & Sirbu, A. (2016). Entrepreneurship In The Tourism And Hospitality Industry. *Management Strategies Journal*, *3*(1), 264–275.

Dahanayake, S. N. S., Biyiri, E. W., & Dassanayake, D. M. C. (2019). Tourism and hospitality undergraduates' internship experience, their satisfaction and impact on future career intention. *Journal of Management Matters*, *6*(1), 33–44.

Diochon, M., Gasse, Y., Menzies, T., & Garand, D. (2002). Attitudes and entrepreneurial action: exploring the link. *Administrative Sciences of Canada 2002, Conference Proceedings*, *23*(21), 1–11.

Echtner, C. (1995). Entrepreneurial training in developing countries. *Annals of Tourism Research*, *22*(1), 119–134. doi:10.1016/0160-7383(94)00065-Z

Esfandiar, K., Sharifi-Tehrani, M., Pratt, S., & Altinay, L. (2019). Understanding entrepreneurial intentions: A developed integrated structural model approach. *Journal of Business Research*, *94*, 172–182. doi:10.1016/j.jbusres.2017.10.045

Fitzsimmons, J., & Douglas, E. (2011). Interaction between feasibility and desirability in the formation of entrepreneurial intentions. *Journal of Business Venturing*, *26*(4), 431–440. doi:10.1016/j.jbusvent.2010.01.001

Fong, V., Wong, I., & Hong, J. (2018). Developing institutional logics in the tourism industry through coopetition. *Tourism Management*, *66*, 244–262. doi:10.1016/j.tourman.2017.12.005

Gamage, A. (2003). Small and medium enterprise development in Sri Lanka: A review. *Masuki Ronso*, *3*(4), 133–150.

Getz, D., & Carlsen, J. (2005). Family business in tourism. *Annals of Tourism Research*, *32*(1), 237–258. doi:10.1016/j.annals.2004.07.006

Guerrero, M., Rialp, J., & Urbano, D. (2006). The impact of desirability and feasibility on entrepreneurial intentions: A structural equation model. *The International Entrepreneurship and Management Journal*, *4*(1), 35–50. doi:10.100711365-006-0032-x

Gurel, E., Altinay, L., & Daniele, R. (2010). Tourism students' entrepreneurial intentions. *Annals of Tourism Research*, *37*(3), 646–669. doi:10.1016/j.annals.2009.12.003

Hisrich, R. D. (1990). Entrepreneurship/intrapreneurship. *The American Psychologist*, *45*(2), 209–222. doi:10.1037/0003-066X.45.2.209

Hisrich, R. D., Peters, M. P., & Shepherd, D. A. (2013). *Entrepreneurship* (9th ed.). McGraw-Hill Education.

Holmgren, C., & From, J. (2005). Taylorism of the Mind: Entrepreneurship Education from a Perspective of Educational Research. *European Educational Research Journal*, *4*(4), 382–390. doi:10.2304/eerj.2005.4.4.4

Hsu, C., Xiao, H., & Chen, N. (2017). Hospitality and tourism education research from 2005 to 2014. *International Journal of Contemporary Hospitality Management*, *29*(1), 141–160. doi:10.1108/IJCHM-09-2015-0450

Keat, O. Y., Selvarajah, C., & Meyer, D. (2011). Inclination towards entrepreneurship among university students: An empirical study of Malaysian university students. *International Journal of Business and Social Science*, *2*(4).

Kirby, D. A. (2005). Entrepreneurship education: Can business schools meet the challenge. *Proceedings of the 2005 San Francisco-Silicon Valley Global Entrepreneurship Research Conference*, 173–193.

Kolvereid, L. (1996). Organizational Employment versus Self-Employment: Reasons for Career Choice Intentions. *Entrepreneurship Theory and Practice*, *20*(3), 23–31. doi:10.1177/104225879602000302

Krueger, N. (1993). The Impact of Prior Entrepreneurial Exposure on Perceptions of New Venture Feasibility and Desirability. *Entrepreneurship Theory and Practice*, *18*(1), 5–21. doi:10.1177/104225879301800101

Krueger, N. Jr, & Brazeal, D. (1994). Entrepreneurial Potential and Potential Entrepreneurs. *Entrepreneurship Theory and Practice*, *18*(3), 91–104. doi:10.1177/104225879401800307

Krueger, N. Jr, Reilly, M., & Carsrud, A. (2000). Competing models of entrepreneurial intentions. *Journal of Business Venturing*, *15*(5-6), 411–432. doi:10.1016/S0883-9026(98)00033-0

Kuratko, D. F. (2009). *Entrepreneurship*. South-Western Cengage Learning.

Kuratko, D. F., Hornsby, J. S., & Naffziger, D. W. (1997). 'An examination of owners' goals in sustaining entrepreneurship. *Journal of Small Business Management*, *35*(1), 24–33.

Lakshitha, H. D. T., & Biyiri, E. W. (2021). *A Study on Tourism and Hospitality Undergraduates' Entrepreneurial Intention. 4th National Research Symposium on Management*, Mihintale, Sri Lanka.

Li, W.LI. (2007). Ethnic Entrepreneurship: Studying Chinese and Indian Students in the United States. *Journal of Developmental Entrepreneurship*, *12*(04), 449–466. doi:10.1142/S1084946707000769

Lin˜a´n, F. (2004). Intention-based models of entrepreneurship education. *PiccollaImpresa/Small Business*, *3*, 11-35.

Liñán, F., & Chen, Y. (2009). Development and Cross–Cultural Application of a Specific Instrument to Measure Entrepreneurial Intentions. *Entrepreneurship Theory and Practice*, *33*(3), 593–617. doi:10.1111/j.1540-6520.2009.00318.x

Liyanage, V. (2020). *Daily News e paper*. Retrieved from Education for entrepreneurship: https://www.dailynews.lk/2020/01/07/features/207687/education-entrepreneurship

Lu, W., Wang, W., & Millington, J. (2010). Comparison of entrepreneurial intention among college students in the USA and China. *International Journal Of Pluralism And Economics Education*, *1*(4), 327. doi:10.1504/IJPEE.2010.037974

Luong, A., & Lee, C. (2021). The Influence of Entrepreneurial Desires and Self-Efficacy on the Entrepreneurial Intentions of New Zealand Tourism and Hospitality Students. *Journal of Hospitality & Tourism Education*, 1–18. doi:10.1080/10963758.2021.1963751

Mirza, J. (2017, September 20). *Why Sri Lanka needs more entrepreneurs*. Retrieved April 27, 2022, from https://www.ft.lk/Columnists/Why-Sri-Lanka-needs-more-entrepreneurs/14-639925#:%7E:text=For%20the%20past%20two%20decades,towards%20business%20amongst%20younger%20generation

Nawaratne, S. (2012). Shifting Paradigms of Higher Education in Sri Lanka. In R. Senaratne & S. Sivasegaram (Eds.), Re-creating and Re-positioning of Sri Lankan Universities to meet Emerging Opportunities and Challenges in a Globalized Environment (pp. 75–95). Academic Press.

Onuoha, G. (2007). Entrepreneurship. *AIST International Journal*, *10*, 20–32.

Peterman, N., & Kennedy, J. (2003). Enterprise Education: Influencing Students' Perceptions of Entrepreneurship. *Entrepreneurship Theory and Practice*, *28*(2), 129–144. doi:10.1046/j.1540-6520.2003.00035.x

Phuc, P. T., Vinh, N. Q., & Do, Q. H. (2020). Factors affecting entrepreneurial intention among tourism undergraduate students in Vietnam. *Management Science Letters*, 3675–3682. doi:10.5267/j.msl.2020.6.026

Ranasinghe, R. (2019). Antecedents of Job Performance of Tourism Graduates: Evidence from State University-Graduated Employees in Sri Lanka. *Journal of Tourism and Services*, *10*(18), 16–34. doi:10.29036/jots.v10i18.83

Rauch, A., & Rijsdijk, S. (2013). The Effects of General and Specific Human Capital on Long–Term Growth and Failure of Newly Founded Businesses. *Entrepreneurship Theory and Practice*, *37*(4), 923–941. doi:10.1111/j.1540-6520.2011.00487.x

Reihana, F., Sisley, M., & Modlik, H. (2007). Maori entrepreneurial activity in Aotearoa New Zealand. *International Journal of Entrepreneurship and Small Business*, *4*(5), 636–653. doi:10.1504/IJESB.2007.014394

Reitan, B. (1997, June). Where do we learn that entrepreneurship is feasible, desirable, and/or profitable. In *ICSB World Conference* (pp. 21-24). Academic Press.

Saadin, M. N., & Daskin, M. (2015). Perceived desirability, feasibility, and social norms as antecedents on hospitality students' entrepreneurial intention in Malaysia: Does gender make a difference? *International Journal of Entrepreneurship and Small Business*, *456*(4), 456. Advance online publication. doi:10.1504/IJESB.2015.070218

Samarathunga, W., & Dissanayake, D. (2018). School Students' Attitude Towards the Career Intention in the Tourism Industry: The Case of North Central Province, Sri Lanka. *Journal of Management Matters*, *5*(2), 1–16.

Scarpetta, S., Sonnet, A., Livanos, I., Núñez, I., Craig Riddell, W., Song, X., & Maselli, I. (2012). Challenges facing European labour markets: Is a skill upgrade the appropriate instrument? *InterEconomics*, *47*(1), 4–30. doi:10.100710272-012-0402-2

Schumpeter, J. A. (1965). Economic Theory and Entrepreneurial History. *Explorations in Enterprise*, 45–64. doi:10.4159/harvard.9780674594470.c5

Scott, M., & Twomey, D. (1988). Long-term supply of entrepreneurs: Student career aspirations in relation to entrepreneurship. *Journal of Small Business Management*, *26*(4), 5–13.

Segal, G., Borgia, D., & Schoenfeld, J. (2002). Using Social Cognitive Career Theory to Predict Self-Employment Goals. *New England Journal Of Entrepreneurship*, *5*(2), 47–56. doi:10.1108/NEJE-05-02-2002-B007

Shapero, A. (1982). The social dimension of entrepreneurship. In C. A. Kent, D. L. Sexton, & K. H. Vesper (Eds.), *The Encyclopaedia of Entrepreneurship* (pp. 72–90). Prentice-Hall.

Singh, I., Prasad, T., & Raut, D. (2012). Entrepreneurial intent: a review of literature. In *Ninth AIMS International Conference on Management* (pp. 201-207). Academic Press.

Solvoll, S., Alsos, G. A., & Bulanova, O. (2015). Tourism Entrepreneurship – Review and Future Directions. *Scandinavian Journal of Hospitality and Tourism, 15*(sup1), 120–137. doi:10.1080/15022250.2015.1065592

Stipanović, C., Rudan, E., & Zubović, V. (2021). *The entrepreneurial intentions of tourism and hospitality students in the face of the covid-19 pandemic*. Tourism in Southern and Eastern Europe. doi:10.20867/tosee.06.48

Tkachev, A., & Kolvereid, L. (1999). Self-employment intentions among Russian students. *Entrepreneurship and Regional Development, 11*(3), 269–280. doi:10.1080/089856299283209

Van Burg, E., Romme, A. G. L., Gilsing, V. A., & Reymen, I. M. M. J. (2008). Creating university spin-offs: A science-based design perspective'. *Journal of Product Innovation Management, 25*(2), 114–128. doi:10.1111/j.1540-5885.2008.00291.x

Veciana, J., Aponte, M., & Urbano, D. (2005). University Students' Attitudes Towards Entrepreneurship: A Two Countries Comparison. *The International Entrepreneurship and Management Journal, 1*(2), 165–182. doi:10.100711365-005-1127-5

Venkatapathy, R., & Pretheeba, P. (2014). Gender, family business background and entrepreneurial intentions in an emerging economy. *International Journal Of Business And Emerging Markets, 6*(3), 217. doi:10.1504/IJBEM.2014.063890

Wang, C. K., & Wong, P. K. (2004). Entrepreneurial interest of university students in Singapore. *Technovation, 24*(2), 163–172. doi:10.1016/S0166-4972(02)00016-0

Weeratunge, N. (2010). Developing Youth Entrepreneurs: A Viable Youth Employment Strategy in Sri Lanka. [E-book] In R. Gunatlilaka, M. Mayer, & M. Vodopivec (Eds.), *The Challenge of Youth Employment in Sri Lanka* (pp. 167–198). World Bank Publications.

Wickramasinghe, V., & Perera, L. (2010). Graduates, University lecturers and employers' perceptions towards employability skills. *Education + Training, 52*(3), 226–244. doi:10.1108/00400911011037355

Wijesundara, W. (2015). An Evaluation of Graduates' Perception on Employment in Tourism and Hospitality Industry. *7th Tourism Outlook Conference/Tropical Tourism Outlook Conference*.

Zhang, S., Li, Y., Liu, C., & Ruan, W. (2020). Critical factors identification and prediction of tourism and hospitality students' entrepreneurial intention. *Journal of Hospitality, Leisure, Sport and Tourism Education, 26*, 100234. doi:10.1016/j.jhlste.2019.100234

ADDITIONAL READING

Fu, H., Okumus, F., Wu, K., & Köseoglu, M. A. (2019). The entrepreneurship research in hospitality and tourism. *International Journal of Hospitality Management, 78*, 1–12. doi:10.1016/j.ijhm.2018.10.005

Jaafar, M., Abdul-Aziz, A. R., Maideen, S. A., & Mohd, S. Z. (2011). Entrepreneurship in the tourism industry: Issues in developing countries. *International Journal of Hospitality Management*, *30*(4), 827–835. doi:10.1016/j.ijhm.2011.01.003

Wang, S., Hung, K., & Huang, W.-J. (2019). Motivations for entrepreneurship in the tourism and hospitality sector: A social cognitive theory perspective. *International Journal of Hospitality Management*, *78*, 78–88. doi:10.1016/j.ijhm.2018.11.018

Zhang, S. N., Li, Y. Q., & Liu, C. H., & Ruan, W. Q. (2020). Critical factors identification and prediction of tourism and hospitality students & entrepreneurial intention. Journal of Hospitality, Leisure, Sport &. *Tourism Education*, *26*, 100234.

KEY TERMS AND DEFINITIONS

Entrepreneurial Event Model: Entrepreneurial event model is a model developed by Shapero and Sokol (1982) to describe the interaction of cultural and social factors which lead to from new businesses by influencing individual's perceptions.

Entrepreneurial Intention: Entrepreneurial intention refers to an individual's willingness to form a new business venture.

Entrepreneurship: Entrepreneurship is a founding a business or businesses while taking financial risks with expectation of making profit.

Entrepreneurship Education: Entrepreneurship education refers to a set of formalized teachings that informs, trains, and educates anyone to promote entrepreneurship awareness, business creation, or small business development.

Perceived Challenges of Entrepreneurship: Perceived challenges refers to the ones belief on the obstructions that impede an individual to start a business.

Perceived Desirability of Entrepreneurship: Perceived desirability defined as the extent to which one finds attractive the possibility of starting a business.

Perceived Feasibility of Entrepreneurship: Perceived feasibility refers to the belief that one possesses the necessary skills and abilities required to start a business.

Social Norms: Social norms refer to the perception of parents, friends, and community on entrepreneurial behaviors of individuals.

Tourism Education: Tourism education is a collection of formalized teachings, which transmit knowledge or foster skills and character traits enabling students for the careers in the industry.

Chapter 2
Entrepreneurship Education in Postgraduate Tourism Programs:
A Content Analysis of Syllabi From Indian Universities

S. C. Bagri
Centre for Tourism and Hospitality Training and Research, India

R. K. Dhodi
Hemvati Nandan Bahuguna Garhwal University, India

Junaid K. C.
https://orcid.org/0000-0002-8577-6320
Hemvati Nandan Bahuguna Garhwal University, India

ABSTRACT

Even though there is an increase in tourism research in India during the last 2-3 decades, researchers within the domain of tourism education made an insignificant contribution to entrepreneurship education (henceforth 'EE') programs. The objectives of this research are to study the current status of EE in tourism, to analyse and compare course title, core concepts, major references, and further readings. This study follows a content analysis design, focusing on an in-depth analysis of syllabi of post-graduation tourism programs in Indian higher educational institutions. The syllabi contents were analyzed using the Atlas.ti. The major findings of this study indicate that in India EE in tourism programs is mostly considered as one of the core modules itself than optional/elective modules and part of other courses. Almost all syllabi have included chapters on basic concepts of entrepreneurship, capital financing, business plan, opportunities, innovations, etc. This finding has major implications for designing innovative entrepreneurship courses in tourism programs.

DOI: 10.4018/978-1-7998-9510-7.ch002

INTRODUCTION

In the new global economy, entrepreneurship has become the central attention of everyone, as entrepreneurs are considered the future of the world, who keep on working on challenging issues creatively to make the world a better place to live. Similar to, how entrepreneurship ideas are recognized or supported by society, entrepreneurship education is also treated as one of the important components in the startup environment/ecosystem along with incubators, innovation centers, venture labs, and funding events (Mcmullan & Long, 1987). But there exists a gap in its intensity depending upon the region, especially the economic status and technological advances of the countries. Moreovér teaching or training for entrepreneurship is facing many challenges including the difference in expectations of stakeholders and the educators (Mwasalwiba, 2010). Similarly, in the case of tourism and hospitality students or industry, in past, most of them have not considered the value of entrepreneurship module in their programs as a very important skill for the future (Ahmad, 2015). Earlier starting own business or small scale venture was challenging when coming to the stage of funding or marketing. Train them for the industry to title as an employee. But things got changed a lot due to technological advancements and government initiatives supporting entrepreneurs. And now they are considered one of the developmental pillars of a country or a community. These days any tourism and hospitality graduates can easily set up their entrepreneurship with minimum capital, they can look for getting funds from big ventures, and can use social media websites to market their products or services. There comes the important role of educators. Educators can help students to find out their passion for entrepreneurship, develop skills, and fully prepare them for taking challenging decisions in their entrepreneurial journey (Deale, 2016). These kinds of innovative or applied education are not only needed for the student's development, but also for ensuring future industrial demands (Zhou, 2017). Every university or administrator has to create a professional platform for students to think out of the box and to develop innovative solutions for different problems faced by existing consumers or society. The university department can prepare talent training plans, entrepreneurship associations among interested students and dual mentorships to foster innovations among students (Zheng, 2019).

Coming to the entrepreneurship education background of India, Raichaudhuri (2005) highlighted that major Indian entrepreneurial schools have begun to provide entrepreneurship education and training, only once after being motivated by the global success of Indian entrepreneurs. India has made greater efforts to promote and nurture entrepreneurship during the period of liberalization that began in 1991 (Rehman & Elahi, 2012). India's current entrepreneurship education is mostly connected to relevant courses. Especially by including modules or chapters on entrepreneurship in engineering and management programs. The fact is that entrepreneurship topics in pure humanities and social sciences programs are rarely seen, compared to the available huge scope for social entrepreneurship in the 21st century. This point is also supported by professor Basu (2014), who said there is an urgent need to develop and promote an effective indigenous entrepreneurship education system and integrated learning platforms in India. To promote entrepreneurship, we need to rethink our education system, pedagogy, curriculum, and other institutions (Yeshawanth & K, 2015). With attention to recent developments, there exists a paradigm shift in student focus on job-creating courses than work-oriented courses in India (Srivastava & Thomas, 2017). Even though reports reflect a good number of students are dreaming to become entrepreneurs, we have to critically think about does our students are prepared for the challenges and failures they may face during the journey to success. The most important thing we need is to create an entrepreneurial spirit in interested students. Entrepreneurs need relentless energy and incurable optimism to get off the less-travelled route and realize their dreams (Gautam & Kumar singh, 2017). Work experience, active participation in incubation activities and adequate mentoring support can boost the entrepreneurial spirit of any student. As tourism programs are usually included with various management models, we can make at least a module on entrepreneurship and proper practicals on the same designed by real entrepreneurs in the sector. Coming to the background of tourism and hospitality education in India, the Ministry of Tourism and the All India Council for Technical Education (AICTE) have played a major role in Human Resource Development and Training in the sector. Different training programs in hotel management, catering and nutrition were started in 1962 by the Government of India in various regions of the country. Likewise, in the year 1982 National Council for Hotel Management and Catering Technology (NCHMCT) was established by the Ministry of Tourism. Moreover to these Indian Institute of Tourism and Travel Management (IITTM) was established to further education and training of tourism sector on 1983. The aim of IITTM was to groom the students for entrepreneurship development and similarly the Ministry of Tourism made efforts to introduce 3 year Diploma in Hotel management with the aim to have more professional entrepreneurship in Hospitality Management, Notwithstanding such efforts, NCERT, Polytechnic, Skill India Mission, and NOO associated with the villages welfare have made efforts to groom the local people to opt tourism and hospitality management for entrepreneurship. The tourism courses are introduced for employment generation and were introduced only in such institutions located whether in and around a tourism circuit or a tourist destination or a tourism-oriented state and because of this the tourism graduates after completing diploma and degree study programs have become manpower in the running tourism plant facilities. Hardly any university made efforts to make the course design entrepreneurship oriented. It was felt necessary when state and central governments introduced policies to provide incentives and concessions running tourism business units and it attracted tourism and hospitality graduates to opt for entrepreneurships. Entrepreneurship education must be mandatory from the beginning in a management related programs and it will strengthen the attitudes, confidence and creative abilities of the students (Bharucha, 2019). A considerable amount of literature has been published on entrepreneurship education and training in India. However, far too little attention has been paid to entrepreneurship education in tourism programs. In this paper, the authors are focused on the analysis of tourism postgraduate program syllabi from various Indian universities. The primary aims of this study are to extract content from currently available entrepreneurship education and training modules in tourism programs offered in India and to analyse the same with different tools. This study is more kind of an exploratory and case study design, with an in-depth content analysis of provided syllabi. For this purpose, the authors have collected the postgraduate syllabus of different tourism departments in Indian universities (25 syllabus approved after screening process for final analysis) and used content analysis by applying ATLAS.ti software. It is hoped that this study will lead to new insights of entrepreneurship education curriculum needs in tourism programs and its further implication in educational institutions.

LITERATURE REVIEW

There exists a very extensive literature on the topic of 'entrepreneurship education, 'entrepreneurship education in tourism and hospitality and 'entrepreneurship education in India'. Similar to the case of entrepreneurship training. Mcmullan & Long (1987) traces the history of entrepreneurship education in the nineties and discuss their answers to questions such as why is entrepreneurship education is important, how it can be unique from related, who will be the students, teachers and what will be the curriculum and methods to measure the success etc. the authors also highlights that entrepreneurship education is a promising strategy for job creation and economic development, yet the nature of education required by new generation aspiring entrepreneurs is not well understood or is minimal in use. In the same vein, Vuuren & Nieman (1999) stated about significance of entrepreneurship education to reduce unemployment by the encouragement of entrepreneurship and self-employment teachings at school and tertiary education levels. They proposed a real content model for entrepreneurship education ie. $E/P = a + bM[cE/S \times dB/S]$, entrepreneurial performance (E/P); motivation (M); entrepreneurial skills (E/S); and business skills (B/S) in a dynamic linear model. The constants a, b, c and d represent some level of skills that each individual has. This particular model identifies that all three constructs (motivation, entrepreneurial and business skills) have to be given attention to ensure the success of entrepreneurship education. There are few studies exploring curricula contents and teaching methods for entrepreneurship education. Sirelkhatim & Gangi (2015) conducted a systematic literature review (SLR) of curriculum content and methods of teaching entrepreneurship and analysed the same using NVivo computer software. The authors further discussed the importance of studying actual results of entrepreneurship education in graduates who already started their businesses. A meta-analysis of entrepreneurial finance courses in U.S. undergraduate courses was conducted by Glackin et al., (2016), who proposed a typology of entrepreneurial finance courses after analyzing the existing course descriptions and syllabi and further the author empirically tested and analyzed this typology. In the same vein, or like a few syllabi analysis studies or methods we have discussed so far, Pittaway (2016) also studied student assessment practice in entrepreneurship education by using a similar methodology or data source, ie. collecting data from course outlines or syllabi of different courses in UK and US since 1980 (up to 2016). Coming to narrow topics of the area, Solomon et al., (2019) conducted a cross-cultural study of social entrepreneurship education in different programs in the USA and Canada. Their exploratory study was focused to express the growing demand for social entrepreneurship courses and topics along with the need for the growth of social entrepreneurship. This view is supported by McNally et al., (2020) who reviewed social entrepreneurship syllabi from various universities around the world and highlighted that educators can positively influence the learner's attitude towards the course before the class begins.

Several studies exploring entrepreneurship education or training in tourism have been carried out by various authors. B. Owusu-Mintah (2014) argues that lack of access to initial capital, lack of entrepreneurship spirit among graduates, and lack of a link between what is studied and startup skills required are major challenges faced by tourism and hospitality graduates. Similarly, Ahmad (2015) found that hospitality and tourism students do not consider the entrepreneurship module to be an important subject of the program. In another case, Sheldon & Daniele (2017) tried to understand the tourism student's perspective on the relevance of entrepreneurship education in the course. And the authors conclude that students support adding entrepreneurship education and training activities within tourism courses as it is considered an important skill to ensure future self-employed. Deininger (2020) conducted an exploratory research study on students' entrepreneurial attitudes and subjective opinions on their control over their entrepreneurial behaviour. Meanwhile, Sahinidis et al., (2019) examined the impact of entrepreneurship education on the business intent of college students in tourism departments. They surveyed 77 students at both the beginning and end of the semester. Regarding teaching methods used in tourism entrepreneurship education, Ahmad et al., (2018) point out that there does not seem to be a single teaching method sufficient to achieve the purpose of the course. But, there has to be a link between theory and practice. Which refers to a combination of different teaching methods to teach a wide range of skills and to keep updated. Ndou et al., (2019) trace the how are the key elements related to entrepreneurship education structured in tourism education programs and also advised on what could be an effective tourism entrepreneurship educational model. Even though these works explore different aspects of entrepreneurship education in tourism and hospitality around the world, very little attention has been paid to similar studies on the Indian subcontinent or country India. But, there are numerous studies on Indian tourism and hospitality education, some of these can relate to or discuss tourism entrepreneurship education in India (such as Bagri et al., 2010; Bagri & Babu, 2011; Dixit & Mawroh, 2019; Gupta & Bhatt, 2017; Kumar, 2018; Ranga Rao, 1995). As far as we know, no previous research has investigated the syllabi analysis of Indian universities focusing on entrepreneurship education in postgraduate tourism programs.

RESEARCH DESIGN

Several methods of syllabi analysis can be found in the relevant literature. Based on current research objectives one of the simplest ways to collect different universities' tourism program syllabi is by downloading them from the university website or department website. But to ensure the available syllabi are up-to-date, the authors further directly contacted with tourism department/centre head or other representatives from each university to mail the updated syllabi. In short, syllabi were collected from both department heads/faculties/instructors and university websites. Certain criteria are used to ensure the collected syllabi are related to research objectives. Criteria for selecting the university syllabi were as follows: i) the syllabus must be on a tourism postgraduate level program, ii) the syllabus must be written in English or an English translation is available iii) the provided syllabus is up to date or currently followed by the university, iv) syllabi must include at least one topics on entrepreneurship and v) syllabus must include a list of reading materials or further references. Authors like Hodson, (1999) and Okumus & Wong (2007) highlighted that 15 cases (syllabi) can be sufficient for content analysis studies. In the initial stage authors recognised around 46 universities in India for the study. Later on, by following the above-mentioned criteria and process, syllabi from 25 universities (N=25 syllabi, including private and government) matched the listed criteria for further study. A complete list of the universities and related details can be found in Figures number 1 and 7. For analysis, in-depth content analysis is carried out on each syllabus selected to respect entrepreneurship topics and variables based on the research objectives. The process has extracted different data categories from each syllabi for easy analysis. To illustrate and do network analysis, a software package 'ATLAS.ti' version 9 for windows 10 has been implanted.

RESEARCH FINDINGS

Outlook on Entrepreneurship Education in Tourism Programs (India)

Figure 1 Provides a bar chart on characteristics analysis of Indian universities with EE in tourism (N=25). As the chart showed, the entire contents of characteristics syllabi/ university/programs are classified into seven categories. And each of these seven categories further shows different features or levels. Reflecting the above results of the sample, *University Category* indicates that, the Syllabi of State universities have included more courses on EE in tourism than Central or Distance/Open or Private universities combined. More than half are from State universities (52%), following Central (32%), Distance Education or Open (12%) and Private (4%) respectively. Expect DE/Open universities (12%, part-time or distance education), *Mode* of programs in EE are designed as in Full-Time structure. For effective Entrepreneurship lessons, syllabi demand an offline or direct interactive learning atmosphere. When analysing the *Program Category*, mostly postgraduate programs in tourism in Indian universities come under three categories such as MTTM, MBA Tourism and MA Tourism. MTTM refers to Masters of Tourism and Travel Management, MBA refers to Master of Business Administration (in Tourism), and MA refers to Master of Arts (in Tourism). Most Indian universities are offering MTTM programs (60%), compared to MBA (36%), and MA (4%) programs. Generally, MTTM programs have more courses on tourism concepts and components, MBA has in-depth courses on management studies, and MA includes courses with topics on history, art and culture. As per the research findings on syllabi analysis, mostly MTTM programs are promoting EE in tourism more than MBA/MA programs. When it comes to the *Type of Course* on each university/syllabi, entrepreneurship courses is preferred as one of the Core Course of the program (64%), in some cases as an Optional or Elective Course (28%) and as part of other core courses (8%) such as marketing, innovation, trade etc. In the case of Optional or Elective Courses, students have a preference to select other alternative courses also (usually which are not directly related to EE). Entrepreneurship courses are often introduced in the final year of the program (i.e., 4th semester, 36% or 3rd semester, 28%) but in some universities, they have included in the first year itself (2nd semester, 20% or 1st semester, 16%). Each entrepreneurship course in tourism has an average of five units/modules and six references/suggested readings per course.

Figure 1. Characteristics of Indian universities with entrepreneurship education in tourism (in %, N=25)

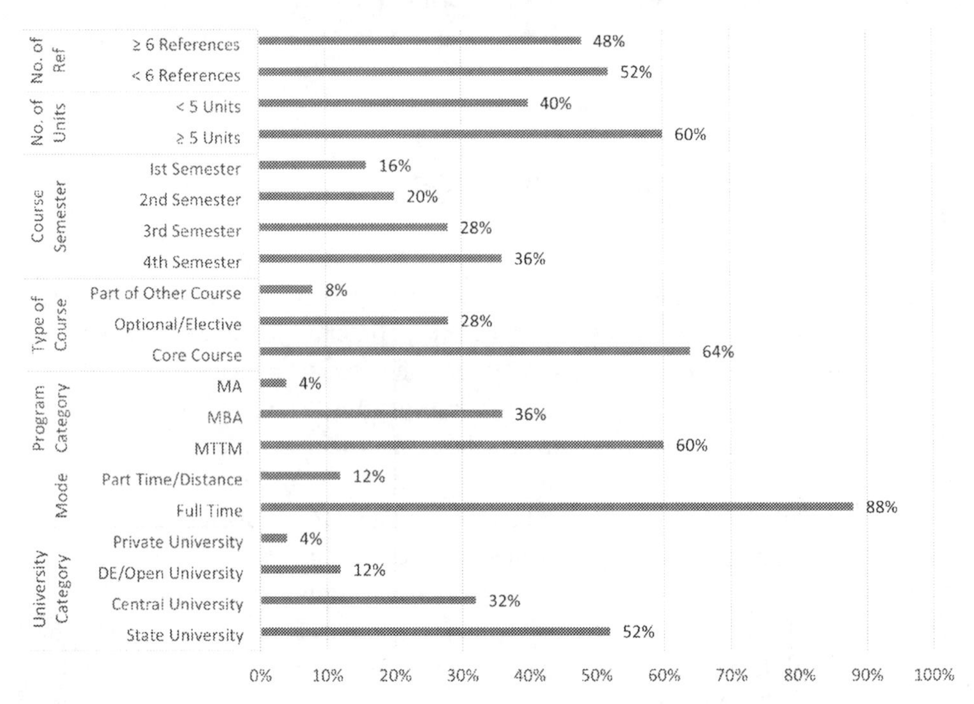

Course Titles and the Syllabi of Tourism Programs

The titles of each course communicate an overall idea of the contents and structure of the course, that is why understanding syllabi are more important before going to topics in content. A word cloud analysis of these titles (N=25, total words/ terms=38) is illustrated in Figure 2. The most common titles of entrepreneurship courses in tourism postgraduate programs are 'Tourism Entrepreneurship' and 'Entrepreneurship in Tourism', both representing more than 5 tokens (13%-21%) in word cloud analysis of ATLAS.ti software. Other most repeated titles include 'Entrepreneurship for Tourism', 'Entrepreneurship Development, and simply 'Entrepreneurship'. Likewise, all of the other titles are either directly coined with the term entrepreneurship or related to different aspects such as 'Venture Creation', 'Trade Management', 'Marketing Management, 'Business Innovations', 'Small Scale', 'Innovation Management', 'Career', and 'Business Plan' etc.

Figure 2. Titles of entrepreneurship course syllabi in tourism programs (word cloud analysis)

Core Concepts in the Entrepreneurship Education Modules

An extensive content analysis of syllabi from 25 universities reflected that the overall contents of the syllabi can be classified into 16 core concepts. All of these core concepts are directly related to EE in tourism. Figure 3 highlights the distributions of these core concepts among all syllabi (in %, N=25) of EE in tourism. Almost all syllabi (96%) have covered 'basic concepts, definitions, and theories' on entrepreneurship or aspects of entrepreneurship in tourism. The topics related to core concepts 'capital financing, business plan, type of entrepreneurship/entrepreneurs, problems and issues faced by entrepreneurs or during entrepreneurship journey, policies and role of government' have been discussed by more than half of the syllabi (52%-68%). Comparatively, around half of the syllabi (48%) have tried to include content on 'qualities of a good entrepreneur and various opportunities for entrepreneurship in tourism'. Only a few syllabi have been considered to include concepts like 'innovations in entrepreneurship, how to manage or monitor the enterprise efficiently, social aspects of entrepreneurship, especially in tourism, the need for professional training, general business environments, and the recent trends in the tourism industry and entrepreneurship. Furthermore, concepts of 'networking and skills' are the least discussed topics in Indian postgraduate tourism entrepreneurship course syllabi.

Figure 3. Core concepts of entrepreneurship course syllabi in tourism programs (in %, N=25).

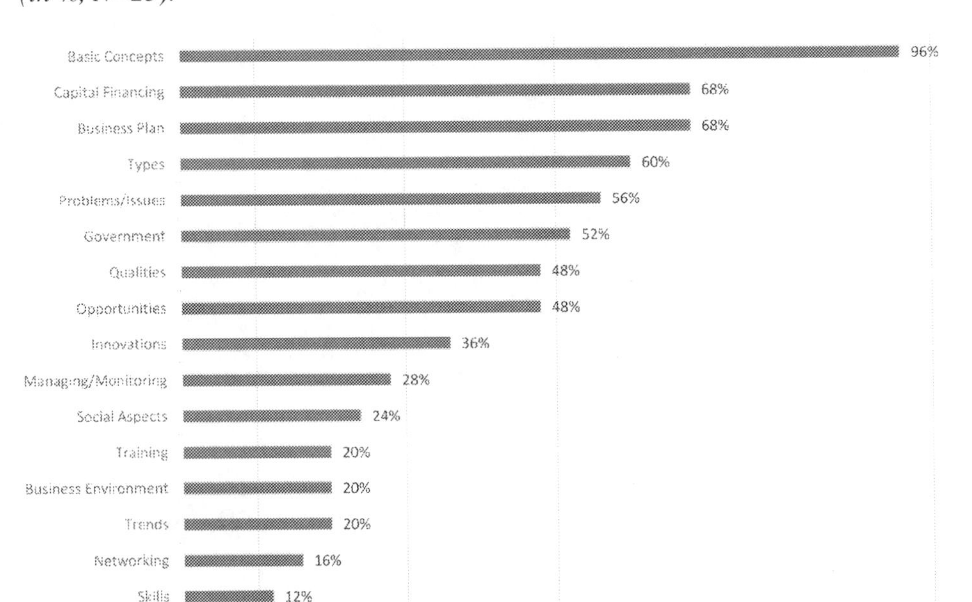

References and Suggested Readings in the Modules

The line graph (Figure 4) shows the number of references and suggested readings of entrepreneurship courses listed in tourism postgraduate syllabi (per year). The year ranges from 1975 to 2020, with publications from 32 unique years included in the overall references and suggested readings list (an average of 3 per year). The highest references are published from the years 2009 (n=8), 2008 (n=6), and the lowest from the years 1975, 1991, 2006, 2018, 2019 and 2020 (n=1). Other than these references to books and journal articles, few syllabi have also mentioned websites with dynamic and up to date contents as an additional reference.

Additionally, the word cloud analysis on names of the authors in references and suggested readings (Figure 5) summarizes popular authors out of a total of 130 authors referred to in these syllabi. The more tokens they represent the more references and suggested readings have authored by that particular author. As the word cloud represents, 'Dr. Vasant Desai' (6 tokens) ranked most, then 'Robert D. Hisrich; Donald F. Kuratko and S. S. Khanka' (3 tokens). Authors like 'CB Gupta, Jan S Cramer, John S Earle, Stephen Page, Peter Drucker, Zuzana Sakova, Jovo Ateljevic, Jeffry A Timmons, Nimit Chowdhary, Barbara Jean Bird, C Mirjam Van Praag, Thomas W Zimmerer, Richard M Hodgetts, and Norman M Scarborough' have contributed at least two references/readings. Authors of websites or web reports in the syllabi references section are not considered in this word cloud analysis.

Figure 4. Publication year of references and suggested readings listed in syllabi, (numbers per year, N=94)

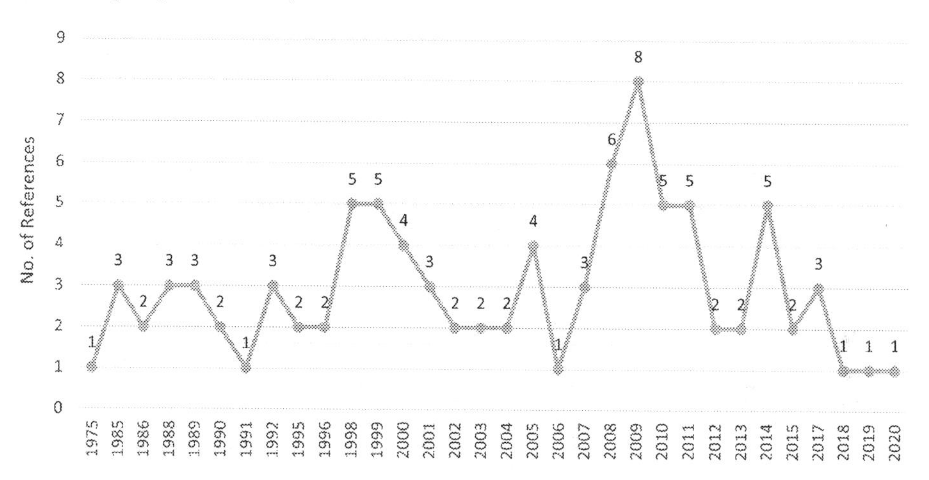

Figure 5. Authors of listed references and suggested reading listed in syllabi (word cloud analysis)

Out of 187 unique terms in titles of references and suggested readings listed in syllabi, the term 'Entrepreneurship' has been highlighted more (46 tokens). Figure 6 illustrates the frequency of terms as per the word cloud analysis of titles of the reference and suggested readings listed in all (N=25) syllabi on entrepreneurship education in tourism. Terms like 'Management', 'Tourism', 'Small Business, 'Entrepreneurship Development', 'Entrepreneur', 'Business', 'Venture', 'New', 'Managing', 'Innovation', 'India', 'Hospitality', 'Entrepreneurial Development', 'Entrepreneurial', and 'Entrepreneurship Management' respectively are other highly ranked terms in the titles (out of total 363 words).

Figure 6. Titles of references and suggested readings listed in syllabi (word cloud analysis)

Network Analysis of Indian Universities with Entrepreneurship Courses in Tourism

Figure 7. Network analysis of Indian universities with entrepreneurship courses on tourism (N=25).
AAKTU: A.P.J. Abdul Kalam Technical University, AMU: Aligarh Muslim University, AU: Alagappa University, BAMU: Dr Babasaheb Ambedkar Marathwada University, CSJMU: Chhatrapati Shahu Ji Maharaj University, CUH: Central University of Haryana, CUHP: Central University of Himachal Pradesh, CUK: Central University of Sikkim, CUKA: Central University of Kashmir, GUG: Garden City University, IGNOU: Indira Gandhi National Open University, IGNTU: Indira Gandhi National Tribal University, KU: Kurukshetra University, MAKAUT: Maulana Abul Kalam Azad University of Technology, MDU: Maharshi Dayanand University, MGU: Mahatma Gandhi University, MKU: Madurai Kamaraj University, PU: Pondicherry University, TU: Tezpur University, UB: University of Burdwan, UJ: University Of Jammu, UK: University of Kashmir, UL: University of Lucknow, UOK: University of Kerala, UOU: Uttarakhand Open University.

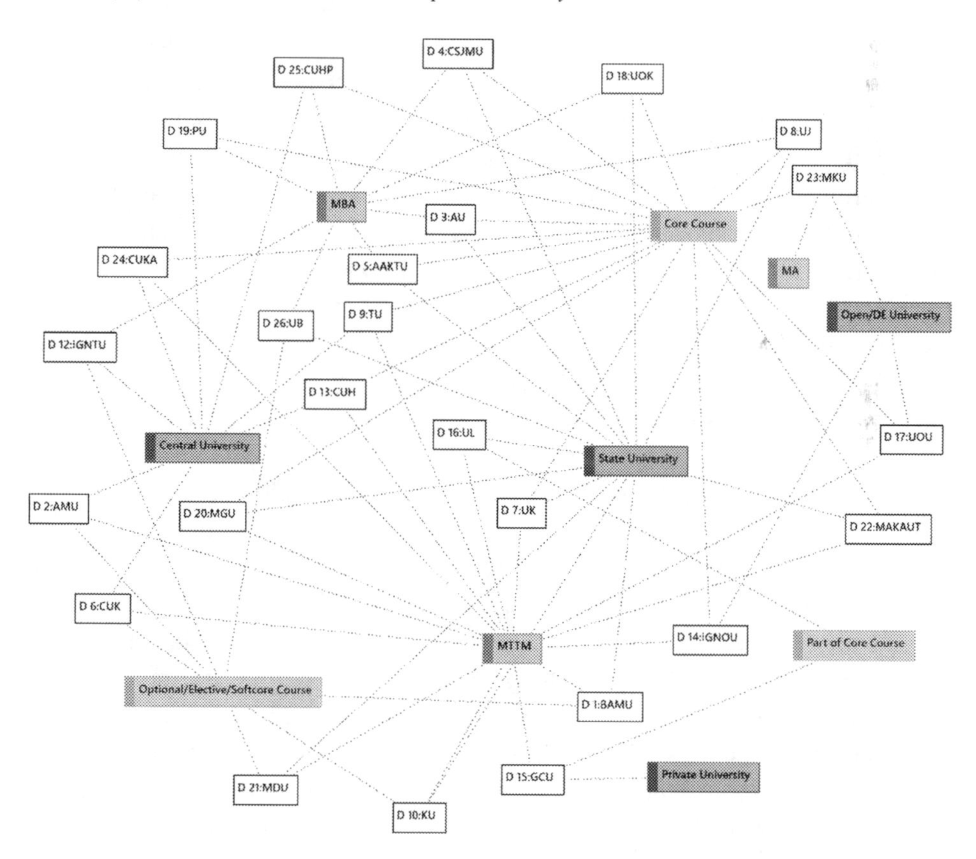

DISCUSSION

Tourism programs with entrepreneurship education and training exhibit great hope for successful graduates than programs without any of these training. As tourism (including allied sectors) is developing to international standards in India at par with the technological advancements, tourism education and training institutions also have understood the great benefits of teaching students the basics of entrepreneurship. The universities that added entrepreneurial lessons as core courses have developed students to think practically about things they have learned in the classroom. By understanding and applying topics like capital financing, business planning, government policies, types of entrepreneurship/entrepreneurs and various opportunities for entrepreneurship in tourism etc. students are now able to differentiate between when, how and why to start a tourism business unit and when not to. Moreover to these, learnings about problems and issues faced by entrepreneurs, real-time case studies, recent trends and innovations are strengthening the students to survive in the sector or their entrepreneurial journey. Industry experts have highlighted that graduates with entrepreneurial knowledge can easily understand the business models and are highly capable to lead the organisation compared to graduates without the same learnings. This further implies that by adding entrepreneurship modules in the tourism programs, we can not only generate innovative entrepreneurship but also capable team leaders, and potential managers who know the business better than normal graduates. Till now most Indian universities with tourism programs have added modules on entrepreneurship education mostly in the fourth semester or final year of the program. But it is interesting to note that the current generation of tourism students are either looking forward to learning the basics of entrepreneurship in the first semester itself or specialised program in tourism entrepreneurship. Universities or institutes can further add more optional modules on each type of tourism and allied business in the specialised program based on the interest of the students. For example, modules on homestay, sustainable travel, luxury tourism, experiential travel, adventure tourism, social entrepreneurship in tourism etc. moreover to the basics, types, and specialisations we have to add modules on recent innovations, the latest technological knowledge, networking skills, multidisciplinary thoughts, and ethics. Coming to the existing contents in the syllabi, the major constraint facing is new or updated references are less due to poor availability of literature on the topics. Especially references having good case studies from Indian context or developing nations. To ensure the successful delivery of tourism entrepreneurship education modules we have to first list out or develop possible adequate quality references. The current scenario reflects that Indian universities or institutions are late in pooling the above resources. This is one of the reasons for not having the entrepreneurship modules as well as incubation centres in some of the highly ranked universities in the country. But it's not too late to work on the same to ensure quality resources for the future generation. Even though while having a lot of weaknesses the universities are bringing the changes to ensure tourism graduates are not only highly employable but also employment creators. The same can be understood from the network analysis of Indian universities with entrepreneurship courses in tourism programs. It is therefore likely that such connections exist between different universities and programs as a result of the nation's intention to make tourism programs more entrepreneurial training in nature to ensure the creation of new ventures in all corners especially rural areas to eradicate poverty and conserve culture & environment through tourism activities. It is interesting to note that in all twenty-five cases of this study defines the need and scope of prompting entrepreneurial training to tourism students in the initial or later stage of their postgraduate programs. The idea of a specialized postgraduate program in tourism entrepreneurship is showing good hope as the country's ministry of education has started working on the implication of the New Education Policy 2020.

CONCLUSIONS AND RECOMMENDATIONS

Remarkably the significance of entrepreneurship in tourism and allied sector have been recognised by the government as part of supporting the local economy, small scale ventures, environment and culture. So far the government have introduced various policies and initiatives which ensure local products and culture are promoted well in domestic and international markets. Initiatives like Vocal for Local, *Aatmanirbhar Bharat* (self-reliant India) etc. are well-recognised examples of the same. Coming to the Indian formal education system, exclusive training on entrepreneurship has not been seen even in the curriculum of popular universities and institutes. Only in recent years have few universities introduced one or two courses in the entire program either as part of the core course or optional course. Even though universities have adapted modules on entrepreneurship at different times, the syllabi with entrepreneurship training have contributed value-added sessions to the entire program. Students started to get an overall idea of what is entrepreneurship and how to start one in the tourism or allied sector. Which further reflected in the department or universities interest initiate startup clubs, entrepreneurship games, expert talks, mentoring sessions, etc. within the campus. Taken together, or from the analysis of the current status of entrepreneurship education in tourism programs, the results suggest that all stakeholders of the tourism sector, including tourism students, are interested in taking part in entrepreneurship education or training and the universities or institutes have started to add the same in their curriculum despite the issues and challenges faced by tourism teachers, students, curriculum designers etc. It is recommended to have vibrant academics and industry experts having experience in entrepreneurship be given opportunities in academic institutions as well as availing the schemes of the Government of India to set up incubation centres. Moreover to that, an extensive study/project report on entrepreneurship education with pan India cases and bottom to top approach is further required to proceed with upcoming entrepreneurship education policies and initiatives. Changing the teaching pedagogy and restructuring the syllabi with the inclusion of case studies centralized around the tourism and allied entrepreneurs can ensure better delivery of entrepreneurial teachings in tourism programs. State and centre governments can also make the provisions with clear and transparent policies of sanctioning subsidies and concessions to graduate entrepreneurs and college start-up initiatives. Additionally, there are a lot of activities, games, competitions, and fests that educational institutions, teachers, and trainers can promote practical application of entrepreneurship learnings. In other words, all stakeholders must try to ensure entrepreneurship education is not only confined to classroom learning, but also beyond the four walls of classrooms. Another key point is that to craft successful entrepreneurs, the proper guidance of good mentors is vital. In the view of the same, entrepreneurship education training can also adapt updated concepts of Guru Shishya approach to teaching and learning. There are numerous questions to be yet answered while coming to the topic, and this research has thrown up many questions in need of further study. As mentioned in the literature review, studies are rarely available on the analysis of entrepreneurship education in tourism programs in India. Seeing that our study encourages a new way to analyse the status of entrepreneurship education, and with this in the mind, the present study reflects the need, scope, and current scenario of entrepreneurship education in tourism programs in Indian universities.

RESEARCH IMPLICATIONS AND LIMITATIONS

Overall the findings of this study have several important implications for planning future tourism curricula of diploma, undergraduate and postgraduate programs. Similarly, the results will help in designing innovative entrepreneurship modules in tourism programs to enrich upcoming tourism graduates to become self-sufficient. Beyond these implications, the research article discusses the importance and need of adding value-based training in vocational or non-vocational programs to ensure the employability of graduates.

Several limitations need to be acknowledged. Firstly, this work is also limited by its consideration of syllabus only from popular private, state or central universities. Further studies can be conducted by including syllabi from more number of educational institutes. With this limited study, it is not known whether undergraduate tourism programs in India also updated the curriculum with modules on entrepreneurship education or not, also the scope and need for the same.

ACKNOWLEDGMENT

The authors very much appreciate the support from the various university administrators and tourism department heads for providing an updated syllabus. The authors appreciate the unknown referee's valuable and profound comments.

DISCLOSURE STATEMENT

No potential conflict of interest was reported by the authors.

Declarations of interest: none.

REFERENCES

Ahmad, S. Z. (2015). Entrepreneurship education in tourism and hospitality programs. *Journal of Hospitality & Tourism Education*, *27*(1), 20–29. doi:10.1080/10963758.2014.998764

Ahmad, S. Z., Abu Bakar, A. R., & Ahmad, N. (2018). An evaluation of teaching methods of entrepreneurship in hospitality and tourism programs. *International Journal of Management Education*, *16*(1), 14–25. doi:10.1016/j.ijme.2017.11.002

Bagri, S. C., & Babu, A. S. (2011). Historical Development of Tourism Education in India: The Case of the Himalayan State of Uttarakhand. *Journal of Tourism*, *12*(1). Retrieved February 1st, 2022, from www.hnbgu.ac.in

Bagri, S. C., Babu, S., & Kukreti, M. (2010). Human resource practices in hotels: A study from the tourist state of Uttrakhand, India. *Journal of Human Resources in Hospitality & Tourism*, *9*(3), 286–299. doi:10.1080/15332841003749227

Basu, R. (2014). Entrepreneurship Education in India: A Critical Assessment and a Proposed Framework. *Technology Innovation Management Review*, *4*(8), 5–10. doi:10.22215/timreview/817

Bharucha, J. (2019). Entrepreneurship education management in India. *International Journal of Business Excellence*, *17*(4), 456. doi:10.1504/IJBEX.2019.099125

Deale, C. S. (2016). Entrepreneurship education in hospitality and tourism: Insights from entrepreneurs. *Journal of Teaching in Travel & Tourism, 16*(1), 20–39. doi:10.1080/15313220.2015.1117957

Deininger, B. (2020). *Entrepreneurship Education in Tourism: A Study on the Institutions of Higher Education in Finland*. Jyväskylä University. https://jyx.jyu.fi/handle/123456789/70047

Dixit, S. K., & Mawroh, H. (2019). Vocational Education and Training for Hospitality and Tourism Industry in India. In Tourism Education and Asia (pp. 35–48). doi:10.1007/978-981-13-2613-4_3

Gautam, M. K., & Kumar Singh, S. (2017). Entrepreneurship Education : Concept, Characteristics and Implications for Teacher Education. *An International Journal of Education, 5*(March), 21–35. https://www.researchgate.net/publication/319057540

Glackin, C., Byrd, K., & Phelan, S. (2016). Contextual considerations in entrepreneurial finance education: A systematic analysis of U.S. undergraduate courses. *Academy of Entrepreneurship Journal, 22*(2), 13–28. Retrieved February 1st, 2022, from https://search.proquest.com/ openview/ b024b5491 fadcccfb 0398b beea 7374f4/ 1?pq- origsite = gscholar &cbl= 29726

Gupta, S. K., & Bhatt, V. P. (2017). Status of Tourism and Hospitality Education in Garhwal Region of Uttarakhand State in India: A Critical Evaluation. *Tourism Development Journal, 16*, 72. http://www.ibef.org

Hodson, R. (1999). *Analyzing documentary accounts*. SAGE Publications. doi:10.4135/9781412983372

Kumar, A. (2018). Hospitality Education in India: Issues and Challenges. *Journal of Hotel and Business Management, 07*(01), 1. doi:10.4172/2169-0286.1000169

Mcmullan, W. E., & Long, W. A. (1987). Entrepreneurship education in the nineties. *Journal of Business Venturing, 2*(3), 261–275. doi:10.1016/0883-9026(87)90013-9

McNally, J. J., Piperopoulos, P., Welsh, D. H. B., Mengel, T., Tantawy, M., & Papageorgiadis, N. (2020). From pedagogy to andragogy: Assessing the impact of social entrepreneurship course syllabi on the Millennial learner. *Journal of Small Business Management, 58*(5), 871–892. doi:10.1080/00472778.2019.1677059

Mwasalwiba, E. S. (2010). Entrepreneurship education: A review of its objectives, teaching methods, and impact indicators. *Education + Training, 52*(1), 20–47. doi:10.1108/00400911011017663

Ndou, V., Mele, G., & Del Vecchio, P. (2019). Entrepreneurship education in tourism: An investigation among European Universities. *Journal of Hospitality, Leisure, Sport and Tourism Education*, *25*, 100175. Advance online publication. doi:10.1016/j.jhlste.2018.10.003

Okumus, F., & Wong, K. K. F. (2007). A content analysis of strategic management syllabi in tourism and hospitality schools. *Journal of Teaching in Travel & Tourism*, *7*(1), 77–97. doi:10.1300/J172v07n01_06

Owusu-Mintah, B., S. (. (2014). Entrepreneurship education and job creation for tourism graduates in Ghana. *Education + Training*, *56*(8/9), 826–838. doi:10.1108/ET-01-2014-0001

Pittaway, L. (2016). *Assessment: Examining practice in entrepreneurship education.* Taylor & Francis. doi:10.1108/00400911211274882

Raichaudhuri, A. (2005). Issues in entrepreneurship education. *Education*, *32*(2), 73–84. Retrieved February 1st, 2022, from http://search.ebscohost.com/ login.aspx? direct = true & profile = ehost & scope = site & authtype = crawler & jrnl = 0304 0941 & AN = 1951 1431 &h = jET8 49Y7 r6NQ hPpC IQc9 J6Rk RSWp YwML arxX xMdR j5Lf MYnx 4FWl w2sP b6sB ti%2 F98a d8uB UCRG iJfH 6xo5 UmyQ %3D% 3D& crl=c

Ranga Rao, G. K. (1995). IITTM: Tourism Education & Training in India. *Tourism Recreation Research*, *20*(2), 75–78. doi:10.1080/02508281.1995.11014753

Rehman, A., & Elahi, Y. A. (2012). Entrepreneurship Education in India – Scope, challenges and Role of B- schools in Promoting Entrepreneurship Education. *International Journal of Engineering and Management Research*, *2*(5), 5–14. www.tie.org

Sahinidis, A. G., Polychronopoulos, G., & Kallivokas, D. (2019). Entrepreneurship Education Impact on Entrepreneurial Intention Among Tourism Students: A Longitudinal Study. Springer. doi:10.1007/978-3-030-12453-3_142

Sheldon, P. J., & Daniele, R. (2017). *Social Entrepreneurship and Tourism.* doi:10.1007/978-3-319-46518-0_1

Sirelkhatim, F., & Gangi, Y. (2015). Entrepreneurship education: A systematic literature review of curricula contents and teaching methods. Cogent Business and Management, 2(1). doi:10.1080/23311975.2015.1052034

Solomon, G. T., Alabduljader, N., & Ramani, R. S. (2019). Knowledge management and social entrepreneurship education: Lessons learned from an exploratory two-country study. *Journal of Knowledge Management, 23*(10), 1984–2006. doi:10.1108/JKM-12-2018-0738

Srivastava, K., & Thomas, P. (2017). Promoting entrepreneurship in higher educational institutions: The role of entrepreneurial methodologies. In Entrepreneurship Education: Experiments with Curriculum, Pedagogy and Target Groups (pp. 247–265). Springer Singapore. doi:10.1007/978-981-10-3319-3_14

Van Vuuren, J., & Nieman, G. (1999). Entrepreneurship Education and Training : a Model for Syllabi / Curriculum Development. *Annual Conference of International Council for Small Business*. https://www.academia.edu/download/31640285/93.pdf

Yeshawanth, R., & K, N. (2015). Entrepreneurship Education in Management Institutes - Need & Challenges. *SSRN Electronic Journal*. doi:10.2139/ssrn.2600605

Zheng, W. (2019). How to carry out innovation and entrepreneurship education for tourism management students? *3rd International Conference on Advancement of the Theory and Practices in Education*. 10.25236/icatpe.2019.307

Zhou, Y. (2017). On the Innovation and Entrepreneurship Education of Undergraduate Tourism Management Specialty in Higher Vocational Education. *Proceedings of the 2017 International Conference on Economics and Management, Education, Humanities and Social Sciences (EMEHSS 2017)*. 10.2991/emehss-17.2017.83

KEY TERMS AND DEFINITIONS

Aatmanirbhar Bharat: Atmanirbhar Bharat Abhiyaan or Self-Reliant India campaign is the vision of new India with the aim to make the country and its citizens self-reliant in all sense.

ATLAS.ti: ATLAS.ti is a computer-assisted qualitative data analysis software that facilitates analysis of qualitative data for qualitative research, quantitative research, and mixed methods research.

Content Analysis: Content analysis is a research tool used to determine whether certain words, themes, or concepts are present within certain qualitative data. Content analysis allows researchers to quantify and analyze the presence, meaning, and relationships of specific words, topics, or concepts.

Diploma: A diploma is a certificate issued by an educational institution that certifies the recipient's successful completion of their studies. Especially short term courses after 10th or 12th standard in India.

Entrepreneurship: The activity of creating a business or businesses, taking on financial risks in the hope of earning a profit.

Hospitality (Industry): Hospitality is a broad sector of the service industry that includes lodging, food and beverage services, event planning, theme parks, travel and tourism. This includes hotels, travel agencies, restaurants and bars. Hospitality is the relationship between a guest and a host in which the host receives the guest with some degree of goodwill, including accepting and entertaining the guest, visitor, or stranger.

Multidisciplinary: The combination or inclusion of several scientific or professional disciplines in approaching a topic or problem.

Postgraduate: Specifies whether to refer to degrees completed after the completion of the first degree. Especially after three or four years of undergraduate degree courses in India.

Syllabi: The subjects in a course of study or teaching.

Tourism: The commercial organization and operation of holidays and visits to places of interest. There are numerous types of tourism based on tourist's interest and market demands.

Undergraduate: A university degree taken after completion of 10th or 12th standard in India.

Vocal for Local: A government of India initiative, the idea is to encourage local industry and consume as locally as possible, and to use the long-term effects of increased demand to develop domestic industry and gradually become self-sufficient.

Chapter 3
Education of Tourism and Hotel-and-Restaurant Specialists in Ukraine

Nadezhda Anatolievna Lebedeva
https://orcid.org/0000-0003-4095-2631
Kherson State Agrarian and Economic University, Ukraine

ABSTRACT

The main aim of the chapter is to describe the professional training of future specialists in tourist and hotel and restaurant service in Ukraine. The object is the training of junior bachelors, bachelors, and masters of services. The subject of the chapter is the conditions of education of future specialists of tourist and hotel and restaurant service in Ukraine. A specialist in the tourism industry and hotel and restaurant business must provide services related to the activities of tourist complexes, restaurants, and hotels to carry out the primary level of management of structural units, operating systems, etc. The novelty of this chapter is to share experiences with colleagues from other countries. Activation of independent cognitive activity of future specialists with the help of project technologies, high level of competence of teachers of higher education institutions, their skill in the implementation of programs, and their harmonious combination in educational and extracurricular activities will contribute to the improvement of entrepreneurship in the field of tourism.

INTRODUCTION

Global trends in social development and competition in the labour market lead to increased requirements for the training of specialists in various fields.

DOI: 10.4018/978-1-7998-9510-7.ch003

As it is well known, the tourism business confidently achieves the first position in comparison with other sectors of the economy in the world. Areas of services such as hotel and restaurant complex, tourism and recreational business can make a significant contribution to the growth of national economies. Accelerated development of this area will contribute to the dynamic expansion of the domestic market as a basis for stable economic growth in some regions, especially in the negative conditions caused by the effects of the global COVID-19 pandemic.

The leading goals of modern higher education institutions of Ukraine are professional training of competent and competitive professionals capable of self-development and self-realization in the chosen profession. So the quality training of future professionals in tourism as a priority component of the hospitality industry is important for the socio-economic development of Ukraine.

Ukraine, in particular the Kherson region, is a unique territory for tourism and recreation, which has enough advantages for the formation and development of powerful resorts and tourist complexes. To service them, there is a need to update the educational process of training tourism professionals, as well as to carry out business activities in this area. In Ukraine, there is a Strategy for the development of tourism and resorts for the period up to 2026 (2017), Laws: “On Tourism” (2020), “On Higher Education” (2019), “On Education” (2017), many legal documents in which the basic requirements are stated. There is a strategy for the development of the Kherson region until 2027, which prescribes a tourist and recreational complex. All this requires the presence of specialists in the field of tourism with entrepreneurship knowlege. Mentioned documents identify the ways of state policy for the development of tourism infrastructure, the importance of the problem of forming the entrepreneurial qualities of specialists in the field of human resources development, which involves improving the training of specialists in tourism and resorts and other areas related to tourism and hospitality. In the XXI century there is a special demand for higher education, in particular for vocational education, due to awareness of its importance for the economic, socio-cultural and spiritual development of civilization, the formation of information and communication society, where knowledge as a specific form of information plays a crucial role. During the years of Ukraine’s independence, the main legislative field of the education sector has been formed, and the legal framework for the creation and development of state standards of vocational education has been developed. The industry standard is a legislative norm in Ukraine and guarantees by the state the right of citizens to quality tourism education.

Thus, the relevance of the topic of this chapter is caused by the rapid development of the tourism and hotel and restaurant industry in Ukraine, the geographical area of which is unique. In Ukraine, there is wide access to the Dnieper waterway. The country has access to two seas at the same time – the Black and Azov Seas.

Accordingly, the state directs its activities to encourage young people to be active, develop innovative products and start a business in the hospitality industry through competitions at the regional and sectoral levels. In higher education institutions of Ukraine, social orders for highly qualified specialists in the field of services and tourism and growth of innovative potential of institutions and enterprises of the hospitality industry, creation of opportunities for small and medium business development within the hospitality industry and unwillingness of specialists to adapt to professional activity. The need for knowledge formation for students is carried out in higher education institutions. The content of educational programs is improved, such as information and methodological supplementation of professional disciplines and development of educational and methodical support, methods (interactive methods, business games, project technologies, visualization methods, educational work with web resources, feedback methods, etc.), organizational forms (traditional and innovative lectures, practical classes, pieces of training, round tables, research work of applicants), teaching aids, which are systematized and implemented in higher education institutions.

The chapter aims to describe the professional training of future specialists in tourist and hotel, in restaurant services in Ukraine. The object is the training of junior bachelors, bachelors and masters of these areas of services. The subject of the chapter is the condition of education of future specialists of tourist and hotel and restaurant service in Ukraine. Tasks are: to study the state of the researched problem and to substantiate the importance of professional training of specialists of tourist, and hotel and restaurant business in Ukraine, to allocate their benefits in the world circle of tourist business.

A specialist in the tourism industry and hotel and restaurant business must provide services related to the activities of tourist complexes, restaurants and hotels, to carry out the primary level of management of structural units, operating systems, etc. In the educational and qualification characteristics of the bachelor there are general competencies (instrumental, interpersonal, system) and professional competencies by production functions (organizational, technological, engineering, control, planning). The analysis of the bachelor's competencies in tourism and hotel and restaurant business allows some improving the educational system of this pedagogical direction. The novelty of this chapter is to share experiences with colleagues from other countries. Creating an atmosphere of a partnership between teachers and students in the educational environment of higher education institutions is based on a project approach. Activation of independent cognitive activity of future junior bachelors, bachelors and masters with the help of project technologies is one of the educational foundations. The high level of competence of teachers of higher education institutions, their skill in the implementation of programs and their harmonious combination in educational and extracurricular activities will contribute to the specialist improvement of entrepreneurship in the field of tourism.

BACKGROUND:

Training of Specialists in «Tourism» and «Hotel and Restaurant Business» in Ukraine

In Ukraine, training is provided in the field of knowledge "24 Sphere of service", "Specialty: 241 Hotel and restaurant business, Educational program: "Hotel and restaurant business" by educational degree as well as "Specialty: 242 Tourism, Educational program: "Tourism":

initial level – junior bachelor;
the first – a bachelor;
the second is a master's degree;
third (educational-scientific / educational-creative) – doctor of philosophy.

Professional training in the areas of "Hotel and Restaurant Business" and "Tourism" in Ukraine is carried out by higher education institutions of III-IV levels of accreditation and institutions of I-II levels of accreditation (colleges, vocational lyceums, higher vocational schools, technical schools, etc.).

"At the present stage of socio-economic development of Ukraine, the urgent problem is to guarantee and enhance the quality of public services. Ensuring and improving the quality of hospitality services is an urgent problem in all countries. Its solution depends to some extent. This is due to the ever-increasing requirements for the training of specialists in the speciality 241 "Hotel and restaurant business" (Klapchuk, 2017, p. 5).

The industry standard of higher education in Ukraine in the field of training "Hotel and restaurant business" and "Tourism" is focused on production functions, typical tasks, professional competencies and socio-personal competencies of the graduate and forms practical skills and experience (Approved standards of higher education, 2020; 2021). There is competence-oriented training, which encourages not only to rethink the goals but requires the search for optimal ways to form the professional competence of the hotel and restaurant and tourism business. Optimization of the process of formation of readiness of junior bachelors, bachelors, masters, doctors of philosophy of tourism, hotel and restaurant business should be realized by activating certain pedagogical conditions. They orient professional preparation on activity in hotel and restaurant business, promote the development of skills of students to subjects and process of cognitive activity. It gives an independent assess the readiness for professional activity, motivates all subjects of the educational process to create a positive psychological microclimate.

"Quality education is very important for an employee of this industry because it depends on the acquired skills and abilities - whether he can keep the client and ignite in him the desire to come and return to this hotel, but also knowledge of ethics of communication with people, conflictology, the flexibility of thinking, ability to resolve conflict situations, which is the key to a successful career in the field of services. Higher education must meet the needs of Ukraine in highly qualified specialists for hotel and restaurant business" (Lebedenko, Solonitskaya, Novichkova, 2021, pp. 436).

Theoretical and methodological principles of the formation of educational standards in the field of tourism were studied by Ukrainian scientist Fomenko (2012). She scientifically substantiated the problem of standardization of professional education in pedagogical theory and practice; developed and theoretically argued the conceptual and methodological principles of formation of Ukrainian standards of tourism education as an organic component of standards of higher professional education (Fomenko, 2012, p.13)

The development of standards of tourism education was based on the scientist's personality-oriented and competence-based approaches. As a result, the semantic paradigm of the future hospitality specialist for tourism was formed,

"which should be qualified as an integrated personal education of the future personality, which enables its ability to professional self-determination, professional self-realization in real changes in the content and nature of work in tourism and prospects of social, scientific and technological progress, development of culture, needs of society and the state" (Fomenko, 2012, p. 15).

In Ukraine, according to Fomenko (2012), the influence of society on tourism education occurs spontaneously because the mechanisms of this are formed as a result of "economic, social and socio-cultural realities" (Fomenko, 2012, p. 375). A directed way of social influence is realized through a system of legislative, economic, organizational decisions at the state level. According to Fomenko (2012), this influence is also manifested in the systematic creation by society and the state of legal, material, social, and spiritual conditions for the formation of future specialists in the field of tourism through self-development and self-improvement.

"The economic sphere affects tourism education by the general standard of living, which is reflected in the degree of satisfaction of material and spiritual needs and demands, and the level of economic development of the state, which depends on quantitative and qualitative parameters of logistics of tourism education" (Fomenko, 2012, p 377).

As a pedagogical phenomenon, tourism education is a system that studies based on social and natural laws of tourism, restaurant and hotel business and entrepreneurship.

"In modern conditions, there is a growing interest in the hospitality industry, in particular in the hotel and restaurant business. The service sector is constantly in need of new staff, so the specialist in the hotel and restaurant business - one of the most popular, prestigious and highly paid professionals. (Lebedenko, Solonitskaya, Novichkova, 2021, p. 436).

As it can be seen from the overview of the scientific issues by Klapchuk (2017), Yakymenko-Tereshchenko, Zhadan, Mardus, Melen, Poberezhna (Yakymenko-Tereshchenko et. al., 2019) in Ukraine, students should know both the legal component of tourism and hotel and restaurant business, and the business fundamentals of doing business in this economic field. It is also important that students must acquire such skills as the ability to use theoretical professional knowledge and practical skills in the organization of activities in the hotel industry, in the modern organization of culinary production in restaurants, planning, implementation of production tasks, management of technological processes of high quality. Also, specialists must have the skills to form a modern system of economic thinking in the field of organization management, taking into account the specifics of the industry and the management of the hotel and restaurant industry, have methods of monitoring and analyzing the marketing environment, choosing the target consumer segment. The use of foreign languages in professional activities and the ability to analyze the effectiveness of positive action on the health of vacationers is mandatory.

The importance of the ability to predict the economic efficiency and effectiveness of projects in the resort business is noted in studies by Stadnytsky, Dzyana, Koropetskaya (Stadnytsky et al., 2013) Medinskaya (2019), Karolop (2020). The skill of decision-making in complex and unpredictable conditions that requires the application of new approaches and forecasting is discussed in the works of Babeshko (2017), Bogonis (2017), Fomenko (2012), Malyuk (2016). Use modern techniques and methods of economic and statistical research, conduct a systematic analysis of macro-and micro-environment of Ukraine, region, city, monitoring of major competitors in the market, analyze business systems and participate in the development of projects to improve them, analyze institutional systems – all these tasks are considered by Kitchenko and Cheremis (Kitchenko & Cheremis 2017), Lukianets and Yevstafiev (Lukianets & Yevstafiev 2019), Oliynyk (2016). They recommend the development of such projects.

Yanchuk, Lubinchak & Vovkolup (Yanchuk et. al., 2020), Kitchenko & Chemerys (2017) propose to evolve a marketing research plan, conduct marketing research to determine the potential consumers, their behavioural characteristics and motivation of demand, communication measures. Korkuna (2020) pays much attention to the skills to justify pricing policy in the face of changes in demand, calculate market capacity, based on the analysis of seasonal factors. Davydova, Pisarevsky, & Ladyzhenska (Davydova et. al., 2012), Zavidna (2017) in the context of quality management of products and services of hotel and restaurant industry address aspects of paperwork related to hotel activities and the need for skills to select, analyze, systematize legal, informational, reporting and statistical materials, to provide voluntary and obligatory certification, to provide quality of hotel services.

Klapchuk (2017) believes that professionals should also have the skills to plan the use of working time, time planning as a resource, use different sources of information, the formation of informative management," - effectively using the capabilities of the automated workplace, quickly process arrays of various information, diagnose management situation in conditions of the limited time;

- on the basis of information support and computer technologies to develop a sufficient number of alternative solutions;
- based on the criteria of socio-economic efficiency and environmental safety, on the basis of scientific methods and models to evaluate alternatives, justify, choose the optimal alternative;
- on the basis of modern software to use electronic tools to optimize solutions;
- monitor changes in legislation, navigate the regulations, ensure the legitimacy of activities;
- ensure the participation of employees at all levels in decision-making;
- to determine the impact of environmental factors on the activities of the organization, to adapt the organization to the rapidly changing environment;
- using regulatory and legal instruments, based on the study of factors of direct and indirect action to organize cooperation with the environment;
- establish, maintain and develop business relationships with other organizations;
- to protect the interests of the enterprise in the system of corporate business;
- to organize the development of a product quality assurance program from design to operation, to implement scientific methods of product quality management;
- to form a bank of standards, technical conditions, to monitor changes in them;

- to organize comparative and analytical monitoring of consumer quality of competitors' products, research of consumer reaction to product quality;
- based on the marketing approach to make recommendations for the introduction of new or changes to existing quality requirements;
- by current legislation and on the basis of standards to maintain the quality of products and services at the appropriate level, to protect consumers from substandard products (Malyuk & Varipaeva (2018);
- to analyze the main indicators of hotel activity and on their basis to forecast the prospects of the enterprise (Paryshkura, 2020);
- analyze trends and prospects for development in the international market; (Klapchuk, 2017, pp. 9-10) (Yakimenko-Tereshchenko et. al., 2019).

"Modern processes of world economic development indicate the strengthening of the role of services in modern society, which is becoming a dominant element of both national and global economic relations. One of the segments of the consumer market in the world's most actively developing is the hotel and restaurant business. This is a complex multifunctional activity, social in nature, should become an important factor in the economic growth of the regions of Ukraine and improve the material well-being of the population, help to overcome territorial disparities in economic development, entrepreneurship in this segment, additional income. The functioning of the market of hotel and restaurant services in Ukraine singles out a set of problems related to the difficulties of transition of enterprises to European standards of service, the problems of improving I level of their competitiveness, efficiency of management and profitability of the business. Under such conditions, there is a need to improve the quality of training, providing the restaurant and hotel industry with specialists who would meet international standards in the field of services" (Yakimenko-Tereshchenko et. al., 2019, p. 3).

Lebedenko, Solonitskaya, Novichkova (Lebedenko et. al., 2021) studied the market of the hotel industry in Ukraine. They determined that despite the quarantine measures it is developing rapidly.

"Investments of private investors in the hotel and restaurant business are growing and its economic efficiency is increasing. This contributes to increasing the number of jobs for professionals in this business. Hotel services are used not only by corporate clients but also by foreign tourists. After all, Ukraine, especially the Odesa region, is an active participant in the economic and social system of the world. Every year it is dominated more and more by the trend of increasing demand for an expanded range of services, including tourism, restaurant and hotel business" (Lebedenko, Solonitskaya, Novichkova, 2021, pp. 435).

According to Lebedenko, Solonitskaya, Novichkova (Lebedenko et. al., 2021), to be efficient and competitive in the global market, the hotel and restaurant business needs professionals who speak foreign languages, know the industry and current trends in traditional hospitality.

"A modern hotel is not only a modern and well-equipped facility with a developed infrastructure, with a restaurant complex, but above all it is presented by competent, qualified, polite hotel staff, ready to meet the needs of guests. The main task of professionals working in modern hotels and restaurants, is the creation and implementation of the latest techniques, provided by the collective efforts of employees of all services, constant and effective control, improvement of forms and methods of service, study and implementation of best practices, new equipment and technologies"(Lebedenko et. al., 2021, p. 436).

Orlova & Shekera (2021) note that the "Standard of Higher Education in the speciality 242" Tourism "for the first (bachelor's) level of higher education" (Approved standards of higher education, 2018; 2020; 2021) provides students with the result "to show the respect for individual and cultural diversity"(Orlova & Shekera 2021, p. 414).

"The peculiarity of this result is that its achievement is important not only for the successful implementation of professional activities by workers in the field of tourism but also involves compliance with some international documents" (Orlova & Shekera 2021, p. 414).

Considerable attention is paid to the achievement of certain competencies and learning outcomes in general in the compulsory disciplines "Geography of Tourism" (Orlova & Shekera 2021, p. 415), "Organization of tourism (Organization of tourist travel)" (Orlova & Shekera 2021, p. 415) and "Organization of tourism (Organization of excursions and animation activities)" (Orlova & Shekera 2021, p. 415). Thanks to all these disciplines, subject competence is formed: "Ability to develop, promote, sell and organize the consumption of a tourist product" (Orlova & Shekera 2021, p. 415), as students learn to create quality tourist products based on individual characteristics and cultural values of tourists. Obligatory knowledge of foreign languages is also the competence of future specialists in the field of tourism and hotel and restaurant business in Ukraine (Shepel & Tretiyk, (2021); Gostryk, Nikitina & Kalashnikova (Gostryk et. al., 2017), Zubar (2016), Korniyaka & Golikova (2015), the work of Yakubenko V., Yakubenko N., Zakharchuk, Arabska K. & Arabska E. (2015)).

Elective course "History of world tourism and the basics of tourism" (Orlova & Shekera 2021, p. 415), primarily aimed at forming a general competence "the ability to preserve and increase moral, cultural, scientific values and achievements of society based on understanding history and patterns of development of the subject area… "(Orlova & Shekera 2021, p. 416), as well as professional competence "understanding current trends and regional priorities for tourism development in general and its special forms and types" (Orlova & Shekera 2021, p. 416). Innovative technologies are being implemented in Ukraine, as noted in the works of Matsuk (2009), Kozik (2017), Bury (2014), Lukyanova, Babushko & Banit (Lukyanova et. al., 2019), Oleynyk (2016)), Frey& Solovey (2018), Yanchuk, Lyubinchak, & Vovkolup (Yanchuk et. al., 2020), Rybchinskaya (2015), Seryogin (2020).

"Activities in the field of tourism work with people, each of whom is an individual, in addition, it is mainly work in an international environment. That is why the disciplines, term papers, practices and other components of the educational program emphasizes the equality of all people regardless of their race, ethnicity, religion, gender and age, political opinion, social status, professional activity, health or other characteristics, future tourism workers must respect this diversity and uniqueness of people at the individual, group and national levels. Appreciate it in native clients, in foreign tourists served in Ukraine, in the local population living in the places of reception of domestic tourists, as well as in their colleagues" (Orlova & Shekera 2021, p. 416).

ENTREPRENEURSHIP DISCIPLINES IN THE FIELD OF TOURISM AND HOTEL BUSINESS IN UKRAINIAN EDUCATIONAL INSTITUTIONS

According to Ivanchenkova & Sklyar (2021), the importance of teaching the discipline "Business planning in the field of hospitality" is the formation of students' general and professional competencies for the successful preparation of business plans and the process of doing business in the hotel and restaurant industry. The scientists (Ivanchenkova & Sklyar, 2021) provide for the acquisition by students of theoretical knowledge and the formation of practical skills in planning the activities of the hotel and restaurant business in modern business conditions. Achievement of the goal is possible under the condition of high-quality mastering of lecture course materials and tasks submitted for practical classes, independent and individual work.

"The main tasks of studying the discipline "Business planning in the field of hospitality" are:

- *formation of the necessary set of theoretical and practical knowledge on the essence of business planning,*
- *presentation of methodological and organizational bases of planning,*
- *definition of methodical principles of functional planning: planning of production, assortment, sale, marketing activity, final results of production and economic activity of the enterprise of the sphere of hospitality,*
- *resource provision, substantiation of the need to update products, organizational and technical development of the enterprise, determination of appropriate methods.*
- *According to the requirements of the educational program, students must know:*
- *theoretical principles, essence, principles and features of business planning in the field of hospitality, its significance in modern conditions of economic development of Ukraine" (Ivanchenkova & Sklyar, 2021, p.407).*

Ivanchenkova & Sklyar (2021) also highlight the system of business planning methods in market conditions, the meaning and content of sections of the business plan of the hospitality company, the organization and procedure for developing plans for hotel and restaurant business, preparation of the necessary analytical data.

"The main issues that have practical significance and should be considered during the study of the course in lectures and practical classes of the discipline:

- *identification of structural patterns of business process development;*
- *determination of sources of profit formation, calculation of the influence of factors on the amount of profit and development of measures for its growth, formation of proposals for reserves to improve activities;*
- *development of a business plan of the enterprise in the field of hospitality and substantiation of its indicators" (Ivanchenkova & Sklyar, 2021, p.408).*

The main competencies of studying are considered as the ability to understand and process ideas and thoughts based on logical arguments and verified facts, the ability to learn new areas, the ability to apply professional and fundamental knowledge of the professional activity. At the same time, scientists identify specific competencies such as "the ability to master the theory and practice of training, the ability to apply them; the ability to analyze trends in the hotel and restaurant industry; the ability to develop market positioning concepts, apply innovative technologies to organize and create customer-oriented hotel and restaurant product (service) to form a positive image, the ability to develop a business plan and calculate its effectiveness for hospitality enterprises, taking into account the requirements and needs of consumers, the ability to use in practice the basics of current legislation in the hotel and restaurant business and monitor changes in this area" (Ivanchenkova & Sklyar, 2021, p.408). Fedosova (2021) considers "Hotel and restaurant business" one of the most prestigious professions of modern times, with which the author of this chapter agrees. According to such opinion, "an expert in restaurant consulting can help restaurateurs to open a new establishment or increase the efficiency of an existing restaurant" (Fedosova, 2021, p. 325). The process of training specialists in the field of restaurant consulting and the algorithm of such a specialist according to Fedosova (2021) is as follows:

- Enterprise audit or Concept development (for new institutions).
- Demand and competitor research.
- Development of a business plan and financial model.
- Development of a strategy for the development and promotion of the institution.
- Project implementation/staff training and project support.

All stages of this work are mastered in the disciplines "Organization of restaurants", "Technology of restaurant products", "Information and communication technologies in the hotel and restaurant business", "Design" and many others. Also during various types of practice, students have the opportunity to spend a lot of time in enterprises, and then after careful analysis and consultation with their managers, they reflect their recommendations for improving the performance of restaurants in their reports" (Fedosova, 2021, p. 326).

"A student understands the algorithm of converting products into profitable dishes. So he can control the processes from the inside, find errors in the operational processes of the kitchen, work with calculations and menus. The student can check the work of both chefs and hall workers, calculate the necessary equipment, control the technological cards, optimize the distribution of raw materials and other" (Fedosova, 2021, p. 326).

Training of specialists in the field of restaurant consulting with the use of information and communication technologies based on the Department of Hotel and Restaurant Business takes place at the Odessa National Academy of Food Technologies. "In the discipline "Information and communication technologies in the hotel and restaurant business, "students study ways to use modern technologies in restaurants and hotels (work with ACS Poster, R-keeper, promotion of restaurants on social networks, targeting, contextual advertising, website development, registration of establishments in Google services, research of competitors with the help of various business tools on the Internet. restaurant consulting, which can develop new concepts and projects of institutions or improve the work of existing enterprises. Thus, it can be concluded that the training program in the field of restaurant consulting using information and communication technologies based on the hotel and restaurant business is effective and very promising" (Fedosova, 2021, p. 326).

According to Pask (2020), the discipline "Engineering in the hotel and restaurant industry" will create new, expand or reconstruct the existing fixed assets of the hotel and restaurant industry based on modern scientific approaches. "In today's world, engineering is understood as works and services, including preparation of technical tasks; conducting research work, drafting project proposals and feasibility study for the construction of industrial and other facilities; conducting engineering research; development of technical projects and working drawings for the construction of new and reconstruction of existing industrial and other facilities, the development of proposals for in-plant and in-shop planning, interoperation connections and transitions, design and engineering development of machines, equipment, installations, devices, products: development of warehouses, alloys, other substances and their testing; development of technological processes, techniques and methods; consultations and author's supervision during installation, commissioning and operation of equipment and facilities in general; consultations of economic, financial or other order" (Paska, 2020, pp. 3).

According to the author of this chapter, additional knowledge of building an effective technological process through innovative engineering solutions and evaluation of the proposed decisions can contribute to the development of a separate business sector in the tourism hotel and restaurant business.

"Over the last decade, Ukraine's major cities have seen a rapid development of the hotel business. Large international chains are coming, the number of small private hotels is growing and old Soviet hotels are being reconstructed. Project management faces such a problem as the proper use and balancing of the three main factors of project implementation, which are the means, quality and timing (Husar, 2020, p.3).

Following the educational and professional training program for masters of speciality 241 "Hotel and restaurant business" the discipline "Project Management in the Hotel and Restaurant Business" should reveal to future professionals an effective methodology for solving problems of project management, as processes of implementation of business ideas, business programs, changes in the initial position of any production system related to investment. The task is to create and develop design-oriented production and commercial systems (enterprises, firms, industries, autonomous production structures, etc.), aimed at the result with predetermined cost and quality characteristics of Ukraine" (Husar, 2020, p. 3). Interdisciplinary links in the study of the discipline are marketing and business economics. According to this program, students must be able to develop and justify the project concept, evaluate the effectiveness of the project taking into account risk factors and uncertainties, use the feasibility study of the project and develop a business plan of the project; to carry out systematic planning of the project at all phases of its life cycle; develop an estimate and budget of the project; find project implementation through tenders, competitions, tenders (Husar, 2020, p. 5). Much attention is also paid to the ability to prepare and conclude supply contracts, organize the optimal procurement and supply procedure, organize project implementation, select an effective "team" for project management, ensure effective control and change management in the project implementation process, its effective completion. The program presents in detail the following topics for mastering:

1. Project management in the management system of hotel and restaurant organizations.
2. Rationale for the project in the hotel and restaurant industry.
3. Project planning in the hotel and restaurant industry.
4. Project time management in the hotel and restaurant industry.
5. Planning of resource provision of the project in the hotel and restaurant economy.
6. Monitoring the implementation of the project in the hotel and restaurant industry.
7. Risk management of projects in the hotel and restaurant industry.
8. Project quality management in the hotel and restaurant industry.
9. Personnel management in projects in the hotel and restaurant industry.
10. Formation of project management strategy of the enterprise.

Zinkova's research (2020) "Pedagogical conditions for the formation of entrepreneurial culture of future professionals in the field of services and tourism" is dedicated to the purpose of entrepreneurial activity in the field of services and tourism, namely: adequate assessment and forecast of tourism and services market needs; the anticipation of new directions of market development, identification of the most promising and popular types of services in the field of hotel and restaurant services and tourist destinations; identification of the optimal volume of production and sale of tourist products and services, taking into account demand, seasonality, environmental conditions; search and creation of new technologies for the production and sale of tourist products and the implementation of services to minimize costs and maximize profits (Zinkova, 2020, p. 44).

"Entrepreneurial culture of specialists in the field of services and tourism - is an integrated personal education based on a system of values and attitudes (beliefs,

attitudes, motives, goals, etc.), due to the peculiarities of activities in the field of services and tourism, implemented in cooperation with others. The concept of "formation of entrepreneurial culture of future specialists in the field of services and tourism" means purposeful modelling of pedagogical conditions that ensure the development of a set of qualities, motives, aspirations, key and professional competencies of personality and determine the readiness of the future specialist in the field of services and tourism to perform professional functions, taking into account the sectoral, economic and socio-ethical principles of entrepreneurship" (Zinkova, 2020, p. 45).

According to Zinkova, entrepreneurial culture, as an integral characteristic of the personality of specialists in the field of services and tourism, in terms of their professional activities provides increased efficiency of professional activities by focusing on improving the quality of services provided to consumers of tourism and hospitality.

"The market for services and tourism is characterized by such features as high rates of development, instability, the presence of various risks, etc. A modern specialist for successful professional self-realization in these conditions must have flexibility, adaptability, creativity, willingness and risk-taking, etc. it is necessary to envisage tasks that will stimulate the formation of qualities relevant to the modern sphere of services and tourism and the labour market in general" (Zinkova, 2020, p. 51).

Zinkova (2020) developed a program of the discipline "Entrepreneurial culture of a specialist in the field of services and tourism: theory and practice", which belongs to the cycle of professional training and disciplines of free choice of students. The content of this discipline covers the theory and practice of business culture in the field of service.

The aim of the course is to form students' general cultural and professional competencies necessary for the realization of the potential of entrepreneurial culture in the field of services and tourism. The development of the ability to create and implement business projects in this area, the formation of skills for organizing the activities of enterprises in the industry, promoting the improvement of professional competence of future professionals" (Zinkova, 2020, p. 51).

The content of competencies according to Zinkova (2020), which should be mastered by future professionals, is such as understanding the social significance of entrepreneurial culture; awareness of the role of entrepreneurship in the development of services and tourism; the desire to qualitatively solve professional problems based on universal values; communication skills; ability to work in a team; tolerance (Zinkova, 2020, p. 243).

It is important to acquire basic knowledge of economics, management and marketing, taking into account the specifics of the industry; mastery of the conceptual content of the category "entrepreneurship" in the field of services and tourism, as well as be able to develop business projects; organizational skills; ability to analyze the services market; willingness to take justified risks; ability to use modern information technologies (Zinkova, 2020, p. 243).

The ability to solve professional problems in uncertain and extreme situations, the skills of productive communication with consumers in the field of services and tourism, the willingness to professional and personal self-improvement are also important factors for success.

Zinkova (2020) offers such methods of methodology and technology as verbal (lecture, conversation, explanation, story, educational discussions, scientific reports), visual (presentation,

intelligence map, "tag cloud", infographics), practical-theoretical (solution of psychological and pedagogical problems, case-study, or method of specific situations), information and communication technologies (Google-class, Google-forms, Padlet), interactive methods (associations, "microphone", "brainstorming", "world cafe", situation modelling, work in small groups, work in pairs, project method), methods of developing critical thinking ("prediction", "reading with marks", "Press") (Zinkova, 2020, p. 246).

"In the process of assessing student achievement, the following methods are used:

- *methods of oral control: individual interview, face-to-face interview, interview, exam.*
- *methods of written control: modular written testing; final written test, essay.*
- *computer control: test programs, final assessment.*
- *methods of self-control: the ability to self-assess their knowledge, introspection*" (Zinkova, 2020, p. 247).

Thus, the training of specialists in the tourism, hotel and restaurant business in Ukraine is quite professional. It provides the market of travel services with quality employees. Educational institutions use innovative technologies, traditional teaching in the educational process, providing a wide range of knowledge, skills and abilities to students that are needed in the process of further employment.

ANALYSIS OF THE UKRAINIAN EDUCATIONAL SUBJECTS IN THE ENTREPRENEURSHIP CONTEXT

The explanatory Cambridge Dictionary defines entrepreneurship as a "skill in starting new businesses, especially when this involves seeing new opportunities" (Cambridge Dictionary, 2022). Entrepreneurship, entrepreneurial activity in many scientific works is presented as an activity in the economic sphere, the result of which is material and spiritual benefits. They arise as a result of the use of property, the sale of goods, the performance of works or the provision of services. Consequently, in the process of training specialists (junior bachelors, bachelors, masters) in the field of tourism and hotel-restaurant business, it naturally becomes necessary to teach subjects that are related to entrepreneurship. There are such as the quality management of products and services of hotel and restaurant business, the geography of tourism, organization of tourism (organization of tourist travel, formation of excursion and animation activities), the restaurant business organization, the technology of restaurant business, information and communication technologies in hotel and restaurant business, design of hotel facilities, the information and communication technologies in the hotel and restaurant business, engineering in the hotel and restaurant business, the project management in the hotel and restaurant business. There are very important studies of such disciplines as marketing, business economics, entrepreneurial culture of services and tourism theory and practice. Summing up the contents of the previous parts of the chapter, the author of this study collected all of the above in figures. Focusing on the Ukrainian standards of higher education, the training of specialists in tourism, hospitality and restaurant business can be presented in Figure 1.

After studying at a higher educational institution in Ukraine, employees of the hospitality, restaurant and tourism business receive many knowledge and skills. The author of this study gives them in the figure. The activity concept covers mandatory knowledge in 17 aspects, as can be seen from Figure 2.

Thus, for the development of entrepreneurship in the sphere of tourism, it is necessary to have highly professional personnel with a set of high-quality knowledge. Such people can develop and improve existing areas of tourism, create new aspects of a business. This is facilitated by curricula and programs of state standards, which were described in detail earlier in this chapter. Without the knowledge, skills and competencies of the staff of the tourism industry as a whole, the development of entrepreneurship is unpromising. Therefore, education determines the improvement of entrepreneurial activity.

Figure 1. Training in the field of knowledge "24 Sphere of service"

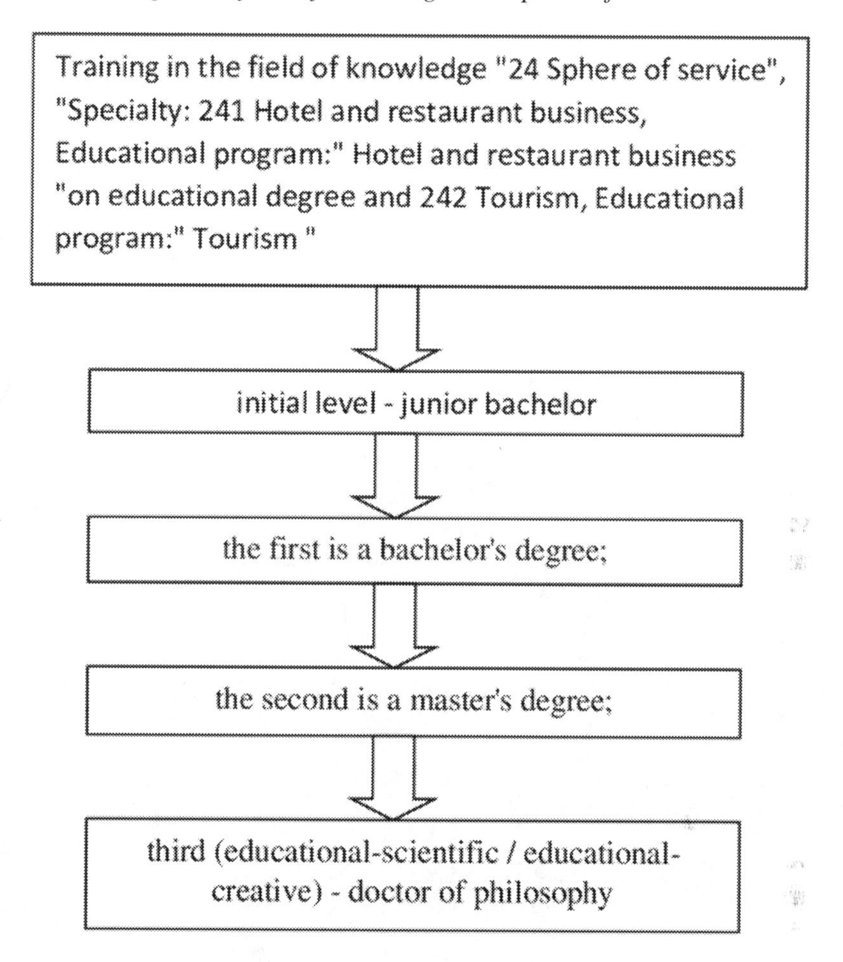

SOLUTIONS AND RECOMMENDATIONS

The Strategy for the Development of the Kherson Region in Ukraine until 2027 (Kherson Regional Council, 2019) states that the Kherson Region is a unique territory for tourism and recreation, which has enough advantages for the formation and development of a powerful resort and tourist complex oriented for foreign tourists as well. The region has access to the Dnieper waterway. It is the only region of Ukraine that has two seas at the same time – the Black and Azov. In the Kherson region are located: the only natural desert in Europe – Oleshkiv sands, the world's largest man-made forest, unique mountain landscapes in the middle of the steppe – Stanislavsky cliffs. The region has 12 resort settlements, more than 450 km of sea coastline, including 200 km of equipped sandy beaches, the longest sandy spit in the world – Arabatskaya Strelka, more than 70 deposits of healing balneological resources (mineral and thermal waters, therapeutic muds, brines of salt lakes), including the unique Lemurian Lake, the therapeutic mud of which has undergone clinical trials, certified and approved for use as a therapeutic and cosmetic product. The city – Skadovsk is a resort of national importance, a centre for children's health and recreation.

Figure 2. Training of specialists in the specialty 241 "Hotel and restaurant business" in Ukraine (summarized by the author of the chapter)

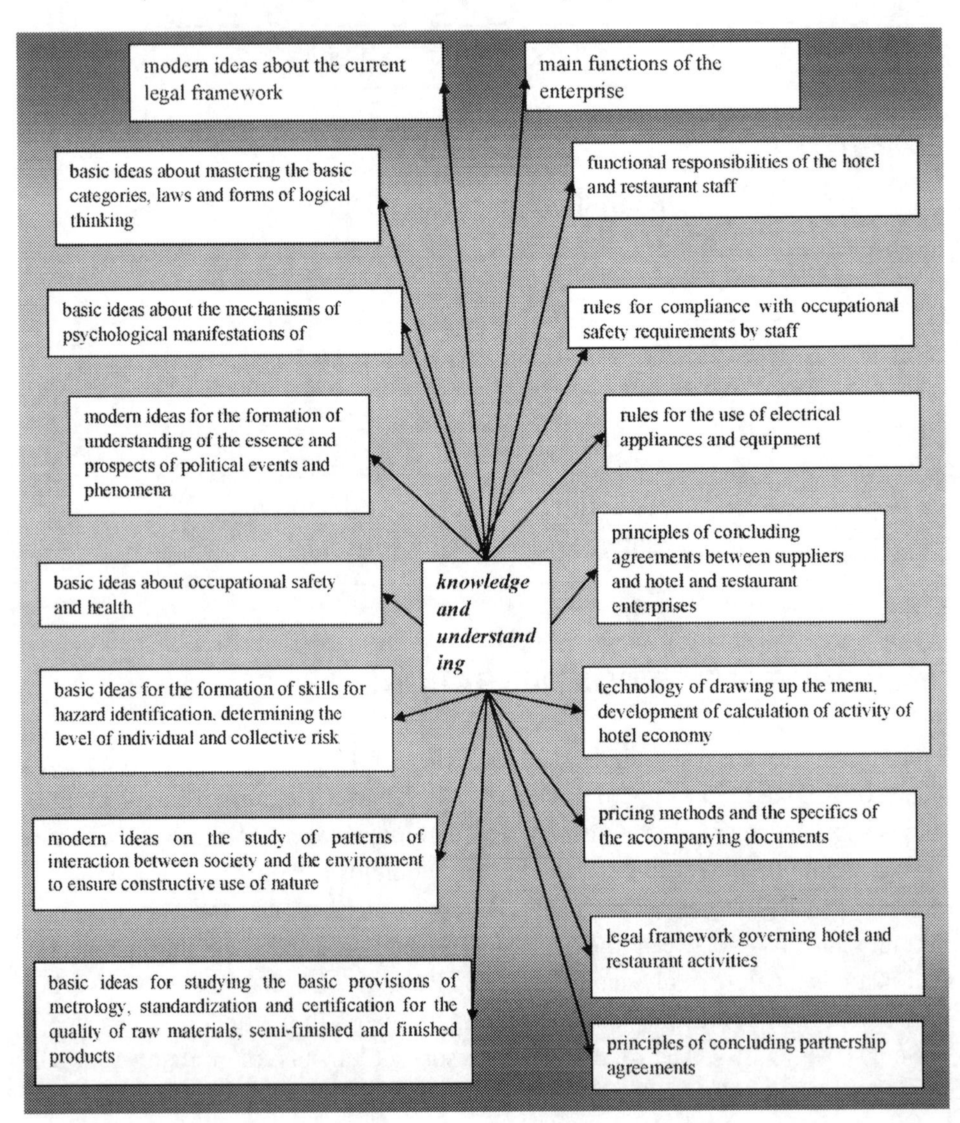

"According to the monitoring, more than 2.2 million tourists visited the region in 2014. In 2018, more than 3.5 million guests came to the region with vivid impressions and unique emotions. In addition, in 2018, more than 20 people visited the Kherson region for private purposes. Top 5 visitor countries of Kherson region - Turkey, Germany, Israel, USA, Japan. It has 51 hotel complexes. The total bed stock - more than 100 thousand places" (Strategy of development of the Kherson area till 2027, p. 77).

Thus, the improvement of education, development of programs aimed at general and professional training of competitive professionals in tourism and hotel and restaurant business, taking into account the agro-economic specifics of the region, which have a research methodology is a promising scientific direction in the Ukrainian educational process.

FUTURE RESEARCH DIRECTIONS

Given the development of tourism trends in the Kherson region in Ukraine, the author believes that this area has significant opportunities to enter the most developed of Europe in terms of tourism and hotel and restaurant business. Kherson region has a favourable geopolitical location, comfortable microclimatic conditions, diverse landscape, unique flora and fauna, historical and cultural, architectural heritage, developed transport network, sufficient human, material, including natural and health resources. In this context, the development of educational institutions, expansion and improvement of educational programs in the field of tourism and hotel and restaurant business are relevant and require further research, theoretical justifications and practical developments. Local research in the field of education of tourism and hotel and restaurant business professionals will contribute to the dissemination of practical experience, which may be interesting in the context of international cooperation in the field of tourism and hotel and restaurant business.

The research would cover all aspects of the problems of entrepreneurial competence formation of future junior bachelors, bachelors, masters of tourism and hotel and restaurant service. The further study requires theoretical and methodological principles of professional training of future professionals, comparative analysis of training systems for hotel and restaurant and tourism services in foreign countries, organizational and pedagogical conditions for the development of their entrepreneurial competence.

CONCLUSION

According to the approved standards of higher education in Ukraine, the requirements for a junior bachelor in tourism and hotel and restaurant business are - the ability of a person to solve typical specialized tasks in a certain field of professional activity or the learning process be responsible for the results of their practices and the activities of others in certain situations. The professional title of works for junior bachelors is as follows: travel agent, guide, maid, administrator, restaurant master, bartender, waiter, steward.

Requirements for bachelor in tourism and hotel and restaurant business are - the ability of a person to solve complex specialized problems and practical problems in a particular field of professional activity; or a capability in the learning process, which involves the application of certain theories and methods of science. The professional title of works for bachelors: a specialist in hospitality at the accommodation (hotels, tourist complexes, etc.), a specialist in hotel business organizer of tourist and hotel activities; hotel service specialist.

Masters must be able to solve complex problems and tasks in a particular field of professional activity and in the learning process, which involves research or innovation. The professional title of works for masters - manager of the hotel industry, tourist complex; head of the branch (s) of the hotel or tourist complex; teacher; guide, recreationist, tourism expert. Based on the scientific works of Ukrainian scientists, the author of the chapter summarizes the existing theoretical experience in the training of tourism and hotel and restaurant services in Ukraine. Ukrainian specialists in the field of tourism and hotel and restaurant business can provide services related to the activities of tourist complexes, restaurants and hotel establishments, carry out the primary level of management of structural units, operating systems, etc. The analysis of the competencies of junior bachelor, bachelor, master in tourism and hotel and restaurant business allows improving the educational system of this pedagogical direction. Creating an atmosphere of a partnership between teachers and students in the educational environment of higher education institutions based on project and innovative technologies contribute to the emergence of world-class tourism and hotel and restaurant business professionals and the improvement of present ones.

ACKNOWLEDGMENT

This research received no grant from any organization and represents teaching and practical experience.

REFERENCES

Approved Standards of Higher Education. (2020). https://mon.gov.ua/ua/osvita/visha-osvita/naukovo-metodichna-rada-ministerstva-osviti-i-nauki-ukrayini/zatverdzheni-standarti-vishoyi-osviti

Babeshko, M. S. (2017). Formation of professionally-specialized competencies of future professionals of hotel and restaurant business. *Psychological and Pedagogical Scientific Collection, 11*. http://pedagogylviv.org.ua/zhurnaly/march_2017.pdf#page=11

Bezruchenkov, Yu. V. (2015). Components of the professional culture of future specialists of the hotel and restaurant industry. *Scientific Bulletin of Donbass*, (1).

Bogonis, O. M. (2018). *Formation of economic competence of future junior specialists of hotel and restaurant service in a professional college* [Doctoral dissertation]. Institute of Pedagogical and Adult Education of the National Academy of Pedagogical Sciences of Ukraine.

Bury, S. A. (2014). *The specifics of technology transfer in the hotel and restaurant business*. http://eztuir.ztu.edu.ua/bitstream/handle/123456789/1561/52.pdf?sequence=1

Davydova, O. Yu., Pisarevsky, I. M., & Ladyzhenskaya, R. S. (2012). *Quality management of products and services in the hotel and restaurant industry*. Tutorial.

Explanatory Cambridge Dictionary. (2022). https://dictionary.cambridge.org/ru/%D1%81%D0%BB%D0%BE%D0%B2%D0%B0%D1%80%D1%8C/%D0%B0%D0%BD%D0%B3%D0%BB%D0%B8%D0%B9%D1%81%D0%BA%D0%B8%D0%B9/entrepreneurship

Fedosova, K. S. (2010). Modern control automation systems in the hotel and restaurant business of Ukraine. *Economics of the Food Industry, 2*, 41-50.

Fedosova, K. S. (2021). Training of specialists in the field of restaurant consulting with the use of information and communication technologies on the basis of the department of hotel and restaurant business. *Odessa National Academy of Food Technologies Collection of materials of the III All-Ukrainian scientific-methodical conference "Ensuring the quality of higher education: improving the efficiency of information technology in the educational process"*, 325-326.

Fomenko, N. A. (2012). *Theoretical and methodical bases of formation of standards of education in the field of tourism* [Doctoral dissertation]. Kyiv University of Tourism, Economics and Law, Kyiv, Ukraine.

Frey, L.V., & Solovjova, O.V. (2018). Current problems of staff training for the hospitality industry. *Current trends and strategies of development of tourist and hotel and restaurant business*, 237.

Gostrik, A. M., Nikitina, N. A., & Kalashnikov, E. A. (2017). *Features of teaching specialized subjects to English-speaking students*. https://repo.odmu.edu.ua/xmlui/bitstream/handle/123456789/9596/Nikitina.pdf?sequence=1&isAllowed=y

Handayani, B., Seraphin, H., Korstanje, M., & Pilato, M. (2019). Street food as a special interest and sustainable form of tourism for Southeast Asia destinations. In *Special interest tourism in Southeast Asia: Emerging research and opportunities* (pp. 81–104). IGI Global. doi:10.4018/978-1-5225-7393-7.ch005

Husar, U. E. (2020). Curriculum in the discipline "Project Management in the hotel and restaurant business" for students majoring in 241 "Hotel and restaurant business". Academic Press.

Husar, U. E. (2020). Project management in the hotel and restaurant business: the program of the discipline of master's degree in the field of knowledge 24 "Service area", specialty 241 "Hotel and restaurant business". Academic Press.

Ivanchenkova, L. V., & Sklyar, V. Y. (2021). The importance of teaching the discipline "Business Planning in Hospitality" for masters of "Hotel and Restaurant Business". *The III All-Ukrainian Scientific and Methodological Conference "Quality Assurance in Higher Education: Improving the efficiency of information technology in the educational process",* 407-408.

Karolop, O. O. (2020). Pedagogical conditions of formation of readyness for professional activity of bachelors of hotel and restaurant business. *Pedagogical Education: Theory and Practice*, *29*, 276-285.

Kherson Regional Council. (2019). Development strategy of Kherson region for the period of 2021-2027. Author.

Kitchenko, E. N., Chemeris, A.V. (2017). Use of marketing tools in the restaurant business. *Technological Audit and Production Reserves, 1*(4), 8-13.

Klapchuk, V. M. (2013a). The program of professional entrance examination for enrollment in the EQL "Master" in the specialty 8.14010102 "Resort Business". Academic Press.

Klapchuk, V. M. (2017b). Hotel and restaurant business (independent work of students): Educational and methodical manual. Faculty of Tourism, Vasyl Stefanyk Precarpathian National University. Ivano-Frankivsk: "Foliant".

Klapchuk, V. M. (2020c). Hotel and restaurant business (independent work of students). Academic Press.

Korkuna, O. (2020). Pricing in the hotel and restaurant business: the procedure for assessing learning outcomes in the discipline of higher education "bachelor" specialty 241 "Hotel and restaurant business" full-time and part-time education. Academic Press.

Korniyaka, A. A., & Golikova, T. P. (2013). Ways to improve the education system in the field of hospitality. *Scientific Bulletin Poltava University of Economy & Trade: Economic Sciences*, *4*(60), 34–38.

Kozik, K. I. (2017). Information technologies of hotel management. Modern information technologies and systems in management: Coll. materials and All-Ukrainian. scientific-practical conf. young scientists, graduate students and students; April 6-7. Kyiv: KNEU.

Law of Ukraine. (2017). *On Education*. https://zakon.rada.gov.ua/laws/show/2145-19#Text

Law of Ukraine. (2019). *On Higher Education*. https://zakon.rada.gov.ua/laws/show/1556-18#Text

Law of Ukraine. (2020). *On Tourism*. https://zakon.rada.gov.ua/laws/show/324/95-%D0%B2%D1%80#Text

Lebedenko, T. E., Solonitskaya, I. V., & Novichkova, T. P. (2021). Modern requirements for the training of specialists for the hospitality industry. National Academy of Food Technologies.

Lukianets, H., & Yevstafiev, V. (2019). Training systems for staff in hotel industry. *VIII All-Ukrainian scientific-practical conference, dedicated to the 135th anniversary of the National University of Food Technology "Innovative technologies in the hotel and restaurant business", March 19 – 20*. Kyiv: NUHT.

Lukyanova, L., Babushko, S., & Banit, O. (2018). Coaching as an innovative technology for personal and professional development of staff. *Rocenka Ukrajinsko-Slovenska*, *2018*, 154–166.

Malyuk, L. P. (2016). Professional ethics and etiquette in the hotel and restaurant business. Kharkiv: KhDUHT.

Malyuk, L. P., & Varipaeva, L. M. (2018). Professional ethics and etiquette in the hotel and restaurant business. Methodical instructions for independent study of discipline by students of a specialty 241 "Hotel and restaurant business". Academic Press.

Matsuka, V. N. (2009). *The system of professional training of specialists in the field of tourism in Ukraine*. http://91.250.23.215:8080/jspui/bitstream/123456789/600/1/sistema_prof_podgotovki.pdf

Medinskaya, S. I. (2019). Competence approach to training specialists in the field of tourism and hospitality industry to increase their competitiveness in national and international markets. *Bulletin of Alfred Nobel University. Pedagogy and Psychology, 2*(18), 208-214.

Morrison, A., & Johnston, B. (2003). Personal creativity for entrepreneurship: Teaching and learning strategies. *Active Learning in Higher Education, 4*(2), 145–158. doi:10.1177/1469787403004002003

Ndou, V., Mele, G., & Del Vecchio, P. (2019). Entrepreneurship education in tourism: An investigation among European Universities. *Journal of Hospitality, Leisure, Sport and Tourism Education, 25*, 100175. doi:10.1016/j.jhlste.2018.10.003

Oleynyk, V. D. (2016). Problems of service of business travelers in Ukraine. Strategic prospects of tourist and hotel-restaurant industry in Ukraine: theory, practice and innovations of development: materials All-Ukrainian. scientific-practical Internet conference, Uman, October 31. University of Horticulture.

On approval of the Standard of higher education in the specialty 242 "Tourism" for the first (bachelor's) level of higher education: the order of the Ministry of Education and Science of Ukraine from 04. 10. 2018 N° 1068. Kyiv.

Orlova, M. L., & Shekera, S. S. (2021). Show respect for individual and cultural diversity: the importance of the program result and the peculiarities of its achievement by students majoring in 242 "Tourism". *Odessa National Academy of Food Technologies Collection of materials of the III All-Ukrainian scientific-methodical conference "Ensuring the quality of higher education: improving the efficiency of information technology in the educational process"*, 414-416.

Paryshkura, Yu. V. (2020) Perspektyvy ta praktyky industriy fitnesu [Perspectives and practices of the fitness industry]. In Scientific-Practical Conf. Kyiv: KNUTD.

Pasichnyuk, V. B. (2020). *Economic and labor law*. http://ep3.nuwm.edu.ua/19288/1/od_gospodarske_i_trudove_pravo%20%2812%29.pdf

Paska, M. Z. (2020). The syllabus of the course of engineering in the hotel and restaurant industry. Educational degree: master Branch of knowledge: 24 Sphere of service Specialty: 241 Hotel and restaurant business. Component of the educational program: free choice of the student.

Paska, M. Z. (2021). *Engineering in the hotel and restaurant industry: syllabus of the course, educational degree: master, field of knowledge: 24 Sphere of service, specialty: 241 Hotel and restaurant business. Academic Press.*

Polchaninova, I. L. (2016). *Metodychni vkazivky do vykonannia kontrolnoi roboty z dystsypliny «Upravlinnia yakistiu produktsii ta posluh v hotelno-restorannomu hospodarstvi» (dlia studentiv 5 kursu zaochnoi formy navchannia napriamu pidhotovky 6.140101 – Hotelno-restoranna sprava)* [Methodical instructions for performance of control work on discipline "Management of quality of production and services in hotel and restaurant economy" (for students of 5th course of a correspondence form of training of a direction of preparation 6.140101 – Hotel and restaurant business)]. Kharkiv: KhNUMH im. O. M. Beketova.

Ratten, V. (2019). Tourism entrepreneurship research: a perspective article. *Tourism Review*. https://www.researchgate.net/publication/338038696_Tourism_entrepreneurship_research_a_perspective_article

Ratten, V. (2020). Coronavirus (Covid-19) and the entrepreneurship education community. Journal of Enterprising Communities: People and Places in the Global Economy. *Journal of Enterprising Communities: People and Places in the Global Economy*, *14*(5), 753–764. doi:10.1108/JEC-06-2020-0121

Rybchynska, A. A. (2015). *E-learning as an innovative tool for training and development of hotel and restaurant business staff.* http://dspace.nuft.edu.ua/bitstream/123456789/20049/1/136.pdf

Seryogina, I. Y. (2020). Modeling of hotel service "Parkour and workout in the hotel" in the study of the discipline "Industrial training of hotel and restaurant business". *Integration of education, science and business in the modern environment: winter disputes: theses add. I International Scientific and Practical Conference, February 6-7, 3,* 165-167.

Sheldon, P. J., & Daniele, R. (2017). *Social Entrepreneurship and Tourism.* Cham: Springer International Publishing. https://www. lusem. lu. se/library

Shepel, M., & Tretiak, V. (2021). *Future tourism industry professionals' cross-cultural communicatiive competence development at foreign language tutorials. Academic Press.*

Stadnytsky, Y. I., Dzyana, O.S., Koropetskaya, T. O. (2013). Features of formation of professional competence of managerial staff of hotel and restaurant economy. *Economic Strategy and Prospects for the Development of Trade and Services, 2*(1), 222-230.

Stahl, T. V., & Kozub, V. O. (2018). Features of the formation of the country's international competitiveness. *Development of food production, restaurant and hotel farms and trade: Problems, prospects, efficiency. International Scientific-Practical Conference,* (2), 105-106.

Strategy for the development of tourism and resorts for the period up to 2026. (2017). https://zakon.rada.gov.ua/laws/show/168-2017-%D1%80#Text

Tkachenko, O. V., Sokolenko, V. M., & Medved, L. M. (2019). *Individualization of education as one of the priority directions of modern pedagogy taking into account individual-typological features of personality.* Retrived from: http://elibumsa.pl.ua/bitstream/umsa/15050/1/Individualization%20_of%20_education.pdf

Tomalya, T. S., & Shchipanova, Y. I. (2014). Quality management in the hotel and restaurant business. *Economy. Management. Innovation*, 2.

Vinduk, A. V. (2017). Features of practice-oriented content of professional training of future specialists in tourism in higher education institutions. *Bulletin of Zaporizhzhia National University. Pedagogical Sciences*, (2), 98–103.

Yakimenko-Tereshchenko, N. V., Zhadan, T. A., Mardus, N. Yu., Melen, O. V., & Poberezhna, N. M. (2019). Hotel and restaurant business. Academic Press.

Yakubenko, V. M., Yakubenko, V. N., Zakharchuk, M. Ya. Ye., Zakharchuk, M. E., Arabskaya, K. L., & Arabskaya, E. L. (2015). Organization, goals and socio-cultural features of foreign language teaching in the system of postgraduate adult education. *Science and Education*, *8*, 223–228.

Yanchuk, T. V., Lubinchak, K. R., & Vovkolup, A. Yu. (2020). The effectiveness of the introduction of marketing technologies in the hotel and restaurant business. *Scientific Bulletin of Uzhhorod National University*, (29), 176–179.

Zavidna, L. D. (2017). Hotel business: development strategies. Academic Press.

Zinkova, I. I. (2020). *Pedagogical conditions for the formation of entrepreneurial culture of future specialists in the field of services and tourism* [PhD dissertation, Vasyl Stefanyk Precarpathian National University", Ivano-Frankivsk]. ProQuest Dissertations and Theses database.

Zubar, N. M. (2016). Formation of competence of teachers of professional training in hotel and restaurant business. *Problems of Methods of Physical-Mathematical and Technological Education*, *1*(7).

Zuccoli, A., Seraphin, H., & Korstanje, M. (2021). *Nuevas Discusiones Alrededor de la Educacuón en Turismo: el Método Pancoe, Laboratorio del Disfrute, Universidad de Palermo*. Revista Latino-Americana de Turismologia.

ADDITIONAL READING

Campon-Cerro, A. M., Harmandz-Mogollon, J. M., & Folgado-Fernandez, J. A. (Eds.). (2019). *Best Practices in Hospitality and Tourism Marketing and Management*. Springer. doi:10.1007/978-3-319-91692-7

Henderson, J. C. (2007). *Managing Tourism Crises*. Elsevier. doi:10.4324/9780080466033

Morrison, A., & Johnston, B. (2003). Personal creativity for entrepreneurship: Teaching and learning strategies. *Active Learning in Higher Education*, *4*(2), 145–158. doi:10.1177/1469787403004002003

Mowforth, M., & Munt, I. (2015). *Tourism and Sustainability: Development, Globalisation and New Tourism in the Third World*. Routlage Taylor & Francis Group. doi:10.4324/9781315795348

Nickson, D. (2007). *Human resource management for the hospitality and tourism industries*. Elsevier. doi:10.4324/9780080469461

Shandova, N. V., & Bylym, O. S. (2018). Resource provision of health tourism. *Naukovyi visnyk Mizhnarodnoho humanitarnoho universytetu. Seriia: Ekonomika i menedzhment,* (31), 12-16.

KEY TERMS AND DEFINITIONS

Black Sea Coast: Within the country of Ukraine, there is a body of water labeled as the Black Sea. The placement of the Black Sea is between Eastern Europe and Asia, known as a beautiful body of water and a vacation location.

Education Strategy: Is a document that defines how the education system will develop.

Hospitality: This is a description of the business sector that supports the housing, feeding and entertainment of visitors, guests, tourists, and travelers. Hospitality is considered to be an industry, inclusive of hotels and restaurants.

Hotel: This is a venue that supports and accommodates different services for visitors and guests, including tourists and travelers. Hotel establishments, within the framework if this discussion, are the focus of attention and are highlighted as venues that can be positively developed so as to support and provide accommodations for eSports tournaments as well as other forms of eSports engagement.

Kherson Region: A region in Ukraine, which has a favorable economic and geographical position, such as access to the Black Sea and the Azov Sea, favorable climatic conditions, picturesque landscapes of the sea coast, and unique landscapes of the Dnieper and Ingulets rivers, significant recreational resources (numerous beaches, reserves of therapeutic mud and lakes).

Restaurant Specialist: Is a person who fully regulates the work of the restaurant and manages the restaurant business.

Specialist: Is an employee whose duties include the availability of specialized education and practical experience in any field.

Chapter 4
Entrepreneurship Education Development in the Context of Tourism in Oman

Mohit Kukreti
https://orcid.org/0000-0003-0067-0103
University of Technology and Applied Sciences, Oman

M. R. Dileep
Pazahassiraja College, University of Calicut, Kerala, India

Aarti Dangwal
Chandigarh University, India

ABSTRACT

An entrepreneurship is a key factor for any country that aims to become competitive in the knowledge-based global market as it is viewed as a means of promoting economic growth, innovation, and creativity. This opinion has given rise to growing interest in establishing entrepreneurship educational programmes by several countries including Oman. The government of Oman has taken tourism as one of the main economic sectors to diversify its oil-based economy. This chapter focuses on the facilities provided by the government of Sultanate of Oman to encourage and motivate growth of new ventures with context to entrepreneurship education, how the government of Oman is monitoring and assessing its initiatives and strategies, planned and implemented to establish entrepreneurship education in tourism context. The chapter also proposed a conceptual framework on entrepreneurship education in tourism context which can be considered by the policy makers to measure the efficacy and efficiency of the entrepreneurship education strategies and policies.

DOI: 10.4018/978-1-7998-9510-7.ch004

INTRODUCTION

An Entrepreneurship plays a pivotal role in boosting economic activities in the country by providing job opportunities and contributing towards the development of the country gross domestic product (GDP). Considering the importance of entrepreneurship towards the economic development, entrepreneurship infrastructure and specifically education are one of the most imperative issues for any country. Within the context of Oman, the government is working to expand its sources to generate revenues and ensure employment for young population by encouraging entrepreneurship education. In this regard, the government of Oman has established institutions which provide different types of support and education to entrepreneurs and would-be entrepreneurs. Entrepreneurship education represents a distinct area of innovative initiatives and approaches in the Arab countries.

The Entrepreneurship and entrepreneurship education have gained a lot of attention in Oman. A number of projects at national, regional or international level have been implemented to promote entrepreneurship and to deliver entrepreneurship education to the youth, unemployed and students. The government of Oman has taken some steps to promote entrepreneurship education. These steps include the availability of loans from Oman Development Bank, (ODB) incubator services, equity funding by the youth fund and development facilities for micro-business offered by SANAD programme. The ODB helps to promote entrepreneurship among young people by lending them soft loans and limiting bureaucracy. The SANAD programme offers a loan of 5,000 Omani Riyal ($ 13,000) (Bindah & Magd, 2016).

The 'SAS' is a national entrepreneurship program in the field of Information and communication technology (ICT). It aims at facilitating the entrepreneurs to enrich the country by establishing IT projects that foster an entrepreneurial spirit in the ICT sector in Oman. The name 'SAS' is derived from a locally used term which refers to any solid foundation like a house foundation. Therefore, "SAS Program" is designed to deliver the entrepreneurship foundation for creating new ICT projects to the students and jobseekers. (Omanuna, n.d.)

It is a well-known fact that tourism has become one of the rapid growing industries worldwide and Oman is no exception to it. It is expected that the country may run out of its oil resources in less than twenty years that is why the government of Oman has started to diversify its economy. Tourism being one of the sectors that has accelerated the economic growth of Oman that's why the country has started to pay more attention to this industry and develop effective strategies for the sustainable development of this sector. The entrepreneurs in tourism business are motivated and highly encouraged, therefore the Sultanate of Oman is paying more attention to tourism entrepreneurship education.

This chapter critically analyses the facilities that are provided by the government of Oman to enhance and encourage the growth of new ventures, the challenges faced by the entrepreneurs in this sector and suggest a conceptual framework on tourism entrepreneurship education in the country. This chapter takes up a qualitative approach to reach the following objectives:

- To examine which strategies are adopted by the government of Oman to encourage entrepreneurship education in context to tourism.
- To analyse how the government of Oman is monitoring and assessing the initiatives and strategies used to implement tourism entrepreneurship education.
- Propose a conceptual framework that can be applied in context to Oman to establish entrepreneurship education.

BACKGROUND

Tourism Business in Oman

According to Mansour et al (2020), the Sultanate of Oman has a number of spatial environments such as mountains, plains, deserts, oases, islands and beautiful coasts which are all potential features for tourism industry. Taking the fact under consideration that Oman is shifting its oil-based economy to tourism (which is basically a shift towards non-production based economy) is because there exist good future prospects for the country in stabilizing its economy (Al- Badi & Khan, 2020). In this context, the tourism entrepreneurship in the Sultanate of Oman is increasing due to the availability of plenty job opportunities and cultural changeability in the country (Sotiriadis & Apostolakis, 2015).

The local population is slowly realising the vast entrepreneurial potential offered by the tourism. Therefore, the tourism entrepreneurship ventures undertaken by the locals are in the form of basic service providing level at the local tourist spots and destinations. This fact is supported by the research entitled "Entrepreneurial Potential of Tourism Sector in Oman" undertaken by students from the College of Economics and Political Science (CEPS), Sultan Qaboos University, Oman. (Oman Observer, 2017). The typology of some basic forms of tourism entrepreneurship ventures are provided in the following table 1.

Table 1. Typology of tourism entrepreneurship ventures in Oman

Café operations business
Fam tourism rental business
Car and Caravan rental business
Guest house catering business
Boat ride operations
Establishing shops for selling handmade baskets, key chains and carpets, traditional pottery, Silver Khanjar knifes, traditional specialties herbs.
Running of B & B (bed and breakfast) establishments
Tour guiding
Tourist taxi operations
Operating refurbished old houses as heritage hotels.
F&B Kiosk operations at the tourist places
Desert camp operations
Business of renting camels and horses for rides
Business of renting Quadra bike, Jet ski, Canoe

Source: Compiled by the Author

The entrepreneurial spirit is in abundance in the local population, however; it can be systematically nurtured further with the help of entrepreneurship education. Also, this requires the entrepreneurs of Oman to pay attention to entrepreneurship education in context with tourism and should start at school level (Al Harthi, 2017; Alsawafi, 2016).

The Sultanate of Oman has started implementing policies to help divert its oil-based economy towards tourism which is a part of its Vision 2040 which is an updated version of Vision 2020. The aim of this vision is to provide conditions for the economic diversification by enhancing or increasing the non-oil production in the country. This calls for a plan to make tourism the next major source of income for Oman after gas and oil. The mission of Vision 2040 states that tourism will facilitate towards economic diversification, preservation of cultural integrity and protection of environment of the Oman (Ministry of Tourism, 2015). The government of Oman has assigned RO 298 million for the development of human resources for industrial sector which also includes tourism industry, the localization drive has met limited success. This could be because of lack of interest towards hospitality business, lack of skills, language barrier and tour guiding (Times of Oman, 2014). As the development of Oman continues the policy makers are turning their attention to the over dependency of the country on oil-revenues and the lack of employment opportunities for the increasing youthful population. Though access to higher education has increased in Oman but one of the consequences of it was that there has been an increase in the number of graduating students looking for meaningful employment which is currently not available. Also, it is not possible to provide all these graduates with jobs in the public sector as it will be expensive and an unsustainable course of action while there being job opportunities in the private sector but many of these positions are occupied by expatriates because of their expertise or perhaps the fresh graduates would see a role under them. In line with the above problem, one potential solution to this problem is to promote entrepreneurship as way to develop private sector in providing employment, diversify the economy and decrease the dependency on oil-revenues (Magd & McCoy, 2014).

Entrepreneurship Education in the Tourism Industry

The tourism industry has been subjected to some fundamental changes due to the alterations in the preferences of consumer and the emergence of new technology (Lew & Williams, 2008). The new technologies have provided platform for creativity and innovation which has influenced the global tourism industry. Innovations like new business models for tourism companies using online auctions, the use of GPS, robotics, iPhones and other types of resources to avail interpretation and guiding services, the use of information and communication technology helps to enhance understanding, attract and make accessibility of heritage sights for the tourists. The emergence of mobile phone technologies also incorporates many tourism applications that have been complemented by the RFID devices (Ndou et al., 2019).

The tourism industry has always been considered by a high percentage of new businesses, ventures and innovative services and products, entrepreneurs in the tourism sector are found to start with limited business skills and innovativeness. According to Zehrer & Mossenlechner, (2008) there is a considerable amount of gap between what educational institutions offer and the needs of the tourism industry. This gap becomes even larger if we think that technology today is not an important part of tourism sector but it has developed a structural reconfiguration of the sector by influencing the way travel is planned, business is carried out and tourism services and experiences are developed and consumed (Neuhofer et al 2014; Del Vecchio et al., 2017). Therefore, creating value needs entrepreneurial actions that rely on a combination of specialized resources, knowledge about different actors, assets and the manipulation of opportunities that depend on technological applications and capabilities as well as scientific and technological knowledge (Bailetti, 2012). This calls for different attitudes, skills and understanding to attain success by exploring various emerging opportunities (Daniel et al., 2017). The work of researchers and scholars in the tourism industry, lack of qualified human capital and the requirement for investing in the training and development of attitudes towards innovation and entrepreneurship are necessary for competitiveness of tourism firms and destinations (Ndou et al., 2019; Neuhofer et al., 2014).

In response to this, the universities and educational institutions have currently expanded their entrepreneurship education offerings, through executive programs and other initiatives dedicated to innovation and development of entrepreneurship (Ahmed et al., 2018). Some of entrepreneurship education initiatives are focused on tourism education programs and researchers have started to take note of this (Daniel et al., 2017; Ahmed et al., 2018). Daniel et al., (2017) explored the case of a program developed to enhance students' entrepreneurial skills through learning-by-doing-approach. The study highlighted the importance of entrepreneurship education for tourism students and states that the students have a lot of interest in getting enrolled in entrepreneurship education courses. Similarly, another study by Ahmed et al., (2018) also presented a critical review of entrepreneurship teaching methods, with focus on the emerging challenges in context with hospitality and tourism programs.

Entrepreneurship in the context of tourism is a welcoming approach that fulfils the need of the growing tourism sector. Tourism sector is one of the economic sectors which needs involvement to a great extent from the entrepreneurial community. In addition, entrepreneurs plan an essential role in the development of tourism due to shared culture for tourism leading to success of this industry (Khan & Krishnamurthy, 2016). In fact, a well-endowed tourism industry cannot evolve successfully without having tourism entrepreneurs. According to a study by Hvidt (2013), Oman is thriving to steer its residence by educating and preparing them to compete for jobs in public and private sectors both. Whereas, the tourism industry has a wide range of jobs available which includes travel agencies, accommodation facilitations, operations, catering services, transportation etc. It can also be seen that Omani students are not interested to take the tourism and hospitality profession even though there lies a good scope and massive job opportunities in this sector. Also, the parents of the students, especially the ones coming from a semi-traditional culture believe that jobs in this industry are servitude and have little future prospects of promotion. This perception arise from the fact that individuals working in this field are seen as uneducated, unmotivated, unskilled, untrained and unproductive. Many positions in the tourism industry needs little experience and low skills (Nikazachenko et al., 2018). For Oman where more young population is unemployment, the focus on entrepreneurship education has become necessary to create job opportunities. Unfortunately, no planning will help if the students are not willing to be self-employed. The Omani society has always claimed to have strived for the spirit of entrepreneurship but recently things have changed (Khan & Krishnamurthy, 2016). In line with this, a survey was carried out by Sultan Qaboos University which showed that the spirit of entrepreneurship has been replaced by a notion of entitlement. This entitlement culture meant how people are continuously seeking for help from the government.

This kind of mind-set has influenced the spirit of entrepreneurship. A number of individuals feel that starting an enterprise is a hard job but to be honest this is a trend that is seen elsewhere too. For example, America which was looked upon as a centre of innovation and creative entrepreneurs is also becoming a victim of this entitlement culture. In context with Oman, although a number of government sponsored programs are available to the emerging Omani entrepreneurs only a few have been made in the tourism sector. This can be due to factors such as role models, lack of proper training, unrealistic setting of goals and planning skills and experience. Moreover, the field of entrepreneurship education in tourism to the best of the author's knowledge remains underdeveloped especially in context with Oman as to how the Omani government analyses the different entrepreneurship education components in this context (Khan & Krishnamurthy, 2016).

Tourism and Entrepreneurship Education in Oman

The Sultanate of Oman is an oil-rich country which is located in the eastern side of Middle-East. As the population of the country grew faster than its economy could sustain, major challenges were faced by the government such as unemployment and provision of opportunities for higher education. To address these concerns the government of Oman looks at entrepreneurship education and self-employment more specifically among young people to handle the challenges and diversifying the economy (Bindah Magd, 2016). For Oman where 78.4% of the population falls under the age of 35 and the unemployment rate is estimated to be 15%, the focus on creating employment or job opportunities is crucial (Ennis, 2015). This seems to be challenging considering the fact that there are 50,000 graduates passing out every year. Therefore, it is necessary to encourage entrepreneurial activity to create job opportunities. But nothing can help if students are not willing to become self-employed (Ennis, 2015). In context with the above, various government-sponsored programs and supporting schemes are available for the upcoming Omani entrepreneurs, but only a handful of attempts have been made in tourism entrepreneurship. This could be because of shortage of role models, lack of trainings, setting unrealistic goals and lack of experience and planning skills (Parambi, 2014).

In line with this, another study conducted by Khan & Krishnamurthy, (2016) aimed to investigate the various factors that constrains tourism student's inclination towards tourism-entrepreneurial activities in Oman. The study found factors like non-discrimination of gender, opportunities related to promotion and physical working conditions play a pivotal role in encouraging students to take up tourism-related career. The empirical result of the study also reflected high risk of accidents, Omani traditional and cultural values and non-tourism spouse preferences seem to discourage tourism among students.

In the previous years, tourists from all around the world have visited Oman because of the breath-taking views and outdoor activities that the Sultanate of Oman provides generously. However, compared to other countries having similar socio-economic conditions like Oman, entrepreneurial potential of tourism industry in the nation has not been given the due consideration it deserved. There exist strong doubts that the residents of Oman are aware of the opportunities this lucrative business of tourism can offer to them (Räisänen, 2018). According to Ibrahim et al (2017), a very important role is played by the government in changing the attitude and mindset of graduates towards entrepreneurship and devising effective entrepreneurship strategies. In order to bring diversification in economy and stimulate private sector, the government agencies and private companies of Oman are collaborating in different entrepreneurship development activities. Taking the importance of entrepreneurship into consideration in terms of economic growth of the country, the government is trying to provide entrepreneurship education for those who have entrepreneurial mindset (Yarahmadi & Magd, 2016).

The Sultanate of Oman is identified as a rentier state and the characteristics of this type of state have implications for the development of entrepreneurship. The theory of rentier state suggests that rentier states receive regular amounts of external rents which are paid by foreign people, governments to individuals of a country (Hanieh 2021). Taking Oman into consideration, these rents mainly come from energy resources available. As the country seeks diversification, therefore according to Vision 2040, Oman looks to expand its non-energy national income from industries such as logistics and tourism. The entrepreneurship in Oman has been considered as a means of contributing to the national diversification plan. There are implications for being a rentier state such as political, cultural, economical and societal. Oman is a monarchy and autocracy state because a small population is involved in generating revenues from it whereas the remaining population is engaged in using the wealth generated (Al Shabibi, 2020).

In Oman after the defence sector, education is the 2nd largest public sector which requires expenditure. The main reason for giving priority to investment in the education sector is to generate job opportunities in the private sector by providing education to the people of Oman (Oman National Centre for Statistics and Information 2018).

An entrepreneurship is a pro-active approach towards boosting productivity and performance of any organization. The tourism industry in Oman is contributing more than 7% and is increasing with the passage of time (Al Abri, et al., 2016). The Oman's economy is mainly dependable on oil-resources just like other Gulf countries are, but in the last few years Oman has shifted towards non-renewable resources and tourism industry has played an essential role by expanding and stabilizing the country's economy as it has beautiful scenic views and places (Sokhalingam, et al., 2013). The tourism strategy of Oman is aligned with the Vision 2040, as it gives more attention to the tourism sector of the country. Oman generates 535,000 jobs in the tourism industry, in line with this, there is a need to shift the burden from the economy as the tourism industry of Oman has a great potential. But there are many challenges faced by the tourism entrepreneurs in Oman (Atef & Al-Balushi, 2015).

Challenges Faced by Omani Tourism Entrepreneurs

A study conducted by Sotiriadis & Apostolakis, (2015) identified several factors such as human capital, lack of technology, support system, government policies and financial constraints as the major challenges faced by entrepreneurs in tourism industry of Oman. Moreover, another problem spotted by Alani et al (2017), is that tourist guide profession is not considered as a prestigious or respectable one in the Omani society but the government has implemented special courses in relation with tourism. The tourism industry in Oman is suffering because of strict policies and lack of support from the government (Saleh & Alalouch, 2015; Baporikar, 2017). Aulia, (2016) and Mansour, et al, (2020) says that Ecotourism is an effective way for sustainable growth of country's economy. Moreover, Alrawadieh et al (2019) and Khan & Krishnamurthy, (2016) in their study states that entrepreneurship education of tourism is much needed in Oman as schools and colleges do not lay emphasize on teaching the students about tourism and its impact on the country's economy.

There is lack of cooperation between the private and government sectors which lead to no strategic alignment. The private sector should collaborate or join hands with the government to improve the tourism industry in Oman by critically analysing the restrains faced by the entrepreneurs in the tourism industry (Ali, et al., 2017). There are different challenging factors which decrease the productivity, performance and the growth of tourism industry in Oman and the role of government in decreasing the negative impact on Oman's tourism industry (Yuksel, 2014). These challenges can be reduced by implementing effective rules and regulations pertaining to tourism by the Omani government (Atef & Al-Balushi, 2015).

Al-Badi & Khan (2020), conducted a study to investigate the challenges faced by the entrepreneurs in the tourism business to develop and grow their businesses in Oman. The study critically examined whether the entrepreneurs in tourism business were encouraged and motivated to develop their business in Oman as well as assess the prospects for the entrepreneurs to enter the tourism industry in Oman. The study found that 3 factors such as initial capital, working capital and good location to be essential for tourism business to establish in Oman. The study also found that the existing rules and regulations are very rigid and strict in order to start tourism business in Oman. Moreover, a lot of time is required to start the operation of this business, seek labour clearance is also not simple for tourism in Oman. Apart from this, cultural values and the physical working conditions are also not encouraging towards tourism-related business and non-preference of spouse from the tourism business is yet another problem for the Omanis to start tourism business.

Technological Support

The advancement in technology has changed the way people travel, these developments provide more interactive and exciting experiences. The Ministry of Tourism of Oman has been working on developing an infrastructure for the tourism industry to raise tourism locally and internationally (Al Muqbali, 2006). According to Vidal, (2019), social media platforms, blogs and different applications play a significant role in planning tours, therefore, tourism business need to adapt them as business models and products to offer attractive packages and services to people. These applications have brought drastic changes in the development of tourism industry by shifting towards e-tourism (Buhalis & Law, 2008). The advancements in the mobile technology creates innovative experiences for the tourist which fosters sustainable competitive advantage for tourism destinations, tourism-related suppliers and create a smart tourism package (Kim & Kim, 2017). Change in the infrastructure of Oman's tourism industry by using technological advancement is necessary to attract tourist (Sazegar et al., 2018). With internet revolution in tourism industry, technological changes will enhance the roadmap to the tourism industry and the way it markets itself (Ozturk, 2020). The start-up businesses if combined with technology can play an important role in increasing tourism business and will ensure its sustainability to avoid the fading effects on both natural and social habitat (Urbančič et al., 2020).

Financial Constraints

One of the major challenges faced by the tourism industry in Oman is the poor financial support and the weak economic conditions (Hilal, 2020). This includes project funding in Oman and managing the tourism business (Al Harthi, 2017). The government of Oman should provide financial and strategic support system to the tourism entrepreneurs so that they are able to boost the tourism industry of the country and able to generate job opportunities which would lift the economic development of Oman (Alani et al., 2017). The youth of Oman have innovative ideas and they need financial support to successfully establish tourism entrepreneurship which would further provide employment chances to many others (Sokhalingam, et al., 2013). The opportunities to generate income-based activities should be provided to local people as a part of development program so as to win their support but due to lack of investment at initial level, the Omanis are behind in the tourism sector. The hesitation by financial bodies to lend loans to entrepreneurs of rural areas restricts them from establishing tourism business. Therefore, lack of adequate and sufficient financial support act as a severe challenge for budding entrepreneurs in tourism business businesses (Ghouse et al, 2017).

Procedure and Formality Difficulties

For tourism industry in Oman to flourish, there is a dire need of improvement in decision-making process at local, regional and international levels with the help of the World Tourism Organization. (Adewale, 2016). The procedures of setting up tourism business in Oman are very time consuming and act as a major barrier (Al Buraiki & Khan, 2018). An entrepreneur who likes to setup a tourism business finds it very complex to cope with these time consuming and complicated procedures, therefore these procedures need to be simplified and less time consuming. Also, policies and rules and regulations pertaining to visas, unavailability of trained tour guides, inadequate maintenance of hotels are some more major challenges faced by the tourism industry in Oman (Aulia, 2016; Baporikar, 2017).

Research Purpose

The purpose of the current research is to find out what strategies were adopted by the government of Oman to encourage entrepreneurship education in the context of tourism, to analyse whether entrepreneurs in tourism business are motivated to develop and grow their businesses and finally to propose a conceptual framework that can be applied in context with Oman to establish entrepreneurship education in tourism.

RESEARCH QUESTIONS

- **RQ1:** What is the current state of entrepreneurship education in tourism industry of Oman?
- **RQ2:** What steps are taken by the Omani government to establish entrepreneurship education in the context of tourism?
- **RQ3:** How the educational programs related to tourism structuring the main components of entrepreneurship education?
- **RQ4:** How is the government of Oman monitoring and assessing the initiatives taken to establish entrepreneurship education in tourism?

INTERNATIONAL ENTREPRENEURSHIP ENVIRONMENT MODEL COMPARISON

The research studies shows that Entrepreneurship Education (EE) is effective in increasing students' entrepreneurial intentions (Vanevenhoven and Liguori 2013) and economic development (Acs et al. 2008). EE typology differs in forms and approaches depending on countries' needs, their political economies, skill formation, and educational systems. The UK, USA, Singapore have been working to enhance the entrepreneurial environment through establishing a number of initiatives and programmes. These countries have a long experience with entrepreneurship and top entrepreneurship indexes (The Global Entrepreneurship and Development Institute 2018). It seems practical for Oman to get influenced from the educational policies and curricula of the more advanced nations in the field of entrepreneurship, as many countries have previously attempted in the area of education. (Al Shabibi, 2020) The following table no 2, provides an introductory overview of Oman's EEP in comparison to the three developed countries' approaches to EE.

The USA and UK does not have a national policy like Oman that requires all HEIs to follow a certain approach that requires EE as mandatory for all undergraduates and post graduate HEIs. Singapore has the comparatively new EE model compared to the UK and USA and it has advanced in delivering EE education due to its high-quality education system. Although, USA has many schools of entrepreneurship due to its huge HE sector, population, and liberal economy, however; schools of entrepreneurship do not exist in Singapore because of low population and less number of HEIs. Finally, the understanding of above Entrepreneurship Education Programme (EEP) models of UK, USA and Singapore will facilitate in perceiving entrepreneurship education well towards contributing to the aim of economic diversification in Oman.

STEPS TAKEN BY THE GOVERNMENT OF OMAN

Government Initiatives towards Entrepreneurship Education and Tourism

In the Gulf Cooperation Countries (GCC) such as Bahrain, UAE, Saudi Arabia, Qatar and the Sultanate of Oman the following activities of Entrepreneurship Education in the Educational Systems of GCC Countries are taking place.

Table 2. The UK, USA, Singapore, Oman entrepreneurship environment model

UK Institution Initiatives	USA Institution Initiatives	Singapore Institution Initiatives	Oman Institution Initiatives
The National Centre for Entrepreneurship in Education offers Entrepreneurial degree programme, National Enterprise Award, Educators Conference.	Lake Erie College - Compulsory or elective entrepreneurship for multidisciplinary program, exposes students to specific entrepreneurial activities for engineering, businesses, etc.	International Enterprise (IE) Singapore - Mainly supports business internationalization.	Oman Government and MOHERI- Ministerial Decree for all HEIs to implement EEP program, MOHE Guidebook Tanfeedh, Riyada, FiveYear Plans, Visions 2020 & 2040, OAAA Quality Reports Study stressing on entrepreneurship
University of Huddersfield Included enterprise education as key theme in its "2015-2018 teaching and learning strategy, Created the Entrepreneur FACETS Framework & the Bolton Thompson Entrepreneur Indicator, enterprise education curricula.	University of Miami - Entrepreneurship program is part of all or some of the Courses. Conducts extensive readings, case studies, guest speakers, and research.	SPRING Singapore - Supports SMEs and Start-ups	Ministry of Manpower- launched 'Fund for the Development of Youth'- offering equity financing, starting at OMR 20,000 SANAD - To fund the establishment SME for the public with maximum of OMR 20,000.
Centre for Enterprise and Entrepreneurship Studies at University of Leeds Offers credited undergraduate elective modules, embeds entrepreneurship in various degrees, offers masters and PhD degrees in enterprise and entrepreneurship.	Babson College - Entrepreneurship program incorporated within curricula, Learning Business commercialization using technology, finding collaborative & innovative entrepreneurship solutions.	The HEAD Foundation and the Human Capital Leadership Institute Provides talent programme in Southeast Asia, including talent entrepreneurs	Nationwide Entrepreneurship **Financial Support** by the **Government Sector**– Al Rafad Fund, Oman Development Bank (ODB), The Research Council Funding program, Ministry of Social Development "Mawarid Al Rizq" Livelihood projects. **Private Sector-** Sharakhah, GroFIN, Towell, Saud Bhawan Group, Zubair Sec
University of Swansea - Teaches one its kind in the UK, the BSc Business Management (Entrepreneurship)	Washington University, St. Louis -Exposing Business major or minor students to the entrepreneurial free-market experience of founding or purchasing a business while at school.	Singapore Institute of Retail Studies (SIRS) - Provides a variety of entrepreneurship courses up to the management level	Nationwide Entrepreneurship **Training Support** by the **Sector** – Public Authority for SME Development (PASMED), The Public Authority for Investment Promotion & Export Development, OCCI, Pubic Authority for Craft Industries. **Private Sector** – Intilaqah, The 'Cell' program of OMIFCO, National Business Center, SAS program, Injaz Oman
Cardiff University - Offers an undergraduate and Master's degree in Entrepreneurship	North Carolina A&T State University - Certificate in entrepreneurship for all university majors, career options, the knowledge & skills application through the Entrepreneurial Internship Programme.	International Enterprise (IE) Singapore	Nationwide Entrepreneurship Financial Support by the Commercial Banks – Islamic bank Financing, Bank Muscat, Bank Sohar, National Bank of Oman (NBO), Bank Dofar, Other forms of financing sales such as 'Murabaha' sale

Source: Modified from Al Shabibi, I. (2020). p 31-38.

Table 3. Experiences and activities of entrepreneurship education in the educational systems of Arab States

Country	Policy and Coordination	Development of Curricula & Study Plan	Training of Teachers & Instructor	Networking and Connectivity	Other Areas
Bahrain	Basic principles of a culture of entrepreneurship in education policies. - Teaching entrepreneurship in Vocational education. - Formal and non-formal education - International partner to facilitate the integration of EPE within the study plans.	Study plans, EPE subjects - Simulation halls of (virtual job market). - EPE Programmes for basic grades - Introduced Entrepreneurship Education in the study plan in partnership with UNIDO.	- Teacher training in cooperation with international organizations and national institutions.	Cooperation with international, regional, and national organizations to support and guide vocational students. - Private & Government sector to Support lead initiatives.	Competition project for young entrepreneurs. - Bahrain Centre for the Development of emerging industries - business service foundation. - Bank of creativity - Tamkeen
Kuwait	- EPE represented in general goals of the various education stages - Ministry of Education adopted educational programs to apply concepts of entrepreneurship.	- School subjects in the field of EPE, including: life skills human rights and the Constitution. - Training package-KAB- for vocational education. - Promote positive educational values project.			
Oman	Education Vision focusing on learning the skills and entrepreneurship - Forming the steering Committee, and the Executive Committee for EPE	Establish an EPE conceptual skills matrix - Prepare EPE activities in the light of the analysis of textbooks - Present activities in Entrepreneurship for students in the Second Cycle and Post Basic Education (Grades 5 to 12) and to include some in the «Your Career Path » books	- Training teachers for the curriculum analysis). - Training life skills teachers, vocational guidance specialists (Later on)	EPE workshop to find out the required specifications in EPE education - Design an educational media campaign in entrepreneurship (later stage)	Entrepreneurship competitions.

continues on following page

Table 3. Continued

Country	Policy and Coordination	Development of Curricula & Study Plan	Training of Teachers & Instructor	Networking and Connectivity	Other Areas
Qatar					- Entrepreneurship Center at the College of North Atlantic - Qatar CNAQ; help the students to explore their self preparations for Entrepreneurship. - Conduct studies and procedural researches in the field of entrepreneurship
Saudi Arabia	Teaching entrepreneurship in vocational education. - Universities, technical colleges and schools included the EPE subjects in the study plans.	Injaz for basic and secondary school. - Secondary education development project included: Life skills-management skills vocational education computer & academic skills.		Cooperation with international, regional, and national organizations and bodies, to facilitate the EPE programmes implementation at schools.	King Saud University initiatives in the field of EPE. - Center for Entrepreneurship, - Saudi Society for Entrepreneurship, - King Saud Fellowship project of entrepreneurship - The International license of Entrepreneurship
United Arab Emirates	- Vision of the Ministry of Education is supportive for educational institutions to adopt "entrepreneurship" Developing the technical infrastructure for schools.	- Promoting school activities to develop the students' life skills, competitive competences. Development of technical and vocational education programmes	Training EPE teachers on teaching and innovative strategies	Activation of community partnership in educational process.	- Strategic initiatives to prepare students for the knowledge society

Source: *Source:* Modified from El Abeer, K. (2013). p 44-57.

The Experiences and Activities of Entrepreneurship Education in the Educational Systems of GCC Countries

In Oman, many efforts have been developed across the country to encourage young people to start their own businesses. The SANAD initiative, which has been a huge success all around Oman, encourages young people to start their own businesses by providing funds and expertise to recent graduates. It was established in October 2001 under the Ministry of Manpower with the goal of people who want to be self-employed are supported by the programme, which relies on accessible mechanisms of training, rehabilitation, funding, and technical and administrative follow-up. It is aimed primarily at young people who are unemployed (Atef & Al-Balushi, 2015). The SANAD incubators programme provides financial and technical assistance to young entrepreneurs from technical colleges who want to start their own businesses. With a head start in the business world, these young entrepreneurs are expected to create their own firms. In each governorate and area, the government has established SANAD offices, which provide technical and administrative assistance to the recipients (Al-Harthi, 2017).

Know About Business (KAB) is a programme that is being implemented in vocational training institutions and technical colleges. Under the auspices of KAB, a package is being offered. The International Labour Organization (ILO) wants to help young people develop skills that will help them succeed in the future and assist them in obtaining a living. KAB's major goal is to teach entrepreneurs in management skills so that they can build an entrepreneurial mind set through entrepreneurship education. The programme aims to enhance young people's entrepreneurial abilities and prepare them not only to start their own firms in the future, but also to work productively in small and medium organisations (SMEs) (Halibas, et al., 2017). The mission of Injaz Oman, a non-profit organisation, is to inspire and prepare young people to prosper in a global market. It is associated with Junior Achievement (JA) all over the world. It gives young people in enterprise education from high school to university a hands-on learning experience. The Injaz Oman's motto is "Assisting People in Improving Their Competitive Performance." The "Intilaaqah" programme is part of the Shell group's LiveWIRE global effort. This programme assists young entrepreneurs by providing them with the necessary training, coaching, and consulting services to help them launch their own enterprises. The training program's goal is to improve the candidate's capacity to conceptualise the business environment by allowing him or her to learn the skills required to run a small business professionally (Pandow & Omar, 2019).

The contribution of Small and Medium Enterprises (SMEs) and the dynamic force of Entrepreneurship in economy of Oman is quite laudable, realising this significance the late Sultan His Majesty Sultan Qaboos Bin Said had directed the convening of the national level convention for SME development. An outcome of this convention was His Majesty's directive to create an Entrepreneurship course for the undergraduate level in Higher Education Institutions (HEIs) of Oman. In 2013, the erstwhile Ministry of Higher Education (MoHE) of Oman which is now known as Ministry of Higher Education, Research and Innovation (MoHERI) had introduced a nationwide module for entrepreneurship and student activities in HEIs in Oman. The team responsible for this module development comprised of members from MoHE, Sultan Qaboos University, Injaz Oman, College of Applied Sciences, Fund for Development of Youth Projects (Sharakah). The aim of this module was to develop the necessary temperament required to nurture Entrepreneurship in Oman (Ministry of Higher Education, 2013). The following table reflects the list of HEIs in Oman imparting Entrepreneurship education either as a course or a degree program and the list of total active enrolments in 2021.

Table 4. List of HEIs imparting entrepreneurship course

Sultan Qaboos University -14428	**Gulf College of Oman - 4898**	**Sohar University - 6293**
University of Technology and Applied Sciences (HCT, CoT, CAS) - 42948	Majan College (University College) - 3254	Sur University College - 1958
Middle East College – 5561	Mazoon College - 2240	University of Buraimi - 2063
Dhofar University - 5582	Modern College of Business and Science - 1854	Waljat College of Applied Sciences - BITS, Oman -1707
University of Nizwa - 7050	Muscat University College- 1060	International Maritime College, Sohar Oman- 1620
Muscat University (MU) – N/A	Royal Guard of Oman Technical College	Muscat University College-1060
Arab Open University - 2831	Scientific College of Design-1330	Caledonian College of Engineering - 3526
Oman Tourism College - 581	Sur University College- 1958	Alburaimi University College - 4740
College of Banking and Financial Studies - 2028	German University of Technology in Oman (GUtech) - 1147	Bayan College - 597
Global College of Engineering & Technology - 57	Al Sharqiyah University - 2115	Oman College of Management & Technology - 876
Vocational Training Colleges - 1645	Al Zahra College for Women – 1736	Oman Institute of Health Sciences - 49

Source: Compiled by the author

The following table reflects the list of HEIs in Oman imparting tourism degree courses to support entrepreneurship in tourism education.

Table 5. List of HEIs offering tourism degree courses

Sultan Qaboos University - BA in Tourism, Hospitality Management, Tourism Guidance (Tour Guiding)
Oman Tourism College- International Diploma in Tourism and Hospitality Management, Professional Certificate in Tour Guiding, Front Office, House Keeping, Culinary, Service & Restaurant Management, Travel Management & IATA programs, Food safety and hygiene, Business languages: English, French & German,s Customer services/ Guest relationship
Colleges of Applied Sciences (CAS)- BBA with majors in Tourism
GU tech - BSc in Sustainable Tourism and Regional Development
Gulf College - BA in Travel and Tourism Management
Sur University College – BBA Hotel Management and Tourism
Majan University College- BA in Business Administration with pathway in Tourism
Al Buraimi University - Bachelor of Tourism and Leisure Management
National Hospitality Institute (NHI)- Diploma in International Hotel Management for existing tourism employees, Certificate in Vocational Courses, Diploma Cabin Crew.

Source: Compiled by the author

The Nizwa College of Technology which is now a part of the University of Technology and Applied Sciences (UTAS) is working on a project called Business Simulation Classes (BSC). Its goal is to provide suitable training and integrate entrepreneurial culture into college academic programmes by allowing students to run a fully operating firm. It provides college students with real-world business experience that is not taught in textbooks or classrooms. In addition to other areas, the UTAS - Colleges of Technology have established programmes for newly hired teachers and lecturers that focus on entrepreneurial education (Moremong-Nganunu, et al., 2018). Following their recruitment, these teachers are sent to get a Master's degree in another country. They work in industry for a few months to get experience and learn entrepreneurship skills, then return to college for a few months of training to learn modern teaching techniques and methods of passing on knowledge and skills to students (Williams, et al., 2015).

Impact of the Initiatives taken by the Government

Taking the above initiatives under consideration, it can be said that The SANAD, SAS initiative has aided in the discovery of youth's creative energies, stimulating investment, assisting small enterprises, and lowering the burden on the state's administrative apparatus. From the government's standpoint, it improves public service delivery while also improving the country's infrastructure by expanding the number of points of presence for citizen services. It helps knowledge workers by providing a unique and innovative business model that is technology-driven and scalable based on public acceptance rates. This has resulted in Omani youngsters being able to work for themselves including tourism ventures as well, with professional training and government backing.

The Know About Business (KAB) programme is being used successfully at vocational training institutions and technical colleges. In order for KAB to be implemented in Oman, it had to be customised so that it could be easily integrated with other programmes.

The Intilaaqah program's initiative has been spread to centres around the Sultanate. In the male-dominated Arab society of Oman, there are a large number of female entrepreneurs. The "Intilaaqah" programme, in particular, has attracted a large number of women who want to start their own micro-business.

MONITORING AND ASSESSING

Despite the success of Oman and several improvements in promoting entrepreneurship skills within the education system, particularly in terms of curriculum development, the impact of the changes has not been assessed to determine how they have contributed to the formation of a generation that is well-rounded for the job market and future life. The programmes designed to assist EPE in teacher education, on the other hand, need to be improved. Collaboration and information exchange among all authorities, for example, could aid in the development of improved practises and the integration of different educational levels. The SANAD offices evaluate small initiatives and their effects on the targeted categories of enterprises on a regular basis, although many of the old programmes need to be re-evaluated (Fatoki & Oni, 2014).

An Entrepreneurship education is a relatively new initiative, with only a few studies addressing entrepreneurship and entrepreneurship education in Oman and the Arab world. However, there have been some lessons learnt and ideas for improvement made. For example, the SANAD programme should be given more resources and infrastructure in order to handle the Herculean task that has been assigned to it. The Intilaaqah programme, on the other hand, is minor in comparison to the number of job seekers and people interested in starting a business in Oman. One of the program's challenges is the nature of the social culture and a lack of understanding of the benefits of self-employment (Alhasni, 2021).

To change that mentality, the local media must instil initiative in young people and citizens must be informed about the programmes. The corporate sector is also instrumental in generating demand for youth investment programmes. Participants in the Intilaaqah programme were drawn to good jobs rather than starting their own enterprises. Interviews with teachers and students in the Know About Business (KAB) programme revealed that the curriculum did not always inspire young people to start their own businesses or work for themselves. Rather, it provides them with real experience and awareness of entrepreneurial opportunities, problems, procedures, traits, attitudes, and abilities. In general, the fund's concept has not been particularly successful in attracting young entrepreneurs. The entrepreneur believes that the fund's engagement in the business administration restricts their decision-making and entrepreneurial flexibility (AL-Hasni & Afifi, 2021).

The role of non-profit organisations in developing a network of entrepreneurship programmes is regarded as critical. The importance of societal sensitization in terms of employment and ownership is recognised, and all stakeholders should play an active role in supporting and promoting small and medium firms to transition from the oil to non-oil sectors. The majority of women's enterprises are small and in the service industry, which is one of the most common issues. Women also lack access to networks where they can share and exchange knowledge (Ahrari-Roudi, 2018).

It can be seen that the government of Oman still needs to devise strategies to bring improvement in promoting entrepreneurial skills within the education system specially focusing on tourism industry as it is making a shift from production-based economy to knowledge-based economy. Therefore, this study has proposed a conceptual framework that can be considered by the policy makers to measure the efficiency and efficacy of the strategies or initiatives devised and implemented towards tourism entrepreneurial education.

PROPOSED CONCEPTUAL FRAMEWORK

The proposed framework can be applied in context to Oman to establish entrepreneurship education in the context of tourism. One of the significant or noteworthy element of this framework is the indicator component which allows the policy makers to measure the efficacy or usefulness of the strategies and policies devised and implemented by them towards stablishing entrepreneurship education in the tourism context.

Figure 1. Conceptual framework
Source: Author

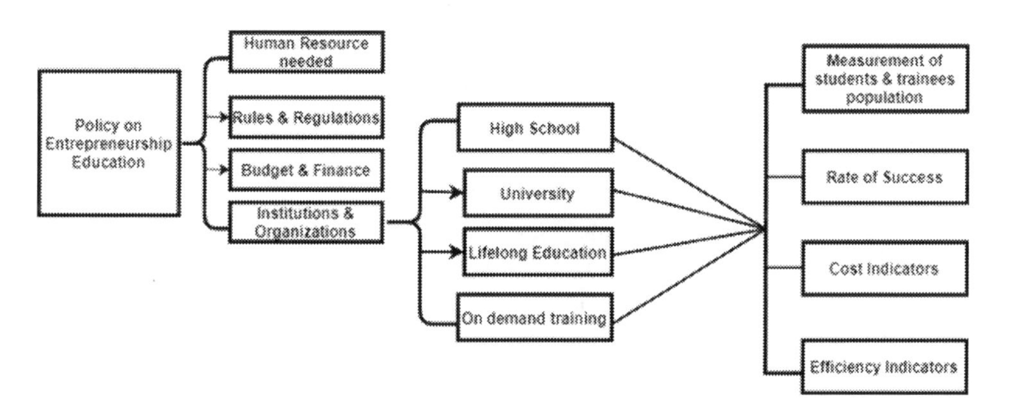

How the Framework Works

The framework shows the following directions:

- The human resources consist of trainers and education providers as they have the experience and expertise at various levels.
- The budgeting and financial issues include the fund resources which are allocated by the policy makers to achieve the set objectives.
- The rules and regulations are for issuing degree or diploma, ensuring academic quality assurance, reporting and other concerns.
- The institutions and organizations are the part of public management authorities of the programs as well as the tourism entrepreneurship education providers.
- The education system can involve various new and existing organizations such as high school which can provide basic training on a broad scale for students to develop entrepreneurial spirit and knowledge. Then, the university level can provide students to compete with the global economic changes and establish a 'can do' entrepreneurial mind-set of students through creative and innovative practices and services.
- The education should not be restricted to age in fact it should be lifelong for all professionals and graduates so as to provide required knowledge and skills to meet the needs of the rapidly growing economy. This can help in the reduction of unemployment that could come because of people's inability to prepare for the changes to come and to keep the competition between the existing workforce at high level.

- The Training on-demand is one of the flexible organizational tools. A wide variety of training levels and areas are covered through this component, intended to be provided as and when the training need is identified.
- The education system indicator can be involved such as, trainees and students' population are the domains in entrepreneurial education policies which should be measured to understand the human resource, budget and financing availability.
- The financial and budgeting measurement for entrepreneurship education policies is provided by cost indicators.
- There is a direct link of efficiency indicators and success rate. If success rate increases the rate of efficiency will also rise and vice versa.

The unemployment and opportunities facilities for higher education institutions are the two main challenges for the government of Oman. These two challenging factors urged and pressurized the government to seek for entrepreneurship and self-employment, specifically among the youth as the main component in handling these challenges and look for the diversified economy. The proposed framework in this chapter could be applied in the context of Sultanate of Oman, to establish tourism entrepreneurship education. The important highlight of this framework is its indicator component which can allow the policy makers to measure the productivity of their policies and strategies towards tourism entrepreneurship education continuously.

DISCUSSION

This study aims to investigate the current status of entrepreneurship education in the context of tourism in Oman, what programs or initiatives have been taken by the government, how it monitored and assessed these initiatives and strategies used to implement tourism entrepreneurship education and finally proposed a conceptual framework to help establish and further enhance entrepreneurship education in Oman. The chapter takes up a qualitative approach to critically analyse the set objectives of the study and to answer its research questions. This is evident from the above literature that Oman has several spatial environments like mountains, plains, deserts, oases, islands and beautiful coasts and they are all potential features for running a successful tourism industry. Now, the question is how to make use of these naturally gifted features to benefit the economy and its people. Here comes the role of tourism industry which can make use of all these potential features to boost the country's economy and provide platform for job opportunities. Taking this fact about Oman under consideration that it is shifting its oil-based economy to tourism which is basically a shift to non-production-based economy and the reason for this change is that there lie a good future prospect for the country to stabilize its economy (Al-Badi & Khan, 2020). This has led to tourism entrepreneurship in the Sultanate of Oman as it will open the door of opportunities as well as cultural changeability in the country. This has forced the entrepreneurs in Oman to pay attention to entrepreneurship education in context with tourism (Al-Harthi, 2017; Alsawafi, 2016).

During 2015 there were 111,500 jobs created in the tourism industry in Oman. These jobs are expected to rise to 164,000 jobs in 2026 (Haque, Patnaik, & et al, 2016). Comparing Oman with other countries around the world having similar socio-economic conditions as that of Oman, entrepreneurial potential of tourism industry has not been given the consideration that it deserved. One of the reasons can be that the residents of Oman are unaware of the opportunities this lucrative business of tourism has to offer. The following table shows the present status of the job seekers and their level of education in the country. The diploma holder and bachelor's degree holder are in majority looking for the jobs. With the support of entrepreneurship education these job seekers could be supported to start their own enterprises in tourism. The contribution of entrepreneurship education to Oman's tourism industry will have a positive effect on creating job opportunities for the nationals.

Job Seekers Rate by Education Status

In context with the above, a substantial role can be played by the Omani government in changing the mind-set and attitude of the youth towards entrepreneurship in tourism and devise effective entrepreneurship strategies. Moreover, the government bodies can join hands with the private sector in arranging various entrepreneurship development activities (Ibrahim et al., 2017). Also, the Omani tourism entrepreneurs are facing a number of challenges like human capital, lack of technology, support system, government policies and financial constraints (Sotiriadis & Apostolakis, 2015; Alani et al 2017; Saleh & Alalouch, 2015; Baporikar, 2017).

However, some initiatives in the form of programs such as SANAD, KAB, ILO, Intilaaqah and BSC are rendered by the government of Oman to help the young tourism entrepreneurs to enhance their skills, and develop their business further. All these programs somehow or the other have helped to attract a large number of individuals who want to start their businesses at micro-level. The study also proposed a conceptual framework to help the policy makers to measure the efficacy or usefulness of the strategies and policies devised and implemented by them towards entrepreneurship education in the context of tourism.

Table 6. Job seekers rate by education status

Item	December 2021			November 2021			
Level of Education	**Total**	**Female**	**Male**	**Total**	**Female**	**Male**	المستوى التعليمي
Less then General Diploma	0.6	0.6	0.6	1.2	0.8	1.3	ما دون دبلوم التعليم العام
General Diploma	2.8	5.9	2.1	3.8	8.1	2.9	دبلوم التعليم العام وما يعادله
Higher Diploma	7.3	14.5	3.1	7.7	14.3	3.8	دبلوم التعليم العالي
Bachelor	5.2	11.4	1.3	4.4	9.8	1.1	البكالوريوس
Master Degree, Ph.D	0.5	1.2	0.1	0.4	0.8	0.1	ماجستير ودكتوراه
Total	**1.9**	**5.6**	**1.1**	**2.5**	**5.8**	**1.7**	الجملة

Source: NCSI Monthly Statistical Bulletin January 2022

FUTURE RESEARCH DIRECTIONS

The future researches can empirically test this conceptual framework to check its applicability, efficiency as well as its implementation into the system. Future studies can focus on conducting interviews with academics, entrepreneurs/industry players and tourism professionals for finding out the need and relevance of tourism education in Oman to compel the government and higher educational organizations to take note.

CONCLUSION

A number of initiatives have been taken by the policy makers and a considerable amount of progress has been made in higher education in Oman since 1970. This is visible with the establishment of the institutions which provide different types of support and education to the current and future entrepreneurs. These measures and initiatives have been taken under the consideration of a number of ministries and agencies in Oman. This chapter has proposed a conceptual model of entrepreneurship education in the context of tourism. It consists of a number of dimensions which the policy makers should refer to when implementing tourism entrepreneurship education. This will undoubtedly aid policymakers in sharpening their attention and knowledge of the youth, as well as higher education institutions in better personalising their education curricula to equip students with the necessary skills to graduate with positive attitudes toward entrepreneurship. The chapter has shed light upon the common approaches towards entrepreneurship success in the context of tourism in

Oman. It can be seen that entrepreneurship education plays a vital role in shaping innovative entrepreneurs and this needs special attention from the policy makers.

SOLUTIONS AND RECOMMENDATIONS

- The government's continuous delivery of strategic support to the tourism entrepreneurs will further facilitate the entrepreneurship.
- The provision of financial aid or support to encourage and motivate tourism entrepreneurs is an important support.
- The government's continuous investment in super-structure projects to increase the scope of tourism in the country will strengthen the tourism entrepreneurship .
- Also, arrangement of more training programs to boost the tourism business in Oman by the government is recommended.
- The government must keep continue transforming the country into an entrepreneurial society. It will take time to reap the benefits of entrepreneurship policy. At all levels, whether its government services, education and training, or business assistance programmes; the Omani government must embrace and emphasise on high standards of quality.
- There is a need for a dedicated government entity to advocate for entrepreneurship issues, and to be the vehicle for driving policies and implementing this agenda. This entity should to work in parallel with various ministries and agencies relevant to the policy. This single authority serves as an advocate for entrepreneurship and high-potential new businesses, and it can help to coordinate government activities, programmes, and organisations that promote entrepreneurship (e.g., technology parks, incubators, business development centres). It has the potential to close the gap in government's appreciation of entrepreneurship in tourism, improve internal agency collaboration and coordination, and provide data, resources, and assistance to entrepreneurs in the tourism.

REFERENCES

Acs, Z. J., Desai, S., & Hessels, J. (2008). Entrepreneurship, economic development and institutions. *Small Business Economics*, *31*(3), 219–234. doi:10.100711187-008-9135-9

Adewale, A. A. (2016). The task, challenges and strategies for the marketing of tourism and relaxation services in Nigeria. *International Journal of Marketing Practices*, *3*(1), 24–32.

Ahmad, S. Z., Bakar, A. R. A., & Ahmad, N. (2018). An evaluation of teaching methods of entrepreneurship in hospitality and tourism programs. *International Journal of Management Education*, *16*(1), 14–25. doi:10.1016/j.ijme.2017.11.002

Ahrari-Roudi, M. (2018). Tourism potential and assessment of its environmental impact on the northern coasts of the Oman Sea, Iran. *Geotechnical Geology*, *14*(1), 131–141.

Al-Abri, S. S., Abdel-Hady, D. M., & Al-Abaidani, I. S. (2016). Knowledge, attitudes, and practices regarding travel health among Muscat International Airport travelers in Oman: Identifying the gaps and addressing the challenges. *Journal of Epidemiology and Global Health*, *6*(2), 67–75. doi:10.1016/j.jegh.2016.02.003 PMID:26948720

Al Badi, O., & Khan, F. R. (2020). Examining Challenging Factors of Tourism Entrepreneurship in Oman using PLS-SEM. *International Journal of Research in Entrepreneurship & Business Studies*, *1*(1), 48–64. doi:10.47259/ijrebs.115

Al Buraiki, A., & Khan, F. R. (2018). Finance and technology: Key challenges faced by small and medium enterprises (SMEs) in Oman. *International Journal of Management, Innovation & Entrepreneurial Research*, 2395-7662.

Al-Harthi, A. S. A. (2017). Understanding entrepreneurship through the experiences of Omani entrepreneurs: Implications for entrepreneurship education. *Journal of Developmental Entrepreneurship*, *22*(01), 1750001. doi:10.1142/S1084946717500017

Al-Hasni, Z. S., & Afifi, G. M. (2021). *Local's Attitudes towards Tourism Development: The Case of Oman.* Academic Press.

Al-Muqbali, A. H. (2006). *Towards More Effective Administrative Training in the Omani Public Sector* [Unpublished Doctoral Dissertation]. School of Education, The University of Manchester (United Kingdom).

Al Shabibi, I. (2020). *Planning for entrepreneurialism in a rentier state economy: Entrepreneurship education for economic diversification in Oman* [Unpublished Doctoral dissertation]. School of Social Sciences, Cardiff University, UK.

Alani, F., Khan, F. R., & Manuel, D. (2017). Need for professionalism and quality service of the Tourist Guides in Oman. *International Journal of Tourism & Hospitality Reviews*, *4*(1), 20–29. doi:10.18510/ijthr.2017.413

Alhasni, Z. (2021). Tourism versus Sustainable Development Goals (SDG) Tourism– an element of economic growth of metropolitan cities, entrepreneurs. *Studies of Applied Economics, 39*(4). Advance online publication. doi:10.25115/eea.v39i4.4587

Ali, Y., Nusair, M. M., Alani, F., Khan, F. R., & Al Badi, L. (2017). Employment in the private sector in Oman: Sector-based approach for localization. *Humanities & Social Sciences Reviews, 5*(1), 1-20.

Alrawadieh, Z., Karayilan, E., & Cetin, G. (2019). Understanding the challenges of refugee entrepreneurship in tourism and hospitality. *Service Industries Journal, 39*(9-10), 717–740. doi:10.1080/02642069.2018.1440550

Alsawafi, A. M. (2016). Exploring the challenges and perceptions of Al Rustaq College of Applied Sciences students towards Omani women's empowerment in the tourism sector. *Tourism Management Perspectives, 20*, 246–250. doi:10.1016/j.tmp.2016.10.004

Atef, T. M., & Al-Balushi, M. (2015). Entrepreneurship as a means for restructuring employment patterns. *Tourism and Hospitality Research, 15*(2), 73–90. doi:10.1177/1467358414558082

Aulia, S. (2016). *The Challenges of Tourism–With Specific Reference to Muscat Region (A Conceptual Perspective)*. Academic Press.

Bailetti, T. (2012). Technology entrepreneurship: Overview, definition, and distinctive aspects. *Technology Innovation Management Review, 2*(2), 5–12. doi:10.22215/timreview/520

Baporikar, N. (2017). Critical review of entrepreneurship in Oman. *Entrepreneurship and Business Innovation in the Middle East*, 147-174. . doi:10.4018/978-1-5225-2066-5.ch008

Bindah, E. V., & Magd, H. A. (2016). Teaching Entrepreneurship in Oman: Successful Approaches. *Procedia: Social and Behavioral Sciences, 219*, 140–144. doi:10.1016/j.sbspro.2016.04.055

Buhalis, D., & Law, R. (2008). Progress in information technology and tourism management: 20 years on and 10 years after the Internet—The state of eTourism research. *Tourism Management, 29*(4), 609–623. doi:10.1016/j.tourman.2008.01.005

Daniel, A. D., Costa, R. A., Pita, M., & Costa, C. (2017). Tourism Education: What about entrepreneurial skills? *Journal of Hospitality and Tourism Management, 30*, 65–72. doi:10.1016/j.jhtm.2017.01.002

Del Vecchio, P., Mele, G., Ndou, V., & Secundo, G. (2018). Creating value from social big data: Implications for smart tourism destinations. *Information Processing & Management, 54*(5), 847–860. doi:10.1016/j.ipm.2017.10.006

Ennis, C. A. (2015). Between trend and necessity: Top-down entrepreneurship promotion in Oman and Qatar. *The Muslim World, 105*(1), 116–138. doi:10.1111/muwo.12083

Fatoki, O., & Oni, O. (2014). Students' perception of the effectiveness of entrepreneurship education at a South African University. *Mediterranean Journal of Social Sciences, 5*(20), 585–585. doi:10.5901/mjss.2014.v5n20p585

Ghouse, S., McElwee, G., Meaton, J., & Durrah, O. (2017). Barriers to Rural Women Entrepreneurs in Oman. *International Journal of Entrepreneurial Behaviour & Research, 23*(6), 998–1016. doi:10.1108/IJEBR-02-2017-0070

Halibas, A. S., Sibayan, R. O., & Maata, R. L. R. (2017). The Penta helix Model of Innovation in Oman: An HEI Perspective. *Interdisciplinary Journal of Information, Knowledge & Management, 12*, 159-172. Retrieved from https://www.informingscience.org/Publications/373

Hanieh, A. (2021). Thinking about Capital and Class in the Arab Gulf Arab States. *Marx in the Field, 3*(1), 77-88.

Haque, A., & Patnaik, A. K. (2016). Contribution of Tourism sector to Oman's GDP. *International Journal of Economics, Commerce and Management*, 185-195.

Hilal, N. (2020). Tourism in the gulf cooperation council countries as a priority for economic prospects and diversification. *Journal of Tourism & Hospitality (Los Angeles, Calif.), 9*(451), 2167–2269.

Hvidt, M. (2013). *Economic diversification in GCC countries: Past record and future trends*. https://www.lse.ac.uk/LSEKP

Ibrahim, O. A., Devesh, S., & Ubaidullah, V. (2017). Implication of attitude of graduate students in Oman towards entrepreneurship: An empirical study. *Journal of Global Entrepreneurship Research, 7*(1), 1–17. doi:10.118640497-017-0066-2

Khan, F. R., & Krishnamurthy, J. (2016). Future proofing of tourism entrepreneurship in Oman: Challenges and prospects. *Journal of Work-Applied Management, 8*(1), 79–94. doi:10.1108/JWAM-06-2016-0008

Kim, D., & Kim, S. (2017). The role of mobile technology in tourism: Patents, articles, news, and mobile tour app reviews. *Sustainability, 9*(11), 2082. doi:10.3390u9112082

Kiswani, A. E. (2013). *Entrepreneurship Education in the Arab States A joint project between UNESCO and StratREAL Foundation, UK Component II: Regional Synthesis Report*. UNESCO. https://unesdoc.unesco.org/ark:/48223/pf0000220305_eng

Lew, A. A., Hall, C. M., & Williams, A. M. (2008). *A companion to tourism*. John Wiley & Sons.

Magd, H. A., & McCoy, M. P. (2014). Entrepreneurship in Oman: Paving the way for a sustainable future. *Procedia Economics and Finance, 15*, 1632–1640. doi:10.1016/S2212-5671(14)00634-0

Magd, H. A., & McCoy, M. P. (2014). Entrepreneurship in Oman: Paving the way for a sustainable future. *Procedia Economics and Finance, 15*, 1632–1640. doi:10.1016/S2212-5671(14)00634-0

Mansour, S., Al-Awhadi, T., & Al-Hatrushi, S. (2020). Geospatial based multi-criteria analysis for ecotourism land suitability using GIS & AHP: A case study of Masirah Island, Oman. *Journal of Ecotourism, 19*(2), 148–167. doi:10.1080/14724049.2019.1663202

Ministry of Higher Education. (2013). Workshop Introducing a Module for Entrepreneurship and Students Activities in Higher Education Institutions in Oman. Ministry of Higher Education (MOHE).

Ministry of Tourism. (2015). *Oman Tourism Alternative.* Vision of Ministry of Tourism. Available at: www.alternativer.co/omantourism.gov.om/sites-like-omantourism

Moremong-Nganunu, T., Rametse, N., Al-Muharrami, S., & Sharma, S. K. (2018). Perceptions towards entrepreneurship and intention to become entrepreneurs: the case of Sultan Qaboos university female undergraduate students. In *Entrepreneurship education and research in the Middle East and North Africa (MENA)* (pp. 215–238). Springer. doi:10.1007/978-3-319-90394-1_12

NCSI. (2022, Jan.). *Monthly Statistical Bulletin*. https://ncsi.gov.om/Elibrary/Pages/Library ContentDetails.aspx?ItemID=Vs6NFz%2B2xQSbfUBfw5b4ng%3D%3D

Ndou, V., Mele, G., & Del Vecchio, P. (2019). Entrepreneurship education in tourism: An investigation among European Universities. *Journal of Hospitality, Leisure, Sport and Tourism Education, 25*, 100175. doi:10.1016/j.jhlste.2018.10.003

Ndou, V., Mele, G., & Del Vecchio, P. (2019). Entrepreneurship education in tourism: An investigation among European Universities. *Journal of Hospitality, Leisure, Sport and Tourism Education, 25*, 100175. doi:10.1016/j.jhlste.2018.10.003

Neuhofer, B., Buhalis, D., & Ladkin, A. (2014). A typology of technology-enhanced tourism experiences. *International Journal of Tourism Research*, *16*(4), 340–350. doi:10.1002/jtr.1958

Observer, O. (2017). *Tapping-the-entrepreneurial-potential-of-omans-tourism-resources.* Available at: https://www.Omanobserver.om/article/82049/Features/tapping–the– entrepreneurial–potential–of-omans-tourism-resources

Oman National Centre for Statistics and Information. (2018). *Statistical Year Book. Statistical Year Book.* National Centre of Statistics and Information.

Omanuna, The Official Oman eGovernment Service Protal. (n.d.). *SAS Entrepreneurship program.* https://www.oman.om/wps/portal/index/bz/ManagingBusiness/SASEP/!ut/p/a1/hc9Nb4JAEAbgX8OVmd1

Ozturk, H. M. (2021). Technological Developments: Industry 4.0 and Its Effect on the Tourism Sector. In *Research Anthology on Cross-Industry Challenges of Industry 4.0, 1464-1487.* IGI Global. doi:10.4018/978-1-7998-8548-1.ch073

Pandow, B. A., & Omar, A. S. (2019). Evaluating Inclination of Youth to Start Enterprise: A Study in Oman. In *Creative Business and Social Innovations for a Sustainable Future* (pp. 133–142). Springer. doi:10.1007/978-3-030-01662-3_15

Parambi, R. (2014). *The case of the missing middle.* Available at: www.muscatdaily.com/ Archive/Business/SME-Development-in-Oman-2y7u

Räisänen, J. (2018). *Changing perceptions of tourism as a respectable career choice for Omani women.* Academic Press.

Saleh, M. S., & Alalouch, C. (2015). Towards sustainable construction in Oman: Challenges & opportunities. *Procedia Engineering*, *118*, 177–184. doi:10.1016/j.proeng.2015.08.416

Sazegar, M., Forouharfar, A., Hill, V., & Faghih, N. (2018). The innovation-based competitive advantage in Oman's transition to a knowledge-based economy: dynamics of innovation for promotion of entrepreneurship. In *Entrepreneurship Ecosystem in the Middle East and North Africa, 491-518.* Springer. doi:10.1007/978-3-319-75913-5_18

Sokhalingam, C. P., Manimekalai, N., & Sudhahar, C. (2013). Entrepreneurial approach to tourism development in Oman. *International Journal of Management*, *4*(3), 48–60.

Sotiriadis, M., & Apostolakis, A. (2015). Marketing challenges in travel, tourism and hospitality industries of the European and Mediterranean regions. *EuroMed Journal of Business, 10*(3), 107–120. doi:10.1108/EMJB-07-2015-0035

Tarkenton, F. (2012). *Culture of entitlement threatens entrepreneurship.* Newsmax. Available at: www.newsmax.com/FranTarkenton/culture-entrepreneurs-America-entitlements/ 2012/09/07/id/451109/

The Global Entrepreneurship and Development Institute. (2018). *Global Entrepreneurship Index.* The Global Entrepreneurship and Development Institute.

Times of Oman. (2014). Oman has tourism challenges to tackle. *Times of Oman.* Available at: www.timesofoman.com/news/37615/Article-Oman-has-tourism-challengesto-tackle

Urbančič, J., Kuralt, V., Ratkajec, H., Straus, M., Vavroš, A., Mokorel, S., & Ilijaš, T. (2020). Expansion of Technology Utilization Through Tourism 4.0 in Slovenia. In *Handbook of Research on Smart Technology Applications in the Tourism Industry* (pp. 229–253). IGI Global. doi:10.4018/978-1-7998-1989-9.ch011

Vanevenhoven, J., & Liguori, E. (2013). The Impact of entrepreneurship education: Introducing the entrepreneurship education project. *Journal of Small Business Management, 51*(3), 315–328. doi:10.1111/jsbm.12026

Vidal, B. (2019). *The new technology and travel revolution.* Retrieved November, 30, 2020. https://www.wearemarketing.com/blog/tourism-and-technology-how-tech-is-revolutionizing-travel.html

Williams, W., Knight, H., & Rutter, R. (2015). A Study of the Convergence between Entrepreneurship, Government Policy and Higher Education in the Sultanate of Oman. *60th Annual ICSB World Conference, Entrepreneurship at a Global Crossroads*, 6-9.

Yarahmadi, F., & Magd, H. A. (2016). Entrepreneurship infrastructure and education in Oman. *Procedia: Social and Behavioral Sciences, 219*, 792–797. doi:10.1016/j.sbspro.2016.05.079

Yuksel, S. (2014). Roadmap Of Recovery Amid Challenges Facing Oman Tourism. *Omani Journal of Applied Sciences, 5*(1), 1–28.

Zehrer, A., & Mössenlechner, C. (2008). Industry relations and curricula design in Austrian tourism master programs: A comparative analysis. *Journal of Teaching in Travel & Tourism, 8*(1), 73–95. doi:10.1080/15313220802441992

ADDITIONAL READING

Ghouse, S., McElwee, G., Meaton, J., & Durrah, O. (2017). Barriers to rural women entrepreneurs in Oman. *International Journal of Entrepreneurial Behaviour & Research, 23*(6), 998–1016. doi:10.1108/IJEBR-02-2017-0070

Tewari, V. (2019). Seasonality in tourism: the case of Oman. *Ottoman: Journal of Tourism and Management Research, 4*(2), 463-476.

KEY TERMS AND DEFINITIONS

Entrepreneur: An entrepreneur is a person who starts a new firm and bears most of the risks while reaping majority of the benefits. Entrepreneurship refers to the process of starting a business. The entrepreneur is frequently portrayed as a pioneer, a provider of novel ideas, products, services, and/or business processes.

Economic Diversification: Economic diversification is the process of transferring an economy's income sources away from a single source and toward an increasing number of sectors and marketplaces. It has historically been used as a tactic to promote positive economic growth and development.

Entrepreneurship: The definition of entrepreneurship is a person who takes action to create a difference in the world. Whether they solve a problem that many people face every day, connect people together in ways no one has done before, or build something new that improves society, all start-up entrepreneurs have one thing in common that is they act.

Entrepreneurship Education: According to the definition of entrepreneurship education, it is a collection of formalised teachings that informs, trains, and educates anyone interested in participating in socioeconomic development through a project to promote entrepreneurship awareness, business creation, or small business development.

Knowledge-Based Economy: A knowledge-based economy is one in which knowledge is produced, disseminated, and used; one in which knowledge is a key factor in growth, wealth creation, and employment; and one in which human capital is the driver of creativity, innovation, and the generation of new ideas, with information and communication technology (ICT) serving as an enabler.

Production-Based Economy: A production-based economy uses labour, capital, goods, and services as inputs to produce outputs of goods or services and is controlled and supervised by an institutional unit.

Tourism Industry: The tourism sector, in its broadest meaning, encompasses any firms that directly supply goods or services to assist business, pleasure, or leisure activities away from home.

Chapter 5
Joy Labs:
Discussing the Advantages and Disadvantages of PANCOE – University of Palermo, Argentina

Maximiliano Emanuel Korstanje
https://orcid.org/0000-0002-5149-1669
University of Palermo, Argentina

María Alejandra Zuccoli
University of Palermo, Argentina

ABSTRACT

The present case study brings reflection on the power of pleasure (joy) to better the classic education system. Whilst pleasure was overlooked as an instrument to make positive feedback in students for classic education, PANCOE (and the laboratory of pleasure) goes in the opposite direction. The laboratory of pleasure stimulates students´ skills and performance through the articulation of pleasurable experiences. The results notably show that those students who participated in PANCOE have better degrees than those who did not take part in the experiment. At the same time, the endorphins liberated by positive interactive communication paves the ways for the rise of pleasurable experiences which dispose from better academic performances. Originally PANCOE was designed to standardize the learning process of foreign students. The goal was chiefly oriented to retain the student reducing the academic desertion, which means the rate of students who fail to earn a degree.

DOI: 10.4018/978-1-7998-9510-7.ch005

1. INTRODUCTION

The term education comes from Latin Educere, which was employed in Ancient Rome with a two-pronged approach. On one hand, it denotes a type of emancipation, or so to speak liberation given by the learned skills, but on another, the word associates to the act of feeding the cattle. The latter meaning mainly marks the ideological nature of education, which is often used as an instrument of domestication –if not massification-. For some reason which is very difficult to precise here, education has evolved according to a positivist dominant paradigm which was based on the Cartesian dualism. Such a dualism emphasized on the division between the mind and emotions (Rozemond, 1988). For the Cartesians, the mandate of the mind subordinates not only the body but also the emotions. Traditional education and Cartesian dualism are inevitably entwined. For traditional education, reasoning situates over human emotionality in the same way that the mind governs the body. In tourism fields, the positivist viewpoint takes the lead in the Academia over other voices and paradigms (Su 2014; Sheldon, Fesenmaier & Tribe 2011; Ayikoru, Tribe & Airey, 2009). Educators give certain prominence to the traditional methods which are drawn to stimulate the skills of students for labour competition. Even if the resulting syllabuses are carefully designed and credited by the national authorities, it is unfortunate the traditional education has serious problems to offer efficient solutions to the new global challenges that are today threatening the industry (Lew 2014). It is noteworthy that major risks as terrorism and political instability seconded by natural disasters or even global virus outbreaks –like the recent COVID-19- without mentioning the effects of climate change ignite a hot-debate revolving around the future of tourism (Sigala 2020; Bagri & Junaid, 2020; Korstanje & George 2021). Without any doubt, big problems need big solutions!

Over the recent years, tourism education has evolved as a promising object of study within the constellations of tourism research. Tourism education not only lays the foundations (curricula) in the process of formation for tourism professionals but also sheds light on the methodological problems of empirical research (Lewis, & Tribe 2002; Tribe 2002). One of the goals of tourism education consists in shortening the gap between theory and practice. Tourism education should be defined as a process that trains the next professionals, policy-makers, researchers and workers in the tourism industry. The learning process is aimed at coping with the nagging problems of the sector as well as the conflicts derived from the interaction of the different stakeholders (Cooper, 2002; Belhassen & Caton, 2011; Paris 2011). Of course, tourism education has developed many methods and techniques but for some reason it leads to an unparalleled crisis. This crisis has been discussed by many studies and works published in leading journals. Academicians and colleagues of all pundits have called the attention to a mix-balanced discussion whilst contemplating the pro and cons of the current tourism higher education. Nevertheless of this fact, tourism education crisis include problems of employability, low-wages paid to workforce as well as students` frustrations once they are incorporated to the front desk staff. Scholars allude to the curricula reformation as a vehicle towards a new type of tourism education in the years to come (Paris 2011; Hsu 2018; Airey 2013).

Having said this, no less true seems to be that digital technologies play a crucial role in the formation of pre and postgraduate students in tourism and hospitality (Morellato, 2014; Buhalis & Law, 2008). Nonetheless of this fact, some critical studies recently caution on the limitations of digital technology to captivate the attention of students. Technology creates standardised forms of knowledge which under some conditions reduces critical thinking (William & Hobson, 1995; Munar & Gyimothy, 2013). One of the paradoxes of tourism education appears to be that much has been written and said about the theme, but little is known in discovering a successful learning process which mitigates the looming threats over the industry. What is more important, the serious challenges (like the pandemic or the climate change) the industry is facing in our days requires innovative but not for these less efficient solutions (Carr 2020; Sigala, 2020; Korstanje & George 2021).

As the previous backdrop, the present case study explores not only problems of classic education in tourism but also the role of pleasure as a key factor towards learning optimization. With basis on the experience of the Joy Labs (Joy Laboratory) a pedagogic centre, which was founded at the University of Palermo to measure and empower students´ skills, this piece describes the different stages and facets of PANCOE which is a new innovative and educative method. The Joy Labs, which was formally approved by Dean Gabriel Foglia in 2012, is headed by Alejandra Zuccoli (the corresponding author). It is important to mention that though food occupies a central position in the experiment, the goals are aimed at strengthen the creativity and entrepreneurship of students (combining the digital platforms with gamification theory). Basically, PANCOE looks to stimulate the students` performance through the combination of different pleasurable experiences. Hence, the present book chapter holds that those pleasurable experiences such as eating, cooking or smelling release endorphins in the body which dispose the involving students to better the academic performance. Participants in this experiment were pre-graduate tourism students coming from neighbouring and Latin American countries who attended the University of Palermo to earn their bachelor degree in Tourism and hospitality.

The book chapter is structured in three main sections. The first contains an in-depth review of specialised literature in education and tourism education. At the same time, this section divides in two sub-sections. One introduces readers in the positivist insight as well as the Cartesian dualism which marks the essence of modern education. The other discusses critically the ebbs and flows of tourism education and its incapacity to resolve the daily problems of tourism industry. At a first glimpse, there is a gap between theory and practice that should be filled. The second part synthesises a case study based on the experience of PANCOE at the University of Palermo, Argentina. In the third section, we enumerate a set of ideas and implications derived from PANCOE as main study-case. The section was inspired in the testimonies of participants as well as other students who have taken part of PANCOE in its different editions. PANCOE puts emphasis in pleasure as a key force towards a new understanding of tourism education and entrepreneurship.

2. LITERATURE REVIEW

2.1 A Short Description

From its outset in Ancient Greece, Stoicism as a school of Hellenistic philosophy, which dates back to 3rd Century B.C, punctuated on the needs of repressing pleasure –or at least the excess of pleasure- for the subject to reach ethics. Without any doubt, this emerging reasoning influenced not only a whole portion of the Hellenic world but also scholastic and even modern philosophy for centuries. At a closer look, Stoics emphasised virtue as the only instrument of education. One century later, in 2nd B.C, Epicurus of Samos founded a new philosophical wave toying with the belief that pleasure was vital for liberating the subject, as well as optimizing his cognitive skills. For Epicurus, pleasure –not pain or suffering- plays a leading role in opening the mind to new knowledge and sensory experiences. The purpose of philosophy rests in three clear-cut pillars: happiness (eudaimonic), a tranquil life (arataxia) and the absence of pain (aponia). Although his thought certainly revolutionised Greek philosophy, his legacy in the fields of education remains in a peripheral position (O´ Keefe, 2014). For some reason, which is very hard to precise here, in tourism education, Epicurus´ works are neither well-known nor widely cited. It is safe to say the specialised literature in tourism education has univocally adopted a positivist viewpoint. The long-dominant paradigm suggests that education that genuine knowledge should be learned through a specific-guided process mainly marked by rules and procedures. In a seminal book which entitles Reproduction in Education, Pierre Bourdieu & Jean-Claude Passeron dissect the complex nature of education. Based on French tradition, authors acknowledge that the shared understandings are transmitted from generation to generation through a mechanism of reproduction. These understandings include norms, expectancies and habits finely articulated in a process of transferring that distinguishes classes, and human groups. Groups work actively to reproduce the existing social structure in order to keep their advantages. In the modern societies, the schooling acts as a mechanism of cultural reproduction beyond the content or the courses that are being taught. This means two important things, education serves as an instrument to operate in the different levels of economy while the student internalizes his future role and position in society. Students, in this way, are formed to perform a role in the social reproduction. Secondly, education conserves the material and financial inter-class asymmetries which are finely ingrained in the capitalist system. For that, schools in the capitalist society need a method of stratification. The syllabuses and academic programs are designed following the codes of the ruling elite. This explains why those who successfully pass the exams belong to privileged classes whereas lower-class students obtain a much poor performance. At the time it includes, the education process makes the inequalities more acute (Bourdieu & Passeron, 1990).

2.2 Tourism Education

Echoing the dualism between the mind and the body, only the reason, which dissociates from emotions, occupies a central position in tourism education. Tourism education is not only based on what Adrian Franklin dubbed as "tourist-centricity" (Franklin, 2014) but also centres on an economic-based paradigm, which means the adoption of the managerial perspective to judge what can be published or not. The managerial perspective dominates a whole portion of the academic curricula in the fields of tourism and hospitality (Korstanje & George 2021). Some voices claimed that tourism education is training future professionals, like tourist agents or guides instead of scientists. Interesting pedagogic methods as life-long learning are systematically excluded from the curricula (Tribe 2002; Cuffy, Tribe & Airey, 2012). From its outset, tourism education starts from the premise that learning should shorten the gap between theory and practice. Likewise, knowledge reproduces professionals educated to solve the problems of the industry (Jafari & Ritchie, 1981; Cooper & Shepherd, 1997). As David Airey & John Tribe (2006) put it, tourism education catalyzes to optimize rational planning as well as overcoming the logic obstacles in tourism epistemology. Tourism education reflects not only the maturation of scientific research but also the emergence of a new enriched curriculum overtly designed to give efficient answers to the nagging problems of the industry (a type of guidebook for good practices). The notable progress of tourism education coincides not only with the growth of the tourism industry worldwide but with to professionalize of the activity (forming qualified staff). Lastly, the problem of education associates with a coherent assessment. To wit, personal-oriented evaluation techniques –centred on the power of digital technologies- should be disposed to stimulate intellectual curiosity. The dissociation between practice and theory was widely documented. Efficiency in tourism education is simply given when the education meets the expectations or at least helps to solve the obstacles of the industry in practical terms (Wang, Ayres & Huyton, 2010). One of the main problems seems to be the multifaceted sub-sectors that integrate the tourism industry without mentioning the multiple and complex demands of the involving stakeholders. In terms of Amoah & Baum: "There is no other industry in the economy that is linked to so many diverse and different kinds of products and services… This then gives rise to the problem of a weak operating framework (Amoah & Baum, 1997: 6).

By this token, Pauline Sheldon, Daniel Fesenmaier & John Tribe (2011) argue convincingly that the Tourism education future Initiative (TEFI) inaugurates a new epoch in education providing an all-encompassing framework of tourism education programs. It kicks off a radical change to accommodate education to give firm responses to the global challenges the industry is now facing. TEFI´s ideals centres on the needs of defining five mainstream values for education: stewardship, ethics, knowledge, mutuality and professionalism. Ethics is defined as the interplay between personal behaviour and those actions striving to make things good associated with cultural values and principles. Rather, knowledge is based on the process of education where the subject develops specific skills and understanding about the problem of the industry. Stewardship refers to the responsibility to care for others for the benefits of future generations. The term here equates to sustainability. Professionalism signals the ability to develop specific skills whilst engaging with guests´ satisfaction. Mutualism is understood as the mutual respect that is evolving at different levels of the organization. This includes self-awareness, open-mindedness, empowerment and critical thinking. These five pillars offered an interesting background that inspired many other works in the fields. Some authors and critical voices have emphasised the introduction of critical theories to overcome the obstacles in higher education system. In fact, these studies have recently alerted on the urgency to adopt a critical insight to create alternative theories which confront directly the status quo (Fuchs 2021). As Belhassen & Caton (2011) adhere, scholars and Academia should move towards a critical pedagogy that improves the curricula in three directions: individual freedom, social justice and business productivity. Although technology helps in boosting education it often creates a technocratic approach that homogenises a major part of the curricula affecting negatively the skill-building process. Above all, few studies emphasise the needs to discuss to what extent management is a skill that can be successfully shared or taught. The classic education lays foundations towards a rational analysis that supports managerial effectiveness instead of stimulating academic engagement, as the authors claim. Instead, the adoption of critical pedagogy allows the training of free individuals who under the auspices of humanism move to social justice. Critical pedagogy resolves the Cartesian dualism where the knower sees in opposition to what should be known and this way controlled. The authors question why the technocratic paradigm has gained further attention in the constellations of tourism. They go on to write, "So what are the reasons why the technocratic educational approach has gained so much success in tourism departments?

It would be reasonable to argue that technocratic curricula in tourism have become self-sustaining because they conform to students' consumer-oriented desires to receive pre-digested units of knowledge and provide them with a comforting sense of certainty that the world is, in fact, well understood. In addition, such curricula also bestow upon universities a "quality control" mechanism as they cast scholars in the role of experts who can, rather tautologically, be evaluated mostly on their ability to transmit the received canon of knowledge entertainingly and engagingly" (Belhassen & Caton, 2014: 1394).

In consonance with the above-cited excerpt, critical pedagogy should incorporate not only the emotionality of students but also postulates a more self-interested path of reciprocity dotted of more social productivity (Belhassen & Caton, 2014). Last but not least, Professor Vishwas Gupta (2016) argues convincingly that the tourism industry sometimes seems to be far from being the vehicle of prosperity and peace policy-makers often proclaim. Authorities allude to tourism prosperity to give further authority and credit to their administration. However, the industry creates more imbalances and problems for locals than authorities recognize. Under the panacea of local economic development no less true is that the negative effects of tourism include unemployment, poverty and inflation for locals. It is difficult to resist the impression that tourism education revitalizes and sanitizes the vices of under-developing economies. This moot point leads to Inui, Wheeler & Lankford (2006) to rethink the economic-based paradigm in tourism education. Per these authors, tourism education evolves to a managerial paradigm that looks for employability as a primary goal. This happens simply because tourism has been widely described as the world´s largest industry. Since the 70s decade, the first academic degree was mainly based on what experts know as the "economic-centred paradigm". These works focused on the economic impact of tourism in society as well as the opportunities of staff to have higher levels of employability. The first pioneering universities which incorporated tourism as an academic career designed the syllabuses to educate the future workforce of the industry. It is safe to say that the curriculum was certainly dominated by a focus on occupational skills whilst pushing the emotional aspect of learning in a peripheral position (Inui, Wheeler & Lankford, 2006). This position invariably was like throwing the bathwater out with the baby. The vocational emphasis explains the obsession of students for reaching a job once the degree is earned (Korstanje & George 2021; Farmaki 2018). Many young people –above all in under-developed economies which are dependant on tourism- decide to study tourism to get a well-paid job. Once graduated, they come across a grim scenario characterised by excessive working hours, low-paid wages as well as labour exploitation. Paradoxically, many students are psychologically frustrated to enter a labour market to compete with others. This negative aspect is the main cause of higher desertion rates in universities (Korstanje 2008).

Daniel et al (2017) call attention to the significant role of entrepreneurship to give students different skills to overcome the obstacles of the employability-based paradigm. Students who start to work in the service sector go across countless difficulties and challenges. The acquired skills they learned in the university do not suffice to deal with these problems. The industry is defined as highly competitive and demanding. Hence, entrepreneurial skills provide students with creating thinking which not only optimises their real performance whilst developing innovative solutions. Ndou, Mele & del Vecchio (2019) remark that entrepreneurs are open to innovative solutions (if not disruptive thinking) for policy-making to adopt sustainable programs. This is the reason why entrepreneur education (EE) is gaining traction in all levels of the industry. EE structures a novel new way of enhancing students´ skills. The problem lies in the fact some countries are not considering the benefits of entrepreneur education or are loath to incorporate it into their programs and syllabuses. As Syed Ahmad (2015) eloquently notes, in Egypt students are not only unfamiliar with EE, the government does not think the entrepreneurship module would be an important aspect of tourism education. The urgency to include EE in classic tourism programs is coincidental with the global threats the industry faces day-to-day. Zhao, Ritchie & Echtner (2011) punctuate that social capital directly correlates to entrepreneurship. To put the same in other terms, social capital not only generates familiarity with tourism business development but also associates positively to the individual´ ability and organizational profitability. By this side, Sheldon, Pollock & Danielle (2017) hold the thesis that social entrepreneurship proposes durable solutions to adopt shifts in the tourist system which are not properly working. For that reason, it is important not to lose sight of the fact entrepreneur education should be widely adopted by university and tertiary institutions (Altejevic & Li, 2017; Fu et al. 2019). Even if scholars have paid considerable attention to entrepreneur education in the dimension of tourism and hospitality, this emerging sub-discipline remains in its infancy.

At a closer look, tourism and entrepreneur education have captivated the attention of countless scholars, situating as buzzwords in the applied research worldwide, but in the literature little attention was given to the powerful role played by pleasure (joy) in the education system. The positivist perspective dominates the main leading and most-cited publications. From this angle, this is where our book chapter makes a seminal contribution to the present book. For the sake of clarity, the current teaching methods do not contemplate the figure of pleasure to boost learning. PANCOE is the first laboratory which experiments with pleasure to potentiate learning skills. Needless to say though promising and illustrative the findings should be limited to the samples and cannot be extrapolated to other universes.

3. PANCOE AS MAIN STUDY CASE

PANCOE is the name of an experimental project which was created by the Economics faculty at the University of Palermo, Buenos Aires, Argentina in 2012. PANCOE articulates with the Joy Labs which was originally oriented to improve the cognitive skills of students through the stimulation of sensory pleasure. Methodologically speaking, we use the term joy and pleasure indistinctively. One operates in the field of endorphins which disposes the body to a pleasurable state whereas joy circumscribes to a durable sate of the mind marked by happiness (well-being).

It is noteworthy that the human senses are five: smell, taste, touch, sight and hearing). Participants in this study were pre-graduate tourism students who have been subject to positive stimulus in smell and taste whilst they were tested in some cognitive skills. At a first glimpse, their skills were notably potentiated through the stimulation of pleasure (joy) experiences in eating or smelling some dishes. Because it innovated in the fields of tourism education, the laboratory received important international recognitions as to be selected as finalist at *Reimagine education awards QS Stars awards 2016 (Wharton College).* It is important not to lose sight of the fact that *t*he laboratory combines fine cuisine, on the hands of well-known chefs with neurosciences and the technology of gamification. In this vein, the laboratory brings students a firm background to improve their academic performances in learning during their careers. In addition, the centre is headed by Alejandra Zuccoli. By a combination of tasting, smelling and cooking or even preparing a meal students release endorphins that dispose students to improve not only their attention but also stimulating their memory. At the time of taking exams, their scoring was notably higher than those students who met with the experiment. What is PANCOE and in what form can be it described?

PANCOE is the name of the method which is distinguished as the only one that deals with pleasure (joy) as a key factor of stimulation and knowledge optimization in the learning process. The term comes from Spanish PAN (Pensamiento automatico naturalizado-Automatic and naturalised thinking) and COE (Comunicacion basada en el estudiante- Communication based on students). To be more precise, the method connects directly with the endorphins of brain exploring not only the students´ skills but also their creativity. The founder of the Joy Labs, Professor Alejandra Zuccoli, drew PANCOE as an emerging and promising experiment to include foreign students coming from different countries. Besides, many of the students who enter the university are certainly educated following traditional methods. The Joy Labs integrates pre-graduate students coming from different Latin American countries as well as social classes. The laboratory puts their innovation and proficiency in the exploration of senses in the foreground of their academic courses. PANCOE has been successfully celebrated 18 encounters gathering well-recognised chefs, tourism and hospitality students as well as professionals from Gastronomy.

As the previous background, the Joy Labsstarts from the premise students are over-exposed to digital technologies. Even if technology often liberates the subject giving him more autonomy no less true seems to be that it standardises the social relations into routine interactions. To some extent, digital technology distracts students at the classroom. This fact inspired Professor Zuccoli to toy with the belief that students seemed to escape mentally from the boring classrooms. Having said this, half of the group was poor grades in the courses. Another additional problem the laboratory successfully resolved was the number of foreign students coming from different cultures and ethnic backgrounds, as Zuccoli concludes. So she asked the following questions: how can teachers organize the syllabus in a multifaceted class? How can teachers replace digital technologies in the classroom for students not to be distracted? How can be a syllabus adapted to foreign students who come from different cultures?

Based on the logic of tourism marketing, PANCOE is a simple methodology dotted with scientific measurements which consist of performing a pleasurable task like cooking, eating a dish or knead bread to optimize academic performance. Participants in the initial experiments came from neighbouring and Latin American countries such as Venezuela, Colombia, Ecuador, Chile and Brazil (only to name a few). Though they shared the same language, Zuccoli argues convincingly that they had different cultural backgrounds and experiences. In view of this, she devoted considerable efforts in deciphering what are their commonalities. All they not only loved cooking but came from the gastronomy industry in their respective countries. The age cohort ranged from 20 to 30 years old. Since many students never culminate successfully in their careers, PANCOE was designed to reduce tertiary education desertion. In so doing, this experiment stimulates and reutilizes the cognitive reserve of endorphins to engage poor grade students but sooner than later it was applied to different classrooms and commissions.

The main goal of the laboratory was associated to integrate the creativity and gifted students with Artificial intelligence and digital social networks as Twitter. Secondly, PANCOE explores and recognizes the smart ideas through the formation of safe social networks. The student´s interaction with others allows a rapid optimization of acquired learning. We coin the term collective intelligence to denote the performance of groups in exams and tests. The experiment was sampled by 870 participants who use regularly twitter (twitter-@holapancoe). The sample divides in active and passive participants. Whilst the former signals to tourism pre graduate students who are subject to PANCOE, the latter refers to students –coming from other universities or areas- who talk and discuss the educative issues but are far from the experiment. The cohort ranges from 18 to 25 years old. Originally the sample was drawn with tourism pre graduate students taking course of Integracion, Ambientacion y communiation (Communication, environmentalism and integration). PANCOE looked to integrate the multisensory of students as well as emotions with academic performance and the digital platforms. PANCOE devotes efforts to transform negative feelings like fear into positive one like joy. Besides, each student imagined its own preferred tourist destination sharing with the others the customs and gastronomy of their own country. We use the term imagined landscape to stimulate pleasure (joy) whilst combining with other methods as cooking, eating or tasting cultural dishes. Students were subject to pictures containing islands, beaches and paradisiacal landscapes. The aim centres on either breaking the humdrum routine or the burden or tensions in a pre-exam stage.

Lastly, the experiment followed three clear facets. The first stage consisted in students creating bread related to identity in twitter. They not only co-created a cultural product characterised from their personal cultural imprint but also interacted and play positively with other peers. In a second facet they eat and taste regional dishes. The breads and dishes followed different cultural traditions from where each student comes from. Each one created a twitter account with 50/60 followers where he or she shared her-his experience whilst cooking or kneading bread. The twitter account was anonymous to potentiate student to express their emotions freely. PANCOE centres on a fluid communication –based on digital technologies- for students to promote their products (dishes or breads). They were encouraged to enter in a branding process where their products were advertised and digitally packaged to be tasted and consumed by others followers. Each product competes with others in egalitarian conditions through twitter. This virtual interaction engaged his-her performance with the academic courses. At the same time, students were bombarded of pictures of paradisiacal pictures and landscape which invited them to travel mentally.

4. DISCUSSION AND RESULTS

Although because of privacy and ethics, their names have been distorted in the present study-case, participants were interviewed in several occasions or at least invited to tell their experiences. Maria (female, 22 years old) said *"the experience was outstanding, thrilling, it was as to apply everything we learned in classroom but in the real life. I did not how to create a twitter account, I learned to use twitter uploading my breads as well as communicating my experiences with unknown others. I was shy to communicate my feelings, PANCOE was a great experience if you ask me"*. Following this, Julieta (female, 20 years old) replies *"to my end, the PANCOE associates directly to the communicative process; each student disseminates a product (a bread) to share a message with professors, students and other peoples. This exhibits a circular model where all we are senders and receivers! The experience interrogated me emotionally situating as a real challenge but it was indeed gratifying!"*

The figure of difference or the radical shift to the traditional education occupied a central position in the Joy Labs. As Rosa puts it, "*it was a strange experiment, innovative, different in essence. Professor Alejandra put to us twitter as an instrument of education and emancipation whilst our products were promoted to the public. Since the twitter account was anonymous it was free to express my feelings.* It was very interesting the previous moment to promote my breads, I did not know who where my followers. My user made public not only the breads but also fine gastronomy. Twitter serves as a fruitful and useful instrument to engage with others". In the same direction, we get with Rogelio (male, 20 years old) who overtly acknowledges that *"PANCOE is great! I never used twitter, it took some time to learn to move in the twitter´s world. Anyway, I created my own avatar, I offered my products whilst interacting positively with other users. This is the type of experience I am willing to make again and again and again!*

The problem of self-esteem and peer valorisation was present in PANCOE as well. Marcelo (male, 20 years old) eloquently claimed that *"I had serious problem to talk with others. This is my Achilles tendon, to the limitations I had because I am not familiar with twitter, one should add I am abroad out of my home. I learned to cook many dishes and I enjoyed getting new experiences during this experiment!*

Finally, Natalia (female, 18 years old) accepts *"PANCOE is a new form of education simply because it basically put me in the Other´s lens. In PANCOE you put as yourself in the other place to improve the relations as well as gaining further understanding on the "Other". Through Twitter and PANCOE I discovered my inner-world"*

The final stage consists in regularly-based exams which were performed orally and by written. Each stage lasted approximately 2 hours. The results were overwhelming, the memory retention increased notably to 33% in students who took part of PANCOE. The graduation rate, which means the number of students who finally earned their degrees, was 40% in students with PANCOE, and 28% in students who did not participate in the experiment.

Amongst the limitations of the study, needless to say, there is some consensus more investigation is needed. In that direction, the study was based on middle-class foreign students, excluding Argentinean peers. In the same way, there is no evidence of results in lower-classes or groups subject to durable psychological deprivations such as students in zones of war, social conflict as well as ongoing political instability or in devastated areas. Promising approaches can be done to marketing issues adapting PANCOE to future products. At the same time, PANCOE would certainly mitigate the negative effects of COVID19 in consumers. PANCOE still remains as an innovative method who credits the important role of pleasure in tourism education.

4.1 Limitations and Next Guides for Research

All experiments and applied research have benefits and problems. To some extent, the obtained outcome in PANCOE cannot be extrapolated to other universes simply because the sample is not statistically representative. To this, one might add the lack of discussion of other qualitative methodologies often used to enhance tourism education. We, rather, start from the premise that the Cartesian dualism which has played a vital role in the current tourism curricula, undermines the importance of joy and pleasure to potentiate the student`s cognitive attention as well as academic performance. Because of time and space, it is very hard to discuss all pedagogic theories in this piece. PANCOE shows a snapshot of the preliminary findings gathered just after the experiment. At the same time, students who have taken part of PANCOE evinced better academic performance in comparison with those who have been excluded from the experiment. PANCOE seems not to be limited to food tourism, or a culinary experience because it stimulates pleasure to boost students` academic performance. In so doing, we have evaluated two key variables: the drop out rates, and the grades for students. Needless to say, this experiment lacks of a long-term evaluation for student which suggests further research in the years to come. Besides, the application of PANCOE to other samples and students in other careers is a much deep issue which needs to be continued. In next empirical layouts, it is important to combine PANCOE with other traditional methodologies in higher education.

5. CONCLUSION

It is important to mention though tourism education shows countless techniques and methods to be applied in the training of the next workforce no less true is that higher tourism education is determined by a strong Cartesian dualism (Cooper & Shepherd, 1997; Qiu, Li & Li 2021). After further review, the present case study brings reflection on the power of pleasure to better the classic education system. Whilst pleasure was overlooked as an instrument to make positive feedback in students for classic education, PANCOE (and the Joy Labs) goes in the opposite direction. The experiment stimulates students´ skills and performance through the articulation of pleasurable experiences. The results notably show that those students who participated in PANCOE have better degrees than those who are not taken part of the experiment. At the same time, the endorphins liberated by positive interactive communication paves the ways for the rise of pleasurable experiences which dispose from better academic performances. Originally PANCOE was designed to standardize the learning process of foreign students. The goal was chiefly oriented to retain the student reducing the academic desertion, which means the rate of students who fail to earn a degree. The results showed that PANCOE not only improved the academic degrees of participants but facilitated their final graduation. Of course, more research should be focused how PANCOE helps to psychologically- disturbed or deprived students who live in zones of war, conflict or disaster as well as whether the same results apply for other groups. Last but not least, though the outcomes are certainly innovative and exhilarating, they cannot be extrapolated to other universes. PANCOE is not based on a statistical representative method. PANCOE is a successful experiment performed by the University of Palermo, Buenos Aires, Argentina.

REFERENCES

Ahmad, S. Z. (2015). Entrepreneurship education in tourism and hospitality programs. *Journal of Hospitality & Tourism Education, 27*(1), 20–29. doi:10.1080/10963758.2014.998764

Airey, D. (2013). Forty years of tourism education and research. *Poznan University of Economics Review, 13*(4), 1-15.

Airey, D., & Tribe, J. (Eds.). (2006). *An international handbook of tourism education*. Routledge. doi:10.4324/9780080458687

Amoah, V. A., & Baum, T. (1997). Tourism education: Policy versus practice. *International Journal of Contemporary Hospitality Management, 9*(1), 5–12. doi:10.1108/09596119710157531

Ateljevic, J., & Li, L. (2017). Tourism entrepreneurship–concepts and issues. In *Tourism and entrepreneurship* (pp. 30–53). Routledge. doi:10.4324/9780080942728-10

Ayikoru, M., Tribe, J., & Airey, D. (2009). Reading tourism education: Neoliberalism unveiled. *Annals of Tourism Research, 36*(2), 191–221. doi:10.1016/j.annals.2008.11.001

Bagri, S. C., & Junaid, K. C. (2020). Ethnic conflict and geopolitics: COVID-19 augmented chaos versus efforts to restart tourism sector. *Skyline Business Journal, 16*(1), 73–81.

Belhassen, Y., & Caton, K. (2011). On the need for critical pedagogy in tourism education. *Tourism Management, 32*(6), 1389–1396. doi:10.1016/j.tourman.2011.01.014

Bourdieu, P., & Passeron, J. C. (1990). *Reproduction in education, society and culture* (Vol. 4). Sage.

Buhalis, D., & Law, R. (2008). Progress in information technology and tourism management: 20 years on and 10 years after the Internet—The state of eTourism research. *Tourism Management, 29*(4), 609–623. doi:10.1016/j.tourman.2008.01.005

Carr, A. (2020). COVID-19, indigenous peoples and tourism: A view from New Zealand. *Tourism Geographies, 22*(3), 491–502. doi:10.1080/14616688.2020.1768433

Cooper, C. (2002). Curriculum planning for tourism education: From theory to practice. *Journal of Teaching in Travel & Tourism, 2*(1), 19–39. doi:10.1300/J172v02n01_02

Cooper, C., & Shepherd, R. (1997). The relationship between tourism education and the tourism industry: Implications for tourism education. *Tourism Recreation Research, 22*(1), 34–47. doi:10.1080/02508281.1997.11014784

Cuffy, V., Tribe, J., & Airey, D. (2012). Lifelong learning for tourism. *Annals of Tourism Research, 39*(3), 1402–1424. doi:10.1016/j.annals.2012.02.007

Daniel, A. D., Costa, R. A., Pita, M., & Costa, C. (2017). Tourism Education: What about entrepreneurial skills? *Journal of Hospitality and Tourism Management, 30*, 65–72. doi:10.1016/j.jhtm.2017.01.002

Farmaki, A. (2018). Tourism and hospitality internships: A prologue to career intentions? *Journal of Hospitality, Leisure, Sport and Tourism Education, 23*, 50–58. doi:10.1016/j.jhlste.2018.06.002

Franklin, A. (2014). Tourist studies. In *The routledge handbook of mobilities* (pp. 94–104). Routledge.

Fu, H., Okumus, F., Wu, K., & Köseoglu, M. A. (2019). The entrepreneurship research in hospitality and tourism. *International Journal of Hospitality Management, 78*, 1–12. doi:10.1016/j.ijhm.2018.10.005

Fuchs, K. (2021). Advances in tourism education: A qualitative inquiry about emergency remote teaching in higher education. *Journal of Environmental Management and Tourism, 12*(02 (50)), 538–543. doi:10.14505//jemt.v12.2(50).23

Gupta, V. (2016). Indian reality tourism-a critical perspective. *Tourism and Hospitality Management*, *22*(2), 111–133. doi:10.20867/thm.22.2.6

Hsu, C. H. (2018). Tourism education on and beyond the horizon. *Tourism Management Perspectives*, *25*, 181–183. doi:10.1016/j.tmp.2017.11.022

Inui, Y., Wheeler, D., & Lankford, S. (2006). Rethinking tourism education: What should schools teach. *Journal of Hospitality, Leisure, Sport and Tourism Education*, *5*(2), 25–35. doi:10.3794/johlste.52.122

Jafari, J., & Ritchie, J. B. (1981). Toward a framework for tourism education: Problems and prospects. *Annals of Tourism Research*, *8*(1), 13–34. doi:10.1016/0160-7383(81)90065-7

Korstanje, M. (2008). Education Issues in Tourism, an analysis of Students expectatives in Argentina. *Tourism Today (Nicosia)*, *8*, 154–166.

Korstanje, M., & George, B. (2021). *The Nature and future of tourism: a post COVID-19 context*. Apple Academic Press.

Korstanje, M. E. (2011). The importance of social sciences in the curricula of tourism students. *Journal of Tourism*, *12*(1), 1–15.

Lew, A. A. (2014). Scale, change and resilience in community tourism planning. *Tourism Geographies*, *16*(1), 14–22. doi:10.1080/14616688.2013.864325

Lewis, A., & Tribe, J. (2002). Critical issues in the globalisation of tourism education. *Tourism Recreation Research*, *27*(1), 13–20. doi:10.1080/02508281.2002.11081352

Morellato, M. (2014). Digital competence in tourism education: Cooperative-experiential learning. *Journal of Teaching in Travel & Tourism*, *14*(2), 184–209. doi:10.1080/15313220.2014.907959

Munar, A. M., & Gyimóthy, S. (2013). Critical digital tourism studies. In *Tourism social media: Transformations in identity, community and culture* (pp. 245–262). Emerald Group Publishing Limited. doi:10.1108/S1571-5043(2013)0000018016

Ndou, V., Mele, G., & Del Vecchio, P. (2019). Entrepreneurship education in tourism: An investigation among European Universities. *Journal of Hospitality, Leisure, Sport and Tourism Education*, *25*, 100175. doi:10.1016/j.jhlste.2018.10.003

O'Keefe, T. (2014). *Epicureanism*. Routledge. doi:10.4324/9781315711645

Paris, C. M. (2011). Social constructivism and tourism education. *Journal of Hospitality, Leisure, Sports and Tourism Education, 10*(2), 103.

Qiu, H., Li, Q., & Li, C. (2021). How technology facilitates tourism education in COVID-19: Case study of Nankai University. *Journal of Hospitality, Leisure, Sport and Tourism Education, 29*, 100288. doi:10.1016/j.jhlste.2020.100288 PMID:34720752

Rozemond, M. (1998). *Descartes's dualism*. Harvard University Press. doi:10.4159/9780674042926

Sheldon, P. J., Fesenmaier, D. R., & Tribe, J. (2011). The tourism education futures initiative (TEFI): Activating change in tourism education. *Journal of Teaching in Travel & Tourism, 11*(1), 2–23. doi:10.1080/15313220.2011.548728

Sheldon, P. J., Pollock, A., & Daniele, R. (2017). Social entrepreneurship and tourism: Setting the stage. In *Social Entrepreneurship and Tourism* (pp. 1–18). Springer. doi:10.1007/978-3-319-46518-0_1

Sigala, M. (2020). Tourism and COVID-19: Impacts and implications for advancing and resetting industry and research. *Journal of Business Research, 117*, 312–321. doi:10.1016/j.jbusres.2020.06.015 PMID:32546875

Su, Y. (2014). Lifelong learning in tourism education. The Routledge Handbook of Tourism and Hospitality Education, 322.

Tribe, J. (2002a). Research trends and imperatives in tourism education. *Acta Turistica*, 61-81.

Tribe, J. (2002b). The philosophic practitioner. *Annals of Tourism Research, 29*(2), 338–357. doi:10.1016/S0160-7383(01)00038-X

Wang, J., Ayres, H., & Huyton, J. (2010). Is tourism education meeting the needs of the tourism industry? An Australian case study. *Journal of Hospitality & Tourism Education, 22*(1), 8–14. doi:10.1080/10963758.2010.10696964

Williams, P., & Hobson, J. P. (1995). Virtual reality and tourism: Fact or fantasy? *Tourism Management, 16*(6), 423–427. doi:10.1016/0261-5177(95)00050-X

Zhao, W., Ritchie, J. B., & Echtner, C. M. (2011). Social capital and tourism entrepreneurship. *Annals of Tourism Research, 38*(4), 1570–1593. doi:10.1016/j.annals.2011.02.006

ADDITIONAL READING

Ahmad, S. Z. (2015). Entrepreneurship education in tourism and hospitality programs. *Journal of Hospitality & Tourism Education, 27*(1), 20–29. doi:10.1080/10963758.2014.998764

Akrivos, C., Reklitis, P., & Theodoroyiani, M. (2014). Tourism entrepreneurship and the adoption of sustainable resources. The case of Evritania prefecture. *Procedia: Social and Behavioral Sciences, 148*, 378–382. doi:10.1016/j.sbspro.2014.07.056

Aktaş, G., & Kozak, M. (Eds.). (2022). *International Case Studies in Tourism Marketing*. Taylor & Francis. doi:10.4324/9781003182856

Ayeh, J. K., Bondzi-Simpson, A., & Baah, N. G. (2022). Predicting Students' Response to Entrepreneurship in Hospitality and Tourism Education: An Application of the Theory of Planned Behavior. *Journal of Hospitality & Tourism Education*, 1–12. doi:10.1080/10963758.2022.2056469

Daniel, A. D., Costa, R. A., Pita, M., & Costa, C. (2017). Tourism Education: What about entrepreneurial skills? *Journal of Hospitality and Tourism Management, 30*, 65–72. doi:10.1016/j.jhtm.2017.01.002

Deale, C. S. (2016). Entrepreneurship education in hospitality and tourism: Insights from entrepreneurs. *Journal of Teaching in Travel & Tourism, 16*(1), 20–39. doi:10.1080/15313220.2015.1117957

Fidgeon, P. R. (2010). Tourism education and curriculum design: A time for consolidation and review? *Tourism Management, 31*(6), 699–723. doi:10.1016/j.tourman.2010.05.019

Igbojekwe, P. A., & Anuñobi, O. U. (2020). Hospitality and tourism education and making of entreprenuers: A review. *International Journal of Research in Tourism and Hospitality, 6*(3), 1–11.

Jaafar, M., Abdul-Aziz, A. R., Maideen, S. A., & Mohd, S. Z. (2011). Entrepreneurship in the tourism industry: Issues in developing countries. *International Journal of Hospitality Management, 30*(4), 827–835. doi:10.1016/j.ijhm.2011.01.003

KEY TERMS AND DEFINITIONS

Cartesian Dualism: The term refers to a philosophical tradition coined by Rene Descartes which emphasized on the logical division of body and mind. At the same time, technique related to cartesian dualism stress on the importance to regulate and subordinate emotionality to logical protocols.

Education: It is a process directed to achieve certain goals while transmitting knowledge and future skills to other generations or citizens

Entrepreneurship: It is defined as a set of practice aimed at combining creative experiences with solutions for the problems of the industry. Based on the concept of change, the term was widely applied in the fields of businesses and management.

Higher Tourism Education: It signals to the set of rules, protocols, infrastructure, and social capital oriented to train the workforce in the industry of tourism and hospitality.

Joy: It is a basic emotion where the subject reaches self-accomplishment or fulfilment.

PANCOE: It is the name of a new experiment conducted by Joy Labs at the university of Palermo, Argentina. The experiment is designed to improve students` academic performance through the stimulation of pleasurable experiences.

Pleasure: It is a state of comfort derived from a good experience or good external stimuli.

Chapter 6
Teaching South Africans How to Become Successful Hosts on Airbnb:
The Case of the Airbnb Africa Academy

Unathi Sonwabile Henama
https://orcid.org/0000-0002-1111-0729
Central University of Technology, South Africa

Lebogang Matholwane Mathole
Tshwane University of Technology, South Africa

ABSTRACT

Due to the tragic past of South Africa, associated with racial profiling and apartheid, the majority of South Africans who were Black were excluded by repressive policies from active participation in the economy. This led to Black South Africans being underrepresented in tourism. The growth of tourism had not benefited the majority of South Africans who happen to be Black. The lack of participation of the previously disadvantaged groups on the Airbnb platform did not resonate with the principles of Airbnb to achieve shared prosperity. In the Black-owned townships such as Khayelisha in Cape Town, Kayamandi in Stellenbosch, and Soweto in Johannesburg, there had been existing tourism businesses especially in accommodation. These guesthouses and homestays were not attracting enough customers to economically benefit the hosts and make these townships viable tourism destinations. The Airbnb Africa Academy was pioneered to train South African homestay and guesthouse owners to register and become successful hosts on the Airbnb platform.

DOI: 10.4018/978-1-7998-9510-7.ch006

INTRODUCTION

The tourism industry is one of the world's largest industries and is big business. Since the end of apartheid in 1994, the government has been seeking to grow the economy and tourism emerged as an economic sector that could assist in growing the economy. Therefore, South Africa also jumped on the tourism bandwagon, like many other countries and destinations. Tourism has since 1994 been a cinderella industry, as its annual growth rate has always exceeded the national growth rate of the economy. Today, tourism is called the ''new gold'' just like how gold mining had driven the economy of South Africa in the 1970s and 1980s.

According to Henama & Apleni (2020) African countries still attract less than 10% of international tourist arrivals. Tourism is associated with the arrival of ''new money'' firstly through tourism expenditure and secondly, through the investments made into the economy to meet the needs of tourists and the tourism value chain. Tourists would consume a multiplicity of goods and products at the destination area, which increases the demand for goods and services. The majority of businesses in tourism are small and medium enterprises and they flourish within the tourism value chain. Governments favour tourism because it's dominated by small businesses, which are known engines of economic growth and job creation because of low barriers of entry in some aspects of the sector. Henama (2017) noted that the tourism industry is appreciated by policy makers because it can create the opportunities for local employment, because it is labour intensive. It creates jobs at a faster rate when compared to other economic sector, and when the number of tourists increase, it leads to an immediate increased demand for tourism labour. ''In the case of South Africa, it is accepted that one permanent job is created with the arrival of eight international tourists'' Henama & Apleni (2020: 284). Marshall (2005) noted that in South Africa, tourism is currently promoted as the panacea of all challenges associated with development, employment and income generation. Tourism is once again gazed upon to help in recovering the economy of South Africa, which had been battered by the COVID-19 pandemic.

SITUATIONAL ANALYSIS: SOUTH AFRICA

The major structural challenges facing South Africa are poverty, unemployment and inequality. ''South Africa faces persistent challenges of inequality, unemployment and poverty. These challenges have overtime been worsened by sustained low levels of investment and growth'' The Presidency (2021:3). The labour instability in South Africa, characterised by high wages, violent strikes and antagonistic labour-employer relationships has further stifled investments into South Africa.

The high rate of crime in South Africa can be regarded as an additional tax, as companies have to allocate additional resources into safety and security, instead of investing in the economy. World Bank (2018) noted young people are particularly affected by unemployment and the youth unemployment rate in the last quarter of 2017 was 51.1 percent – down from 52.2 percent in the previous quarter. The high unemployment rate experienced by South Africa does not bode well because of the demographic dividend, where the vast majority of citizens are young people. This happens when the labour absorption potential of the South African economy is at its lowest, meaning that the unemployment will be a reality for many South African youth. South Africa has a skill deficiency that is stifling the growth of the economy. The World Bank (2018) noted that the legacy of "Bantu education" continues to deprive South Africa of the skills it urgently needs, resulting in low competitiveness, high unemployment, and wage inequality. Improving access to quality education for all in South Africa is critical, however, the schooling system produces poor educational outcomes.

The initiatives that would alleviate the high rate of unemployment will include upskilling South Africans with the skills necessary to fill the many vacancies that exist. In addition, promoting entrepreneurship education to be incorporated into the schooling system, to create the institutionalisation of entrepreneurship. Entrepreneurship education is important for a developing country such as South Africa which has deep structural challenges, namely poverty, stubborn unemployment and the most unequal country in the world. Naturally entrepreneurship would be gazed as an opportunity to alleviate the high rate of unemployment and grow the economy. Unfortunately, small businesses have a high failure rate in South Africa. ''South Africa has a stubborn unemployment rate which is a major contributor towards poverty… The low levels of entrepreneurship in South Africa are further stifled by the high failure rate of small businesses within 5 years of operating'' Henama (2019: 31). The unreliable electricity supply had become the biggest threat to the economy of South Africa, a challenge that been facing South Africa since 2008. The challenges in electricity generation by state owned ESKOM, has deteriorated the trading conditions in South Africa, reducing the productive capacity of the economy. Companies are experiencing additional costs pressures by seeking alternative energy sources such as solar energy and generators when there are blackouts and loadshedding.

THEORETICAL FRAMEWORK: TOURISM LIFESTYLE ENTREPRENEURSHIP (TLE)

An entrepreneur is someone that commands land, resources and capital to create a business by providing either a product or a service, and it can be regarded that entrepreneurship is laced with taking on financial risk in the hope for profit and business growth. The process of setting up the business undertaking is defined as entrepreneurship.The tourism industry is promoted because of the positive economic impacts such as immediate jobs that it crates because of its labour-intensive nature, the promotion of small businesses as the majority of tourism businesses are primarily small in nature and being a catalyst for entrepreneurship because of the low barriers of entry in some aspects of the tourism industry. Wang, Hung & Huang (2019) noted that tourism offers opportunities to start up various types of business, especially small or microbusinesses, which appeal to both sole proprietors and families. Many people involved in other economic sectors, prepared their enterprises, hobbies and work for tourism consumption combining experiences such as farms into farm tours, tea plantations into tea tourism tours and places of troubled history for heritage tourism, justice tourism and cultural tourism.

Furthermore, the owners of these existing enterprises may be attracted by the appeal of tourism, to diversify income generation, but may not have a desire to grow beyond their smallness, informality and flexibility. These existing enterprises may not be desire growth prospects, rather they may be anti-growth as the business may be used to provide sufficient cash-flow to maintain lifestyle. This form of entrepreneurship which is dominated by lifestyle domains (lifestyle goals) instead of growth domains (commercial goals). In the case of the lifestyle entrepreneurs, there is a convergence of lifestyle and commercial interest, where the lifestyle interests take precedence. Airbnb has the ability to create an opportunity for people to create an additional income stream. According to Rentalscaleup (2022) Airbnb noted that 20% of hosts are either educators or healthcare professionals. The Airbnb platform had presented itself as a great opportunity to develop tourism lifestyle entrepreneurs.

Entrepreneurial Education

Teaching entrepreneurship education is vital for inculcating the ethos of entrepreneurship and to trigger entrepreneurial action to create sustainable businesses. Entrepreneurship education is important to stimulate the development of businesses that would create jobs, improve the Quality-of-Life and standard of living for citizens across the world. According to Isaacs et al. (2007) entrepreneurship education can be defined as the purposeful intervention by an educator in the life of a learner to impact entrepreneurship qualities and skills to enable the learner to survive in the world of business. Entrepreneurship education would make so much sense in a country such as South Africa with the stubborn structural challenges such as poverty, unemployment and inequality. Isaacs et al. (2007) noted that the key to success of establishing a culture of entrepreneurship in South Africa is education. And this means entrepreneurship education. The Global Economic Monitor (GEM) reports reflects on the high failure rate of entrepreneurs usually under 5 years. ''Given South Africa's unemployment problem, the role of effective entrepreneurship education is seen to be indispensable in the future economic prosperity of the country'' Isaacs et al. (2007: 625). Gautam & Singh (2015) noted that there are a number of non-governmental organisations (NGOs) that specialize in entrepreneurship education and training. These NGOs may be better placed to understand the needs of the market and clientele they serve with entrepreneurship education. NGOs can therefore play a leading role in delivering entrepreneurship education. Entrepreneurship education can only succeed when the teachers and educators are also schooled in the pedagogy of entrepreneurship education.

Airbnb

Serrano et al. (2020) noted that Airbnb is the most powerful peer-to-peer company in short-term rental (STR) tourist accommodation without owning any establishments around the world. Peer-to-peer accommodation platforms are online marketplaces that allow the lease or rent of accommodation spaces for a fee. ''To book or rent a space, one must have an Airbnb profile. When interested in a space, the tourists will send the host a reservation request and/or message to express interest, possibly ask questions and possibly provide information about the travel party. The host then may respond and ask any questions of the tourist or if a reservation request has been made then the host can accept the reservation'' Mhlanga (2019: 445). According to Henama (2018) Airbnb is a win-win for consumers (clients) and renters (hosts) where the owners earn an extra income and renter books accommodation at a lower price. Airbnb has been able to disrupt commercial tourism accommodation providers, especially hotels. ''Airbnb is an online marketplace and hospitality service that enables people to list, discover, ad book accommodation around the world. Founded in 2008 in San Francisco, California, Airbnb supports accommodation for over three million lodging listings in over 190 countries worldwide'' NERA Economic Consulting (2017: 1). Bivens (2019) noted that Airbnb makes money by charging guests and hosts for short-term rental stays in private homes or apartments booked through the Airbnb website. According to Genesis Analytics (2018), Airbnb has generated an estimated R8.7 billion in economic impact in South Africa, whilst providing over 22000 jobs across the country. Walker (2019) noted that South Africa is ranked 22nd on the on the list of 30 countries in which the travel and accommodation form has the largest impact, totaling R9.7 billion. Henama (2018) noted that in the case of South Africa, Airbnb listed accommodation have grown by more than 250%. Genesis Analytics (2021) noted that Airbnb contributed almost R11 billion to the GDP of South Africa, supporting 28 000 economy wide-jobs and have experienced a growth rate of 10% from the year 2017. From a South African's contextual data retrieved by World Travel and Tourism Council (2018), the following statistical findings were drawn:

- 65% of home hosts are women
- 82% of guests say they are more likely to return due to Airbnb
- 95% of hosts recommend local businesses to their guests
- 80%+ of hosts engage in eco-friendly practices

From Airbnb Africa Academy to Airbnb Entrepreneurship Academy: Entrepreneurship Education in Action

The tourism trade in South Africa is dominated by established tourism business entrepreneurs, which are vertically and horizontally integrated and they benefit from the bulk of the tourism expenditures in South Africa. The growth of Airbnb in South Africa had continued in the same trajectory as guesthouses and bed-and-breakfast establishments, dominated by listings in wealthy suburbs. The majority of tourism businesses are owned by White South Africans, and there is a slow pace of transformation in the tourism industry. The slow rate of transformation in the tourism industry has been a major challenge facing South Africa. The spatial distribution of tourism zones are primarily in well-developed and serviced areas that under apartheid, where classified as areas exclusively for White South Africans. ''Airbnb's success in Johannesburg has largely been in the Northern Suburbs with isolated pockets in gentrifying areas such as Braamforntein and Maboneng while access to amenities such as the Gautrain and the corporates in downtown Johannesburg also see the number of listings rise'' Niselow (2019:55). Furthermore, Niselow (2019) indicated the highest number of Airbnb listings are in Rosebank and Sandton. The initial entry of Airbnb in South Africa reflected ownership patterns that further entrenched the tourism expenditure patters that are in high-end, and established tourism zones, excluding areas located in previously disadvantaged communities. Considering the history of South Africa, associated with the skewed distribution of wealth and assets as part of the legacy of apartheid, the majority of tourism zones are located in localities that were exclusively for White South Africans. Because of these spatial challenges that reflect themselves in Airbnb listings in the South Africans context, seeking hosts outside the established tourism zones was important as part of healthy tourism and entrepreneurship, which Airbnb is very passionate about it.

Because Airbnb sought to create authentic experiences that are located in communities, the absence of Airbnb hosts in previously disadvantaged communities (PDCs), where the vast majority of Black South Africans reside, did not give a comprehensive picture of South Africa. The Airbnb Africa Academy (AAA) was established and piloted in South Africa, combining skills development and training for would-be hosts'' Henama (2021:283). AAA focused on emerging entrepreneurs in under-resourced communities by creating opportunities for them to list on the Airbnb platform after being trained by Airbnb on how to be successful hosts. By training local communities through the AAA, it opens up a whole new avenue from these communities to benefit from tourism through Airbnb. Airbnb gazes this as being their contribution towards healthy tourism. Airbnb piloted the AAA to achieve geographic spread of Airbnb guests and tourists to underserviced areas which had not on the Airbnb platform to benefit from tourism. The first graduates from the AAA graduated in 2019 in Cape Town, included 38 owners of tourism enterprises that participated in the three month training period. The training included tourism and entrepreneurship training, beginning with a two-day immersive training. The 38 owners of tourism enterprises came from the under-services areas in terms of tourism assets such as Langa, Khayelitsha, Bo Kaap, Kayamandi, Gugulethu and Rondebosch. The NGO that Airbnb partnered with was ABCD Concepts, a lifestyle marketing tourism start-up based in Khayelitsha.

The gaze was that there were a paucity of Airbnb hosts in formerly black-only townships and rural areas and Airbnb sought to mitigate this challenge by developing a training and skills development programme, the AAA to teach these communities on how to be successful Airbnb hosts. The training undertaken by AAA seeks to level the playing ground by training potential hosts in rural and under-resourced communities across South Africa. The success of the AAA in South Africa, has led to the programme being expanded to Kenya in Eastern Africa, which is a major tourism destination on the African continent. According to Airbnb (2017) the AAA was an intentional economic and social empowerment programme through in townships such as Langa, in the Western Cape. Airbnb's success with the AAA can be attributed on recruiting passionate people that seek to be hosts and using the expertise of non-government organisations to assist in delivering the 3 month programme and support to would be hosts. The AAA's first graduates were announced and presented during the Airbnb organised Africa Travel Summit at Gugu S'thebe Arts and Culture Centre in Langa, a township in Cape Town, which was hosted in 11-13 September 2018. The AAA was announced during the Africa Travel Summit as a $1 million investment by Airbnb to promote and support community-led tourism projects in Africa. The AAA was piloted with 12 communities in Cape Town and Johannesburg in 2017 and it has been expanded to other provinces, specifically KwaZulu-Natal. The first dates in 2018 for the hosting of the AAA, where 30th to 1 August in Johannesburg and Cape Town from 2st August to 4th August in Cape Town. The Airbnb Africa Academy was established in 2017 to offer hospitality and technology training that would increase the representation of Airbnb in underserviced area as part of a $1 million investment to promote inclusive tourism. According to

Airbnb (2021) the programme has trained 225 individuals, earned hosts in excess of R200 000 in income, and more than 30 communities were involved.

The AAA was structured as follows:

- Two days of training on subjects covering how to become a successful tourism entrepreneur, evaluating the tourism potential in local communities, navigating the Airbnb platform, understanding the expectations of Airbnb guests and how to become Superhosts as noted by Airbnb (2021):
- Each participant is provided with the opportunity to experience the Airbnb platform first hand, participating in an Experience and spending the night in a home listed on Airbnb as noted by Airbnb (2021):
- Airbnb developed with Edge Digital with the Airbnb Africa Academy Hosting Toolkit, which is a 150 page step-by-step guide, to assist hosts and co-hosts in rural and township to be successful on the Airbnb platform.
- The training is free of charge and would-be participants would have to apply to the specific NGO for acceptance to the AAA.
- Airbnb will work with a technology advanced non-government organisation during the training and the post-training technology support for a period of three months.
- The training during the AAA would focus on hospitality and technology.

According to Airbnb (2021), the AAA model has dual approaches:

- Build out training and curriculum materials addressing the unique challenges of under-resourced communities in Africa.
- Empowering partner organisations embedded in high-tourism communities to train and support emerging entrepreneurs to succeed on the Airbnb platform.

The Airbnb Africa Academy Hosting Toolkit has the following content for imparting knowledge and skills:

Irvine Partners (2021) noted that during the COVID-19 pandemic, Airbnb was able to distribute R1 million in financial relief to Airbnb Africa Academy hosts and had become dependent on Airbnb as a source of income for themselves and their families. Airbnb (2020) notes that R25 000 was paid out to each of the 45 graduates of the Airbnb Africa Academy. The success story of the AAA, has meant that there would be greater demand for training would-be entrepreneurs by Airbnb. To mitigate the demand-and-capacity constraints, the AAA would be delivered in collaboration with one of best tourism and hospitality schools in South Africa, the University of Johannesburg. The AAA has partnered with the School for Tourism and Hospitality (STH) at the University of Johannesburg to expand the AAA to accommodate at least 1000 students over the next three years. This would ensure that the AAA benefits from the vast intellectual capital at the University of Johannesburg, whilst the university would have benefit from a successful community project, which is one of the pillars for reporting to the National Department of Higher Education (DHET). The University of Johannesburg's School for Tourism and Hospitality would continue with entrepreneurship education in its collaboration with Airbnb on the AAA.

- Entrepreneurial education
- Professional photography
- Tourism and hospitality skills training
- Technology training
- Hosting tips

Table 1. Hosting toolkit contents

1. Airbnb	What is Airbnb?
	How was Airbnb started?
	Why people use Airbnb
	What are the opportunities that Airbnb presents?
	The benefits of Airbnb
	Airbnb glossary
	How travellers book homes and experiences
2. Homes	Hosting
	Co-hosting
	Reviews
	Top tips for being a Superhost on Airbnb
3. Experiences	What is an experience?
	What is a qualifying experience?
	Tips for looking after your guests?
	Other things you need to know
4. Tips to navigate the Airbnb app	Getting started
	Hosting mode
	App basics
	Questions from hosts
	Experiences
5. FAQ	

Source: Airbnb (2016a)

- Experiential leanring
- AAA was made to be a host-success programme

A graduate of the AAA, can do the following:

- Be confident in using the Airbnb application and website.
- Empower the hosts to tell their personal story on the Airbnb platform.
- Publish on the Airbnb platform a Home or Experience listing that stands out.
- Become part of the Airbnb community and belong to a network of tourism entrepreneurs around the world.

As part of the three month period of training and support includes the use of an Airbnb Coach that with the following:

- Help with the hosting process.
- Telling the story that guests will enjoy.
- Help with changes on your Airbnb listing.
- Offering suggestions.

Airbnb Entrepreneurship Academy

The success of the AAA, which was piloted in South Africa and expanded to Kenya, some of the leading tourism destinations on the African continent, led to a realisation that this programme can be extended across all territories where Airbnb operates. The AAA which was launched in 2017, was changed to become the Airbnb Entrepreneurship Academy, as the skills development and capacity building of the AAA was successful in entrepreneurship education and ensuring 'Access with Success' for those who products were accepted on the Airbnb platform. The Airbnb Entrepreneurship Academy imparts skills, practical tools and technology support just like the AAA. The goal of the Airbnb Entrepreneurship Academy are to empower the next generation of emerging tourism entrepreneurs by partnering with non-profit organisatios, small business centres and academic institutions. According to IOL (2021) noted that the Airbnb Entrepreneurship Academy was able to lower barriers to entry and welcoming new hosts onto the platform by empowering groups typically excluded from the benefits, like those living in rural and township communities. Through such initiatives, Airbnb has democratized the global hospitality industry by enabling millions of homeowners to become business owners. The intention of the Airbnb Entrepreneurship Academy was to have an impact specifically in the township tourism sector, because it receive little to scant support to exploit its unexplored potential. The Airbnb Entrepreneurship Academy is associated with the following capacity building programmes:

- Digital skills building.
- Mentorship from existing Airbnb hosts.
- Marketing support.
- Professional photography.
- Partnering with leading non-profit organisations, small businesses and academic institutions across the globe to empower fragile communities.

The Airbnb Entrepreneurship Academy has extended to the following countries:

- United States.
- India.
- South Africa.
- Kenya.
- Colombia.
- Thailand.
- People's Republic of China.
- South Korea.

Airbnb (2020) noted that to date the Airbnb Entrepreneurship Academy has trained more than 300 hosts and earned hosts more than R2.8 million in 18 months.

University of Johannesburg School of Tourism and Hospitality

The University of Johannesburg is a University of Technology (UoT) based in the CBD of the City of Johannesburg. The success of the Airbnb Africa Academy led to the expansion to the Airbnb Entrepreneurship Academy, which has been expanded to many localities where Airbnb operated. Airbnb, the booking platform partnered with University of Johannesburg's School of Tourism and Hospitality. The Airbnb Entrepreneurship Academy will be expanded through the partnership with University of Johannesburg, by seeking to train atleast 1000 students over the next three years. This expands to the developmental mandate of Airbnb for health tourism which has a local impact, whilst achieving by sheer coincidence achieves entrepreneurial education.

Airbnb Academy Fund

The COVID-19 pandemic ravaged the tourism industry in almost all destinations. Airbnb responded by setting up an Airbnb Academy Fund that paid out R1 Million to hosts in need. According to Airbnb (2020) noted that a total of 45 graduates of the Airbnb Africa Academy received R25 000 each, because they could not host. Genesis Analytics (2021) noted that from 2016 to 2019, the number of active hosts on the platform in Soweto increased by 508% and in Tembisa by 200%. The townships remain underserviced by Airbnb due to the low number of hosts, when compared to the population density of the townships.

Wi-Fi Access through Ikeja

Data poverty is a major challenge in South Africa due to the high costs of data. The artificially expensive data makes the costs of doing business expensive. This cost burden is more profound for small business, especially for those operating in the sharing economy and digital economy. The provision of free Wi-Fi can be regarded as a basic human right, due its institutional use in society. The most economically depressed areas in South Africa, such as the townships are most disadvantaged when it comes to access to Wi-Fi and fibre networks to make communication easy. Airbnb was very much cognizant of these challenges, and it understood that the success of Airbnb hosts was dependent on having reliable internet access. To alleviate the Wi-Fi challenge, Airbnb partnered with a local network provider Ikeja to roll out free Wi-Fi hotspots. The Wi-Fi hotspots would be prioritized at least 100 Airbnb Africa Academy hosts and their communities for free Wi-Fi according to MyBroadband (2021).

Ikeja would provide unlimited internet access for the Airbnb Africa Academy hosts and their guests. Ikeja was a perfect partner for Airbnb because it focuses its business model in serving the underservices townships of South Africa. The business model of Ikeja sought to connect, empower and uplift the underserviced disadvantaged communities located primarily in South Africa's townships. According to Ikeja (2022) it owns and build its own bespoke wireless infrastructure for townships in South Africa. Ikeja is important to Airbnb by tacking the digital divide by providing affordable Wi-Fi. By providing internet connectivity through Ikeja as a partner, Airbnb has provided an enabling environment for the success of entrepreneurship enterprises under training and listed under the Airbnb Africa Academy. This home grown company's base has the majority of its operations in the Western Cape Province, where Cape Town is the capital city, and Cape Town has the majority of Airbnb listings on the African continent. The partnership with Ikeja would decrease the cost of doing businesses for the data-intensive business of

Airbnb, making it easier for them to operate their businesses without the challenge of high data costs.

CONCLUSION AND RECOMMENDATION

Tourism will remain a major economic sector for South Africa. It's already been noted that tourism is regarded as a cure-all and panacea for many of the challenges the country is facing such as poverty, unemployment and inequality. Tourism which is regarded as an economic messiah, would be expected to lead the recovery of the economy which has been ravaged by the COVID-19 pandemic. The sharing economy will continue to grow, as mode switching will continue to shape the evolution of tourism transactions. The major challenge facing Airbnb is ensuring that it lobbies for favourable legislation in South Africa and bring finality to the regulatory grey areas around the operation of Airbnb in South Africa. The sharing economy has been able to create a plethora of jobs and economic opportunity in South Africa. In the absence of jobs and economic opportunity, many are considering the sharing economy as the new engine of opportunity. This has meant that the sharing economy is gazed upon for success. The AAA is a great success story for entrepreneurship education in the case of the Global South, in South Africa. AAA was established to fill a gap in the market and level the playing field by training would-be entrepreneurs from rural areas and under-represented areas on the Airbnb platform in the previously disadvantaged areas, called townships in South Africa.

The AAA can be regarded as an ''Access with Success'' programme as much effort is made to capacity build the would-be hosts with all the skill, knowledge and expertise to succeed on the Airbnb platform. The training sought to build skills and competences that would ensure that a new generation of entrepreneurs, indicating the success of entrepreneurship education in the case of the Global South. South Africa is in a better position to grow sharing economy. The phenomenon is new and practical to all individuals who can be well informed and trained on how to practice sharing of their resources for a greater benefit. The success of sharing economy in major cities is well-positioned to influence/spread out to other parts of the country for an all-inclusive practice and value. Therefore, the future and success of Airbnb in South Africa is entirely up-to its citizens to refute. The success of the Airbnb Africa Academy led to the development of the Airbnb Entrepreneurship Academy, a success story in the Global South that has been expanded to all localities where Airbnb operates. The robustness and success in Entrepreneurship Education by Airbnb had led to an initiative developed for the Global South, expanded for all localities where Airbnb operates. This provided a reflection that Entrepreneurship Education is imperative in all localities, as a means for empowering communities to become successful on the Airbnb platform. The outcomes of being successful on the Airbnb platform include creating an additional revenue stream, improving their Quality-of-Life and standard of living.

This reflects the entrepreneurship success story that Airbnb has been able to develop, initiate and succeed in developing tourism entrepreneurs. The greatest contribution of the Airbnb Entrepreneurship Academy in Entrepreneurial Education is by lowering the barriers of barriers to tourism entrepreneurship especially for excluded groups that have a low presence in the tourism supply chain. The inclusion of underserviced areas and exclude groups into the tourism value chain through the Airbnb has been able to disperse the positive developmental benefits of tourism and making more destinations accessible. This has the positive impact of leading to the geographic spread of tourists through the Airbnb platform, due to the inclusion attempts through the Airbnb Entrepreneurship Academy. Airbnb has therefore developed tourism in non-traditional tourism areas, promoting rural areas and building hosting capacity in townships according to Genesis Analytics (2021). Entrepreneurship education is about creating a critical mass of new entrepreneurs which could improve a country GDP, create employment opportunities and assist in promoting entrepreneurship opportunities for economic prosperity especially in the Global South.

REFERENCES

Adamiak, C. (2019). Current state and development of Airbnb accommodation in 167 countries. *Current Issues in Tourism*. Retrieved from: http://urn.kb.se/resolve?urm=nbn:se=umu:diva-167097

Africa Ignite. (2020). *Tourism Development*. Retrieved from: https:www.africaingnite.co.za

Africa Ignite. (2021). *Contact Us*. Retrieved from: https://africaingnite/co.za

Airbnb. (2016a). *Airbnb Hosting Toolkit: Airbnb Africa Academy*. Retrieved from: https://www.airbnb.com

Airbnb. (2016b). *Overview of the Airbnb community in South Africa*. Retrieved from: https://www.airbnb.com

Airbnb. (2017). *Overview of the Airbnb Community in Africa*. Retrieved from: https://www.airbnb.com

Airbnb. (2019). *Africa!Ignite brings the Airbnb Africa Academy to Durban*. Retrieved from: https://www.airbnb.com

Airbnb. (2020). *Airbnb Academy Fund pays out R1 million to hosts in need in South Africa*. Retrieved from: https://www.airbnb.com

Airbnb. (2021). *The Airbnb Entrepreneurship Academy*. Retrieved from: https://www.airbnb.com

Anagnos, C. (2019). *Crony Capitalism Threatens Airbnb in South Africa*. Retrieved from: https://www.aier.org/article/crony-capitalism-threatens-airbnb-in-south-africa

Apleni, L., Vallabh, D., & Henama, U. S. (2017). Motivation for tourists' participation in religious tourism in Eastern Cape: A case study of Buffalo City, South Africa. *African Journal of Hospitality, Tourism and Leisure*, *7*(1), 1–16.

Batat, W., & Hammedi, W. (2017). Collaborative consumption as a feature of Gen-Y consumers: Rethinking youth tourism practices in the sharing economy. In *Advances in Social Media for Travel, Tourism and Hospitality*. Routledge. doi:10.4324/9781315565736-18

Belk, R. W., Eckhardt, G. M., & Bardhi, F. (2019). Introduction to the Handbook of the Sharing Economy: the paradox of the sharing economy. In *Handbook of the Sharing Economy*. Edward Elgar Publishing. doi:10.4337/9781788110549.00005

Bivens, J. (2019). *The economic costs and benefits of Airbnb: No reason for local policymakers to let Airbnb bypass tax or regulatory obligations*. Economic Policy Institute.

Bredvold, R., & Skalen, P. (2016). Lifestyle Entrepreneurship and their identity construction: A study of their tourism industry. *Tourism Management*, *56*, 96–105. doi:10.1016/j.tourman.2016.03.023

Briggs, K. (2018). The New Blame Game: How Airbnb Has Been Mis-regulated as the Scapegoat for Century-Old Problems. The Business, Entrepreneurship & Ta. *Law Review*, *2*(1), 1–21.

Da Costa, M. T. G., & Carvalho, L. M. C. (2011). The Sustainability of Tourism Supply Chain: A Case Study Research. *Tourismos*, *6*(2), 393–404.

Dragomir, C. C., & Panzaru, S. (2015). The relationship between education and entrepreneurship in EU Member States. *Review of General Management*, *22*(2), 55–65.

Fayolle, A. (2009). Entrepreneurship Education in Europe: Trends and Challenges. *OECD LEED Programme. Universities, Innovation and Entrepreneurship: Good Practice Workshop*. Retrieved from: https: www.oecd.org/datao

Forgacs, G., & Dimanche, F. (2016). Revenue challenges for hotels in the sharing economy: Facing the Airbnb menace. *Journal of Revenue and Pricing Management, 15*(6), 509–515. doi:10.105741272-016-0071-z

Gautam, M. K., & Singh, S. K. (2015). Entrepreneurship Education: Concept, Characteristics and Implications for Teacher Education. *Shaikshik Parisamvad, 5*(1), 21–35.

Genesis Analytics. (2021). *The contribution of Airbnb to inclusive growth in South Africa*. Retrieved from: https://www.genesis-analytics.com

George, R. (2020). *Marketing Tourism in South Africa* (6th ed.). Oxford University Press.

Goga, S. (2020). *The Impact of Digital Platforms on Competition in the South African Tourism Industry*. Industrial Development Think Thank.

Griggio, C., & Oxemswardh, A. (2021). Human capital and sustainability challenges for Airbnb Bed and Breakfast lifestyle entrepreneur. *Scandinavian Journal of Hospitality and Tourism, 21*(3), 286–312. doi:10.1080/15022250.2021.1927828

Henama, U.S. (2017a). International Migration and National Tourism Industry Development: The Case of South Africa. *The EurAseans: Journal of Global Socio-Economic Dynamic, 2*(3), 72-82.

Henama, U. S. (2017b). Marikana: Opportunities for Heritage Tourism. *African Journal of Hospitality, Tourism and Leisure*, *6*(4), 1–16.

Henama, U. S. (2018). Disruptive entrepreneurship using Airbnb: The South African experience. *African Journal of Hospitality, Tourism and Leisure*, *7*(1), 1–16.

Henama, U. S. (2019a). *The Sharing Economy in South Africa's Tourism Industry: The Case of Uber-Hailing Taxi Services. Oncioiu, I. Improving Business Performance through Innovation in the Digital Economy*. IGI Global.

Henama, U. S. (2019b). *Tourism as Neoliberal Messiah: The Case of South Africa. Nadda, V., Azam, M. & Mulindwa, D. Neoliberalism in the Tourism and Hospitality Sector*. IGI Global.

Henama, U.S. (2021). eCommerce within the Tourism Industry in the Global South: The case of sharing economy in South Africa. *Advances in Digital Marketing and eCommerce*, 280-290.

Henama, U. S., & Apleni, L. (2020). *Religious Tourism in Africa's Global South: Indigenous African Traditional Spirituality. In Global Development of Religious Tourism*. IGI Global.

Herrington, M., & Kew, P. (2018). *Global Entrepreneurship Monitor*. Retrieved from: www.seda.gov.za/

Ikeja. (2022). *Welcome to Ikeja*. Retrieved from: https://www.ikeja.co.za

IOL. (2017). *Airbnb and Ikhaya le Langa partner to help entrepreneurs thrive*. Retrieved from: https://www.iol.co.za/travel/africa

IOL. (2021). *Airbnb contributes more than $550 million to SA economy*. Retrieved from: web.sabc.co.za/sabc/home/channelafrica/details?id=c79a6d87-6bd6-46a8-bb14-e8b053a922a5&title=Airbnbcontributes

Irvine Partners. (2021). *Hosts on Airbnb awarded funds to help see them through the COVID crisis*. Retrieved from: https://irvinepartners.co.za/hosts

Isaacs, E., Visser, K., Friendrich, C., & Brijlal, P. (2007). Entrepreneurship education and training at the Further Education and Training (FET) level in South Africa. *South African Journal of Education*, *27*, 613–629.

Koh, E., & King, B. (2017). Accommodating the sharing revolution: A qualitative evaluation of the impact of Airbnb on Singapore's budget hotels. *Tourism Recreation Research*, *41*(4), 409–421. doi:10.1080/02508281.2017.1314413

Lackeus, M. (2015). *Entrepreneurship in Education: What, Why, When, How*. Retrieved from: https: www.oecd.org/datao

Letsebe, K. (2018). *Airbnb makes good on $1m Africa investment*. Retrieved from: https://www.itweb.co.za/content/GxwQDM1AWJpM1PVo

Li, Z., Chen, H., & Huang, X. (2020). Airbnb or Hotel?:A Comparative Study on the Sentiment of Airbnb Guests in Sydney–Text Analysis Based on Big Data. *International Journal of Tourism and Hospitality Management in the Digital Age*, *4*(2), 1–10. doi:10.4018/IJTHMDA.2020070101

Mani, M. (2015). Entrepreneurship Education: A Students' Perspective. *International Journal of E-Entrepreneurship and Innovation*, *5*(1), 1–14. doi:10.4018/ijeei.2015010101

Marchant, B., & Mottiar, Z. (2011). Understanding Lifestyle Entrepreneurs and Digging Beneath the Issues of Profits: Profiling Surf Tourism Lifestyle Entrepreneurs in Ireland. *Tourism Planning & Development*, *8*(2), 171–183. doi:10.1080/21568316.2011.573917

Marshall, S. (2005). Making Money with Memories: The Fusion of Heritage, Tourism and Identify Formations in South Africa. *Historia (Wiesbaden, Germany)*, *50*(1), 103–121.

Mhlanga, O. (2019). Peer-to-peer travel: Is Airbnb a friend or foe to hotels. *International Journal of Culture, Tourism and Hospitality Research*, *13*(4), 443–457. doi:10.1108/IJCTHR-05-2019-0087

Mody, M., & Gomez, M. (2018). Airbnb and the Hotel Industry: The Past, Present and Future of Sales, Marketing, Branding and Revenue Management. *Boston Hospitality Review*. Retrieved from: https: www.bu.edu/bhr

Molefe, L. P., Tauoatsoala, P., Sifolo, P. P. S., Manavhela, P., & Henama, U. S. (2018). The effects of tourism supply chain management on practices on tourism operations in Pretoria, South Africa. *African Journal of Hospitality, Tourism and Leisure*, *7*(1), 1–16.

Moneyweb. (2017). *Namibia tells Airbnb hosts to register or face jail*. Retrieved from: https://www.moneyweb.co.za/news-fast-news

Morrison, A. (2006). A contextualization of entrepreneurship. *International Journal of Entrepreneurial Behaviour & Research*, *12*(4), 192–209. doi:10.1108/13552550610679159

Mussi, G. A. (2017). *When consuming becomes collaborative: Airbnb Case Study*. ISCTE Business School.

MyBroadband. (2021). *Airbnb launches fee WI-FI in South African townships*. Retrieved from: https://mybroadband.co.za/news/wireless/415762

Ndofirepi, T. M. (2020). Relationship between entrepreneurship education and entrepreneurial goal intentions: Psychological traits as mediators. *Journal of Innovation and Entrepreneurship*, *9*(2), 1–20. doi:10.118613731-020-0115-x

NERA Economic Consulting. (2017). *Airbnb's Global Support to Local Economies: Output and Employment: Prepared for Airbnb*. Retrieved from: https://www.nera.com

Niselow, T. Y. (2019). *The location and the nature of Airbnb listings in Johannesburg and their impact on property prices and the availability of long term rental stock* [Masters Thesis]. University of Witwatersrand.

Peters, M., Frehse, J., & Buhalis, D. (2009). The importance of lifestyle entrepreneurship: A conceptual study of the tourism industry. *PASOP*, *7*(2), 393–405. doi:10.25145/j.pasos.2009.07.028

Presenza, A., Yucelen, M., & Camillo, A. (2015). Passion before profits in hospitality ventures: Some thoughts on Lifestyle Entrepreneur and the case of "Albergo Diffuso". *Sinergie*, *34*, 221–239.

Ravenelle, A. J. (2020). Digitalization and the hybridization of markets and circuits in Airbnb. *Consumption Markets & Culture*, *23*(2), 154–173. doi:10.1080/10253866.2019.1661244

Rentalscaleup. (2022). *How Airbnb wants to unlock the next generation of Hosts*. Retrieved from: https:www://www.rentalscaleup.com/airbnb-unlock-the-next-generation-of-hosts

Serrano, L., Sianes, A., & Ariza-Montes, A. (2020). Understanding the Implementation of Airbnb in Urban Context: Towards a Categorization of European Cities. *Land (Basel)*, *9*(12), 1–32. doi:10.3390/land9120522

Set, K., Yaakop, A. Y., Hussin, N. Z. I., & Mohd, B. (2015). Understanding Motivation Factors of Tourism Entrepreneurs in Tasik Kenyir. *International Academic Research Journal of Social Science*, *1*(2), 248–254.

Shereni, N. C. (2019). The tourism sharing economy and sustainability in developing countries: Contribution to SDGs in the hospitality sector. *African Journal of Hospitality, Tourism and Leisure*, *8*(5), 110.

Sifolo, P. P. S. (2020). Tourism supply chain management: A catalyst to development in Africa. The Gaze. *Journal of Tourism & Hospitality (Los Angeles, Calif.)*, *11*(1), 126–139.

Tapper, R. & Font, X. (2008). Tourism Supply Chains: Report of Desk Research Project for the Travel Foundation. *Environment Business and Development Group,* 1-23.

The Presidency. (2021). *The South African Economic Reconstruction and Recovery Plan*. Retrieved from: https://www.gov.za/sites/default/files/gcis_document/202010/south-african-economic-reconstruction-and-recovery-plan.pdf

Van Pletzen, D. (2019). *Improving Tax Compliance in the Sharing Economy: A focus on Airbnb in South Africa* [Masters Thesis]. University of Johannesburg.

Van Raatle, D., Parsons, S., & Hendrickse, K. (2018). Recommendations for Improving Tax Compliance by South African Airbnb Hosts. *2018 South African Accounting Association. Natioonal Teaching and Learning and Regional Conference Proceedings*, 255-271.

Visser, G., Erasmus, I., & Miller, M. (2017). Airbnb: The emergence of a new accommodation type in Cape Town, South Africa. *Tourism Review International*, *21*(2), 151–168. doi:10.3727/154427217X14912408849458

Volgger, M., Pforr, C., Stawinoga, A. E., Taplin, R., & Matthews, S. (2018). Who adopts the Airbnb innovation? An analysis of international visitors to Western Australia. *Tourism Recreation Research*, *43*(3), 305–320. doi:10.1080/02508281.2018.1443052

Walker, A. (2019). *Airbnb believes it has a R10 billion impact on South Africa's economy*. Retrieved from: https://memeburn.com/2019/07/

Wallace, L. K. (2020). *The Cultural Influence on Sharing Economy Services: The Case of Airbnb* [Honours Thesis]. The University of Southern Mississippi. Retrieved from: https:Aquila.usm.edu/honors_theses/

Wang, S., Hung, K., & Huang, W. J. (2019). Motivations for entrepreneurship in tourism and hospitality sector: A social cognitive theory perspective. *International Journal of Hospitality Management*, *78*, 78–98. doi:10.1016/j.ijhm.2018.11.018

World Bank. (2018). *Jobs and Inequality*. Retrieved from: https://thedocs.worldbank.org/en/doc/798731523331698204-0010022018/original/SouthAfricaEconomicUpdateApril2018.pdf/

Chapter 7
Skill India Mission Programme in the Hospitality Management for Quality Products and Services

A. Suresh Babu
Government Arts College, Ooty, India

Junaid K. C.
https://orcid.org/0000-0002-8577-6320
Hemvati Nandan Bahuguna Garhwal University, India

Satish Chandra Bagri
Centre for Tourism and Hospitality Training and Research, India

ABSTRACT

Service quality is highly related to the quality of training given to the workers and stakeholders. As the requirements of skills are changing in every industry along with the global trends, initiatives like 'Skill India' missions have gone through many changes. This paper analyses the 'Skill India' mission particularly in hospitality and allied sectors. The authors have conducted a broader analysis and critical evaluation of various policies, schemes, initiatives, trends, future perspectives, and challenges in skill training in the hospitality sector. For this purpose, numerous studies, regional study findings, news articles, government reports, official publications, and in-depth interviews with experts have been conducted. The study highlights the existence of a skill gap, major constraints in skilling the youth, quality of skills trained, skilling marginalised, private-public partnership, entrepreneurship initiatives, eSkill opportunities after training, feedback systems, etc. In general, these results suggest that an intensive skill gap exists in many sectors and departments.

DOI: 10.4018/978-1-7998-9510-7.ch007

WHY SKILL DEVELOPMENT PROGRAMMES?

India, an emerging economy, shows a paradigm shift in the areas of infrastructure, education, healthcare, tourism and hospitality, research, automobile, manufacturing, science and technology, through its great vision to lead the world. Among many industries which contribute to the nation's economy, the hospitality sector plays a formidable role in driving India towards self-sustenance, with an annual growth rate of 14% (not considered for the pandemic period) along with the information technology sector. Employee efficiency, being a significant factor possessing strong influence and measurable repercussions over the hospitality sector and the nation as whole, but surprisingly, the number of quality employment and share of the sector are inversely proportional. Interestingly, there happens to be a record footfall of tourists, which is significant for the hospitality sector to grow, but the gap is becoming more wider between the demand and supply, however, the sector has high understanding towards quality manpower and their share in enhancing guest experience, signals the necessity of rejuvenation on policies pertaining to the sector, revisiting the existing guidelines to energise the expectations of the guests and involved stakeholders. Purchasing behaviour of Indians show positivity, leading in experiential travel, especially among the rising middle class and their income, fuelled by avocational occupations. In the year 2020, India had around 1702 hospitality outlets ranging from star category hotels to bed and breakfast establishment with the offering of 102154 rooms (Mot, 2021 report) with the average employee per room covering all types of hospitality establishments was 1.8 (India Hotel Industry Survey 2020, FHRAI) considered to be serious dearth of quality human resources, specifically on skill shortage.

Acquiring skill is viewed as an art, which encompasses interest, dedication, commitment and being competitive continuously, however, the present perception of acquiring skills draws attention towards studying, training and getting certified, though it plays a significant role, the interest factor and continuous upgradation makes their opportunity successful. Interestingly, technology has given enough scope for enhancing the skill through e-learning and assessments. Demanding interpersonal skills has become crucial in the hospitality sector, expecting multitasking, crisis management, time management and teamwork from the youth aspirants to become competent assets, thus creating an urgent intervention to equip skills among the youth of the country. Skill India is a futuristic mission of the government of India to develop the youth population and define their strengths and opportunities in the hospitality management area.

REVIEW OF LITERATURE

This section reviews the literature related to 'Skill India' initiatives and the Indian Hospitality sector. Government organizations have always played a major role in initiating skill development programs throughout the decades. Indian scenarios of the same have been discussed in studies of Jamal and Mandal (2013) by mapping various government initiatives towards skill development in the country. And it is found that lack of skilled force is present in all levels and types of organisations. Fruitfully the authors have also suggested mechanisms to fill the skill development gap with suitable examples. Applying the same in the current generation of human resource environment again needs more calculations and clarifications. Similar research is contributed by Das (2015), which further critically examined national skills development initiatives in India based on the demand for skilled manpower in SMEs. The authors claimed lack of 'awareness' and 'monitoring mechanism' as the major reason why these national programs have not reached targeted beneficiaries. Chenoy (2013) explored the status, scope, and need of private-sector partnerships with NSDC-funded institutions to establish skill development activities in rural or deep roots of India. In this analysis, it is highlighted on opportunities for skill development as a sustainable business and beyond (social enterprise initiatives). The author has also focused on the social inclusion aspects of skill development initiatives regarding different models that can be practiced in organisations. Likewise, studies by Mehotra et. al., (2014) cross-examined skill-related issues of Indian and German companies (mostly private, including manufacturing and service sector). This study has worked on adapting/transferring the dual system of German to the Indian context and workable recommendations on the Indian system of skills development. The results ensured the existence of skill gaps, skill-related issues, and the need for improvement on various initiatives. Issues of skills gap have been discussed by various authors including Srivastava and Hasan (2016). Commenting on private-public partnership, FDI (foreign direct investments) also have been impacted by the introduction of 'Skill India' and 'Make in India' programs (Khan and Pal, 2016; Gaur and Padiya, 2017). The authors underscore that if India is looking for employment generation through FDI, the nation must first generate a skilled workforce. Because it will result in a better standard of living, more employability, and poverty eradication. Again the challenge is not only generating a skilled workforce but also skilling the existing workforce which is crores in number. Jagadisha (2016) researched Ministry of Skill Development and Entrepreneurship initiatives and highlighted best practices that can be utilised in the skill development ecosystem of India, especially by international collaborations. When the study of Siddiqui and Siddiqui (2016) analyzed the importance of skill development courses in Higher Education Institutions (beyond technical and vocational education), Venkateshwarlu et.al. (2016) tries to understand the role of distance education (particularly IGNOU) in skill development training using technological advancements. Both initiate the thoughts on the importance of all educational stakeholders' participation in skill development other than a single government-funded institution. Iyengar and Mishra (2017) conducted a SOAR (Strengths, Opportunities, Aspirations, and Results) analysis of the 'Skill India' mission initiatives and concluded that it will take more years to see aggregate results of skill training at national levels. The works of Malik and Gupta (2017) summarised that, in addition to the skill gap, the gaps in skill needs, skill measurement, and skill production is high in India. This further demands different applications and approaches to the 'Skill India' mission and initiatives. Another interesting study by Afroz (2018) investigated employees' attitudes toward the skill India campaign has mentioned that employees are more motivated to create jobs and attain growth once after skill training, they also believe that proper skill training will boost their performance in the organisation benefiting both themselves and the organisation. According to Debpriya (2019) to overcome the challenges of implementing skill India initiatives, the administration must focus on long-term sustainable approaches rather than any kind of short-term gains based on political propaganda and bias. The author made extensive research on issues and challenges of implementation of the "Skill India Movement" at the ground level by conducting round-table discussions and questionnaires etc. Auxilia (2021) took a sample of above 250 respondents for understanding Indian youths' perception on skill development programs and their effect on their career growth. This underlined the importance of providing regular and quality skill training for better results, which further questions whether the government institutions delivering quality training under the 'Skill India' mission or not.

Other aspects which have been discussed by scholars on the 'Skill India' program include its contribution to rural development, women empowerment, and digital skilling. Previous studies have emphasized skill training for women, especially in rural areas for uplifting women communities. The study by Koul (2013) was on women's participation in vocational training programs and the author further suggests various measures to boost the same. Similar to other study results, lack of awareness among the target group is seen as the biggest challenge ever faced. Recent works of Kannadhasan (2020) also support the above statement on various schemes that governmental organisations have already initiated but the mission has not yet been completely accomplished. Rani and Agrawal (2020) contribute a descriptive idea of how the Skill India mission helps to empower women and achieve gender equality in the nation by promoting various schemes. Researchers have ensured that the skill training has improved opportunities for women communities, like increased skills enabled women to 'choose' work from a pool of different tasks which earlier they didn't have (Brännström, 2020). Likewise, Digital skilling is another niche area all stakeholders of skill India mission have to work on. According to Anancentres2016) both 'Skill India' and 'Digital India' initiatives have to go hand in hand to ensure up to date skill development of human resources in the nation. Likewise, Aruna (2015) recommends the need for an 'E-Skilling' ecosystem in India in the background of "Digital India" successful initiatives. The author also examined the importance of better plans and strong leadership to further the development of skills in various sectors.

There have been numerous studies investigating skill India initiatives in the hospitality and tourism sector. Kavita and Sharma (2011) analysed the key skills that the Indian hospitality industry demands and the existing skills of hospitality graduates. By admitting Chi-square and Anova technique for analysing the data, the authors concluded that students found a lack of skill in most of the departments in the hospitality sector (ie. Human Resources, Food and Beverage, Front Office, Food Production, and Housekeeping). And also further suggested how the education and training system has to respond to reduce the skill gap. A study by Manoj (2013) on KTDC (Kerala Tourism Development Corporation) and its efficiency of given training show that organisations have to ensure frequent training for all levels of employees as fast-changing trends, technology and systems exist in every sector. Other studies evaluated the requirements of skills and talents in the hospitality sector to renovate the initiatives like 'skill India'. The case study of Assam was conducted by Mokhalles (2018) to provide an overall status of skill requirements in the sector. As per the author, the hospitality sector has to work on training for new skills and skill up-gradation for existing employees to improve their service delivery. The study conducted by Sharma and Sharma (2019) focuses on analyzing the 'skill India' initiative with ground realities particular to culinary skills. And the results suggest aligning academic standards and curricula with international quality frameworks and the latest updates. The statement is further supported by the recommendations of Dixit and Mawroh (2019). Experts have also noted that employee and employer expectations are mismatched in many cases of hospitality organisations (Kumar, 2019). In this scenario, the question of how 'Skill India' becomes a solution to the urgent need for skilled labour in the hospitality sector is deeply discussed by Tiwari and Munjal (2019). Their work has added more ideas to the need for professionally skilled labour in the Indian hospitality sector. Scope of Corporate Social Responsibility (CSR) in the context of the 'Skill India' initiative is a different approach evaluated by Sharma and Mishra (2019), and the results draw the improvement in employee motivation and job retention due to CSR practices (skilling subordinates or uneducated workers). Kumar and Chansoria (2021) studied the gap between the skills demands of the hospitality sector and the supply by academia in the region. The research evidence summarised that hospitality training in India has seen great improvements in adapting technologies and training methods, but still, the syllabus is not uniformly followed in all training centers, and a significant gap exists between the industry and academia. Previous studies were limited to understanding 'Skill India' initiatives in its early stage and less focused on sub-themes of the same. Some of the interesting questions in this context are i) major constraints to skill the youth of the country, ii) quality of the skilled youth, iii) skilling the rural population and marginalised communities, iv) budget, investment, and v) feedback systems and practices. This paper addresses 'Skill India' mission in Hospitality Management for quality products and services, so far lacking in the scientific literature.

RESEARCH DESIGN

Studies on Skill India mission and outcomes in hospitality management are lacking in the main literature. There is no systematic study to evaluate the Government of India 's skill Development programme launched for the promotion of Skilled manpower in the tourism and hospitality sector. The objective of the present study is to analyse the 'Skill India' Mission and its initiatives in hospitality and allied sectors. In terms of the hospitality sector, this work specifically concentrates on aspects of skill training initiatives to ensure quality products and services. Additional general research objectives are i) to critically analyse the Government of India's Skill Development programme, ii) to examine the importance and significance of the ongoing Skill Development programme in hospitality management, iii) to evaluate the role of the Government of India's National Skill Development Mission, and iv) to critically analyse the benefits and ongoing constraints of 'Skill India' capacity building programmes. The data in this work mostly consists of secondary in nature and is analysed in a descriptive style. For this purpose, numerous literatures, regional study findings, news articles, government reports, official publications, and in-depth interviews with experts have been conducted. The authors also performed additional data collection with case study analysis. Based on the collected information, the authors have further analysed the data to find out the skill gap and reality of skilling initiatives in the actual field.

GOVERNMENT OF INDIA'S SKILL DEVELOPMENT PROGRAMMES

Government of India has taken up a mission to develop skill capacity among its citizens through its various arms duly created by the Ministry of Skill Development and Entrepreneurship with the objective of narrowing the gap between demand and supply. The Ministry has promised itself with the 3-tier approach, namely Skill, Re-skill and Up-skill, to make future ready workforce and entrepreneurs, thereby emerging as the world's skill capital significantly. The Government of India has kick-started this mission with the youth, providing a holistic milieu to sync their aspirations with that of the nation's goals, as the government felt the youth as the guiding stars for nation-building. This mission, with the successful nascent experience of 7 years has energised the youth with distinguished skillsets focussing on fostering industrial growth and self-reliance. It is the honest objective of the responsible government to ensure its youth emerge with self-confidence to face the competitive world besides being a pioneer to the world countries. It is learned that the country requires 109 million workforces for the 24 sectors by 2022, from the India Skill report of 2018, which highlights the necessity and significance of the 'Skill India' Mission, with the objectives such as Institutional training, developing infrastructure, training the trainers, ensuring employment, and sustaining the livelihood. This mission is expected to train 10 million youths annually to deploy them across diverse sectors, with the sizable percentage headed towards the service sector through diverse programs and apprenticeships, in particular the hospitality sector. The significance showered upon the service sector has resulted in the creation of the Apprenticeship Act and the National Apprenticeship Promotion Scheme (NAPS) in the year 2016 to ensure employers are encouraging apprenticeship, which has been seen a good response from the youth. Alongside creating different arms to ensure skill development, it has charted out a New Education Policy – 2020 providing special impetus on vocational education and training, arguing for "vocal for local" enabling start-ups to glorify the local flavours in their education and entrepreneurial ventures. The propagation of "vocal for local" is propagated among school students to encourage them to have high regard for the diversity found around them. Equally, the government endorses and analyses the problem of increasing unemployment rate which has risen to 12.6% from 9.3% for the June quarter of 2021-22. The Covid -19 pandemic has fueled an increased rate of unemployment over the past couple of years, among the urban and rural youths. Having learned that the tourism and hospitality sector faced serious threats due to pandemics, forced the participating stakeholders with the support of government agencies to offer varied short-term courses related to hospitality, preferably online courses with robust guidelines for assessment. As there is a gamut of areas in the field of hospitality and in its outlets, the workforce specialising in different areas has become imperative and reflected in the variety of courses such as Baker, Barman, and Cloud Kitchen Cooks offered to pursue. Presently, there are 4-year Bachelor's degree in Hotel Management and 3-year diploma in Hotel Management duly governed by the All India Council of Technical Education (AICTE), whereas a 3-year B.Sc. degree in hotel management is governed by state universities apart from various certificate courses focussing various functional areas of hospitality outlets (Annual Report, 2020-21, Ministry of Skill Development and Entrepreneurship, Govt. of India).

DETAILS OF HOSPITALITY MANAGEMENT COURSES OFFERED IN STATES

Hunar se Rozgar (Skill to employment) is hands on the skill development program, especially concentrated on tourism and hospitality, launched in the year 2009-10, for the youth belonging to economically weaker sections of the society between the age group of 18-28 preferably. It is a 6-8-week program offered by the Ministry of Tourism, Government of India under its funded institutions like the Indian Institute of Tourism and Travel Management (IITTM) and other states government-sponsored hospitality and tourism institutions. Programs are offered in compliance with the directions and guidelines issued by the government of India, skill development is ensured under 3 categories namely 1. for fresh entrants with the training of 200 hours, 2. Re-skilling and up-skilling programs with the training of 16 hours, 3. Recognising and certifying the vocational skills possessed by the aspirants through informal and experiential learning. Also, certificate courses related to core and allied areas of the hospitality sector like Food and Beverage service steward, Room attendant, Front office associate, Kitchen steward, bakery and confectionary, and Housekeeping through Tourism ministry sponsored Institutes such as the Institute of Hotel Management (IHM) and Food Craft Institutes (FCI). Following are the major training programs launched under *Huner Se Rozgar* scheme 1. Food and Beverage (6 weeks), 2. Food Production/bakery (8 weeks) 3. Front Office (6 weeks) and 4. Housekeeping (6 weeks).

DISCUSSION

Hospitality, one of the fascinating industries, contributes a major chunk of young minds in their deliverables, expects equally the sharp minds and easy learners and believes in teamwork. From the psychological perspective of young minds, being tough to cope with the amount of bonding with their teammates and socialising skills. It is strongly believed that education shapes the individual and develops necessary skills to work for a sector, but the scenario in hospitality education resumes many debates and differences right from the syllabi content and pedagogy of various programs.

Hospitality pedagogy is always debatable, inviting focus on various aspects that hospitality education is designed to offer. Expectation and demand from the industry are quite contrary to the content of the program, its cited as the war between practical vs theory, as the hospitality program offered at the higher education level concentrates more on the management and theoretical aspects, whereas the gained theoretical expertise does not suit the industry requirements.

Table 1.

Delhi NCR - [96]	Uttarakhand - [32]	Chandigarh - [11]	Jammu and Kashmir - [3]
Tamil Nādu - [93]	Kerala - [28]	Assam - [7]	Sikkim - [3]
Maharashtra - [66]	Madhya Pradesh - [23]	Chhattisgarh - [6]	Bihar - [2]
Uttar Pradesh - [63]	Telangana - [19]	Goa - [6]	Nagaland - [2]
Punjab - [43]	Orissa - [18]	Meghalaya - [5]	Puducherry - [2]
Haryana - [39]	Gujarat - [15]	Arunachal Pradesh - [4]	Dadra and Nagar haveli - [1]
Rajasthan - [36	Himachal Pradesh - [14]	Jharkhand - [4]	Mizoram - [1]
West Bengal - [36]	Andhra Pradesh - [12]		
Karnataka - [35]			

(Source: Annual Report, 2020-21, Ministry of Skill Development and Entrepreneurship, Govt. of India)

Hospitality education in the country is governed and regulated by various national and state agencies, more diversification is found in the hospitality programs offered such as 4-year Bachelor's degree in Hotel Management and 3-year Diploma in Hotel Management duly governed by the All India Council of Technical Education (AICTE), whereas 3-year B.Sc. degree in hotel management is governed by state universities bringing wide differences in the curriculum and pedagogy. The combination of subjects, practicals, and internships do have wide differences in the programs offered at degree and diploma levels leaving scope for debates and discussions. The present hospitality education system not only brings differences in the syllabi but also differs in the assessment part too. The mode of admission is also not similar at least between private and government institutions. A centralised entrance test is applicable for diploma courses offered by the Institute of Hotel Management (IHM), governed by the Ministry of Tourism, Government of India. Having such dissimilarities, the job opportunities are at stake for the students. Also, students tend to be less motivated at the job-hunting ground with the prevailing dissimilarities that need to be rectified. Learning at the institutional level should be motivated through Technology, Entertainment, and Design (TED) talks aimed at enriching learning experiences, organizing industrial visits and innovation labs, and displaying hospitality quotes across the campus.

Technically speaking, most hospitality education is more of the explicit knowledge, emphasising articulated, codified, and language-based, whereas, tacit knowledge is non-verbal, practical, and experience-based. Collins (2010) opine tacit knowledge is the accumulation of individual "know-how" while explicit knowledge is the fact-based aggregation of shared "know-that." Considering functions of the hospitality sector, it is understood that the presence of both knowledge in the aspirants proves to be effective to lead the industry, also, the institutes imparting hospitality education should also train the students on both tacit and explicit knowledge. Hospitality trainers should also deal with Blue Ocean Strategy (BOS) to inculcate its traits and its applications in the hospitality industry. Inputs of BOS are identifying guest value perceptions, innovating distinctive added-value offerings, developing new market segments, branding, re-branding, creating a unique hotel ambience, adjusting distribution channels, and establishing strategic alliances (Yang, 2012)

So, the present hospitality education system needs to be revisited. Also, there is a serious signal among the majority of the youth population preferring the informal sector rather than joining the formal sector, which should be vice-versa. Another problem, in attracting the youth to the hospitality sector is its way of operation, as it's totally a cumbersome job, which involves round the clock presence of employees, and unsocial working hours, makes the aspirants withdraw and change their careers. As the hospitality sector is changing its face towards technology-driven services, there happens to be a reduction in the workforce nor the workforce should be tech-savvy. This is a grey area among most of the aspirants who do not have strong access to technology, nor allow themselves to learn and train. Also, the absence of cognitive skills and a strong knowledge base seems to be a worrying factor toward skill development among hospitality aspirants. The absence of Job security and poor retention strategies by most of the hospitality players stands as a reason for such poor show by youth towards this industry, unlike IT and ITES companies, hospitality firms do not practice employee-friendly practices aimed at stress management, work-life balance, financial and non-financial benefits, societal respect and gender equity, etc. however, there are many noteworthy organisations, creating overwhelming satisfaction to both guests and employees, but it's very minimal, as most of the hospitality business in the country is more of standalone firms who run the show on the basis of the available human resources who are mostly less trained and learned. It's clear from the above discussions that industry is largely fragmented, diversified, and complex, which paves way for the youth to prefer the industry as their career.

Quality of service in hospitality stands of utmost significance in enhancing the brand and acquiring a strong customer base, having said this, quality could be achieved through rigorous and continuous training and brainstorming exercises for the employees and the new recruits, both in house and external training sessions should be given to the students and the aspirant youths, so that the objective of the hospitality business of respecting the guest (*athithi devo bhava*) shall be achieved. However, not all training institutes offering hospitality education has the provision of offering a stipulated 6-month training period during their course of study, and less than that period of training will not yield quality in the aspirants for achieving excellence. The departments in the hospitality outlets, though require and expects varying skills from the job seekers, but the present expectation is towards collective skills who can learn and grasp thing easier and bring in innovativeness in the deliverables, so the creativity, innovativeness, enthusiasm, leadership, high commitment, and integrity towards the taken-up job are expected within the youth. Though the above said quality is neither achieved nor developed in the shorter span, it is equally a two-way process as the aspirants should satisfy themselves with those traits while choosing hospitality as their career. Training should also concentrate on staying competitive, value creation, scenario-based learning, and microlearning, which can be measured by the effectiveness and output approach.

Such as important training is given by the in-house HR department to its employees continuously, but it is to be accepted that certain training organisations and agencies do offer certifications enabling the aspirants to excel and expertise in their taken-up assignments, it is to be made mandatory to get certified by such agencies which again makes industry easier to find a talented pool. Few certifications offered in the USA are as follows

- CRDE: Certified Rooms Division Executive
- CHSP: Certified Hospitality Sales Professional
- CHS: Certified Hospitality Supervisor
- CHRM: Certified Hospitality Revenue Manager

Equally, hospitality institutes should be equipped with good labs and facilities to train the students and should have an in-house hotel to provide live exposure and understand the modalities of a hospitality business. Also, there should be an MoU with major hotel chains to share the expertise of the hospitality trainers with both students and staff. There should always be a train the trainers' program which can pave the way in achieving skilling the youth. The Government of India, under the Ministry of Tourism, is offering a program named "*Hunar Se Rozgar Tak*" (skill to employment) and an "Entrepreneurship programme" towards capacity development among young talents to join the hospitality trade. The above said programs are made aware to the youths of the nation and motivated to join and assist to land up in jobs after successful completion of the course and training. The course receives good patronage from the youths as it is financially supported by providing stipends, specially targeted to the rural youth, who could not join the colleges and universities formally.

'Skill India' mission is considered to be a futuristic and progressive step of the Indian government aimed at developing skills among the youth to lead the country and be self-reliant through partnering with state governments, industry, NGOs and academia to ensure holistic growth across the country. It is also witnessed positive consensus among the above stakeholders to seal positive deliverables as employment generation. The Ministry of Skill Development and Entrepreneurship (MSDE), Government of India has taken up several additional roles through multiple organizations and skilling schemes, namely PMKVY (*Pradhan Mantri Kaushal Vikas Yojana*), PMKK (*Pradhan Mantri Kaushal Kendra*), NSDC (National Skill Development Corporation), NCVT (National Council for Vocational Training), JSS (*Jan Shikshan Sansthan*), NIESBUD (National Institute for Entrepreneurship & Small Business Development), IIE (Indian Institute of Entrepreneurship), and Directorate General of Training (DGT).However, there are significant challenges to achieving the same in the economic and social volatility. People perceive the programs and training offered under this mission as meant for those who were distanced from formal education and the present Government of India's New Education Policy-2020 makes provision to pursue courses aimed at acquiring skills and even deposit the credits in the academic credit bank. Also, coordination among varying assessment agencies and departments proves to be worrying and leads to inconsistency in deliverables, which poses a serious challenge to the enrolled aspirants and job offering agencies. The balance between the formal education and vocational system is at great stake, and acceptance between them towards supply is widening besides low awareness among the youth to join the mission, especially among women. However, there are certain schemes, like *Jan Shikashan Sansthan* (JSS), " People's Education Institute'' which provide vocational training to non-literates, neo-literates as well as school drop-outs in rural regions by identifying skills that have a relevant market in that region, has seen 89% of female beneficiaries, irrespective of the fact that the Scheme is not a female-centric scheme. It is also challenging to attract demand-based curricula and curricula-based trainers for consistent service. Though these challenges are significant, the need for human resources is increasing every year and makes the stakeholders concentrate to eradicate the challenges. It is clear that tourism, hospitality, and travel signify 4.9 million incremental human resource requirements in the last 5-year (2017-22) period (annual report-2020-21, skill development and entrepreneurship ministry).

In order to attain the objectives of skilling the youth, Sector Skill Councils (SSCs) under the National Skill Development Corporation were set up as autonomous bodies with the team representing industry leaders in the respective sectors to standards, developing competency framework, conducting train the trainer programmes, affiliate vocational training institutes, conduct skill gap studies in their sector, assess and certify trainees on the curriculum aligned to the National Occupational Standards developed by them. Accordingly, the Tourism and Hospitality Skill Council was set up to ensure quality training and skill development among the youths. Considering the importance of English in the tourism and hospitality sector, necessary English training in the name of English, an Employability and Entrepreneurship Training (EEE) module was introduced covering Digital Literacy, Financial Literacy, Employability, and Entrepreneurship. In addition to this, through various channels including Print advertisements, Bulk SMS, social media, and workshops at College and University levels. Capacity-building drives were initiated to attain collective development among youth, but it is worrying to see the wide gap between the enrolled and placed numbers.

Table 2. Skill development initiative and progress

Targets allotted	Enrolled	Trained	Certified	Placed
9,681	9,449	8,836	7,460	4,848

Source: Annual report 2020-21 Skill development and Entrepreneurship Ministry, Govt. of India.

As a continuous exercise of reaching the youth, the government has introduced the e-skill India program by reaching the youth through a digital platform offering around 850 courses through 35 knowledge partners, in 10 languages comprising 1.6 million minutes of online content, but only a few courses are well received by the youth, which needs a strong intervention in the process of delivery. However, this program is well partnered with top companies including Microsoft, IBM, British Council, Amazon, etc., and offers mobile applications too. It follows stringent practices in identifying the training institutes based on the facilities, quality, innovation, faculty strength, placement records, and following are the steps followed.

- Training Partner Registration & Training Centre Creation
- Accreditation of Training Centre
- Affiliation of Training Centre's Added Job Roles
- Continuous Monitoring
- Renewal of Accreditation

After the huge allocation of funds, different autonomous bodies working under the aegis of Skill Development and Entrepreneurship Ministry and its associated initiatives, it has recorded notable enrolments and changes among the youth.

Top 3 sectors are IT-ITES, Electronics, and Healthcare contributing ~60% of the total enrolments on eSkill India.

Figure 1. e-skill India interface

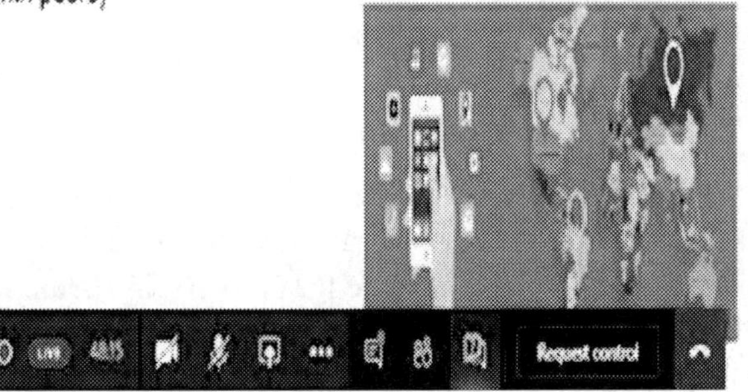

India is progressing as a most sought-after destination for international tourists, with a respectable international tourist of 2.74 million (2020), decreasing by 74.9% compared to 2019 due to the Covid-19 pandemic and expected to rise in the future. Another challenge with the rural tourist spots and hospitality outlets are failing to attract trained and young talent, as all the trained pool of youth are willing to work in the cities and metros, very limited or untrained or semi-trained are working in the rural area hospitality outlets. Though the skill India mission provides a greater chance to learn and train, youth are provided jobs as apprentices in many organisations, and post-completion of the apprenticeship, they could not land any job as organisations do not consider an apprenticeship as experience. This again makes the youth search for other ways of living, considered to be the practical obstacles for the enrolled aspirants.

Figure 2. e-skill India mobile app interface

Figure 3. eSkill India in different sectors (India)
Source: Annual report 2020-21 Skill development and Entrepreneurship Ministry

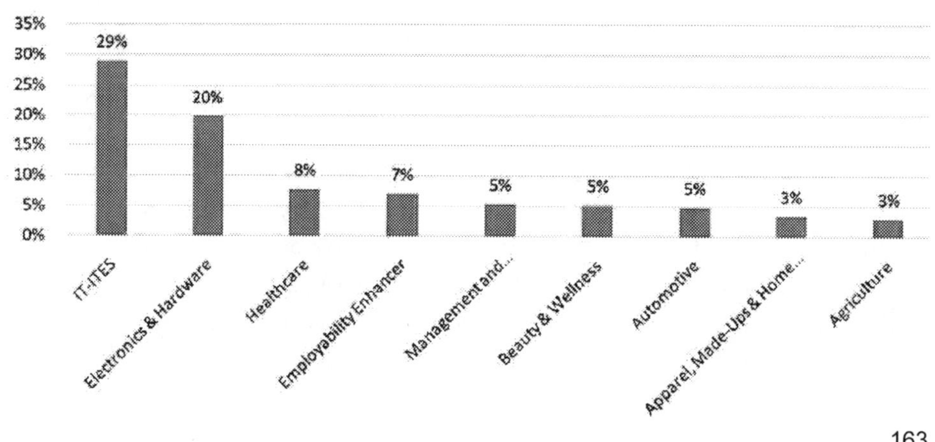

CONCLUSION

Hospitality industry has evolved technologically sound in the last 15 years, which has shown considerable evidence in terms of growth and satisfaction of guests. Also, technology driven services happen to be the USP of certain international hospitality chains. However, challenges and growth are inseparable for the hospitality industry with the volatile competitive environment. There are increased critical factors affecting the skills of job aspirants, and a serious decline in attracting the skilled youth as well, expecting greater intervention from academics and practitioners. Unlike academics, the government of India has taken the responsible act of skilling the youth through various schemes, although they are yet to attain their successful acceptance and implementation. Further, recognising the collaborative contribution in forecasting the demand for skilled employees will enable the government to admit in its offerings, which will eventually enable them to get placed. The major challenge to ensure effective implementation of skill India mission is demand uncertainty, which can lead to excessive allocation of funds in a given financial year. Also, the different schemes found in the 'Skill India' mission, provide a chance to have multiple enrolments by an individual leads to duplication of data and require the system of information sharing, where information about the enrolled youths across the entire ministry will fulfil the objective of ensuring wider reach. 'Skill India' mission is more concentrated on providing training and courses only on certain functions of hospitality operations, they should introduce cost control, supply chain management, inventory management, revenue management, Customer relationship management and ICT enabled CRS and GDS, and upcoming technologies such as Artificial Intelligence, Virtual and Augmented reality, Internet of Things and Block Chain technology so that the skill mission would achieve its objective among the youth as they are more tech-savvy. However, it is accepted that the 'Skill India' mission has created interest among the youths and has to go miles to ensure its reason for creation.

Limitations, Implications and Future Research

The results demonstrated and discussed in this work provide an understanding of the 'Skill India' initiative in the hospitality sector with insights on the significance of skilling, reskilling and upskilling. The findings of this study have numerous important implications for planning upcoming hospitality skill development initiatives and training activities. All stakeholders (employees, employers, trainers, academicians, students, researchers, industry experts, private sector, government organisations, NGOs, trade associations, local residents, activists etc.) in the hospitality sector and allied sectors can adapt the current study findings in various stages of their project discussions, design and execution. Few limitations exist in the current study beginning with a descriptive analysis of a wide topic. The work is limited by its consideration of the hospitality skill development mission and lack of on-field long term case analysis. It is not well clear whether the existing skill gap will decrease compared to earlier or will increase due to various reasons including the issue of the digital divide etc. Further investigation is necessary to explore and forecast changing demands of work skills in the hospitality sector and training methods to be adopted by the training centers/institutions. Future studies could fruitfully explore this issue more by utilising participant research tools.

REFERENCES

Afroz, A. (2018). Employees Aspiration Towards Skill Development in Uttarakhand: A Study of Needs and Findings. *OJAS, 13*.

Ananthesh, H. (2016). Role of" skill india program" in realizing" digital India mission. *Splint International Journal of Professionals*, *3*(6), 78.

Aruna, A., & KR, D. M. K. (2015). *Enabling E-Skilling in India through Digital India and Skill India Programs*. Academic Press.

Auxilia, P. M. (2021). *Indian Youths' Perception on Skill Development Training Programs for Career Growth*. www. ijrpr. com

Brännström, S. (2020). *What's the problem with Women not Working? A Critical Analysis of the Skill India Development Mission & Explanations on Female Labor Force Participation*. Academic Press.

Chenoy, D. (2013). Public–private partnership to meet the skills challenges in India. *Skills Development for Inclusive and Sustainable Growth in Developing Asia-Pacific,* 181-194.

Chenoy, D. (2016). Skill development in India: A transformation in the making. *India Infrastructure Report*, *2012*, 237–245.

Collins, H. (2010). *Tacit and Explicit Knowledge*. The University of Chicago Press. doi:10.7208/chicago/9780226113821.001.0001

Das, A. (2015). Skills Development for SMEs: Mapping of Key Initiatives in India. *Institutions and Economies*, *7*(2), 120–143.

Debpriya, De. (2019). Issues and challenges in implementing the skill India movement: Training partner perspective. *Worldwide Hospitality and Tourism Themes*.

Dixit, S. K., & Mawroh, H. (2019). Vocational education and training for hospitality and tourism industry in India. *Tourism Education and Asia*, 35-48.

Gaur, A. D., & Padiya, J. (2017). A Conceptual Study of "Skill India" Mission Bridge to "Make in India" Program. Editorial Advisory Board, 52.

Iyengar, V., & Mishra, D. K. (2017). Skilling for inclusive growth: SOAR analysis of 'Skill India 'Mission. *International Journal of Applied Business and Economic Research*, *15*(16), 209–221.

Jagadisha, T. (2016). Opportunities and Challenges of Skill Development Programmes in India: An Analysis. Skill India and Development: Emerging Debates, 170.

Jamal, T., & Mandal, K. (2013). Skill development mission in vocational areas–mapping government initiatives. *Current Science*, 590–595.

Kannadhasan, S. (2020). Women Empowerment and Economic Development Schemes through Skill India. Skill India: A Catalyst to Nation Building, 72.

Kavita, K. M., & Sharma, P. (2011). Gap analysis of skills provided in hotel management education with respect to skills required in the hospitality industry: The indian scenario. *International Journal of Hospitality and Tourism Systems*, *4*(1), 31.

Khan, M. I., & Pal, M. (2016). Foreign Direct Investment and Labour Process in India: The Role of 'Make in India 'and 'Skill India" Programmes. *International Journal of Multidisciplinary Research and Development*, *3*(8), 396–403.

King, K. (2012). The geopolitics and meanings of India's massive skills development ambitions. *International Journal of Educational Development*, *32*(5), 665–673. doi:10.1016/j.ijedudev.2012.02.001

Koul, M. (2013). Skill development through government initiatives: Anything for women? *Current Science*, *105*(2), 146.

Kumar, A. (2019). Skill India: Bridging the Gap in Skills of Hospitality Sector Manpower. *Emerging Trends in Indian Tourism and Hospitality: Transformation and Innovation, 140.*

Kumar, P., & Chansoria, M. (2021). Assessment of Hospitality education in terms of Lacking Skill Development in Meeting the demand of Industry: An Integrative review. *Revista de turism-studii si cercetari in turism*, (31).

Malik, A., & Gupta, S. (2017). Bridging the skill gap: An overview of skill India campaign. *Asian Journal of Research in Social Sciences and Humanities*, *7*(7), 271–283. doi:10.5958/2249-7315.2017.00385.9

Manoj, A. S. (2013). A Study on the Efficiency of Training in Hospitality–A Kerala Tourism Development Corporation (KTDC) Experience, Trivandrum, Karela. *International Journal of Advanced Research in Management and Social Sciences, 9*.

Mehrotra, S., Raman, R., Kumra, N., & Röß, D. (2014). *Vocational Education and Training Reform in India: Business Needs in India and Lessons to be Learned from Germany*. Working paper.

Mokhalles, M. M. (2018). Skill Gap Analysis: A Review of Hospitality Sector in Assam. *Journal of Rural and Industrial Development*, *6*(1), 49.

Rani, P., & Agrawal, R. (2020). Women Empowerment Through Skill India to Achieve Gender Equality–A Review. Skill India: A Catalyst to Nation Building, 140.

Sadgopal, A. (2016). 'Skill India 'or Deskilling India: An Agenda of Exclusion. *Economic and Political Weekly*, 33–37.

Sharma, S., & Mishra, P. (2019). Hotel employees' perceptions about CSR initiatives and there potential to support the skill India initiative. *Worldwide Hospitality and Tourism Themes*, *11*(1), 78–86. doi:10.1108/WHATT-10-2018-0064

Sharma, S., & Sharma, R. (2019). Culinary skills: the spine of the Indian hospitality industry: Is the available labour being skilled appropriately to be employable? *Worldwide Hospitality and Tourism Themes*, *11*(1), 25–36. doi:10.1108/WHATT-10-2018-0061

SiddiquiD. M.SiddiquiA. (2016). *Integrating the NSDC Agenda in the Higher Education Institutions: A New Model for Employability Skill Development*. Available at SSRN 2744609. doi:10.2139/ssrn.2744609

Srivastava, A. I., & Hasan, A. (2016). Bridging the Skill Gap in India: Challenges and Solutions. JIMS8M. *The Journal of Indian Management & Strategy*, *21*(1), 45–54. doi:10.5958/0973-9343.2016.00007.7

Tiwari, S., & Munjal, S. (2019). What are the key challenges that the Indian hospitality industry is facing in search of skilled labour? *Worldwide Hospitality and Tourism Themes*, *11*(1), 99–102. doi:10.1108/WHATT-10-2018-0063

Venkateshwarlu, N., Sharma, R., & Agarwal, A. (2016). Skill Development Training Programme: A Case Study of IGNOU. *Global Journal of Enterprise Information System*, *8*(4), 66–70. doi:10.18311/gjeis/2016/15775

Yang, J. (2012). Identifying the attributes of blue ocean strategies in hospitality. *International Journal of Contemporary Hospitality Management*, *24*(5), 13–27. doi:10.1108/09596111211237255

KEY TERMS AND DEFINITIONS

Athithi Devo Bhava: *Treating guest as god.*

E-Skilling: E-skilling is the process of enabling an individual on the nuances of digital learning.

Employee Efficiency: Employee efficiency is the ability that he/she possess to accomplish the given task effectively.

Experiential Travel: Experiential travel is the activity of travelling to a destination with an exclusive objective of experiencing the history, socio-cultural delicacies practically beyond mere destination visit.

Hospitality Management: Hospitality management is the broad area covering various dimensions ensuring effective functioning of accommodation outlets such as hotels, resorts, and its associated units.

Hunar se Rozgar: "Skill to employment" is hands on the skill development program, especially concentrated on tourism and hospitality, launched in the year 2009-10, for the youth belonging to economically weaker sections of the society between the age group of 18-28 preferably.

Jan Shikashan Sansthan **(JSS):** "People's Education Institute'' which provide vocational training to non-literates, neo-literates as well as school drop-outs in rural regions by identifying skills that have a relevant market in that region.

Multitasking: It's a quality of an employee, who is an expert is diversified areas of operation, an organization demands.

Re-Skilling: It's the process of enabling employees to equip with new skills tom perform a new job.

Rozgar Mela: Is a Hindi term representing "employment fair" unites the job seekers and employers, sensitized, and mobilized to ensure effective employment opportunities.

Service Quality: Service quality is the concept flashing the relationship between the expectation and performance of services extended to guests. It's also expressed as the extent to which the organization meets the expectation of guests need.

Skill Gap: Skill gap refers as the shortage of essential traits and the gap between the expected qualities and existing quality within employees.

Skill India: Skill India is a promising mission of government of India to energize, empower youth to become skillful employees and entrepreneurs.

Skills: Skills refers to the primary and secondary talents and traits to perform a particular assignment given to employees.

Up-Skill: Where employees learn additional skills to discharge his/her allotted work.

Chapter 8
TVET System and Tourism in Oman:
Present and Future Outlooks

Mohit Kukreti
https://orcid.org/0000-0003-0067-0103
University of Technology and Applied Sciences, Oman

Mohammed Ali Ahmed Obaid
University of Technology and Applied Sciences, Oman

ABSTRACT

Technical and vocational education and training (TVET) is an important contributor to the sustainable economic development to achieve Sustainable Development Goals (SDGs) and Oman Vision 2040. TVET is expected to facilitate the insertion of young people and adults into the labor market and their career progression. The tourism and hospitality sector is a priority sector for a country's Tanfeedh plan for economic diversification. This chapter highlights the historical and existing practices in the Oman's TVET system that can be considered as enterprise-based learning that includes apprenticeship, OJT for students and workers of different ages. This chapter focusses on the practical attempts to incorporate work-based learning leading to identification of the strengths, weakness, and opportunities for all the people concerned. It highlights the present situation and future outlook of technical and vocational education and training in the tourism and hospitality sector in Oman.

DOI: 10.4018/978-1-7998-9510-7.ch008

1. INTRODUCTION

Oman occupies a strategic location in the Arabian Peninsula surrounded by countries such as Yemen, Saudi Arabia, and United Arab Emirates (UAE). It has a vast coastline touching three main seas namely the Sea of Oman, the Arabian Sea, and the Arabian Gulf. The Sultanate of Oman has 11 governorates/administrative regions (Muscat, Dhofar, Musandam, Al-Buraimi, Al-Dhakhilyiah, Al-Batinah North, Al- Batinah South, Al-Sharqiyah North, Al-Sharqiyah South, Al Dhahirah, Al-Wusta) with a population of approximately 4.5 million (2.9 million males and 1.5 million female) and including 2 million expatriate residents.

The Sultanate of Oman is a high-income country with plethora of natural resources including hydrocarbons and frankincense. Since Oman is surrounded by the sea from the three sides hence, it has many marine resources and modern strategic port infrastructure. In 2016, GDP stood at US$66.29 billion and the gross national income (GNI) per capita was US$18,080. (UNESCO, 2019)

The country's present education system is divided into three levels namely basic, secondary, and tertiary education. In 1997, the basic education program was introduced and consists of two cycles; the first cycle covers grades from 1 to 4 and the second cycle covers grades from 5 to 10. During the second cycle, there are two years of post-basic education (secondary education). Basic and secondary education is obligatory for all children. In addition, there are a number of prestigious private schools, and the majority of schools are private educational establishments. (UNESCO, 2019)

The Ministry of Higher Education Research and Innovation (MoHERI) administers the free of charge higher education for all locals. The Sultan Qaboos University was established in 1986. In 1994, Colleges of Education (CoE) were established, and to facilitate Oman's diversification of economy drive, these education colleges were transformed into to Colleges of Applied Sciences (CAS) in 2007. In 2001, Oman industrial colleges were transferred to Colleges of Technology (CoT). In 2020, both CAS and COTs were merged under the largest public sector institution entitled University of Technology and Applied Sciences. In addition to the government higher education institutions, there are many private sector HEIs in Oman offering higher education programs in all disciplines.

1.1 Methodology

Brown (2006) has mentioned literature review validity measures as intent/purpose, scope, authority, audience, and format. While conducting the secondary source-based research, all these measures were duly considered. Internet websites of Oman Ministry of Higher Education, Manpower; Educational Council; CAS; COT were used for online searching of the information. No primary data was collected therefore, formal ethical approvals were not required. Secondary data sources are duly acknowledged, and the research questions postulated were: what type of historical and present TVET practices are available in Oman? What is the present situation and future-outlook of technical and vocational education and training in the tourism and hospitality sector in Oman? Based on these questions the following objectives are formulated:

- To highlight the historical and present practices in Oman's TVET system as an enterprise–based learning.
- Compare between technical and vocational education in the public and private sectors.
- To highlight the present situation and future outlook of TVET system in the tourism and hospitality sector in Oman.
- To provide recommendations for improving the TVET system in Oman.

1.2. Literature Review

An Entrepreneurship is the most powerful and important economic tool which the world has seen lately as it contributes to innovativeness, competitiveness, economic development, employment creation for the well being of the society and the country. According to Valerio et. Al (2014) an entrepreneurship can be defined as a process of starting a lawful business to make money.

According to Verheul, Wennekers, Audretch and Thurnik (2001), there are variety of factors such as economic and social factors that explains the level of entrepreneurship. To support entrepreneurship, economic and social development, Technical and Vocational Education and Training (TVET) system plays an important role.

According to Pittaway & Cope (2007) Government's role is important in bringing efficiency in the entrepreneurship education in the country however; Cho & Honorati (2014); and Martin et al., (2013) advocated private sectors involvement in the entrepreneurship education. Therefore, both government and private sectors are important stakeholders in the entrepreneurship education development in any country including Oman.

UNESCO (2015) has defined TVET as, those aspects of education which in addition to general education involves the study of science and technologies and acquisition of practical skills, attitudes, understanding and knowledge relating to occupation in various sectors of economic life. It transforms people from an 'educational to 'functional' world of education (Maclean & Pavlova, 2013). This can be ensured if the TVET system should be concerned about effective integration of entrepreneurial education into all vocational education stages to generate committed and capable entrepreneurs (Shikalepo, 2019).

In Oman also, according to Education Council, TVET plays an important role in the overall economic development and education in Oman (Educational Council, 2016). However, it should be remembered that according to Ramdzan et al., (2020) it can't be assumed that the TVET students will have an ambition to become entrepreneurs in the future.

TVET system can be considered as organizational based practical learning, that includes apprenticeship, OJT for students and workers of different ages. Since Oman is trying to develop niche tourism to achieve its vision 2040 and UNSGs; therefore, the proper understanding and development of TVET system is quite essential. TVET system will compliment and strengthen the vocational training and education in Oman to contribute towards quality human resource development in tourism. This chapter focusses on the practical attempts to incorporate work-based learning to help identify strengths, weakness, and opportunities for all stakeholders. It highlights the present situation and future outlook of technical and vocational education and training in tourism and hospitality sector in Oman.

2. TECHNICAL AND VOCATIONAL EDUCATION IN OMAN

2.1 TVET Mission, Strategy and Legislation

Many people in Oman consider public sector jobs as the best employment opportunity due to the lucrative benefits offered by government and the limited working hours. This is an area of concern and therefore planners and policymakers in Oman are making various efforts to change this notion. One such effort involved modifications to the private sector employment rules and improvements to the Oman Labor law. Formal education and lifelong learning are focused more to equip the citizens with the required knowledge, skills, attributes, and competencies to work successfully in the private sector. This shift was designed to develop an entrepreneurial mindset among the youths and encouraging entrepreneurship for self-employment.

The decline in economic activity and employment opportunities usually led countries to give more attention to TVET education. Accordingly, there is a high level of government involvement in providing TVET programs and high degree of expectation about the outcomes of TVET education. The TVET system in Oman has been tailored to meet the above requirements as well as the local employment needs. The Oman government is developing TVET system to respond to the various economic challenges, economic diversification, and unemployment.

Oman expects TVET to become the first choice for students and employers by providing high-quality education and research that facilitates Oman's endeavor of economic diversification and development. Oman interprets TVET missions to deliver high-quality technical education and vocational training and to produce competent professionals to enter labor market to significantly contributes to the overall economic, socio-cultural, and environmental development of Oman.

TVET in Oman aims to:

- Achieve excellence in governance and administration based on principles of sound ethics.
- Offer best quality of educational and training opportunities as per the labor market needs, so as to provide Omani society with competent and professional graduates.
- Provide outstanding essential services to students.
- Provide up-to-date learning resources for students to develop their educational, job related and social skills.
- Ensure that the facilities are managed, used, and developed in an innovative way.
- Ensure well established and standardized financial planning and management.
- Develop its staff by providing opportunities for professional and personal growth and development, rewarding hard work and fostering leadership skills and innovative thinking.
- Achieve and sustain a national and regional reputation for excellence in specialist technological and applied research of benefit to Omani society.
- Foster an open and fruitful relationship with public and private sector organizations and with the community at large.

To provide a high-quality workforce that meet the labor market needs and achieve the target level of performance and productivity, the following policies have been implemented for TVET system in Oman:

- Adoption of an open and flexible educational and training system that allows career progression and continuously helps to develop the skills of Omani labor.
- Adoption of advanced TVET system to keep up with the market demands and latest technological developments.
- Efforts to increase the participation of female workers.
- Conducting audits of the efficiency of TVET to meet the requirements of the labor market and making necessary adjustment to the programs wherever applicable.

The present TVET system in Oman is an outcome of several legislative changes and developments in the form of Royal Decrees and Ministerial Decisions regarding as mentioned below:

- In 2001, the Ministry of Workforce was responsible for TVET education in Oman according to Royal Decree No. 108/2001. The Ministry of Workforce became responsible for the development of Technical Colleges and public and private Vocational Institutes.
- On 20th May 2001, the Higher Education Council rename "Muscat Technical Industrial College" to "The Higher College of Technology" to award Bachler degree, and "The Technical Industrial Colleges as "Colleges of Technology" to award the National Technological Diploma.
- The most recent By-laws for the Colleges of Technology and Vocational training Centers were published by Ministerial Decision No. 72/2004 on 21st March 2004 for the Colleges of Technology and Ministerial Decision No. 429/2008 on 16th September 2008 for the Vocational Training Centers. Few amendments were made to the By-laws through Ministerial Decrees.
- In 2020, a Royal Decree No. 76/200 was issued to merge Colleges of Technology and Colleges of Applied Sciences under a new university named as "University of Technology and Applied Sciences".
- In 2020, a Royal Decree No. 98/2020 was issued to transfer the Directorate General of Vocational Training, and the Directorate General of Occupational Standards and Curriculum Development from the Ministry of Manpower to the Ministry of Higher Education, Research, and Innovation (MoHERI).

2.2 TVET Structure in Oman

10th grade pass students can either continue their education to post-basic school education (grade 11 & 12) or opt to vocational training. The Post-basic education encourages provides students with life-skills and information about the different specializations available in HEIs. 12th grade pass students can join any of the following education and/or training programs:

- Academic universities and colleges
- Colleges of Technology
- Vocational Education

In general, TVET system in Oman is composed from three categories shown in figure (1):

- Technological education
- Vocation Education
- Occupational Standards and Testing Center

Figure 1. Structure of TVET system in Oman
Source: Designated by the Authors

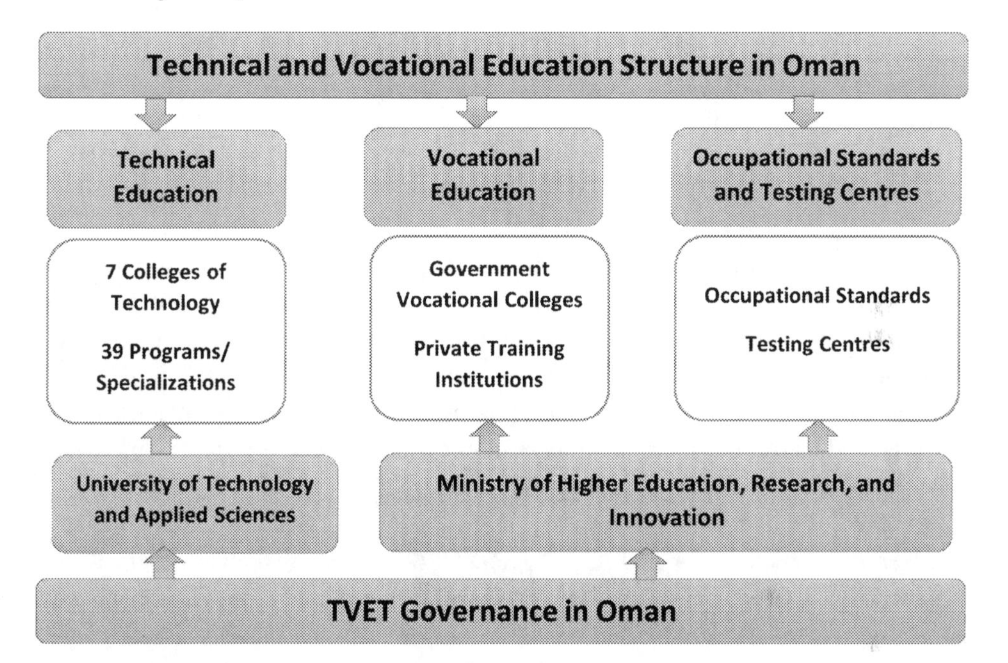

2.3 Technological Education

The Technological Education in Oman aims to develop a quality workforce by qualifying general diploma graduates in the light of the requirements of the job market. It offers a vide verity of Majors/specializations such as Pharmacy, Engineering, Information Technology, Fashion and Design, Applied Sciences, Business, and Photography.

Technological Education in Oman started in 1984 with one college only under the name "the Oman Technical Industrial College". After that, four Industrial Technical Colleges in Musanna, Nizwa, Ibra and Salalah were established. In 2001, the Technical Industrial Colleges were upgraded to five Colleges of Technology; one of them is Higher College of Technology in Muscat, which offers a Bachelor of Technology. In 2005 Shinas and in 2007 Ibri College of Technology were set up, resulting in total 7 technological colleges distributed geographically across the country. In 2018 a new college of technology in Musandam was established. (Educational Council, 2016)

According to Educational Council (2016), the Technological Education began with limited intake of 65 male and female students. Now, the annual average general diploma student's intake is approximately 9,000 males and females constituting 32,2% of students enrolled under the Government expenses. The number of registered students in all seven Colleges of Technology is 40,000 male and female students. As for the 2017/2018 academic year, the number of graduates reached 5891 across all Majors.

2.3.1 The Structure and Governance of Technological Education

The Ministry of Manpower was supervising the governance and development process of all seven Colleges of Technology in Oman. To provide high quality education, the Ministry developed the infrastructure including buildings, services, facilities for education & training, Laboratories for engineering and IT, workshops for practical, contemporary educational technology and latest computers, electronic database for references, audio-visual aids, smart boards, etc. The Ministry concentrated on training students through practical workshops, training periods, various programs to build student's capacity, grants and scholarships.

In 2020, a government university with headquarters in Muscat named the "University of Technology and Applied Sciences" was established as per the Royal Decree No. 76/200. The university has legal personality, enjoys financial and administrative independence, and included competences, allocations, assets, rights, obligations, and holdings all the Colleges of Technology and all the Colleges of Applied Sciences.

2.3.2 Specializations and Qualifications

At the Colleges of Technology, students' progress through several levels. Upon acceptance, the student is enrolled on the foundation program, focusing mostly on English, Mathematics, IT and life skills. After successfully completing the foundation program, students move to specializations at the level of diploma of technology, with possible progression to Advanced Diploma of Technology and Bachelor of Technology. Students that do not achieve the requirements for progressing to a higher level are offered industrial training (On-the-Job Training), whereby they undergo intensive training supervised by college-based tutors and industry-based practitioners. The Colleges of Technology worked in cooperation and coordination with the labor market, to offer contemporary programs and specializations for better employability. A total of (39) approved specializations, as shown in table (1) below. (UNESCO-UNEVOC, 2013).

The Colleges of Technology offers three common programs: Engineering with (16) approved specializations making up 41% of the total; Information Technology and Business Studies with (7) specializations for each making up 18% of the total. The Higher College of Technology offers, in addition to the programs mentioned, Applied Science Program with (6) specializations making up 15% of the total, and Pharmacy, Photography, and Fashion Design, making up altogether 7.7% of the total number of programs. (Educational Council, 2016)

The above table reflects the Diploma, Advance Diploma offered by the Colleges of Technology. They also offer bachelor level academic degree in Technology in all specializations excluding Photography, Fashion Design, Pharmacy, and some engineering specializations such as Refrigeration and Air Conditioning, and Oil and Gas Engineering.

Eight weeks On the Job Training (minimum 300 hours OJT) relevant to the specialization at various public and private sector corporations is considered as an essential part of the educational process.

2.3.3 Student Distribution on Specializations based on the Requirements of the Labor Market

To facilitate Omanisation (nationalization of the work force), the Colleges of Technologies admit the largest number of General Diploma graduates. Figure (3) as shown below, presents that for meeting the job market requirements, the largest proportion of students are allocated in Engineering specializations (48.6%). In fact, according to the economic indicators largest expatriate percentages are in Construction Sector and in Transformational Industry, both related to the Engineering Field.

2.3.4 Quality of Technological Education

All the educational activities at the Colleges of Technology are based on the quality standards issued by the Oman Academic Accreditation Authority. Quality Assurance committees and Quality Department at the Ministry supervise quality assurance process in the Colleges of Technology. The Quality Department reviews self-assessment reports and conducts periodical monitoring visits to the Colleges. Furthermore, the DG of Technological Education supervises the establishment and development of systems and policies for the practical educational systems and their related activities. (Educational Council, 2016)

Table 1. Accredited specializations delivered at the colleges of technology

No.	Specializations	No.	Specializations
Engineering Program			
1	Architecture	9	Civil Engineering
2	Computer Engineering	10	Electronics & Telecommunications Engineering*
3	Industrial Engineering**	11	Chemical Engineering
4	Electrical Engineering	12	Mechanical Engineering
5	Mechatronics Engineering	13	Engineering Drawing (Draftsman)
6	Land Surveying	14	Quantity Surveying
7	Oil & Gas Engineering	15	Refrigeration and Air Conditioning
8	Biomedical Engineering	16	Aircraft Engineering**
Information Technology programs			
17	Information Systems	21	Information Security
18	Software Development	22	Networking
19	Software Engineering	23	Multimedia**
20	Database Systems		
Business Studies Programs			
24	Office Management	28	Human Resources Management
25	Marketing	29	E-Business Administration
26	Accounting	30	Certified Accounting Technicians
27	Legal Insurance Qualifications**		
Applied Sciences Programs			
31	Applied Biology	34	School Laboratories*
32	Environmental Sciences	35	Occupational Health and Safety **
33	Applied Chemistry	36	Industrial Hygiene**
Other Programs			
37	Assistant Pharmacy	39	Fashion Design
38	Photography		

* Discontinued Approved specializations.

** Undelivered Approved specializations.

Source: Educational Council (2016): Technical and Vocational Education in the Sultanate of Oman. Oman: Diwan of Royal Court, D.G of Telecommunication and Information System. www.educouncil.gov.om. Accessed on May 02, 2022.

Figure 2. Teaching, training, and transition between the levels of the technological education programs
Source: *Educational Council (2016): Technical and Vocational Education in the Sultanate of Oman. Oman: Diwan of Royal Court, D.G of Telecommunication and Information System. www.educouncil.gov.om. Accessed on May 02, 2022.*

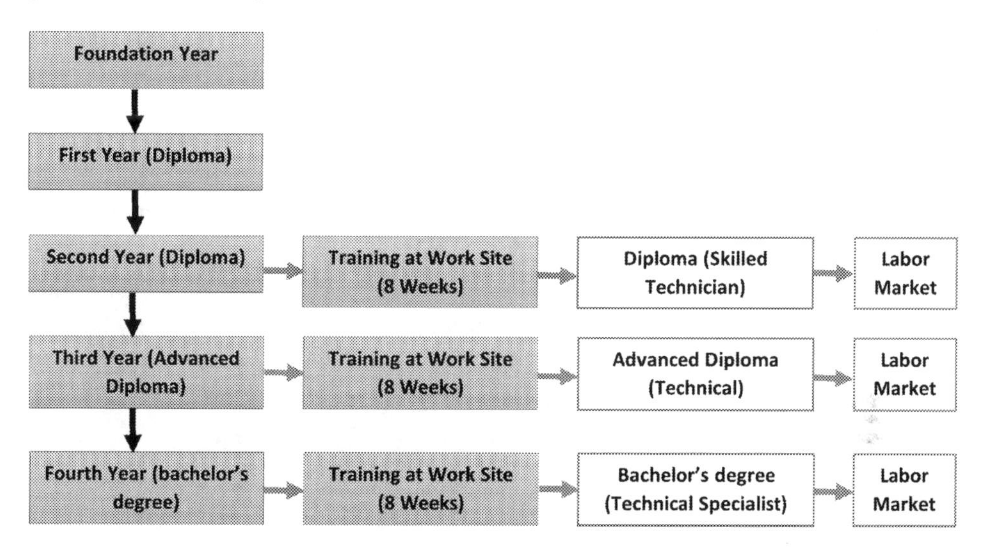

Figure 3. Students distribution among technical programs
Source: *Designated by the Authors.*

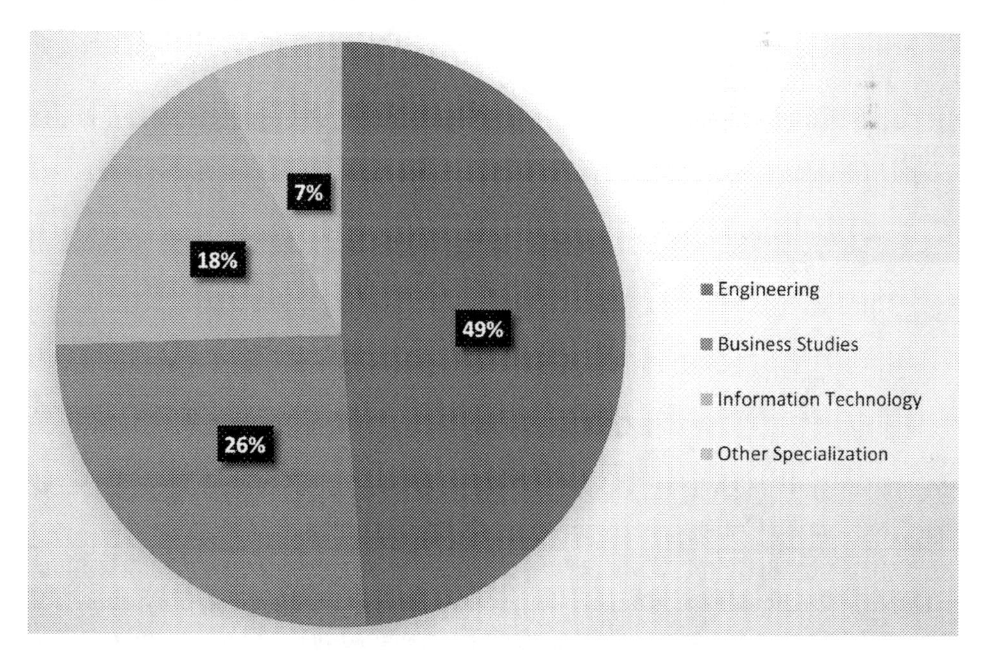

2.3.5 Student Participation in the Educational Process, Support for Innovation and Entrepreneurship

The Colleges of Technology engage students in educational and knowledge development process through listening and addressing their concerns, grievances, opinions, provide communication channels to encourage research projects and innovations. The students participation and involvement is made possible through the ***Student Councils*** (activated in 2011, to help students in education, training and services, communicating with administration and officials in colleges as well as the Ministry, organizing co-curricular activities and programs); ***Annual Student Gathering:*** (aim to develop creativity, innovation and entrepreneurship, competitive spirit, entertainment and cultural activities); ***Student Applied Research Projects*** (aims to conduct different innovative entrepreneurial projects, experiments and research projects in association with the Research Council and other research institutions); ***Student Participation and Achievements in Competitions*** (national, region and international competitions, international Contests and challenges)

2.4 Vocational Education

2.4.1 Background

As stated above, the vocational education in Oman was under the governance of the Ministry of Manpower and subsequently in 2020 transferred to the Ministry of Higher Education, Research, and Innovation.

Vocational training centers attract the school leavers and prepare them in the following ways:

- First year: Limited skills
- Second year: Skilled
- Third year: Craftsman

From September 2012, Vocational Training Centers started offering the Post-secondary Vocational Diploma which consists of a one-year foundation program and a two-year diploma program. Some students that successfully complete the Vocational Diploma may be allowed, depending on their performance, to continue their study at the Colleges of Technology at Bachelor Level.

As indicated in figure (1), there are two types of vocational education and training in Oman: government vocational colleges and private institution. The government of Oman seeks to ensure the good quality of vocational education and training system and pursues to implant competitive concepts and business entrepreneurship to achieve strategic goals that have been planned for a period of ten years (2016-2025).

Since the significance of vocational education and training is shown in most of the countries through the high percentages of the public education students, who have been enrolled and trained in vocational institutions. According to the Educational Council (2016), the followings represent the strategic objectives of the vocational education and training in Oman:

- Increasing the number of enrolled students in vocational education and training for the skilled labor market.
- leading and supervising human resources to the vocational education and training sector in modern ways.
- Provide all the required resources to the trainers, employees, and as per modern technical requirements of the worksites.
- Developing vocational education curriculum aligned with the labor market.
- Developing vocational education and training courses and qualifications according to national, regional, and international standards.
- Assuring the quality of the vocational education and training colleges according to the national and international standards.
- Executing financial and environmentally sustainable practices of the vocational education and training.

2.4.2 Government Vocational Education and Training System

TVET colleges are considered highly important for building and improving the skills of the Omani citizen to fulfill UNSDGs and Oman Vision 2040. Vocational training can facilitate the growth levels by creating opportunities for employment and entrepreneurship. According to Edcuational Council (2016), Vocational education and training programs are provided through three certificates offered by the government vocational colleges:

- *Vocational Diploma Certificate:* obtained by the student after completing all the necessary prerequisites of the Vocational Diploma program.
- *Certificate of Professional Competence:* awarded to those trainees who fulfills the requirements of the apprenticeship pathway.
- *Training Course Certificate:* awarded to those students who join the following vocational training courses:
    - Workers and employees' upgrading competence courses.
    - Job seekers, or those who seek to change their careers.
    - People with special needs.

- Local community development.

The governmental vocational colleges were established by the Ministerial decision (244/2015). As Shown by figure (4), there are different pathways of vocational education and training in the governmental vocational colleges to meet the requirements of Oman labor market. These pathways include: Vocational Diploma Pathway, Vocational Apprenticeship Pathway, and Training Course Pathway. Graduates of the vocational diploma can peruse their studies in technological colleges in certain specializations of technological education according to specific standards. (Educational Council, 2016)

a) Vocational Diploma Pathway

Graduates with vocational education diploma study for three years. Vocational diploma includes a constituent program/curriculum in English, Physics, Chemistry, Mathematics and six academic semesters on vocational programs/curriculum. The student obtains a Vocational Diploma Certificate after the successful completion of three years. Vocational Diploma Certificate is equal to the Technological Diploma Certificate, according to the Civil Service Council decree number (1/2015). It allows the graduates to join the labor market in their specialization and gives them the opportunity to continue their high technological education.

b) Vocational Apprenticeship Pathway

Vocational apprenticeship pathway qualifies education system dropouts who are below 18 years of age and are job seekers to obtain a certificate of professional competence, with three levels (semi-skilled, skilled, and professional). This training is implemented in the two locations of:

- Government Vocational Colleges to acquire the basic vocational skills (practically and theoretically).
- Workplaces to acquire the advanced vocational skills required by the trainee after graduation and joining the labor market.

This pathway is applied based on a tripartite agreement between the Vocational College, workplace, and the trainee.

Figure 4. Vocational education and training pathways in government vocational colleges

Source: *Educational Council (2016): Technical and Vocational Education in the Sultanate of Oman. Oman: Diwan of Royal Court, D.G of Telecommunication and Information System. www.educouncil.gov.om. Accessed on May 02, 2022.*

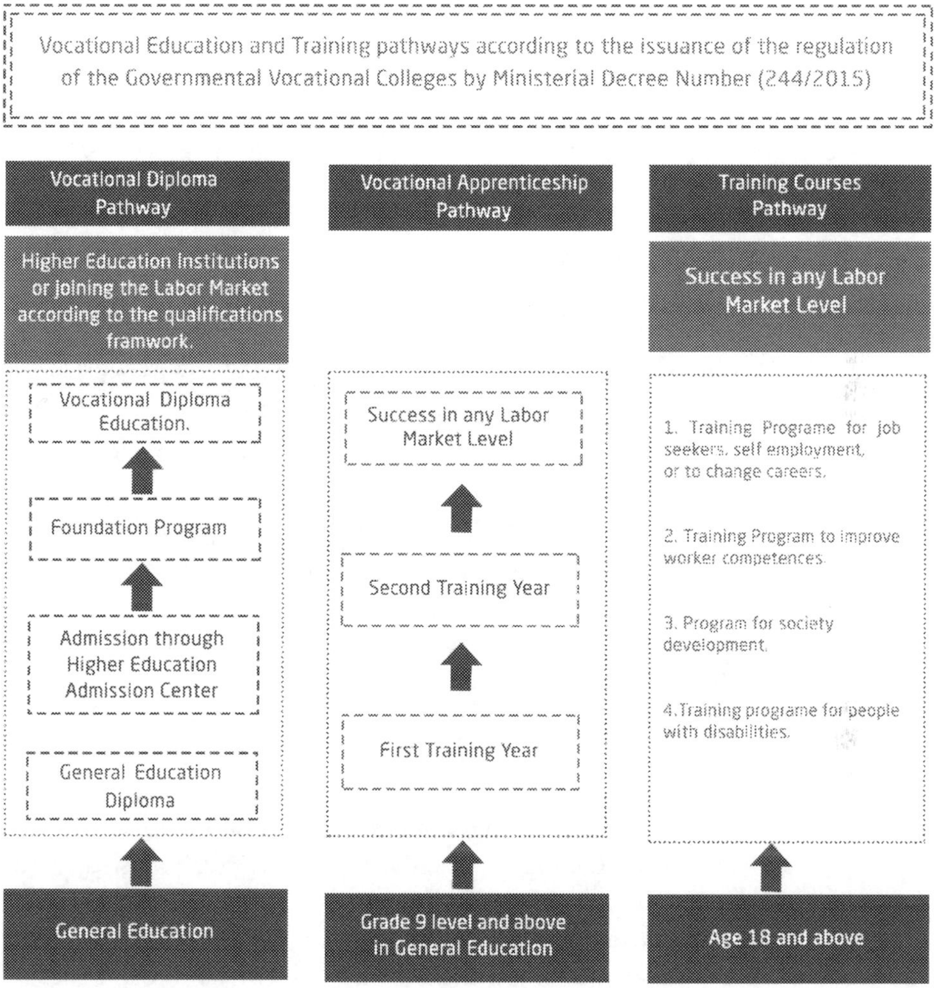

Vocational Education and Training pathways according to the issuance of the regulation of the Governmental Vocational Colleges by Ministerial Decree Number (244/2015)

Vocational Diploma Pathway

Higher Education Institutions or joining the Labor Market according to the qualifications framwork.

Vocational Diploma Education.

Foundation Program

Admission through Higher Education Admission Center

General Education Diploma

General Education

Vocational Apprenticeship Pathway

Success in any Labor Market Level

Second Training Year

First Training Year

Grade 9 level and above in General Education

Training Courses Pathway

Success in any Labor Market Level

1. Training Programe for job seekers, self employment, or to change careers.

2. Training Program to improve worker competences.

3. Program for society development.

4.Training programe for people with disabilities.

Age 18 and above

c) Vocational Training Courses Pathway

This pathway includes the following training programs:

- Competence Upgrading Programs: workers join this pathway to improve and enhance their skills. This training is part of the lifetime learning policy adopted by the Ministry.

- Local Community Development Programs: Citizens are enrolled regardless of their age and gender to be qualified with vocational skills they may need in their homes and workplaces such as, simple electrical wiring, plumbing, painting walls and doors, sewing, embroidery, etc. This training is part of the Ministry's Education for All Policy.
- Training Programs for the Rehabilitation of the Disabled: This training is a part of the Ministry's policy of non-discrimination and for those wishing to be enrolled in the sector of education and vocational training. These programs grant students with vocational Qualification of specific level and specialization.
- Training programs for job seekers and those who are willing to change their careers or start their own projects are implemented within the framework of the lifetime learning policy and the encouragement of entrepreneurship. The term of the course must not be less than one week, and not exceeding nine months, according to the nature of the profession and the required level.

Programs and Specializations Offered by Governmental Vocational Colleges

As shown in Table (2) and table (3), there are several programs offered by the vocational colleges with different approved specializations and majors.

2.4.3 Vocational Education and Training in Private Training Institutions

Private Training Institutes can be categorized into four groups:

- *Private institutes (individuals / companies):* The premises set up for the purpose of vocational training, in accordance with the conditions stipulated in the bylaw of private training institutions.
- *Centers within private establishments:* The premises located within an establishment or a group of facilities to train employees through specific courses or training programs according to their needs.
- *Training services offices (individuals / companies):* They hold lectures, seminars, conferences and workshops, and work on refining and developing cognitive, mental, and informational skills. Such courses do not exceed 25 training hours, or one week in the maximum.
- *Training Units within private educational institutions:* Implementation of programs within the activities of private universities and colleges.

Table 2. Approved vocational diploma specializations

No.	Technical section	Specialization in Arabic Language
1	Electrical Engineering	Household Electrician
		Industrial Electrician
2	Electronics Engineering	Maintenance of Electronics
		Mechatronics
3	Air-conditioning & Refrigeration Engineering	Household Air-Conditioning
		Industrial air-conditioning
4	Automotive Technology Engineering	Automotive Maintenance Technology
		Automotive Painting
		Automotive Body Repair
5	Mechanical Engineering	Operation Mechanics
		Industrial Maintenance
6	Welding & Metal Fabrication Engineering	Welding & Metal Fabrication
7	Construction & Building Engineering	Steel Fitting & Shuttering Concretes
		Draftsmanship
		Design & Décor
		Building Management & Maintenance
		Painting & Décor
8	Woods Technology Engineering	Joinery
		Furniture and Design
		Upholstery
9	Agriculture Technology	Plant Production
		Food Processing Technology
10	Beauty & Care	Beauty Care& Hair Dressing
11	Business Studies	Specialized Sale & Marketing

Source: Educational Council (2016): Technical and Vocational Education in the Sultanate of Oman. Oman: Diwan of Royal Court, D.G of Telecommunication and Information System. www.educouncil.gov.om. Accessed on May 02, 2022.

Table 3. Fisheries specializations

No.	Technical section	Specialization in Arabic Language
1	Aquaculture	Fish Farming
2	Fisheries Development	Fisheries Extension and Quality Control
3	Ship Building & Repair	Ship Building & Repair Models
4	Navigation Technology & Fishing Gears	Skipper of Deep-Water fishing vessels
5	Fishing Engineering	Engineering of Deep-Water Fishing Vessels
		Engineering of Coastal Fishing Vessels

Source: Educational Council (2016): Technical and Vocational Education in the Sultanate of Oman. Oman: Diwan of Royal Court, D.G of Telecommunication and Information System. www.educouncil.gov.om. Accessed on May 02, 2022.

As Shown in figure (5), there are four licensing areas in the private vocational training institutions:

- *The commercial field:* The field of commercial and administrative activities and specialties, which includes administrative and financial sciences, information technology, language teaching and others.
- *Industrial field:* The field of industrial activities and specialties with practical training and auxiliary theoretical sciences, which include mechanics, blacksmithing, carpentry, electricity, construction, and others.
- *Craft field:* The field of activities and handicrafts, with manual, or cosmetic practice, which include tailoring, household economics, beautification, shaving, hospitality, and others.
- *Special programs field:* Activities and specialties of special nature, which require the supervision of official bodies in the Sultanate such as: areas of fisheries, livestock, veterinary assistance, meteorology, agricultural fields, medical assistance, legal fields, and others.

Figure 5. Licensing areas of vocational education in the private institutions
Source: *Educational Council (2016): Technical and Vocational Education in the Sultanate of Oman. Oman: Diwan of Royal Court, D.G of Telecommunication and Information System. www.educouncil.gov.om. Accessed on May 02, 2022.*

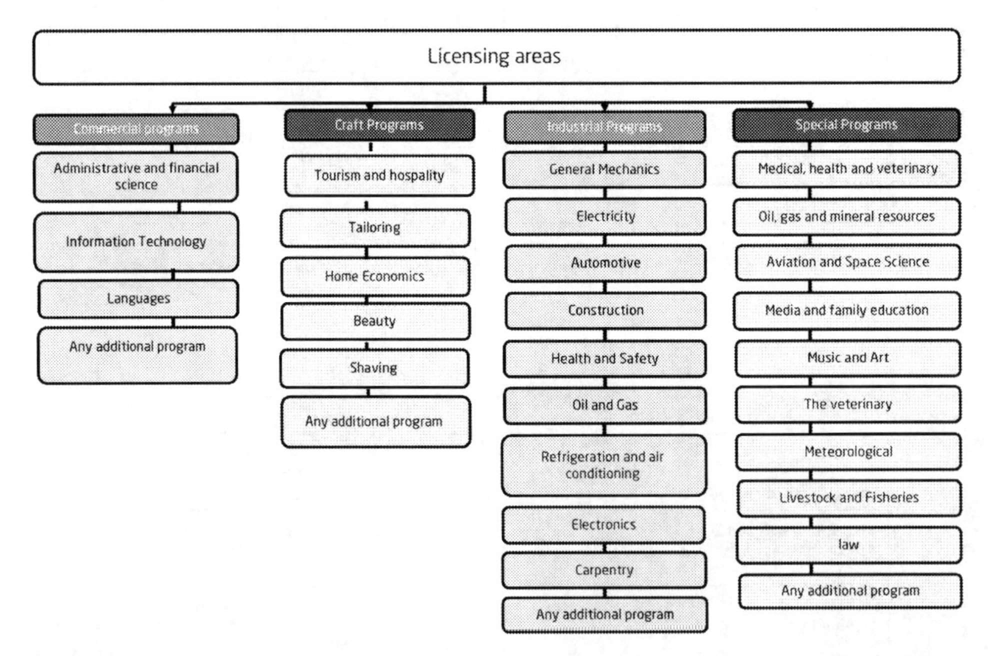

Licensing Stages of Private Training Institutions

The association with the Ministry of Commerce and Industry to render licensing applications of private training institutions began on 31/12/2017, to carry out the following:

- Investors shall apply for a training license to the Ministry of Commerce and Industry (invest easy portal).The application is dispatched to the Ministry of Manpower to undergo the stages of checking the documents submitted, and then after a satisfactory audit visit, it is finally approved by the Ministry of Manpower.
- The private training institution will start the implementation of the training activity after the approval of its administrative and training staff, the certification of training activities, in accordance with the following mechanisms:
    - The mechanism of accreditation of the administrative and training staff: The administrative and training staff shall be accredited in accordance with the regulations mentioned in the bylaw of the private training institutions.
    - Program Accreditation Mechanism: Programs shall be approved in accordance with the applicable regulations by specialties and after meeting all program requirements.
- Upon completion, the training certificates are approved, provided that the trainees are registered in the system so that the competent officer can match the name of the trainee from the ID card and training certificate with the electronic system.

As indicated in table (4), there are many licenses offered to the private vocational and training institutions. Approval issued by the government, to ensure that a private training institution is eligible to organize and implement vocational training courses, or programs, or training services in a specific field, in a certain Governorate or area.

Supervision and field follow-up of training activities implemented in private training institutions:

Technical supervision and training quality assurance are carried out by the Ministry of manpower to ensure the proper implementation of training activities, through various field visits. There are different types of field visits to private training institutions:

- *Licensing visit:* It is paid to grant a license to a new private training institution
- *Evaluation and Follow-up visits:* Shall be paid on regular basis to private training institutions, in accordance with a program prepared in advance to evaluate and follow up the private training institution, in terms of management documents, material and human resources, training plan, curricula, tests and evaluation.
- *Counseling visits:* Such visits are paid at the request of the private training institution for the purpose of guidance.
- *Classification visits:* The purpose of these visits is to determine the classification category of the private training institution. In this regards, the private training institutions can be classified into four classes as follow:
    - ***First Class:*** privileges for the implementation of international training programs and opening branches and/or special programs.
    - ***Second Class:*** privileges for the implementation of opening branches and/or special programs.
    - ***Third Class:*** Privileges for the implementation of general programs.
    - ***Fourth Class:*** this class shall be reclassified after six months from the date of the first classification, and its license shall be revoked if it receives the same class.

The classification process is carried out through careful evaluation according to the classification form prepared by the Directorate for this purpose, as follows:

- The administrative documents
- Human resources
- Financial resources
- Vocational guidance
- Training plan curricula and programs
- The exams and general assessment

Table 4. Types of licenses for private vocational education

License name	License code	Legal form of commercial registration	Description	Commercial activity	Commercial activity code
Private vocational training center, within establishments	LD-578	Company	The premises inside an establishment or a series of establishments set for the training of employees through certain training courses, or programs.	Vocational training centers	852202
Private Vocational Training Institute (Private Programs)	LD-574	Individual firm	Activities and specializations of a special nature, which require supervision from official authorities in the Sultanate, such as fisheries, livestock, assisting veterinary, meteorology, agricultural, assisting medical and legal. fields… etc	Vocational and administrative training institutes	854907
	LD-575	company		Music Education Institutes	854201
Private Vocational Training Institute (Commercial)	LD-570	Individual firm	Commercial and administrative activities and specializations, including the administrative and financial sciences, information technology and language teaching.... etc	Vocational and administrative training institutes	854907
	LD-571	company		Language and Computer Education Institutes	854902
Private Vocational Training Institute (crafts)	LD-572	Individual firm	Crafts activities and specializations featuring a manual or cosmetics practice, such as tailoring, household economics, cosmetics, haircutting, hospitality...etc	Vocational and administrative training institutes	854907
	LD-573	company			
Private Vocational Training Institute (Industrial)	LD-567	Individual firm	Industrial activities and specializations which include practical training and assisting theoretical sciences such as mechanics, blacksmithing, carpentry, electricity, construction… etc.	Vocational and administrative training institutes	854907
	LD-569	company			
Training Services Offices	LD-577	company	Seminars, conferences, and workshops, which do not exceed 25 training hours	Training services	854905
	LD-576	Individual firm			
A training unit in private educational institutions	LD-579	company	The premises at private higher educational institutions for practicing training works	Training services	854905

To review the conditions of establishing a private training institute, please refer to the license simulator at the Invest Easy Portal on: www.business.gov.om.

2.5 Occupational Standards and Testing Center

2.5.1 Background

As per the Government's Instructions work has commenced to draft a set of occupational standards for a number of vocations, which are prioritized in the vocational training programs. This was carried out through coordination with a global think tank (The German International Cooperation Agency, GIZ) from 2005 until 2011(The consultancy period) to design the structural hierarchy of the center and identify its requirements for human resources. In 2011, the ministerial order no. (76/2011) was issued, stipulating the establishment of the occupational standards and tests center to be in charge of developing the occupational standards system for all vocations across the different skill levels. It also plans and manages the vocational competency tests system, vocational and technical training programs and curricula and trains the participants using advanced scientific methods. This center serve as a reference for the development process of governmental and private sectors as well as for education and training institutions, it was affiliated directly under the Ministry's undersecretary for Technological Education and Vocational Training. (The Educational Council, 2016).The center is made up of six main departments:

- Advanced occupational standards department.
- Testing and diploma department.
- Trainee counseling and guidance department.
- Vocational and industrial relation department
- Labor market and training research department.
- Finance and administrative affairs department.

2.5.2 Requirements of Occupational standards Development:

The Vocational training and education system in Oman, sought to produce a competent and highly skilled national workforce for the labour market in line with country's education system. This system aims to equip the labour force with the necessary technical skills and knowledge via OJT. The persistent need for occupational, national standards can be explained by the following factors:

- The increasing complexity in the work environment.
- The rapid growth of all types of economic activities, due to the information and technology revolution in the developed countries, which deeply rippled into the developing countries, reducing the information and skills acquired

by individuals acquire and the ongoing need for employee's development and progress in various vocational fields.

- The emergence of new vocations due to the rapid technological advancement.

2.5.3 Occupational Standards Concept and its Development Methodologies

The occupational standards, as agreed upon by most definitions, is

"An accurate and clear standard description of the competences (know-how, skills, trends, and behaviors) that the incumbent should have to skillfully fulfill the tasks with the results of the mastered performance being identified." (Educational Council, 2016)

As such, occupational standards represent the regulations that govern the preparation, employment, and movement processes of manpower, making them necessary. Sometimes, occupational standards are taken for job description. The latter, however, is only a component of the former, if not the main one. The job description is a detailed description of the tasks and duties that the incumbent should fulfill, listing the conditions necessary for the job, such as academic and professional qualifications and the vocational category and field. The occupational standards, however, present a wider description of the occupation, including the following elements (some change can be expected based on the methodology used to produce the standards):

- Duties and tasks of the occupation.
- The required competences, know-how, skills, trends, and behaviors.
- Implementation steps.
- Implementation tools and equipment.
- Relevant safety and security laws and regulations.
- Training methodology and standards (in some methodologies).

There are several methodologies to be adopted to develop the occupational standards. They differ in terms of work mechanisms and the goals to be attained by developing the standards in the concerned country, and as per the priorities identified by decision-makers. The most common and important methodologies are the following:

- Functional Analysis Methodology.
- Dacum Methodology

- Work Process Analysis

The last is the most recent and the one the Ministry of Manpower and the Occupational Standards and Testing Center adopted to develop 60 occupational standards for a number of vocations across the different skill levels. Further developed was a set of 10 tests, as seen in the table (5).

Table 5. Occupational standards and fields

Number	Vocational Field	Number of occupational standards	Number of occupational tests
1	IT services	3	-
2	Engineering drawing using computers	4	-
3	Travel and Tourism	2	-
4	Sales	3	-
5	Hospitality	4	2
6	Agriculture	4	-
7	Livestock	2	-
8	Media technology	4	-
9	Mechanical Services	5	2
10	Refrigerating and Air-Conditioning	3	2
11	Drivers	1	-
12	Vehicles	4	1
13	Electricity	3	2
14	Electronics	4	-
15	Carpentry	1	1
16	Constructions	7	-
17	Fisheries	3	-
18	Sewing	3	-
Total		**60**	**10**

Source: Educational Council (2016): Technical and Vocational Education in the Sultanate of Oman. Oman: Diwan of Royal Court, D.G of Telecommunication and Information System. www.educouncil.gov.om. Accessed on May 02, 2022.

The occupational standards methodology has recently been updated to keep abreast of the requirements of the current phase. The Center has developed a new set of occupational standards for the oil and gas sector in cooperation with the Oman Petroleum Services society (OPAL). In this context, several technical workshops were organized with the participation of more than 165 experts concerned and more than 30 business sites of several companies for have been visited for the same purpose. Occupational standards have been developed for seven professional fields:

- Welding and manufacturing.
- Occupational Safety and Health.
- Lift and unload operations.
- Engineering maintenance and installation of electrical and mechanical equipment.
- Maintenance of buildings and facilities.
- Engineering of mechanical industries.
- Specialization management of engineering clients.
- Drilling and excavation.

Coordination is underway with other sectors to develop occupational standards such as the automotive sector represented by the National College of Automotive Technology and the Logistics Sector represented by the ASYAD Group.

3. TOURISM EDUCATION AND TVET SYSTEM IN OMAN

As indicated in the previous sections, tourism higher education is one of the academic areas which is included under the TVET system in Oman.

Under the umbrella of the University of Technology and Applied Sciences (UTAS), a new bachelor's degree program named as "Tourism and Hospitality Management" will be offered in the academic year 2022/2023. This program aims to provide nationally and internationally recognized qualification in Tourism & Hospitality Management and equip students with the knowledge, real-life experiences, and skills to enable them for successful careers in tourism and hospitality.

The aim of tourism and hospitality management program is to provide recognized qualification in tourism and hospitality management, equip students with knowledge, real life experiences and skills to enable them for successful careers in tourism and hospitality industry, and make a positive contribution to society by demonstrating a high level of proficiency in their specialization area. The program assists students in acquiring knowledge and linking tourism studies to relevant subjects such as marketing, finance, hospitality services, service management, product development, ticketing, airline operations, airport operations, tour guiding, statistics and economics of tourism, tourism development and sustainability, entrepreneurship, and human resource management. The program qualifies graduates for positions in private and public tourism organizations, both nationally and internationally.

The objectives of tourism and hospitality management program include:

- Equip students with knowledge and real-life perspective, experiences, Tourism & hospitality skills, practical competencies, managerial and leading capabilities, and developing their analytical thinking, interpersonal skills, and communication skills.
- Qualify students for employment in various tourism and hospitality enterprises in entry-level supervisory and management positions at the national and international levels.
- Train and educate students on areas of the tourism and hospitality industry such as customer services, tour guiding, hotel operations, events, and general functional areas of management.

The Tourism and Hospitality Management program is designated to enable students to:

- Demonstrate an understanding of the knowledge, concepts, theories, and principles of the tourism and hospitality industry.
- Apply knowledge in dealing with the management, planning and policymaking, operations, marketing and sustainability of tourism and hospitality products, services, attractions, destinations, tourism enterprises and events.
- Exhibit an understanding of the functions, management and operation of airlines, tour guiding, airports, tour operators, hotels, resorts, recreation facilities, events, and food and beverage departments.
- Adapt modern technologies relevant to the tourism and hospitality industry.
- Establish critical thinking skills and academic skills and knowledge for lifelong learning for a successful career in the tourism and hospitality industry.
- Implement creative thinking skills to develop rational practical solutions to problems in the workplace.
- Develop scientific research to provide solutions to problems relevant to the tourism and hospitality industry.
- Obtain interpersonal, intercultural, and cross-cultural communication competencies and work effectivity as an individual and in multidisciplinary teams.
- Think, act, and lead professionally and ethically in diverse work settings and environments.
- Apply entrepreneurial skills and lead business enterprises effectively and successfully.

As per the Tourism and Hospitality Management study plan, there are three levels od study: Diploma for those students who can complete the first two years, Advanced Diploma for one year after diploma for those students who get GPA 2.5 or more in the first and second years, and bachelor's degree for one year after advanced diploma for those students who get GPA 2.75 or more in the third year.

As per indicated in table (6), diploma program is composed from 20 courses with 60 credit hours, advanced diploma is composed from 30 courses with 90 hours, and bachelor's degree is composed from 42 courses with 126 hours.

Table 6. Structure of tourism and hospitality management program

Programs	University Requirements	College Requirements	Major Requirements	Total
Diploma in Tourism and Hospitality Management	12 Credit Hrs. (4 Courses)	27 Credit Hrs. (9 Courses)	21 Credit Hrs. (7 Courses)	60 Credit Hrs. (20 Courses)
Advanced Diploma in Tourism and Hospitality Management	15 Credit Hrs. (5 Courses)	30 Credit Hrs. (10 Courses)	45 Credit Hrs. (15 Courses)	90 Credit Hrs. (30 Courses)
Bachelor of Business Administration in Tourism and Hospitality Management	18 Credit Hrs. (6 Courses)	39 Credit Hrs. (13 Courses)	69 Credit Hrs. (23Courses)	126 Credit Hrs. (42 Courses)

Source: UTAS (2022). Tourism and Hospitality Management program Audit. Oman: University of Technology and Applied Sciences, Oman.

As indicated in table (7), the contact hours of tourism and hospitality programs are divided into theoretical contact hours and practical contact hours. The practical contact hours represent the higher portion (53.8% in average) in comparing with the theoretical portion (46.2% in average). In addition to the practical contact hours, work-based learning (WBL) experience is a basic component of tourism and hospitality management degrees. Student must pass the internship course before getting the diploma or advanced diploma or bachelor. Internship course is about spending eight weeks as work-based learning in one of the tourism and hospitality organizations as a fulfillment of graduation.

The graduation project (GPR) is another component for getting bachelor's degree. The graduation project is intended to develop research capability, to address specific real-life problems within various contexts of tourism and hospitality industry. It develops and consolidates the ability to recognise the problem, undertake statistical analysis, evaluate, select and implement the appropriate course of action within the specified area of research. It further provides graduates with an opportunity to showcase their ability and skills to carry out highly independent research and prepares them to be employable graduates.

Table 7. Contact hours of tourism and hospitality management program

Programs	Theory Hours		Practical Hours		Total
	Number	Percent	Number	Percent	
Diploma in Tourism and Hospitality Management	38	46.3%	44	53.7%	82
Advanced Diploma in Tourism and Hospitality Management	58	47.5%	64	52.5%	122
Bachelor of Business Administration in Tourism and Hospitality Management	78	44.8%	96	55.2%	174

Source: UTAS (2022). Tourism and Hospitality Management program Audit. Oman: University of Technology and Applied Sciences, Oman.

In addition to offering diploma, advanced diploma and bachelor's degrees in tourism and hospitality management program, training courses in tourism and hospitality are provided by private training institutes under the craft program.

Students at UTAS conduct different research projects in tourism and hospitality field under the supervision of lecturers. These research projects are funded by the Research Council. These efforts of UTAS will not only encourage innovativeness, creativity, entrepreneurship development nut also quality training and education to help in the economic diversification of Oman. As Oman is bestowed with the plethora of attractive tourism attractions, therefore the above academic and training endeavors shall further strengthen the vocational training and education to contribute towards quality human resource development in tourism in Oman.

4. RECOMMENDATIONS AND FUTURE OUTLOOK

A variety of interdependent factors influence and shape the provision of TVET education and Work-Based Learning (WBL) experiences. These factors both facilitates as well as hinder the magnitude and take-up of TVET system locally and internationally. Therefore, there is a need for a range of aligned and interdependent initiatives. These factors involve:

- Types and quality governance, laws, rules and regulations.
- Social engagement of employers, workers unions, and professional bodies at local and regional, and national level.
- Types of SMEs and MSMEs in these countries.
- Financing provisions for example sharing of costs and access to reimbursement.
- The quality and type of TVET System and its alignment to the labour market.

- The cultural and belief system shaping the participation of stakeholders in the TVET system.

The Omani TVET system has been adapted to meet local needs and cultural sensitivities and economic challenges such as unemployment. The main focus is to ally the provision of TVET system with the present and emerging labour market. However, consistent with the concern to align educational experiences with job and occupational outcomes, the Government manage the system to ensure that work-based learning (WBL) experiences are relevant to educational outcomes and further facilitate in achieving UN SDGs and Vision 2040.

The key purpose of TVET system is to build the nation's human resource capacities to be more innovative and entrepreneurial. So, the legislative and administrative requirements for students to have access to and complete extensive periods of workplace experience relevant to their programs are implemented.

The development of TVET system in ensuring entrepreneurship in Oman is a major success. The vocational training system is now appealing a good number of students, as school graduates are now paying attention to technical education and making it as their preference amongst other HEIs in the country. Despite this success, below are some recommendations for improving the TVET system in Oman. The recommendations provided here arising from the synthesis and analysis of the research studies and associated documents issued by the UNESCO and Oman government:

- Developing legislative and institutional frameworks under which sustainable and quality TVET system can be developed and progressed with the help of various public and private sector stakeholder to support quality work-based learning.
- More motivations might be provided to attract more students in the vocational education track. One of the important suggestions in this regard is considering grade 9 as a qualification certificate and set admission criteria for joining the secondary stage. Only students with higher marks can join secondary education and the remaining students might be sent to the vocational education. Moreover, there is a need for restructuring the admission system in vocational education to accept students after grade 9, especially who cannot join the secondary education.
- Develop and implement country specific local systems and enablers such as sharing of costs, kinds, and duration of workplace learning, and how they can be supported by the stakeholders.
- The Government, HEIs and stakeholders should take necessary actions to augment the position and status of TVET system and the occupations it serves. This can be ensured by encouraging the view that OJTs and practical

skills and knowledge are legitimate, useful, and highly significant for various occupations.

- Audit the curriculum and regularly update it based on labor market's skills requirements. Additionally conduct research studies for improving the effectiveness and efficiency of the TVET system.
- Public and private sector's capacity should be developed to provide effective practical on job learning experiences to the students entering labor market. This can be ensured by providing support for practical learning and providing recognition to those who undertake this mission.
- Support and encourage to global work-based learning scheme through research and promotion, this would facilitate entrepreneurship, employment, creativity, and innovation among the participants.
- Accept and adopt the traditional model of apprenticeship within the TVET system.
- Align TVET provisions with employment and entrepreneurship opportunities through introducing employment-enhancing initiatives to TVET programs related to people's needs and needs of workplace employing them. This includes upgrading of teaching pedagogy, occupational relevance, and designing and implementing local enterprise development programs.
- Increase the Omanization ratio in technical and vocation careers. This may occur by encouraging Omanis to accept jobs and entrepreneur opportunities at vocational and technical levels and qualifying Omanis to work as academic and support staff in vocational and technical education using ambitious plans and proper budgeting.
- Build sustainable partnership among all the stakeholders locally, regionally, nationally and globally to secure alignments between models of practical work-based learning, developing skills for local enterprises, and strategies to promote engagement in TVET by all the stakeholders.
- Encourage engagement between TVET institutions and the labour market. Stronger links between TVET institutions and various enterprises, including SMEs and MSMEs can be encouraged to develop an understandings for symbiotic benefit for developing required KSAs and employment, and entrepreneurship in the Country.
- Make certain that the feedback covering all aspects of the trainees should be provided by the training providing companies to the TVET Institutes for further quality education development.
- Apply various strategies of both shorter-term and long-term to develop the industry and occupational expertise, and pedagogic skills of TVET resource persons, familiarize them to the current employment and entrepreneurship

practices. Ensure effective associations of various stakeholders to support TVET system.

- Support and connect with research and
- Evaluate TVET policies and practices at the national, regional, and local levels with the help of research and conducting critical appraisals of the socio-cultural and economic initiatives being conducted in other countries that might be applicable to Oman.

REFERENCES

Al-Ghassani, A. M. (2010). A case study of Oman. In M. Masri, M. Jemni, A. Al-Ghassani, & A. A. Badawi (Eds.), *Entrepreneurship Education in the Arab States* (pp. 47–72). UNESCO.

Al-Harthi, A. S. (2017). Understanding Entrepreneurship Through the Experiences of Omani Entrepreneurs: Implications for Entrepreneurship Education. *Journal of Developmental Entrepreneurship*, *22*(1), 1–20. doi:10.1142/S1084946717500017

Al-Mujaini, A. (2018). *An Investigation on Modules of Work-Based Learning (WBL) Programmes Implementation for Youth in Oman*. The UNESCO Regional Bureau for Education in the Arab States.

Brown, R. B. (2006). *Doing your dissertation in business and management: The reality of research and writing*. Sage Publications.

Cho, Y., & Honorati, M. (2014). Entrepreneurship programs in developing countries: A meta-regression analysis. *Labour Economics*, *28*, 110–130. doi:10.1016/j.labeco.2014.03.011

Educational Council. (2016). *Technical and Vocational Education in the Sultanate of Oman*. Diwan of Royal Court, D.G of Telecommunication and Information System. www.educouncil.gov.om

Maclean, R., & Pavlova, M. (2013). Vocationalization of secondary and higher education: pathways to the world of work. *Revisiting global trends in TVET: Reflections on theory and practice*, 40-85.

Martin, B. C., Mcnally, J. J., & Kay, M. J. (2013). Examining the formation of human capital in entrepreneurship: A metaanalysis of entrepreneurship education outcomes. *Journal of Business Venturing*, *28*(2), 211–224. doi:10.1016/j.jbusvent.2012.03.002

Ministry of Commerce and Investment. (2022). *License simulator*. Invest Easy Portal. www.business.gov.om/

Ministry of Higher Education. (2010). Colleges of Applied Sciences Bylaw. Ministerial Decision No. 13/2010, Ministry of Higher Education.

Ministry of Higher Education. (2021). *Student Guide for Joining Higher Education Institutions for the academic year 2020/2021*. Ministry of Higher Education, Research and Innovation.

Ministry of Manpower. (2004). Colleges of Technology Bylaws. Ministerial Decision No. 72/2004.

Ministry of Manpower. (2011). *Bylaws and Regulations of Private Vocational Training Institutes and Centers*. Ministry of Manpower.

Ministry of Manpower. (2011). *Overview of Vocational Training*. Ministry of Manpower.

Ministry of Manpower. (2012). Amendments of Colleges of Technology Bylaws. Ministerial Decision No. 17/2012.

Ministry of Manpower. (2019). *Vocational Education and Training Pathways*. Ministry of Manpower, General Directorate for Vocational Training. www.manpower.gov.om/

Pittaway, L., & Cope, J. (2007). Entrepreneurship Education a Systematic Review of the Evidence. *International Small Business Journal*, *25*(5), 479–510. doi:10.1177/0266242607080656

Ramdzan, A. S., Arasinah, K., & Zuraidah, Z. (2020). Entrepreneurship education: Unemployment issues, people's wellbeing, and entrepreneurial intentions among TVET graduates in Malaysia. *International Journal of Psychosocial Rehabilitation*, *23*(4), 953–965.

Royal Decree. (2007). Organizing Colleges of Applied Sciences. Royal Decree 62/2007.

Royal Decree. (2020a). *Amending the Name of the Ministry of Higher Education to the Ministry of Higher Education, Research, and Innovation, Determining Its Competences, and Adopting Its Organizational Structure*. Royal Decree 98/2020.

Royal Decree. (2020b). *Establishing the Ministry of Labor and Determining Its Competences and Adopting Its Organizational Structure*. Royal Decree 89/2020.

Royal Decree. (2020c). *Establishing the University of Technology and Applied Sciences*. Royal Decree 76/2020.

Shikalepo, E. E. (2019). Sustainability of entrepreneurship and innovation among TVET graduates in Namibia. *International Journal for Innovation Education and Research*, *7*(5), 133–145. doi:10.31686/ijier.vol7.iss5.1484

UNESCO. (2014). *Technical and Vocational Teachers and Trainers in the Arab Region: A Review of Policies and Practices on Continuous Professional Development*. The United Nations Educational, Scientific and Cultural Organization.

UNESCO. (2015). *Technical Vocational Education and Training*. Retrieved from http://www.unesco.org/new/en/newdelhi/areas-of-action/education/technical-vocational-education-and-training-tvet/

UNESCO. (2019). *Reviewing Work-Based Learning Programmes for Young People in the Arab Region: A Comparative and Longitudinal Analysis*. The UNESCO Regional Bureau for Education in the Arab States.

UNESCO. (2020). *UNESCO Recommendation concerning Technical and Vocational Education and Training (2015)*. The United Nations Educational, Scientific and Cultural Organization.

UNESCO-ILO. (2020). *Decent Work Country Programme Sultanate of Oman*. International Labor Organization, Regional Office for the Arab States. www.ilo.org/

UNESCO-UNEVOC. (2013). *World TVET Database Oman*. UNESCO-UNEVOC International Centre for Technical and Vocational Education and Training. www.unevoc.unesco.org/

UNESCO-UNEVOC. (2019). *Innovation in TVET.* The UNESCO-UNEVOC International Centre for Technical and Vocational Education and Training. www.unevoc.unesco.org/

UTAS. (2022). *Tourism and Hospitality Management program audit*. University of Technology and Applied Sciences. www.cas.edu.om/

Valerio, A., Parton, B., & Robb, A. (2014). *Entrepreneurship Education and Training Programs around the World: Dimensions for Success*. World Bank Publications. doi:10.1596/978-1-4648-0202-7

Verheul, I., Wennekers, S., Audretsch, D., & Thurik, R. (2001). An eclectic theory of entrepreneurship. *Tinbergen Institute Discussion Papers*.

ADDITIONAL READING

UNESCO. (2010). *Guidelines for TVET policy review*. United Nations Educational, Scientific and Cultural Organization.

UNESCO. (2015). *EFA Global Monitoring Report 2015: Education for All 2000–2015 – Achievements and Challenges*. United Nations Educational, Scientific and Cultural Organization.

KEY TERMS AND DEFINITIONS

Entrepreneur: Entrepreneurs are the risk bearers, innovators, self-reliant learners that set up their own enterprises to drive the society economically and socially by fulfilling its needs and requirements.

Entrepreneurship: Is the creative tendency to start small and medium businesses, startups, intrapreneurship, or social entrepreneurship by creating innovative products and services for the society to stimulate economic development.

Occupational Standards: These standards depict an occupational profile and defines the necessary knowledge, skills, and attitudes, required for successfully performing occupational duties and responsibilities.

Technological Education: Technology is the application of practical knowledge to manage materials and tools with the help of various scientific techniques. In technology education students are taught about the knowledge and practices pertaining to the technical information to enhance human skills and abilities.

Tourism: Definitions of tourism can be thought of as either demand-side definitions, or supply-side definitions. From demand-side point of view, UNWTO defined tourism as "the activities of persons travelling to and staying in places outside their usual environment for not more than one consecutive year for leisure, business, and other purposes' (WTO & UNSTAT, 1994). From Supply-side point of view, Leiper (1979) suggested that 'The tourist industry consists of all those firms, organizations and facilities which are intended to serve the specific needs and wants of tourists' (p. 400).

TVET: TVET is an abbreviation that stands for technical and vocational education and training. It is an education that in addition to the general education equip students with the required employment related technical and scientific knowledge and skills to become successful in the labour market.

Vocational Education: It is intended to prepare "work ready" graduates. It delivers practical and application-based education to develop relevant skills, knowledge, and abilities to successfully fulfil the labor market requirements.

Chapter 9
Entrepreneurship in Tourism Education:
The Case of Ethiopia and Kenya

Agnes D. Historia
Cavite State University, Philippines

Bonface O. Kihima
Technical University of Kenya, Kenya

Mohit Kukreti
https://orcid.org/0000-0003-0067-0103
University of Technology and Applied Sceinces, Oman

ABSTRACT

Hospitality and tourism requires varying degrees of skills that allow for quick entry into the workforce and business for trainees. It is one of the most diversified industries in the world because of the wide number of different occupations and professions involved in it. With increasing change in both the domestic as well as the global market, technology and customer expectations of the industry itself, the requirements of the hospitality and tourism have also undergone significant transformation. With these ever increasing changes in the industry, graduates are expected to possess more than just specialized knowledge and skills, but also the capacity to be proactive and to see and to respond to problems creatively and autonomously. This chapter critically looks at the place of entrepreneurship education within the hospitality and tourism programs in Ethiopia and Kenya. It adopts a qualitative study by way of unstructured interviews and secondary data analysis. It concludes by proposing various strategies to achieve this, notably an outcome-based system and industry-based learning models.

DOI: 10.4018/978-1-7998-9510-7.ch009

INTRODUCTION

Tourism as an economic sector has the potential for higher growth prospects worldwide through economic linkages and multiplier effects. International arrivals, grew exponentially to reach 1.5 billion in 2019 (UNWTO, 2020). According to UNWTO (2011), international tourist arrivals worldwide are expected to reach 1.8 billion by 2030. The growth trajectory of the industry has continued to stimulate Gross Domestic Product (GDP) for many economies with increased international trade; a boost in international investments; increased infrastructure development among others (World Bank, 2017). The contribution of direct employment in the tourism and travel industry is estimated to grow at an average of 1.9 percent per annum, compared to total employment growth of 1.2 percent each year and predicted to continue through to 2022 (WTTC, 2020).

Since the advent of the first inns and taverns in the 1700s, tourism has grown to the level and need for formal training (Qiu, Dooley & Xie, 2020). Being a highly labor-intensive sector, tourism depends on a well-trained workforce to deliver quality service to clients. With the modern-day client described as sophisticated, dynamic, and highly knowledgeable (Boniface, 2001), the advent of tourism education was to meet the demand for a qualified workforce. However, over the years, and in many countries, there is a lack of sufficient training capacity for the tourism industry (UNCTAD, 2011). In addition, the focus has been on employment rather than on entrepreneurship, leaving the core aspect of decision-making within the sector in the hands of non-professionals who dominate the sector as entrepreneurs and investors. This chapter calls for entrepreneurship education to be at the core of tourism programs.

Knowledge in entrepreneurship would enable tourism graduates to develop dynamism to serve the ever-changing tourism industry. For instance, in Uganda's Bigondi village, just like in many community-based tourism projects in Kenya, Lepp (2008) noted that despite the available opportunity to cater to the dining needs of the visitors, the residents did not make an effort to take advantage of the existing market. This is a typical example of a lack of entrepreneurial spirit in the sector. With entrepreneurship education, such scenarios could be replaced with a deliberate move of capitalizing on the existing opportunities for the betterment of the sector while appealing to the client (Kihima, 2015).

Over the years, the tourism industry has been characterized by fixation and refusal to change (Boniface, 2001), exemplified by lack of product diversification, dull and unappealing community-based tourism projects, lack of tangible innovation in the sector, and having same itineraries over the years (Kihima, 2014). The inertia exhibited in the sector may be attributed to a lack of entrepreneurship or initiative among the tourism graduates. In most cases, such graduates only fit into the existing structures and models as opposed to coming up with new paradigms that can modernize the sector. The modern-day client who is discerning and looking for in-depth exposure (World Bank, 2010), would adequately be served by a graduate who is entrepreneurial and innovative.

The dynamic nature of tourism is influenced by several change factors. Such include the dynamic human element, sophisticated nature of the client; technological and environmental concerns, and crises within the operating environment among others. This, therefore, calls for a transformative agenda to handle diverse and unexpected scenarios. An example would be the sharing economy platforms in the accommodation and transport sector that opens the traveler or visitor to numerous possibilities while away from home (OECD, 2016). Such dynamism is putting pressure on traditional tourism businesses, hence the need to innovate to maintain competitiveness. The modern challenges of the COVID-19 pandemic, also need to be catered for to understand the new consumer and innovatively meet the demand

Moreover, as the number of visitors continues to increase, so is the consciousness to preserve the environmental integrity of destinations and attractions. Without such consciousness, the influx creates distribution challenges where tourism activity is often concentrated in major attractions and ecologically vulnerable areas. Thus, new business models need to be developed to mitigate the impact of tourism and enable the long-term sustainability of destinations and businesses. For instance, Kihima (2014) noted that of the 52 national parks and reserves in Kenya, only 6 accounted for 70% of the total visitation. This is still true to date despite many years of tourism training in Kenya. Tourism programs, therefore, need to be re-tooled and aligned to innovative managerial and planning approaches for destinations and facilities to stay competitive (Buhalis & Costa, 2005). This could happen if training institutions go beyond teaching what only exists in the industry but also explore future scenarios concerning the sector while proposing potential areas of improvement.

Entrepreneurship in tourism education entails primarily creating a skill concerning the industry. It is about initiating an education program that is capable of making one practice the tourism trade in an independent manner. It involves creating a 'thinking doer' as well as a 'doing thinker' who can fit, blend, improve and innovate within the real world environment. This chapter, therefore, aims at discussing the place of entrepreneurship education within the tourism courses as well as identifying missing links in training.

THEORETICAL FRAMEWORK

Active engagement of students is at the core of course delivery. Such can be exhibited through case studies, site visits, solving real-life issues, and linkages with the industry through guest speakers among many other modes of delivery. According to Kearsley and Schneiderman (1998), the Engagement Theory is a framework for learning that states that students must be engaged significantly in learning activities. This theory emphasizes cooperative learning whereby learners draw support and learn from each other, communicate with others, and obtain help on tasks being undertaken. This enables them to help others solve problems and make progress together. Such cooperation and exchange can result in creative activities, and strengthen the continuation of study at the same time (Lu, 2019). This would then create a human capital pool of skilled people so that they can sustain professional and progressive behaviors.

Methods

This work was based on personal experiences and encounters as researchers, scholars, and tourism lecturers. It resulted from unstructured discussions with industry professionals and lecturers from across the training institutions. Such discussions centered on the role of entrepreneurship education in tourism schools. The respondents included hotel managers, tour consultants, government tourism officers, sites and monument curators, community project leaders, conservation managers, and tourism and entrepreneurship lecturers. Except for the tourism and entrepreneurship lecturers, the discussions took place mainly during the assessment of students on industry placement between 2016 and 2021.

Different visits were done randomly to different sites depending on the availability of a trainee on attachment and the allocation of the researchers to visit a particular organization. In total, 20 respondents participated in the study with each respondent session averaging one hour. The respondents involved individuals who have experienced lived and interacted with students in class and the working environment. This was done by obtaining information that helped describe the existing phenomena and thus allowed an in-depth investigation into the subject under study. This approach was considered appropriate as the selected subjects were deemed to be privy to information on tourism teaching.

As indicated by Mayaka and Prasad (2012), such an approach provides an important insight into the ongoing discourse in a non-intrusive, unrestricted environment. These authors note that 'such unsolicited views can be relied upon to make a substantive contribution to a subject matter (p. 1). Thus, this allowed the researchers to engage with the social world and to view it from the inside out to clearly understand it (Gray, 2004). The method included taking notes during such interactions and discussions, and comparing and contrasting them to get a common theme. Arguably, qualitative research has gained prominence as a mode of inquiry into social issues (Ospina & Parry, 2004). Such is grounded in the world of experience where conclusions in the social world are derived from other means than statistical analysis. This methodology tries to approach reality without preconceived ideas and pre-structured models and patterns (Sarantakos, 2013).

TOURISM ENTREPRENEURSHIP EDUCATION

The Case of Ethiopia

Tourism training in Ethiopia started in the 1960s with the establishment of The Hotel and Tourism Training Institute in 1961 with support from the Government of Israel. In 1969, the Catering & Tourism Training Center (CTTC) was also created to produce skilled manpower in the tourism industry in collaboration with the Israeli government. In 2003, former CTTI invigorated the need for education for a higher degree. It started with a Bachelor in Tourism Management in the Region of Amhara in 2003 in the province of Gondar. The former Gondar University (now called the University of Gondar or UoG).

TVET-System in Ethiopia is outcome-based. It benchmarks from the world of work in the delivery of tourism education. This ensures that learners acquire the necessary competencies (skills, knowledge, and attitude) required in the working place. Technical and Vocational Education and Training (TVET) in Ethiopia is offered by different providers at various qualification levels. On one hand, private and public TVET concentrate on producing professional middle-level technical graduates at the post-Grade 10 levels. On the other hand, the non-formal TVET programs offer employment-oriented TVET programs to various target groups, including school leavers, people in employment, school dropouts, and marginalized groups in the labor market.

The need to improve the TVET delivery system in line with the quality management system was conceptualized. This ensured that the TVET system was in line with international best practices. Such included the need to replace the current curriculum-centered approach and move toward an occupational standard-based system. The result was to create a competent, motivated, adaptable, and innovative workforce in Ethiopia. Public sector intervention is therefore necessary for defining what needs to be taught, to whom it should be taught, and who teaches it. Such interventions facilitate demand-driven, high-quality technical and vocational education and training, relevant to all sectors of the economy, at all levels, and to all people.

The Kenyan Context

The training in tourism courses in Kenya date 1964 when the then Kenya polytechnic now, Technical the University of Kenya established the department of Institutional

Management at the TVET level. Currently, several middle-level colleges offering tourism programs at artisan, certificate, and diploma levels with a clear progression path from certificate to post-graduate level operate in Kenya. Since the 1990s, Kenyan Universities began to offer tourism undergraduates. The tourism sector has now grown to a level of being a major revenue earner and a contributor to the country's GDP as well as employment (Rogerson & Rogerson, 2019). Currently, over 20 Universities offer academic programs in tourism with the face of tourism training being the Kenya Utalii College (KUC) which was established in 1975 and operates under the ministry in charge of tourism.

However, challenges still abound in the sector; notably a shortage of adequately trained and skilled staff suitable for the job market (Francis, Wamathai, Wandaka & Jilo, 2020). This, therefore, calls for strategic re-alignment and harmonization of tourism curriculum and standards to meet the expectations of the industry (Ndiuini & Baum, 2020). Another challenge has been matching training with the expectations of the employers in the industry (Kabii, Wamathai, John, & Jilo, 2019; Muge, Sempele, and Kiplagat, 2019), due to the development of training curricula by educators with minimal or no input from the practitioners.

DISCUSSIONS

Entrepreneurship in Tourism Education

Due to the multifaceted nature of tourism, its training requires varying degrees of skills that allow one to enter the workforce and business. It is one of the most diversified industries in the world because of the wide number of different occupations and professions involved. Due to the wide variety of programs taught at different academic levels, as well as its sector-specific focus, an agreement about the core tourism curriculum is far from having been reached. Zehrer & Mossenlechner (2008, p. 73) note that "...there appears to be a considerable gap between what educational institutions offer as management level tourism education and the needs that are expressed by the tourism industry". Consequently, soft competencies, such as communication skills, problem-solving abilities, and reasoning are often considered more essential than hard ones by companies (Sisson & Adams, 2013).

The lack of required skills is one major problem facing the industry (Ivkov, Simon, Tepavčević, and Stojković, 2020). In some cases, a mismatch of employee skills and tasks given causes dissatisfaction. Moreover, working within the tourism industry typically requires professionals to work in a fast-paced environment that deals with people daily. In essence, the industry requires excellent customer service skills (Weber, Lee & Crawford, 2020), where the employee not only understands the customer's needs but is also able to deliver a positive customer service experience at all times. A good understanding of business and what drives business success is a great advantage for people working in the tourism industry.

For instance, Rohwerder (2020) decries the constant churning out of University graduates who do not fit in the job market since the skills they have do not match with the job market in Kenya. The fitting here is not just being able to work in the day-to-day operations but also being able to innovate, advise on the next steps in case of a crisis, offer a strategic direction to the sector, and being able to get involved in a pre-opening of a facility among other aspects. Training programs should therefore adequately prepare the workforce to meet not only the present but also future demands of the industry (Wanjiku, 2020).

With the dynamic nature of the industry (Boniface, 2001) the requirements of tourism have also undergone significant transformation (Griffin, 2020). It is recognized that as the growth of tourism increases, so will the increased demand for a qualified labor force (Wanjiku, 2020). However, although this growth prospect is envisioned to increase in the coming decade, the greatest concern continues to be that of the quality of human resources. These concerns are diverse, including inter alia: mismatched qualifications, lack of specialized skills, the weak link between the training providers and the skill users, and challenging work conditions characterized by low pay and high turnover (Yusof, et al 2020). According to Makumbirofa & Saayman (2018), these challenges have promoted poor services attributed to inadequate training and supply of skilled workers, especially in developing countries.

Entrepreneurial Skills Development

The growth of entrepreneurship education programs is evident in most higher education institutions worldwide (Goldin & Katz, 2009). Their integration into tourism studies is reinforced by the recognition that tourism is a business subject. Notably, tourism courses at the University level in the recent past have been housed in the schools of business with an emphasis on the business side of tourism. This however presents a challenge of finding a balance between the business side of tourism and the liberal thinking to promote deep learning of tourism as a subject (Jamal, Taillon, & Dredge, 2011).

Within tourism programs, there is a tendency to focus on one subject called 'tourism entrepreneurship' at the tail end of the studies while forgetting to inculcate entrepreneurial skills from the very beginning. More often than not, the output in such a course is a business plan that is often written with little or no guidance from the lecturer and is not even tested to find out its viability. In other words, the business idea is rarely implemented, making it a theoretical exercise. Consequently, aspects of creativity, innovation, and entrepreneurship are at the periphery of tourism teaching. For instance, Muge, Sempele, and Kiplagat (2019) found out that there was a disconnect between the curriculum and market needs due to the expenses involved. This is exemplified in many ways. Such include limited practical hours for Food production students, static menus presented over and over again in the hospitality training restaurants with a total lack of creativity; lack of adequate field trips among tourism students hence little or no exposure at the time of graduation.

Elsewhere at a policy level, relevant measures have been put in place to promote entrepreneurial skills, as well as enable direct investment in the creation of structures to support entrepreneurship education. For instance, in 2006, the recommendation of the European Parliament and the Council on key competencies for lifelong learning recognized a 'sense of initiative and entrepreneurship as one of the eight key competencies all individuals need for personal fulfillment and development, active citizenship, social inclusion, and employment. With this, an individual can turn ideas into actions, innovate, take risks as well as manage projects. The need to rethink tourism education blended with entrepreneurship is therefore necessary. This should go beyond the traditional and theoretical pedagogical forms of educational practice notably the 'education about entrepreneurship approach' (Pittaway & Edwards, 2012). Such an approach makes entrepreneurship education a mere academic exercise that gives little or no insights into the real world of entrepreneurship. More elaborate approaches can be put forward notably 'education for entrepreneurship's approach' and 'education through entrepreneurship approach. Such encourages pedagogy that is learner-centered, process-based, experiential, and socially situated (Gibb, 2003). It also allows the learner to have contact with real entrepreneurial experiences such as Industry based learning where the learner is attached to an institution for three months to gain hands-on experience.

In the case of tourism programs, Ahmad (2015) argues that currently the focus and process of education are too mechanistic and do not promote or encourage entrepreneurial behavior. Examples abound of tourism graduates who cannot sell a tour package to a client; pastry graduates who cannot start their cake-making business; even most University hospitality training restaurants do not break and no emphasis is placed on this aspect. This points to the lack of entrepreneurship in tourism training with tourism teaching being more of a classroom affair and theoretical. Most courses end at the 'knowing stage', how to do an itinerary, how to do reservations, ticketing, how to make a cake, food production, how to serve in the restaurant, etc. Little time is given to exposure through site visits and guest lectures hence limiting the business aspect of the program as well as the realities of entrepreneurship. Thus, the purpose of teaching entrepreneurship in tourism programs should be to give the students exposure, as well as to help the learners to discover the possibilities and various opportunities in the business world. Currently, in Kenya, few tourism graduates remain employed in tourism organizations and less than 5% become independent entrepreneurs within the sector.

Industry Exposure

According to Anderson & Sanga (2019), there is a significant disparity between the tourism education provided by institutions and the skills required by the industry. It has not been easy for institutions to fit into the industry training needs (Ghani and Muhammad, 2019). This may be attributed to the fact that the training curriculum takes time to evolve. This has led to a disparity between tourism education given and skills sought. Despite this, it has not been easy for institutions to identify needs and requirements and the involvement of industry in curriculum design (Morozov and Morozova, 2020). One way to bridge this gap is through Work Integrated Learning (WIL) or Industry Based Learning. To be effective, these approaches require a properly structured program with clear learning outcomes and objectives from the training institution. The quality of placement, the range of opportunities would all play a significant role in maximizing the benefits. Evidence from the field reveals that this aspect has not been well taken care of. In most cases, the industry exposure is limited to 12 weeks for the entire four-year program. Moreover, the trainee may be given irrelevant tasks, not in line with the training and may also be given one repetitive task throughout the attachment period limiting learning. Unfortunately, much of this exposure during industry-based learning prepares one for the world of employment as opposed to entrepreneurship.

One notable concern is the lack of industry experience by the teaching staff (Dellova, 2019). This compromises the aspect of teaching for the real world. In some cases, there is a lack of properly qualified lecturers employed to present tourism courses at universities, technical colleges, and especially private colleges (Yusof et al, 2020). Moreover, unlike other professional fields like engineering, medicine, and law, more often than not most lecturers in tourism are not practitioners. This, therefore, limits the mentorship of graduates in the profession. The absence of a well-defined tourism professional body does not help matters either. Given these gaps, the involvement of industry practitioners as training resource persons at academic institutions would be of the essence. Institutions should also introduce an industry placement experience for the academic staff for a prescribed duration of time. To anchor students deeper into entrepreneurship, there is a need to prepare the students adequately for the industry by developing contacts in the industry (Najar and Bukhari, 2017). Also, there is a need for entrepreneurship lecturers to have some knowledge of the uniqueness of the tourism sector.

CONCLUSION

More reflections and analyses are required to get structured views from students, lecturers, and tourism practitioners. Future research should consider the collection of primary data and the application of relevant theories to discuss the subject at hand. Moreover, further research should be done to ascertain the effectiveness of tourism curricula in preparing the learner for entrepreneurship. Also, there would be a need to determine the hindrances of tourism graduates in starting their tourism enterprises. Due to the complexity and multiplicity of views needed to answer the research question at hand, this study was limited in that the researchers relied on their observations, experiences, and interactions with key actors

This chapter proposes a review of the delivery of tourism programs with a focus on entrepreneurship. It proposes among others 'Learning to be', which focuses on nurturing entrepreneurial attitudes and skills, through a project-based learning methodology (Daniel et al., 2017). In this program, tourism students are challenged to develop viable solutions to real-case problems as they are in real organizations. One such other method is Problem-Based Learning (PBL) which is a student-centered approach in which students work in groups to solve an open-ended problem (Heuchemer, Martins, Szczyrba, 2020). Industry-based learning is also another aspect practiced where it allows students to utilize key skills and knowledge in the academic environment while building professional networks and refining transferrable skills (Ilyas, Semiawan, 2017).

REFERENCES

Ahmad, S. (2015). Green Human Resource Management: Policies and Practices. *Cogent Business & Management*, *2*(1), 1–13. doi:10.1080/23311975.2015.1030817

Anderson, W., & Sanga, J. J. (2019). Academia–industry partnerships for hospitality and tourism education in Tanzania. *Journal of Hospitality & Tourism Education*, *31*(1), 34–48. doi:10.1080/10963758.2018.1480959

Bennett, D. (2019). Meeting society's expectations of graduates: Education for the public good. In *Education for Employability* (Vol. 1, pp. 35–48). Brill Sense.

Boniface, P. (2001). *Dynamic tourism, journeying with change*. Channel View Publications. doi:10.21832/9781873150368

Buhalis, D., & Costa, C. (Eds.). (2005). *Tourism Business Frontiers*. Butterworth Heinemann. https://goo.gl/uv1V6a

Daniel, D. A., Costa, R. A., Pita, M., & Costa, C. (2017). Tourism Education: What about entrepreneurial skills? *Journal of Hospitality and Tourism Management, 30*(March), 65–72. doi:10.1016/j.jhtm.2017.01.002

Dellova, R. I. (2019). Student Workplace Competency: Industry Outcomes-Based Assessment in Selected Higher Education Institutions Offering Tourism and Hospitality Courses. *APCoRE Journal of Proceedings.*

Francis, K., Wamathai, A., Wandaka, J. K., & Jilo, N. (2020). Analysis of the skills gap in the tourism and hospitality industry in Kenya. *Journal of Tourism Management Research, 7*(1), 42–51. doi:10.18488/journal.31.2020.71.42.51

Ghani, E. K., & Muhammad, K. (2019). Industry 4.0: Employers' Expectations of Accounting Graduates and Its Implications on Teaching and Learning Practices. *International Journal of Education and Practice, 7*(1), 19–29. doi:10.18488/journal.61.2019.71.19.29

Gibb, A. (2003). In Pursuit of a New 'Enterprise' and 'Entrepreneurship' Paradigm for Learning: Creative Destruction, New Values, New Ways of Doing Things and New Combinations of Knowledge. *International Journal of Management Reviews, 4*(3), 233–269. Advance online publication. doi:10.1111/1468-2370.00086

Goldin, C., & Katz, L. F. (2009). The Race Between Education and Technology. *The Journal of American History, 96*(1), 246. Advance online publication. doi:10.2307/27694819

Gray, E. G. (2004). *Doing research in the real world.* Sage Publications Inc.

Griffin, W. C. (2020). Hospitality faculty: Are we meeting the demands of industry? *Journal of Teaching in Travel & Tourism, 20*(4), 1–22. doi:10.1080/15313220.2020.1746225

Heuchemer, S., Martins, E., & Szczyrba, B. (2020). Problem-Based Learning at a "Learning University": A View from the Field. *The Interdisciplinary Journal of Problem-Based Learning, 14*(2). doi:10.14434/ijpbl.v14i2.28791

Ilyas, I. P., & Semiawan, T. (2017). Industrial-Based Learning (IBL): Promoting Excellent on Polytechnics and Vocational Higher Education. Academic Press.

Ivkov, M., Simon, V., Tepavčević, J., & Stojković, I. (2020). Expectations and satisfaction of hospitality students with employment in hospitality industry. *Turizam, 24*(2), 57–67. doi:10.5937/turizam24-24810

Jamal, T., Taillon, J., & Dredge, D. (2011). Sustainable tourism pedagogy and academic-community collaboration: A progressive service-learning approach. *Tourism and Hospitality Research, 11*(2), 133–147. doi:10.1057/thr.2011.3

Kabii, F., Wamathai, A., John, K. M., & Jilo, N. (2019). Analysis of the Skills Gap in Tourism and Hospitality Industry in Kenya. *Asean Journal on Hospitality and Tourism, 17*(2), 95–105. doi:10.5614/ajht.2019.17.2.3

Kearsley, G., & Shneiderman, B. (1998). Engagement Theory: A Framework for Technology-Based Teaching and Learning. *Journal of Educational Technology, 38*, 20-23.

Kihima, B. O. (2014). Unlocking the Kenyan tourism potential through park branding exercise. *Tourism Recreation Research, 39*(1), 51–64. doi:10.1080/02508281.2014.11081326

Kihima, B.O. (2015). Community and Tourism Entrepreneurship: Toward a Viable Community Based Tourism Initiatives in Kenya. *The East African Journal of Hospitality, Leisure and Tourism.*

Lepp, A. (2008). Tourism and dependency: An analysis of Bigondi village, Uganda. *Tourism Management, 29*(6), 1206–1214. doi:10.1016/j.tourman.2008.03.004

Lu, W. (2019, September). Exploration on the problems and deepening ways of International Exchange and Cooperation in Colleges and Universities. In *2019 3rd International Seminar on Education, Management and Social Sciences (ISEMSS 2019)*. Atlantis Press. 10.2991/isemss-19.2019.71

Makumbirofa, S., & Saayman, A. (2018). Forecasting demand for qualified labour in the South African hotel industry. *Journal of Economic and Financial Sciences, 11*(1). Advance online publication. doi:10.4102/jef.v11i1.189

Mayaka, M. A., & Prasad, H. (2012). Tourism in Kenya: An analysis of strategic issues and challenges. *Tourism Management Perspectives, 1*, 48–56. doi:10.1016/j.tmp.2011.12.008

Morozov, M., & Morozova, N. (2020, January). Innovative Staff Training Strategies for the Tourism and Hospitality Industry. In *5th International Conference on Economics, Management, Law and Education (EMLE 2019)* (pp. 393-396). Atlantis Press.

Muge, C. C., Sempele, C., & Kiplagat, H. (2019). The Impact of Curriculum Content on the Quality of Food and Beverage Training in Selected Technical and Vocational Education and Training Institutions in the Western Region, Kenya. *East African Journal of Education Studies, 1*(1), 28–32.

Najar, A. H., & Bukhari, S. A. M. (2017). Gap Analysis in Hospitality Education and Industrial Requirements. *International Journal of Engineering and Management Research, 7*(4), 170–173.

Ndiuini, A., & Baum, T. (2020). Underemployment and lived experiences of migrant workers in the hotel industry: Policy and industry implications. *Journal of Policy Research in Tourism, Leisure & Events*, 1–23.

OECD Publishing. (2016). OECD Tourism Trends and Policies 2016. OECD Publishing.

Ospina, S., & Parry, K. (2004). Qualitative research. In G. Goethals, G. Sorenson, & J. Burns (Eds.), *Encyclopedia of leadership* (pp. 1280–1285). SAGE Publications.

Pittaway, L., & Edwards, C. (2012). Assessment: Examining practice in entrepreneurship education. *Education and Training, 54*(8/9). doi:10.1108/00400911211274882

Pranila & Irin. (2010). *Technical and Vocational Education and Training in Ethiopia*. International Growth Center.

Qiu, S., Dooley, L. M., & Xie, L. (2020). How servant leadership and self-efficacy interact to affect service quality in the hospitality industry: A polynomial regression with response surface analysis. *Tourism Management, 78*, 104051. doi:10.1016/j.tourman.2019.104051

Rogerson, C. M., & Rogerson, J. M. (2019). How African is the African Journal of Hospitality Tourism and Leisure? An analysis of publishing trends for the period 2011-2018. *African Journal of Hospitality, Tourism and Leisure, 8*(2), 1–17.

Rohwerder, B. (2020). *Inclusion Works Kenya Situational Analysis June 2020 update*. Academic Press.

Sarantakos, S. (2013). *Social research* (4th ed.). Palgrave Macmillan. doi:10.1007/978-1-137-29247-6

Séraphin, H., Ambaye, M., Capatina, A., & Dosquet, F. (2018). DRA Model and Visual Online Learning Material in Tourism. *International Journal of Hospitality and Tourism Systems, 11*(1).

Sisson, L., & Adams, A. (2013). Essential Hospitality Management Competencies: The Importance of Soft Skills. *Journal of Hospitality & Tourism Education, 25*(3), 131–145. doi:10.1080/10963758.2013.826975

United Nations Conference on Trade and Development (UNCTAD). (2011). *Bilateral Investment Treaties: Kenya's Total number of Bilateral Investment Treaties 143. Concluded by 1 June 2011*. Retrieved 22.01.2011 from: http://archive.unctad.org/sections/dite_pcbb/docs/bits_kenya.pdf

UNWTO. (2011). *Tourism toward 2030, Global overview*. UNWTO.

UNWTO. (2020). *International Tourism Highlights, 2020 edition*. UNWTO.

Wanjiku, C. P. (2020). *Effects of Employee Behavioral Factors on HACCP System Practices in Four and Five Star Rated Hotels in Nairobi County, Kenya* (Unpublished Dissertation).

Weber, M. R., Lee, J., & Crawford, A. (2020). A suggested best practices for enhancing performance of soft skills with entry-level hospitality managers. *Anatolia*, *31*(1), 76–87. doi:10.1080/13032917.2019.1703770

World Bank. (2017). *World Development Report, Governance and the Law*. World Bank Group.

World Bank Group. (2010). *Kenya's tourism: polishing the jewel, Finance and Private Sector Development, Africa Region Summary Report, 2010*. Author.

World Travel and Tourism Council (WTTC). (2020). *Travel and Tourism, Global Economic Impact and Trends 2020*. WTTC.

Yusof, M. F. M., Wong, A., Ahmad, G., Aziz, R. C., & Hussain, K. (2020). Enhancing hospitality and tourism graduate employability through the 2u2i program. *Worldwide Hospitality and Tourism Themes*.

Zehrer, A., & Moessenlechner, C. (2008). Industry Relations and Curricula Design in Austrian Tourism Master Programs: A Comparative Analysis. *Journal of Teaching in Travel & Tourism*, *8*(1), 73–95. doi:10.1080/15313220802441992

ADDITIONAL READING

Tarekegne, W. M., & Gelaneh, A. H. (2019). The Integration of Entrepreneurship Education into Ethiopia Universities Formal Curriculum. *International Journal of Research in Business and Social Science*, *8*(2), 61–73.

KEY TERMS AND DEFINITIONS

Education: Is the process of facilitating learning and acquiring knowledge, skills, principles, ethics, beliefs, and attitudes. Educational methods include teaching, training, storytelling, discussion, and face-to-face research.

Entrepreneurship: Is an entrepreneurial process to discover/create a new method, idea, or product. It has the ability and skill to produce something as capital and risk take place.

Learning: Can be defined as a process where individuals receive stimuli and responses that lead to adaptation to the environment.

Skills: Are the capacity or ability of a person, meaning it is the things he can do because he is an expert and has enough knowledge about it.

Tourism: Refers to the act of traveling by a person, going to different places or regions of a country, it is to see the scenic environment, it is said that a person who traveled 50 miles or 80.5 kilometers away from his residence referred as a tourist as per World Tourism Organization.

Chapter 10
Rural Entrepreneurship Skill Development Through Regenerative Tourism in Channapatna, Karnataka

Ananya Mitra
Amity University, Kolkata, India

ABSTRACT

With the increasing popularity of the tourism industry, a significant rise and development of destination and managing crowds has always remained a challenge that contributed to global tourism costs rise and pressure on local resources. The concept of regenerative tourism focuses on promoting the concept of leaving behind something better than the present. Regenerative tourism supports the industry to be reborn and continuously renew itself avoiding human intervention. Regenerative tourism acknowledges co-existing natural and social environmental set-ups and is planned such that local land and people get back from whatever they have invested for tourism development. Channapatna, the toy town of Karnataka, may see a further glorious future if the concept of regenerative tourism can be applied in the region. The town lies in an already existing tourism circuit, and regenerative tourism would show new avenues of rural entrepreneurship opportunities. In lieu of this, the chapter discusses in detail the scope of skill development in the Channapatna region of Karnataka.

DOI: 10.4018/978-1-7998-9510-7.ch010

INTRODUCTION

In the southern part of Karnataka, around 54 kilometres from Bengaluru on the Bengaluru-Mysuru Highway lies Gombegala Ooru, the toy town popularly known as Channapatna. The toys bearing roots from the Tipu Sultan era are GI-tagged products that not only Karnataka, but the entire India boasts about (Economic Survey Of Karnataka, 2021). From traditional lacquer-coated dolls, horses, bangles to recently added versions like models of ISRO spacecraft the variety of the toys are huge and mind boggling. However, with lack of fresh wood supply, fund issues, steeply rising competition from factory made plastic toys and lack of alternative livelihood options have left the next generation in a dilemma whether to continue with the tradition of toy-making. Under such circumstances tourism opportunities in the region have shown a ray of hope.

Tourism is the most vibrant industry that has shown a growth pattern in most of the situations. The prime feature of the industry is that it can be developed in almost every corner of a nation, especially in a country like India that has an abundance of tourism resources. Trade in tourism services and tourism activities in general have the potential to become an engine for growth and economic development. Tourism can also be a driving force in efforts to combat poverty (ITB, 2016). Tourism is also being recognised as a source of employment. It is a highly labour-intensive industry offering employment to both the semi-skilled and the unskilled. Being a service industry, it creates employment opportunities for the local population. This aspect of provision of employment becomes more important in developing countries where the level of unemployment and under-employment tends to be high more so post pandemic era.

The major issue in skill development, up-skilling or re-skilling rural population lies in its heterogeneous nature with a labour force consisting of youth, women, school dropouts, disabled, minorities, and tribal groups (Regenerative Travel, 2020). The study aims to present regenerative tourism as a way even beyond sustainable tourism that facilitates skill ecosystems to be created and policies are put in place for linkages and achieving high employment potential in the Channapatna region.

Sustainable approaches of tourism development have been working relentlessly to develop local communities. Regenerative tourism shows a further step ahead. Various strategies for rural entrepreneurship skill development can be achieved using regenerative approaches of tourism. The Rural Entrepreneurship Skill Development through regenerative approaches of tourism mainly focused on clean energy solutions and other sustainable practices. This would help develop technical knowledge and entrepreneurial skills, for the local community to set up their own enterprise or earn a living thus improving their living standards.

BACKGROUND

To proceed with the research work it is of utmost importance that the terms that would be used repeatedly must be inferred properly to avoid any future confusion.

Figure 1. Regenerative tourism

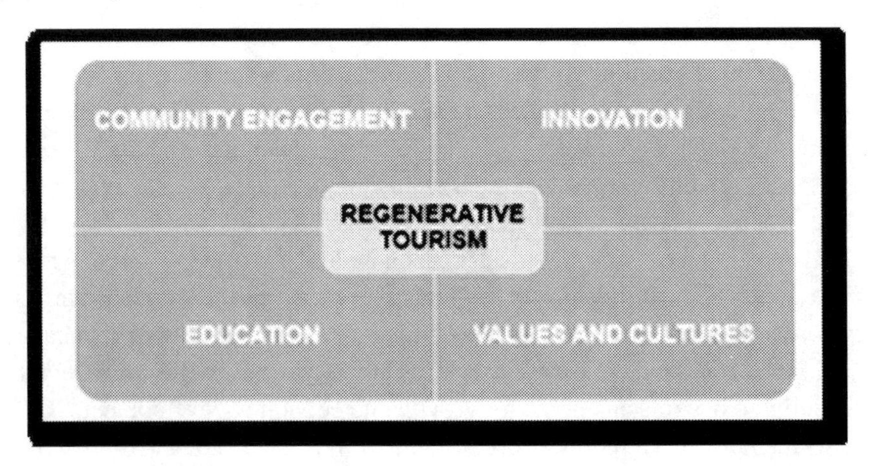

Regenerative tourism: Sustainable tourism in all good faith shows a bright future, but it yet to find solutions for many developmental hurdles. Also sometimes are overly idealistic. However, regenerative tourism is a better solution under such a scenario. It must not be undermined that the current generation must prosper so that they aspire for a prosperous future for the generations to come. One thing is absolutely clear is that development is necessary for overall growth and regenerative tourism neither aspires to slow down or stop development. On the contrary it looks out for options on how development can be done to revive the economy keeping a check on the costs paid for that and finding practical solutions for that. Regenerative tourism believes in revival, a continuous process, probably that's the key that both current and future generations need to be taught. Mother Nature has given us resources to be used. Currently people are overusing it, sustainable tourism recommends optimum use, however, regenerative tourism goes one step forward by recommending optimum use along with repayment to the local land and people for what has been taken from them.

As per the definition of Anna Pollock (2019) "*Regenerative tourism is not anti-growth*", as quoted in 2019, "*it simply asks that we grow the things that matter most to us in ways that benefit the entire system and never at the expense of others*". She further adds "*At its simplest, regeneration is about creating the fertile conditions conducive for life to thrive*". Regenerative businesses prosper by contributing to life-affirming prospects. Regenerative approach is more holistic that advocates welfare of the entire ecosystem including environment, community, culture, education, and innovation. Regeneration promotes human activities in which the population must live comfortably, create innovatively, support the dependent communities, and uphold the culture and value system. This is the only way true development would happen and our next generations would also be trained for paradigm shift in the understanding of development in its truest form.

Regenerative tourism has scope even beyond sustainable tourism: Sustainable tourism approach focuses on long term, ecologically bearable development that conserves resources. The following most important focus is preservation and promotion of the local culture and fostering the local society and their means. It also concentrates on generating employment and financial viability to the local economy. Thus, the local environment, society and its culture, and the indigenous economy act as the urgencies in sustainable development of tourism. The main idea of developing sustainable tourism is diminishing the negative tourism impacts and expanding the positive effects through tourism to the local society, environment, and the economy. All around the world, service providers of tourism and tourists themselves are becoming more and more conscious of sustainable tourism that not only ensures the lengthier life of the tourism product but also gains the local communities involved. The models of Reduce, Reuse and Recycle are extensively used. Sustainable tourism and its environmental, economic, and social benefits are well-known and required by tourists. Studies also disclose that tourists are willing to support the cause of sustainable tourism even if that entails shedding extra money from their wallet. Thus, sustainable tourism products, even at a greater price, are in excellent demand. It also suggests a conscious decision by tourists assuming sustainable tourism: they do it with a viewpoint of capitalizing on nature and society for generations to come.

The major aims of sustainable tourism are as follows:

1. Economic viability – Ensuring the competitiveness and viability of tourism destinations and businesses. This will help the tourism industry in long-term prosperity and supply of benefits.
2. Local prosperity – Maximising host destinations' economic prosperity through tourism contribution, including the locally retained share of visitor expenditure.
3. Employment quality – Strengthening the pay levels, service conditions and job availability without any caste, creed, or gender bias. Also consolidating the number and quality of jobs created or maintained by the local tourism industry.

4. Social equity – Seeking from tourism a fair and extensive distribution of social and economic benefits to the host community that includes improved opportunities for services and income available to locals, especially the poor.
5. Visitor fulfilment – Providing a fulfilling, safe and satisfying experience to all visitors, irrespective of their caste, creed or gender or any other discriminatory factors.
6. Local control – Engaging and involving the local stakeholders in crucial activities like planning, managing and decision making for the future prospects of the destination.
7. Community wellbeing – Sustaining and strengthening the elements determining the locals' quality of life; this mostly include amenities influencing life support systems, social structures, the right to resources and avoidance of all social degradation or manipulation.
8. Cultural richness – Respecting the authentic culture and traditions, historic heritage and uniqueness of the host communities.
9. Physical integrity – Maintaining and improving both urban and rural landscapes as well as avoiding the physical and visual degradation of the environment.
10. Biological diversity – Conserving wildlife as well as its habitats and other natural areas while simultaneously minimising damage to these.
11. Resource efficiency – Minimising the utilisation of rare and non-renewable resources for developing and operating facilities and services pertaining to tourism.
12. Environmental purity – Minimising tourism-generated waste disposal and tourism-related air, water, or land pollution.

The major aims of Regenerative tourism are as follows:

1. Custom tourism as a tool for the well-being of the locals through revitalization and sustainability, especially bringing in micro-scale initiatives rather than macro-scale regeneration plans.
2. Regenerative tourism focuses on giving back to the local land and the people. It contributes proactively to regeneration of communities and its cultures and heritage, of places and its landscapes and overall well being.
3. Regenerative approaches attempt to create positive outcomes and way forward for both cultural and natural resources and just not promote lesser damage.
4. Regenerative approaches focus beyond the sole motive of growth or profit but operationally accepts the existence of post-capitalism economies and markets.
5. Regenerative tourism chooses for holistic development over mere economic progress and thus advocates deconstructing the existing commercial practices in tourism with a more all-inclusive approach.

6. Regenerative tourism emphases on qualitative more than quantitative development thus, concentrations on overall development in place of growth of any destinations or a specific market alone.

Regenerative tourism approaches concentrate on inclusive community participation and advocates the fact locals would take pride and protect destinations if included and would protest and destroy if excluded. The essence of the destination that makes it a unique product in the market is the local historical background and community stories. This eventually nurtures a greater sense of community ownership and empowerment and leads to inclusive tourism practices.

Figure 2. Balance between Sustainable tourism & Regenerative tourism

RESEARCH METHODOLOGY

The study is done based on both primary and secondary research. In primary research, mostly observation methods have been adopted along with interviewing and interacting with the locals. In the secondary method various sources are being well reviewed to collect data. The following figure explains the methodology in detail.

Figure 3. Research Methodology

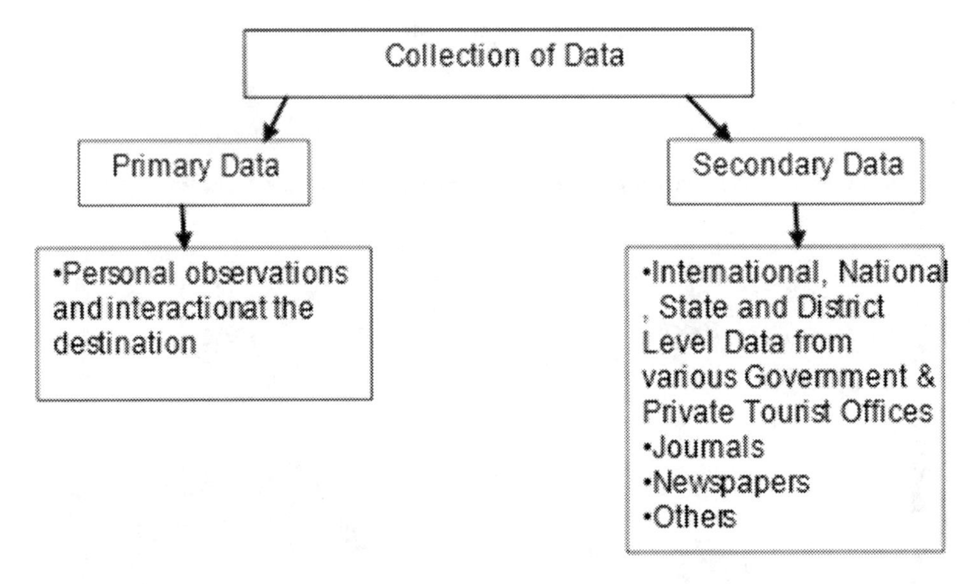

REVIEW OF LITERATURE

With increasing popularity of the tourism industry, mass-tourism propensity saw a significant rise and development of destination and managing crowd has always remained a challenge that even led to global rise in the tourism costs (Epler Wood et al., 2019). Tourism, depending on limited resources, has been an extractive economy. The tourism industry has almost no hurdle to the entry that competes on any product's cost, and the return reduces due to stiff competition and the seasonality factors (Pollock, 2019). However, the individual cost contribution of tourists' is difficult to ensure as the economic measure of destination health is based on an inadequate set of indicators (Epler Wood et al., 2019). With global tourism spread, accessing the negative tourism impacts, has taken a backseat. As per the UNWTO-UN Environment Report of 2019 only 11% of the governments have effectively implemented the sustainable tourism measures in their National Tourism Administrations.

Continuous transcending into a renewed form amidst dynamic life conditions is what marks the strength of regenerative conditions for life (Hutchins, 2019). Owen (2007) was the first to introduce the term 'regenerative' under a tourism framework. The concept of regenerative tourism works in the same principle where conditions are provided for the industry to reborn and continuously renew itself and transcend into a new form without much human intervention (Pollock, 2019). Regenerative tourism acknowledges the fact of co-existing natural and social environmental setups and is planned such that the local land and people get back from whatever they have invested for tourism development. However, this set up brings up a concern for the tourism industry as there is a caravan of allied industry that coexists along with tourism. The obvious hurdles that bring up worry lines on the forehead of tourism planners is the extent of human intervention, destination and service management challenges and the overall product development and their marketing and promotional strategies that by all probability would intrude on the natural recovery processes of tourism.

STATEMENT OF PROBLEM

A clear formula to a perfect regenerative tourism set up is to affirm that the tourism health is directly proportional to destination health which to a great extent is determined by the hospitable and tolerance level of the host community. De-growth can never be a route to development. Thus, the route to development must go through reviving resources, revitalizing the economy, and rejuvenation for the entire society.

The point that needs immediate unaltered attention is to see that the human resource involved in conducting and implementing the new practices for updated tourism practices must be unskilled and reskilled too (WTTC, 2016). Probably alone classroom teaching may not just do the trick. But the need of the hour is to affirm and confirm the fact that most of the industry and the allied industry would come together to do the needful. This would not only lead to brighter and much updated tourism services but also encompass the goals of inclusive tourism.

STUDY AREA: CHANNAPATNA, KARNATAKA

Channapatna, a small city located around 54 km south-west of Bengaluru on the Bengaluru-Mysore state highway in the district of Ramanagara. The city has a prominent Tamil influence pertaining to its proximity to the Tamil Nadu border.

The place is well-known for its wooden toys and crafts and lacquer ware. The place is famous for its picturesque surroundings, but it has become more renowned for its striking wooden toys and hence also entitled as ‘City of Toys’. There are several traditional as well as contemporary industries located here which manufacture and market these toys worldwide. Channapatna has brought together all sorts of ritualistic, ornamental, and utilitarian products that reflect both style and aesthetic value that the indigenous artisans of Karnataka can flaunt in the international market giving a tough competition to even the Chinese toy market.

Figure 4. Location Map

Channapatna, has made its own niche for the toy market in the global market. People across national and international borders flock to acquire handmade sustainably made wooden items. A major contribution of Channapatna to be able to curve out its niche is dependent on the artisans and the indigenous techniques used to make the products. The foundation of the wooden toys in Channapatna can be traced back to the sovereignty of Tipu Sultan (Ajith, C, 2017) . It is believed to have invited artisans from yesteryear Persia to train the native artisans in the manufacturing of wooden toys. For nearly two centuries ivory-wood was primarily used in the creation of these toys. However, sandalwood and rosewood were also intermittently used.

Later, a family of master-craftsman from Channapatna who lives in a small village called Muniyaponna Doddi, situated 80 km south-west of Bengaluru made the craft grow to the next level. They trained the local boys and eventually developed their indigenous workshop. In due course these successful toymakers upgraded to producing toys using lathe machines and reached out to the iconic Cauvery Arts Emporium on M.G road in Bengaluru city to buy their toys. This was the beginning of the large-scale production of toys that has made its presence in the global market currently. To estimate roughly 90% of the toys made by the artisans of Channapatna are procured online by multinational companies and are used as corporate gifting (Govt of Karnataka, 2022). The scope of the toy is not restricted to this.

Figure 5. Toys of Channapatna

With proper planning and promotion, the toy industry has much scope to grow beyond this and even develop various allied scope of business to develop. As of the statistics published by the Hindu as of 2020 almost 3000 families are involved in the toy making in Channapatna (Naseer. T, 2020). Developing regenerative tourism can help in process and even bring in the required attention and funding to the development of the art and the artisans. This attracts a substantial number of tourists to the destination that is quite a good number in comparison with the other districts. It can be noted that Ramanagara district attracts 2.39% of the total tourist arrivals in the state as per the district-wise tourist footfalls statistics of Karnataka in the year 2017 by the government sources (Channapatna City Municipal Council, 2021).

THE STAGES FOR DEVELOPING ENTREPRENEURSHIP SKILL THROUGH REGENERATIVE TOURISM IN CHANNAPATNA

There are basically three steps involved in the whole process of developing entrepreneurship skills in Channapatna – Exploration, Resolution and Application. Let's see the steps one by one.

1. **Exploration –** This step gives a reality check to the entire scenario. Before taking any step towards development, assessing the current scenario of the situation is absolutely mandatory. This exploration step exactly does the same. The long-drawn practices are recorded and then analysed to affirm the future steps to be taken. This is a very essential step as the success of the next steps of course much depends on the right analysis done in this step. With increased demand of child and eco-friendly toys in the global toy market, the craftsmen have to access scope to enhance production keeping the indigenous flavour intact.
    i. **Analysing available skill set –** Each place has a unique entrepreneurial pattern, and the skillset of the locals are developed accordingly (Skill Development and Training. n.d.). For instance, the skillset of the population of a place located near a river or a sea is very different from people living on a hill. The unique selling point of the Channapatna toys is its no-compromise with traditional methods of toy making in the region. Thus, the upskilling and reskilling process must adhere to the same. The next generations must focus more on packaging the products at international level with eco-friendly materials to enhance the attractiveness of the toys.
    ii. **Analysing the required skill set to establish rural tourism –** To establish rural tourism in core areas it is very important that the locals are involved. To involve the locals with the tourism industry, especially the rural ones, accessing their skillset is essential. This is to make the developmental process in tandem with the existing resources. The skillset of the locals is always as per the availability of the local resources, and very rarely exported from outside more so in case of the rural areas. Thus, the skill of the tourism industry and its stakeholders would lie in aligning these skill sets with the tourism ones so that the locals can be collaborated easily with the tourism industry with basic training. The nearby tourist

attractions like JANAPADA LOKA can be tagged in to pull more crowds to the destination.

iii. **Analysing the skill gap –** In majority of the cases the gap lies in making the collaboration between aligning the primary sector people with the tertiary sector skills. The major people in the rural areas depend on primary sector activities like farming, agriculture, fishing, and such others for their livelihood. To skill them up for a tertiary sector, that is for the service industry is where the challenge lies. Skilling is not the only challenge here; another major challenge lies in preparing the locals in accepting the importance and benefits that tourism would bring up in their basic livelihood and ensuring the fact that the ill-effects can be handled judiciously. As per the study the main attraction of the toys are its eco-friendly nature and kids-friendly design. But the improvement scope lies in packaging, promoting and in reachability of the product to the global market. The local crafts must actively take part in this otherwise the corporates would take out the entire benefit if involved directly. Thus, skilling the locals becomes mandatory.

2. **Resolution –** This is the most important of all the steps considering the fact all the decisions regarding developing the local skillset as per the industry standards so that both host and guest community can gain out of it, is to be decided in this stage. One thing must be concluded that the balance between these two can probably be brought in only through establishing regenerative tourism in the destination.

   i. **Deciding the right re-skilling/ up-skilling toolkit –** As discussed earlier in the chapter, the major hiccup in skilling the locals is to pull them out from an absolute primary sector mindset to a more service oriented tertiary sector behaviour. For instance, in Channapatna toy-making is the main livelihood and a major portion of the locals are involved in the same, they are already skilled in their business. Their main source of earning would be selling these toys in the nearby market. If regenerative tourism is developed in the area, the locals would earn from selling the toys, moreover, they can involve in taking the tourists on a tour to their extensive work-shops, briefing them about the nitty-gritties of the entire toy-making process and several other interesting trivia's, they can involve in giving their one extra room for a homestay, selling the organic colours or hand-made jewelleries or other essentials involved in making these toys to the tourists. Channapatna needs to have their own skilling toolkit based on the local requirements.

   ii. **Deciding specific action plan –** As seen in the above discussion, each place has its own entrepreneurship skills and thus unique entrepreneurship skill development strategies are required. Thus, one thing is very clear: such an action plan will be unique for each place and one overall plan may not work well for the purpose. In lieu of the above example of Channapatna and establishing tourism in the form of regenerative development once the probable tourism entrepreneurship scopes are established and skill gaps are understood, the next step is to decide an appropriate skill development plan to bridge the gap. The skill development action plan required in the current case is probably to establish language and communication training and train the locals on the basics of hospitality to start with.

iii. **Deciding the training authority –** Once the relevant training programs to be conducted are decided the next big step is to decide how these trainings are going to be conducted. In lieu of this deciding the training authority is very important. This is very vital as funds are needed for any training. As per the principles of regenerative tourism the industry must give back the locals and thus the industry and the business houses cannot deny their responsibility in training the locals and involve them actively. A major role also must be played by the local government authorities. Other people who may join hand for a greater success of the noble endeavour are the NGOs, the local universities, and institutes through projects like HUNR-SE-ROZGAR, the allied industries who would be benefitting with tourism development of the site or from some private business house through their CSR activities.

Figure 6. Developing Rural Entrepreneurship Skill through Regenerative Tourism

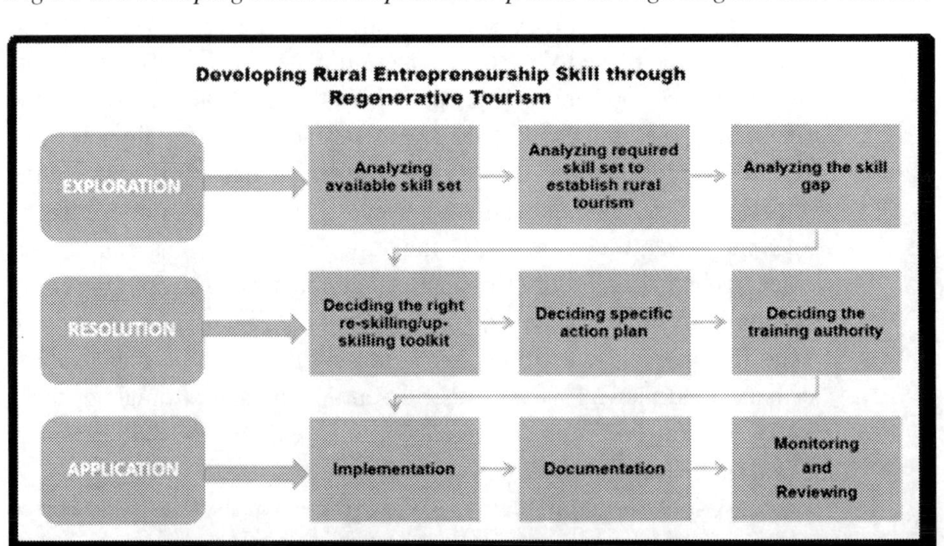

3. **Application –** The final stage is implementation of the customized plans and ensure its smooth running. Any endeavour however noble it might be duped if there is no proper implementation and monitoring. Thus, the final stage mostly concentrates on that.
    i. **Implementation –** The most important stage in any plan or project is the implementation. All hard-work and plan may go in vain once the implementation is not done correctly. As said planning virtually and doing it is a faraway process. Until a plan is being done in real the actual potential of the action plan cannot be assessed. Thus, the correct implementation, its time frame, the real-life acceptance of the plan by the people denotes the success of the plan. Channapatna has already got the limelight in the global market a proper plan implementation would help it establish a permanent market share in global toy market as well as pull in tourists through regenerative tourism.
    ii. **Documentation –** Documentation is sometimes a much-neglected step in plan implementation but is essential for future references, learning purposes, legal viewpoint and for any kind of further changes or developments in the action plan.
    iii. **Monitoring and Reviewing –** Once the action plan is implemented, the work does not end there. Following up with regular updates and comparing the statistics with expected results, taking feedback from both host and guest community, taking actions on problem areas and constant development is something that ensures the long run success of the action plan.

BENEFITS OF REGENERATIVE TOURISM IN UPGRADING SOCIO-ECONOMIC LIFESTYLE OF INDIGENOUS CRAFTSMEN IN CHANNAPATNA

A tool for the well-being of the locals: As of 2017, almost 72,000 people in Channapatna, were engaged directly and indirectly in the making of these toys. The Channapatna toys are completely locally handled from manufacturing, marketing to its export. The **GI certificate** granted by Geographical Indications Registry protects the handicraft from being exploited.

Focus on giving back to the local land and the people: According to the person in charge of research, quality and a few other functions at Maya Organic, a Bengaluru-based NGO that owns a factory in Channapatna, the demand has significantly gone up in the past few years till the pandemic could pull the brakes. A significant number of local and global customers prefer these toys over the China-made ones.

Maya Organic says exports mainly to the UK and other parts of Europe, however, is exploring the US market as well recently.

Promoting lesser damage: The biggest USP of the Channapatna toys is the fact that they are eco-friendly. The toys are made up of wood, coloured with vegetable colours and polished by blades of a particular locally grown grass. The factory set up is also in a home environment located mostly in the backyards or empty place in or near the houses of the artisans. The toy making practice does not generate any health issues for the artisans or environmental pollution. The toys are cent percent child friendly without any chemicals or sharp edges.

Focuses beyond the sole motive of growth or profit: The toy-making craft have scope beyond mere selling of the products.

Figure 7. Michele Obama in Channapatna
Source: Deccan Herald

The toys give opportunity to less educated locals to earn their living. The handicraft and its unique making process are recognized worldwide and make the presence of India felt in the global toy market. Success is more than just making toy. The actual accolade lies in certain distinctions pertaining to being eco-friendly, child-friendly, pollution-free and being home-grown. The simple instance that proves the fact is that the first Lady, Michelle Obama purchased the Channapatna toys during her visit to India (DHNS, 2010). The residents of Channapatna are cooperative in helping and guiding the tourists thus can be developed as professional guides.

Holistic development: The location of Channapatna on the Bengaluru- Mysuru highway gives the town the greatest physical integrity as the accessibility of the place plays a major role in attracting the tourists. The nearby destinations can also be connected and promoted as a tourism circuit. The sightseeing sites near Channapatna are Maloor Aprameya Swamy Temple, Kengal Anjaneya Swamy Temple, Kanva Maharshi Math, Brahmanya Theertha Brundavan, Kanva Reservoir, Bettada Timmappa, Igloor Barrage, Bevoor Mutt, Revana Siddeswara Betta, Kokkare Bellur bird sanctuary etc.

Emphases on qualitative more than quantitative development: Channapatna, a well-known name in the World Toy Market earned its name by upholding its unique manufacturing style. The artisans have earned international recognition, the demand has increased but the artisans have maintained their indigenous making process. From collection of the wood, its processing, making the organic colours to making the final saleable product the process is unaltered. The old legacy of Indian toy making has spread worldwide through the popularity of the Channapatna toys keeping the cultural heritage of toy making intact.

Community ownership and empowerment: The toy-making practice has been going on for more than 200 years now and is continued as an inherited art-form. Artisans involved are maintaining the tradition till today. However, they have upgraded the art keeping in pace with the modern toy-market demand but not compromising on the production method. Seemingly, they produce various mathematical games and puzzles that are sourced by big corporations to impart knowledge and education for the under privileged children of the evolving markets of the world.

Women empowerment: The women folk is closely related to the entire process of the toy making, particularly making the organic colours, painting the wooden products, application of lacquer, jewellery designing process. Active participation of women artisans including a large group of self-employed artisans. Introduction of electric lathe machines in the process has encouraged many more female artisans to join in.

CHALLENGES OF SKILL DEVELOPMENT IN CHANNAPATNA

Skill development is not an easy task, especially when it comes to a dynamic service industry like tourism. The major point of contention is that there are various layers of issues that may crop up. Skill development training usually includes training teamwork, responsibility sharing, developing self-initiative apart from improving their professional, soft and technical skills. But the hindrance on the way of setting up these skills lies in basically three factions. They are as follows –

Low quality education – Channapatna is a City Municipal Council city in Ramanagara district. Literacy rate of Channapatna city is 84.70 % as per the 2011 Census Report with male literacy around 88.13 % and female literacy rate around 81.28 %. The overall quality of tourism education has been not up to the standard to deal with the global market. As per popular belief a major reason for this is that the inception of tourism education has been under the umbrella of allied streams like history, commerce and event management. The major issue in such cases is that the curriculum is much influenced by the parent stream and various technical papers of tourism have been neglected. This was particularly the first generation of tourism education. Gradually as it was accepted as an individual full-fledged subject the scenario was altered. However, there are still major issues pertaining to the training where the majority of the courses emphasize theoretical learning over practical ones and lab work is rare. Industry interfaces of the students are very brief, and many institutes lack modern equipment. Most of the placement that the students at the institutes get are based on personal recommendations and no proper liaison between the institutes/ universities and the industry for placement usually exists. Moreover, promotion of the tourism courses at school level is rare and thus awareness of the scope of this course is very limited among parents and the wards. Therefore, the admission rate for the course has always suffered and even various institutes don't see this course as a profitable one to run. This also leads to low-paid tourism faculties thus compromising the overall tourism education system. This runs like a vicious circle of difficulties to grow the course. To highlight a basic issue, a student from Channapatna who would want a professional degree in Tourism would have to travel to either Bengaluru or Mysuru for the same.

Low employability – The tourism industry records a high number of non-formalized jobs. Also, usually there is a tendency of the industry to appoint non-tourism-trained people for administration and management level of jobs. Many times there are mismatches with industry requirements and newly passed-out candidates from the institutes and the universities. Thus, the employability quotient is under question many times. The career guidance facilities are very meagre in most of the cases. Tourism is such a vast industry, and the job opportunities are very high, but the problem occurs as the process of recruitment from either side is not streamlined and as mentioned earlier many allied courses candidates are selected for the tourism industry job openings (OECD, 2018). This mostly happens as there is low output of trained, employable candidates as compared to the industry requirements and there is no formal strong labour union to liaison the process. Another major issue is the employability quotient of the locals and the training required for them. The artists of Channapatna are trained by the Handicrafts Corporation and an amount of rupees one lakh loan is provided per artisans which includes 50 % subsidy, but that is not enough looking at the current demand.

Ineffective government policies – Low level involvement to skill up the tourism workforce may be considered the major issue of government policy implementation. Funding the local authorities (government/ private/ NGOs) to up-skill and re-skill the local workforce and provide funding for formal tourism courses may change the course of action of the entire industry. The government must compulsorily involve industry experts for tourism policy formulation, tourism education and tourism training processes. Government certification to all trained workforce through government initiatives can work out as a big motivation across.

Therefore, one thing is clearly projected that if the above three issues are well handled then the overall rural entrepreneurship skill development process especially through regenerative tourism can be well achieved.

PROMOTING FUTURE SCOPE OF RURAL ENTREPRENEURSHIP SKILL DEVELOPMENT IN CHANNAPATNA

Channapatna toys are confined only in a few states of South India- The toys of Channapatna are confined only to South Indian states but must be promoted in other parts of India. The handicrafts of India need to be highlighted among the people so that there is an increase in sales of the handicrafts. This would also give the toy artisans an extended job opportunity as trainers.

Channapatna toys must be kept in Duty free shops at the Indian International airports- The duty-free shops are prime locations where the tourist gets attracted. Most of the airports have international brands on display, so that the Government can initiate and display the handicrafts of Karnataka- Channapatna toys. This would give an enhanced scope to sell the indigenous products.

There must be a tie up with fashion houses to promote new fashionable wooden toys of Channapatna- The Channapatna handicrafts are focusing on making fashionable accessories for girls like wooden bangles, earrings etc. These fashionable articles can be sold at famous fashion houses to attract a greater number of girls.

Summer camps can be held for kids to create an awareness about the making of eco-friendly toys- The kids get attracted and love summer camps which can be one of the main promotional aspects. The kids can be shown and help make a toy of their choice and take it back home as a souvenir. By doing such activities the kids and their parents can focus on Channapatna toys.

Channapatna people should give importance to foreign tourists – The local people must focus and attract foreigners towards their handicrafts. The local toy making must be highlighted and make sure the foreign tourist purchases the toys. A potential foreign market opening can be noticed for the toys as Chinese toys lose their popularity.

The Tourism Ministry should pay more attention towards promoting the handicrafts in a large-scale basis- The tourism ministry must uplift the handicrafts of Karnataka and make necessary strategies to promote Channapatna toys globe wide (Ministry of MSME, 2016). The rich culture of handicraft making needs the extra effort of promotion so that each person of India and of the globe gets to know about the toys. The online buying of these toys has made it easier for the handicraft lovers to buy products and get it couriered to the desired destination. There are few leading online sites like firstcry.com, hoops.com and shopping.indiatimes.com. This indirectly promotes the products also.

There is a lot of scope of Resorts in the village which will increase the tourist inflow automatically- The village is a very quiet and calm place to live in. Resorts can have a lot of scope there. Resorts can focus on making toy making as a part of an activity to attract a lot of tourists. The tourists can stay back in Channapatna and witness the art and learn the making of art. The village stands on the Bengaluru – Mysuru highway that is a prime tourist spot. A new bypass road connecting Channapatna has made travel to the destination easier. Resorts can make a 1-day package tour and take them around the village and Mysuru for a visit.

The cultural triangle must be developed to preserve the heritages of Karnataka for the Future Generation- The cultural heritage near Channapatna is – Jananpadloka – Channapatna – Mysuru. These 3 places are a hot spot of culture and promote culture in their own ways. Jannapadloka is a place where folk dance is promoted and taught to people, Channapatna is a cultural place where handicrafts are promoted, Mysuru has been regarded as a cultural capital which has a rich background of history. A tourism hinterland may even be grown connecting the nearby mulberry gardens for sericulture near Ramanagara, the Silk City.

CONCLUSION

To sum up, the study extensively focusses on employability in rural areas and entrepreneurship being the most logical solution. To achieve this rural entrepreneurship skill development is a must. This has many faced benefits to develop the local economy, local livelihood, local living standards, scope of tourism, reduced tourist satisfaction gap and overall, a much-anticipated win-win situation for locals, government, and the industry as well. Regenerative tourism being a much progressive approach in comparison to sustainable tourism, is the most appropriate approach to achieve rural entrepreneurship skill development.

There are several issues in achieving the desired results. It has always been hard to fill up the vacancies that are more widespread in rural regions. The major reason behind this is because they lack the practical, technical, interpersonal skills that tourism employers need. This occurs as the rural areas fall short in retaining and attracting talent and providing education and training. Job providers have shown their displeasure in getting talents especially for management and leadership roles or mentoring and customer-oriented services. The tourism industry also faces difficulties to handle age and gender issues of the rural workforce because of demographic reasons.

Another major barrier in skill development particularly in the soft skills and the language training arises from non-availability of higher education. Other rural concerns include arranging for connectivity and logistics for smooth skill development processes and thereafter maintaining regular contact for any refresher programs if needed. Thus, the inception of regenerative tourism would give a fresh insight and opportunity for the locals to grow. It is believed that if tourism does not contribute to the local people, society, environment, and economy then it is exploitative in nature and cannot be considered as fair tourism. Regenerative tourism brings us back to our roots and eventually give an overall development. The case study on Channapatna is a pilot study how regenerative development can bring in success to various potential rural areas around India. Thus, skill development negating all odds and bringing up and promoting regenerative tourism becomes the need of the hour.

REFERENCES

Ajith, C. (2017, November 19). *This Karnataka village has been making wooden toys since Tipu Sultan's time.* https://scroll.in/article/858249/crafting-joy-this-karnataka-village-has-been-making-wooden-toys-since-tipu-sultans-time

Channapatna City Municipal Council. (2021). *City Population Census 2011-2021; Karnataka*. https://www.census2011.co.in/data/town/803239-channapatna-karnataka.html

DHNS. (2010). *Michelle spends $25 on Channapatna toys*. Deccan Herald. https://www.deccanherald.com/content/111225/michelle-spends-25-channapatna-toys.html

Economic Survey of Karnataka 2020-21. (2021). *Planning, Programme Monitoring and Statistics Department*. https://des.karnataka.gov.in/storage/pdf-files/CIS/Economic%20Survey%202020-21_Eng_Final_R.pdf

Epler Wood, M., Milstein, M., & Ahamed-Broadhurst, K. (2019). *Destinations at risk: the invisible burden of tourism*. The Travel Foundation.

Govt of Karnataka. (2022). *Tourists Foot Falls Karnataka*. https://karnataka.data.gov.in/catalog/tourists-footfalls-karnataka 3#web_catalog_tabs_block_10

Hutchins, G. (2019). *Regenerative leadership*. eBook Partnership.

ITB. (2016). *World Travel Trends Report 2016–2017*. Berlin: Messe Berlin.

Ministry of MSME. (2016). *District Industrial Profile of Ramanagara*. https://msmedibangalore.gov.in/files/Ramanagar.pdf

Naseer, T. (2020, May 8). *Channapatna toy makers have been hit badly by the lockdown*. The Hindu. https://www.thehindu.com/society/talk-of-the-toy-town-the-channapatna-artisans-are-in-dire-straits/article31533199.ece

OECD. (2018). *Organisation for Economic Co-operation and Development (OECD). Tourism Trends and Policies*. OECD.

Owen, C. (2007). *Regenerative tourism: a case study of the resort town Yulara*. Open House International.

Pollock, A. (2019). Flourishing beyond sustainability. *ETC Workshop in Krakow*.

Regenerative Travel. (2020). *Taking Regenerative Tourism to Scale - Everyone has a Role to Play*. https://www.regenerativetravel.com/impact/taking-regenerative-tourism-to-scale-everyone-has-a-role-to-play

Skill Development and Training. (n.d.). *NITI Aayog*. Retrieved October 20, 2021, Ch (5) from https://niti.gov.in/planningcommission.gov.in

WTTC (World Travel and Tourism Council). (2016). *Global Talent Trends and Issues for the Travel and Tourism Sector*. WTTC.

ADDITIONAL READING

Duxbury, N. (2021). (Re)articulating culture, tourism, community, and place: Closing remarks. In N. Duxbury (Ed.), *Cultural Sustainability, Tourism and Development: (Re)articulations in Tourism Contexts*. Routledge.

Higgins-Desbiolles, F., Carnicelli, S., Krolikowski, C., Wijesinghe, G., & Boluk, K. (2019). Degrowing tourism: Rethinking tourism. *Journal of Sustainable Tourism, 27*, 1926–1944.

Hoxie, C., Berkebile, R., & Todd, J. A. (2012). Stimulating regenerative development through community dialogue. *Building Research and Information, 40*, 65–80.

Mitra, A. (2018). *Steps towards Sustainable Tourism: Explore, Don't Exploit*. Cambridge Scholars Publishing.

KEY TERMS AND DEFINITIONS

Regenerative Tourism: Regenerative tourism is a sensitive and un-exploitative way to deal tourism resources so that the industry must pay back through contribution for the local economy and the population.

Reskill: Skilling the unemployed demography with some new type of training to provide employment.

Rural Development: Rural development is the upgradation process or endeavour through which the livelihood process, living standard, quality of living, economic standards of a rural area and its demography are improved.

Rural Entrepreneurship: Rural entrepreneurship is process of engaging the rural population for some remunerative or profit-oriented activity, business, or service. This in the long run works well to stop the rural-urban migration and unnecessary crowding and pressure on urban resources.

Skill Development: Skill development is the process of proving skill training appropriated through skill gap studies.

Sustainable Tourism: Sustainable tourism inducts the thought of optimum utilization of the available resources to ensure conservation of tourism resources for the future without compromising the current industry needs.

Upskill: Skilling the workforce with some new type of training or advanced version of the existing knowledge to upgrade the workforce and increase productivity.

APPENDIX

Figure 8. Conventional tourism v/s Sustainable tourism

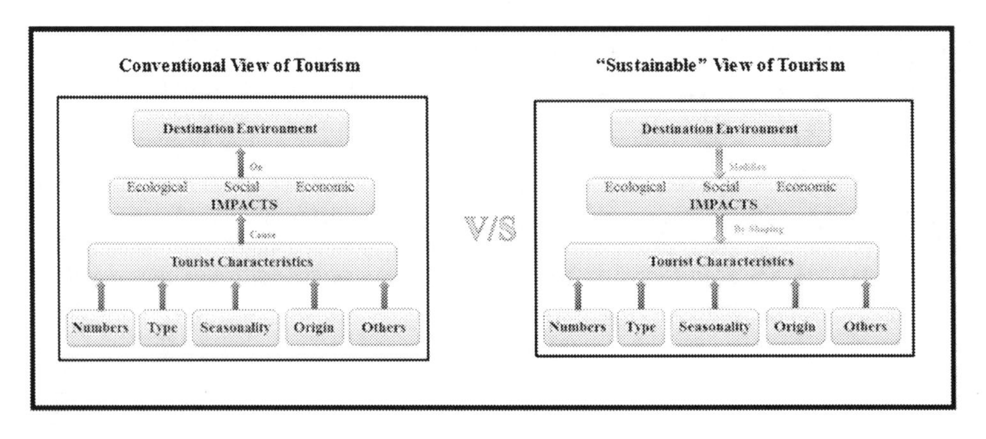

Figure 9. Sustainable tourism v/s Ecotourism

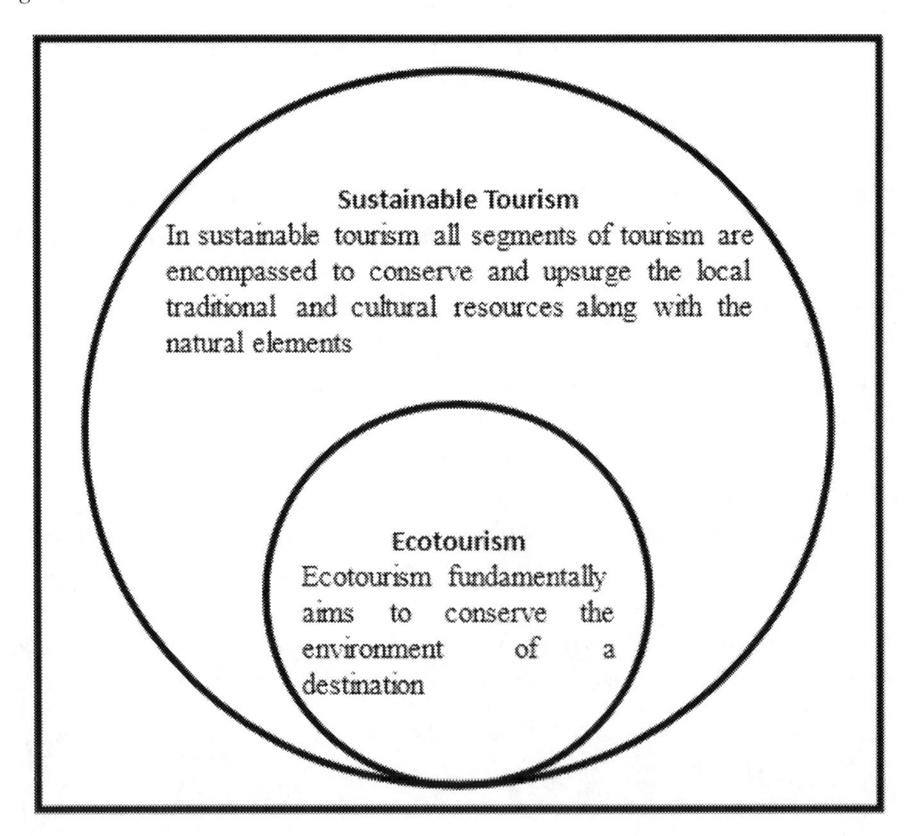

Figure 10. Sustainable tourism v/s Regenerative tourism

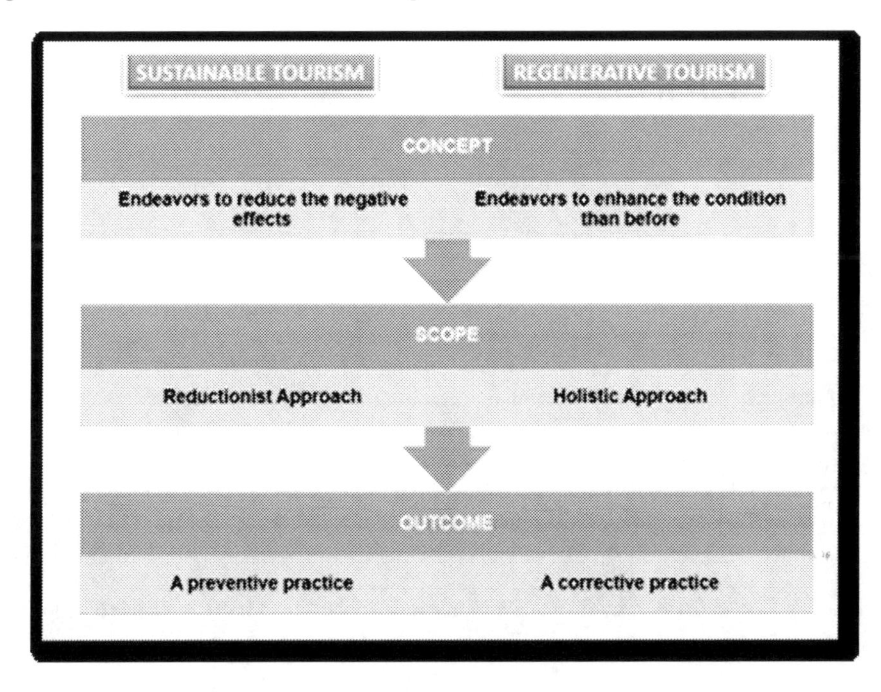

Compilation of References

Achchuthan, S., & Nimalathasan, B. (2020). scholars and undergraduates perspective regarding level of entrepreneurial intention of the management undergraduates in the university of Jaffna, Sri Lanka. *Academicia: An International Multidisciplinary Research Journal*, *10*(6), 1118. doi:10.5958/2249-7137.2020.00718.1

Acs, Z. J., Desai, S., & Hessels, J. (2008). Entrepreneurship, economic development and institutions. *Small Business Economics*, *31*(3), 219–234. doi:10.100711187-008-9135-9

Adamiak, C. (2019). Current state and development of Airbnb accommodation in 167 countries. *Current Issues in Tourism*. Retrieved from: http://urn.kb.se/resolve?urm=nbn:se=umu:diva-167097

Adewale, A. A. (2016). The task, challenges and strategies for the marketing of tourism and relaxation services in Nigeria. *International Journal of Marketing Practices*, *3*(1), 24–32.

Africa Ignite. (2020). *Tourism Development*. Retrieved from: https:www.africaingnite.co.za

Africa Ignite. (2021). *Contact Us*. Retrieved from: https://africaingnite/co.za

Afroz, A. (2018). Employees Aspiration Towards Skill Development in Uttarakhand: A Study of Needs and Findings. *OJAS, 13*.

Ahmad, N. H., Ramayah, T., Mahmud, I., Musa, M., & Anika, J. J. (2019). Entrepreneurship as a preferred career option. *Education + Training*, *61*(9), 1151–1169. doi:10.1108/ET-12-2018-0269

Ahmad, S. (2015). Green Human Resource Management: Policies and Practices. *Cogent Business & Management*, *2*(1), 1–13. doi:10.1080/23311975.2015.1030817

Ahmad, S. Z. (2015). Entrepreneurship education in tourism and hospitality programs. *Journal of Hospitality & Tourism Education*, *27*(1), 20–29. doi:10.1080/10963758.2014.998764

Ahmad, S. Z., Bakar, A. R. A., & Ahmad, N. (2018). An evaluation of teaching methods of entrepreneurship in hospitality and tourism programs. *International Journal of Management Education*, *16*(1), 14–25. doi:10.1016/j.ijme.2017.11.002

Ahrari-Roudi, M. (2018). Tourism potential and assessment of its environmental impact on the northern coasts of the Oman Sea, Iran. *Geotechnical Geology*, *14*(1), 131–141.

Airbnb. (2016a). *Airbnb Hosting Toolkit: Airbnb Africa Academy*. Retrieved from: https://www.airbnb.com

Airbnb. (2016b). *Overview of the Airbnb community in South Africa*. Retrieved from: https://www.airbnb.com

Airbnb. (2017). *Overview of the Airbnb Community in Africa*. Retrieved from: https://www.airbnb.com

Airbnb. (2019). *Africa!Ignite brings the Airbnb Africa Academy to Durban*. Retrieved from: https://www.airbnb.com

Airbnb. (2020). *Airbnb Academy Fund pays out R1 million to hosts in need in South Africa*. Retrieved from: https://www.airbnb.com

Airbnb. (2021). *The Airbnb Entrepreneurship Academy*. Retrieved from: https://www.airbnb.com

Airey, D. (2001). Education for hospitality. Search of Hospitality, 276–292. doi:10.1016/B978-0-7506-5431-9.50019-6

Airey, D. (2013). Forty years of tourism education and research. *Poznan University of Economics Review, 13*(4), 1-15.

Airey, D., & Tribe, J. (Eds.). (2006). *An international handbook of tourism education*. Routledge. doi:10.4324/9780080458687

Ajith, C. (2017, November 19). *This Karnataka village has been making wooden toys since Tipu Sultan's time*. https://scroll.in/article/858249/crafting-joy-this-karnataka-village-has-been-making-wooden-toys-since-tipu-sultans-time

Ajzen, I. (1987). Attitudes, traits, and actions: Dispositional prediction of behavior in personality and social psychology. *Advances in Experimental Social Psychology*, *20*, 1–63. doi:10.1016/S0065-2601(08)60411-6

Ajzen, I. (1991). The theory of planned behavior. *Organizational Behavior and Human Decision Processes*, *50*(2), 179–211. doi:10.1016/0749-5978(91)90020-T

Al Badi, O., & Khan, F. R. (2020). Examining Challenging Factors of Tourism Entrepreneurship in Oman using PLS-SEM. *International Journal of Research in Entrepreneurship & Business Studies*, *1*(1), 48–64. doi:10.47259/ijrebs.115

Al Buraiki, A., & Khan, F. R. (2018). Finance and technology: Key challenges faced by small and medium enterprises (SMEs) in Oman. *International Journal of Management, Innovation & Entrepreneurial Research*, 2395-7662.

Al Shabibi, I. (2020). *Planning for entrepreneurialism in a rentier state economy: Entrepreneurship education for economic diversification in Oman* [Unpublished Doctoral dissertation]. School of Social Sciences, Cardiff University, UK.

Al-Abri, S. S., Abdel-Hady, D. M., & Al-Abaidani, I. S. (2016). Knowledge, attitudes, and practices regarding travel health among Muscat International Airport travelers in Oman: Identifying the gaps and addressing the challenges. *Journal of Epidemiology and Global Health*, *6*(2), 67–75. doi:10.1016/j.jegh.2016.02.003 PMID:26948720

Alani, F., Khan, F. R., & Manuel, D. (2017). Need for professionalism and quality service of the Tourist Guides in Oman. *International Journal of Tourism & Hospitality Reviews*, *4*(1), 20–29. doi:10.18510/ijthr.2017.413

Al-Ghassani, A. M. (2010). A case study of Oman. In M. Masri, M. Jemni, A. Al-Ghassani, & A. A. Badawi (Eds.), *Entrepreneurship Education in the Arab States* (pp. 47–72). UNESCO.

Al-Harthi, A. S. A. (2017). Understanding entrepreneurship through the experiences of Omani entrepreneurs: Implications for entrepreneurship education. *Journal of Developmental Entrepreneurship*, *22*(01), 1750001. doi:10.1142/S1084946717500017

Al-Hasni, Z. S., & Afifi, G. M. (2021). *Local's Attitudes towards Tourism Development: The Case of Oman*. Academic Press.

Alhasni, Z. (2021). Tourism versus Sustainable Development Goals (SDG) Tourism–an element of economic growth of metropolitan cities, entrepreneurs. *Studies of Applied Economics*, *39*(4). Advance online publication. doi:10.25115/eea.v39i4.4587

Ali, Y., Nusair, M. M., Alani, F., Khan, F. R., & Al Badi, L. (2017). Employment in the private sector in Oman: Sector-based approach for localization. *Humanities & Social Sciences Reviews*, *5*(1), 1-20.

Al-Mujaini, A. (2018). *An Investigation on Modules of Work-Based Learning (WBL) Programmes Implementation for Youth in Oman*. The UNESCO Regional Bureau for Education in the Arab States.

Al-Muqbali, A. H. (2006). *Towards More Effective Administrative Training in the Omani Public Sector* [Unpublished Doctoral Dissertation]. School of Education, The University of Manchester (United Kingdom).

Alrawadieh, Z., Karayilan, E., & Cetin, G. (2019). Understanding the challenges of refugee entrepreneurship in tourism and hospitality. *Service Industries Journal*, *39*(9-10), 717–740. doi:10.1080/02642069.2018.1440550

Alsawafi, A. M. (2016). Exploring the challenges and perceptions of Al Rustaq College of Applied Sciences students towards Omani women's empowerment in the tourism sector. *Tourism Management Perspectives*, *20*, 246–250. doi:10.1016/j.tmp.2016.10.004

Altinay, L., Madanoglu, M., Daniele, R., & Lashley, C. (2012). The influence of family tradition and psychological traits on entrepreneurial intention. *International Journal of Hospitality Management*, *31*(2), 489–499. doi:10.1016/j.ijhm.2011.07.007

Amoah, V. A., & Baum, T. (1997). Tourism education: Policy versus practice. *International Journal of Contemporary Hospitality Management*, *9*(1), 5–12. doi:10.1108/09596119710157531

Anagnos, C. (2019). *Crony Capitalism Threatens Airbnb in South Africa*. Retrieved from: https://www.aier.org/article/crony-capitalism-threatens-airbnb-in-south-africa

Ananthesh, H. (2016). Role of" skill india program" in realizing" digital India mission. *Splint International Journal of Professionals*, *3*(6), 78.

Anderson, W., & Sanga, J. J. (2019). Academia–industry partnerships for hospitality and tourism education in Tanzania. *Journal of Hospitality & Tourism Education*, *31*(1), 34–48. doi:10.1080/10963758.2018.1480959

Ang, S. H., & Hong, D. G. P. (2000). Entrepreneurial spirit among East Asian Chinese. *Thunderbird International Business Review*, *42*(3), 285–309. doi:10.1002/1520-6874(200005/06)42:3<285::AID-TIE2>3.0.CO;2-5

Apleni, L., Vallabh, D., & Henama, U. S. (2017). Motivation for tourists' participation in religious tourism in Eastern Cape: A case study of Buffalo City, South Africa. *African Journal of Hospitality, Tourism and Leisure*, *7*(1), 1–16.

Approved Standards of Higher Education. (2020). https://mon.gov.ua/ua/osvita/visha-osvita/naukovo-metodichna-rada-ministerstva-osviti-i-nauki-ukrayini/zatverdzheni-standarti-vishoyi-osviti

Aruna, A., & KR, D. M. K. (2015). *Enabling E-Skilling in India through Digital India and Skill India Programs*. Academic Press.

Atef, T. M., & Al-Balushi, M. (2015). Entrepreneurship as a means for restructuring employment patterns. *Tourism and Hospitality Research*, *15*(2), 73–90. doi:10.1177/1467358414558082

Ateljevic, J., & Li, L. (2017). Tourism entrepreneurship–concepts and issues. In *Tourism and entrepreneurship* (pp. 30–53). Routledge. doi:10.4324/9780080942728-10

Aulia, S. (2016). *The Challenges of Tourism–With Specific Reference to Muscat Region (A Conceptual Perspective)*. Academic Press.

Autio, E., Keeley, R. H., Klofsten, M., & Ulfstedt, T. (1997). Entrepreneurial intent among students: testing an intent model in Asia, Scandinavia and USA. *Frontiers of Entrepreneurship Research, Babson Conference Proceedings.*

Autio, E., Keeley, R., Klofsten, M., Parker, G., & Hay, M. (2001). Entrepreneurial intent among students in Scandinavia and in the USA. *Enterprise and Innovation Management Studies*, *2*(2), 145–160. doi:10.1080/14632440110094632

Auxilia, P. M. (2021). *Indian Youths' Perception on Skill Development Training Programs for Career Growth.* www. ijrpr. com

Ayikoru, M., Tribe, J., & Airey, D. (2009). Reading tourism education: Neoliberalism unveiled. *Annals of Tourism Research*, *36*(2), 191–221. doi:10.1016/j.annals.2008.11.001

Babeshko, M. S. (2017). Formation of professionally-specialized competencies of future professionals of hotel and restaurant business. *Psychological and Pedagogical Scientific Collection, 11*. http://pedagogylviv.org.ua/zhurnaly/march_2017.pdf#page=11

Bagherifard, S. M., Jalali, M., Jalali, F., Khalili, P., & Sharifi, S. (2013). Tourism entrepreneurship: Challenges and opportunities in Mazandaran. *Journal of Basic and Applied Scientific Research, 3*(4), 842–846.

Bagri, S. C., & Junaid, K. C. (2020). Ethnic conflict and geopolitics: COVID-19 augmented chaos versus efforts to restart tourism sector. *Skyline Business Journal, 16*(1), 73–81.

Bailetti, T. (2012). Technology entrepreneurship: Overview, definition, and distinctive aspects. *Technology Innovation Management Review, 2*(2), 5–12. doi:10.22215/timreview/520

Baporikar, N. (2017). Critical review of entrepreneurship in Oman. *Entrepreneurship and Business Innovation in the Middle East*, 147-174. . doi:10.4018/978-1-5225-2066-5.ch008

Bardolet, E., & Sheldon, P. (2008). Tourism in archipelagos: Hawaii and the Balearics. *Annals of Tourism Research, 35*(4), 900–923. doi:10.1016/j.annals.2008.07.005

Basu, A., & Virick, M. (2008). Assessing entrepreneurial intentions amongst students: A comparative study. In *VentureWell. Proceedings of Open, the Annual Conference* (p. 79). National Collegiate Inventors & Innovators Alliance.

Batat, W., & Hammedi, W. (2017). Collaborative consumption as a feature of Gen-Y consumers: Rethinking youth tourism practices in the sharing economy. In *Advances in Social Media for Travel, Tourism and Hospitality*. Routledge. doi:10.4324/9781315565736-18

Begley, T. M., Tan, W. L., Larasati, A. B., Rab, A., & Zamora, E. (1997). The relationship between socio-cultural dimensions and interest in starting a business: a multi-country study. *Frontiers of Entrepreneurship Research, Babson Conference Proceedings.*

Belhassen, Y., & Caton, K. (2011). On the need for critical pedagogy in tourism education. *Tourism Management, 32*(6), 1389–1396. doi:10.1016/j.tourman.2011.01.014

Belk, R. W., Eckhardt, G. M., & Bardhi, F. (2019). Introduction to the Handbook of the Sharing Economy: the paradox of the sharing economy. In *Handbook of the Sharing Economy*. Edward Elgar Publishing. doi:10.4337/9781788110549.00005

Bennett, D. (2019). Meeting society's expectations of graduates: Education for the public good. In *Education for Employability* (Vol. 1, pp. 35–48). Brill Sense.

Bezruchenkov, Yu. V. (2015). Components of the professional culture of future specialists of the hotel and restaurant industry. *Scientific Bulletin of Donbass*, (1).

Bindah, E. V., & Magd, H. A. (2016). Teaching Entrepreneurship in Oman: Successful Approaches. *Procedia: Social and Behavioral Sciences, 219*, 140–144. doi:10.1016/j.sbspro.2016.04.055

Bird, B. (1988). Implementing Entrepreneurial Ideas: The Case for Intention. *Academy of Management Review, 13*(3), 442–453. doi:10.5465/amr.1988.4306970

Bivens, J. (2019). *The economic costs and benefits of Airbnb: No reason for local policymakers to let Airbnb bypass tax or regulatory obligations*. Economic Policy Institute.

Blake, A., Sinclair, M. T., & Soria, J. A. C. (2006). Tourism productivity: Evidence from the United Kingdom. *Annals of Tourism Research, 33*(4), 1099–1120. doi:10.1016/j.annals.2006.06.001

Bogonis, O. M. (2018). *Formation of economic competence of future junior specialists of hotel and restaurant service in a professional college* [Doctoral dissertation]. Institute of Pedagogical and Adult Education of the National Academy of Pedagogical Sciences of Ukraine.

Bolton, B., & Thompson, J. (2004). Entrepreneurs, Second Edition: Talent, Temperament, Technique (2nd ed.). Butterworth-Heinemann.

Boniface, P. (2001). *Dynamic tourism, journeying with change*. Channel View Publications. doi:10.21832/9781873150368

Bourdieu, P., & Passeron, J. C. (1990). *Reproduction in education, society and culture* (Vol. 4). Sage.

Brännback, M., Carsrud, A., Elfving, J., Kickul, J., & Krueger, N. (2006, July). Why replicate entrepreneurial intentionality studies? Prospects, perils, and academic reality. In SMU Edge Conference, Singapore.

Brännström, S. (2020). *What's the problem with Women not Working? A Critical Analysis of the Skill India Development Mission & Explanations on Female Labor Force Participation*. Academic Press.

Bredvold, R., & Skalen, P. (2016). Lifestyle Entrepreneurship and their identity construction: A study of their tourism industry. *Tourism Management, 56*, 96–105. doi:10.1016/j.tourman.2016.03.023

Briggs, K. (2018). The New Blame Game: How Airbnb Has Been Mis-regulated as the Scapegoat for Century-Old Problems. The Business, Entrepreneurship & Ta. *Law Review, 2*(1), 1–21.

Brown, R. B. (2006). *Doing your dissertation in business and management: The reality of research and writing*. Sage Publications.

Buhalis, D., & Costa, C. (Eds.). (2005). *Tourism Business Frontiers*. Butterworth Heinemann. https://goo.gl/uv1V6a

Buhalis, D., & Law, R. (2008). Progress in information technology and tourism management: 20 years on and 10 years after the Internet—The state of eTourism research. *Tourism Management, 29*(4), 609–623. doi:10.1016/j.tourman.2008.01.005

Bury, S. A. (2014). *The specifics of technology transfer in the hotel and restaurant business*. http://eztuir.ztu.edu.ua/bitstream/handle/123456789/1561/52.pdf?sequence=1

Carr, A. (2020). COVID-19, indigenous peoples and tourism: A view from New Zealand. *Tourism Geographies, 22*(3), 491–502. doi:10.1080/14616688.2020.1768433

Carton, R. B., Hofer, C. W., & Meeks, M. D. (1998). *The Entrepreneur and Entrepreneurship: Operational Definitions of Their Role in Society*. Academic Press.

Channapatna City Municipal Council. (2021). *City Population Census 2011-2021; Karnataka*. https://www.census2011.co.in/data/town/803239-channapatna-karnataka.html

Chenoy, D. (2013). Public–private partnership to meet the skills challenges in India. *Skills Development for Inclusive and Sustainable Growth in Developing Asia-Pacific,* 181-194.

Chenoy, D. (2016). Skill development in India: A transformation in the making. *India Infrastructure Report*, *2012*, 237–245.

Cho, Y., & Honorati, M. (2014). Entrepreneurship programs in developing countries: A meta-regression analysis. *Labour Economics*, *28*, 110–130. doi:10.1016/j.labeco.2014.03.011

Ciochina, L., Iordache, C., & Sirbu, A. (2016). Entrepreneurship In The Tourism And Hospitality Industry. *Management Strategies Journal*, *3*(1), 264–275.

Collins, H. (2010). *Tacit and Explicit Knowledge*. The University of Chicago Press. doi:10.7208/chicago/9780226113821.001.0001

Cooper, C. (2002). Curriculum planning for tourism education: From theory to practice. *Journal of Teaching in Travel & Tourism*, *2*(1), 19–39. doi:10.1300/J172v02n01_02

Cooper, C., & Shepherd, R. (1997). The relationship between tourism education and the tourism industry: Implications for tourism education. *Tourism Recreation Research*, *22*(1), 34–47. doi:10.1080/02508281.1997.11014784

Cuffy, V., Tribe, J., & Airey, D. (2012). Lifelong learning for tourism. *Annals of Tourism Research*, *39*(3), 1402–1424. doi:10.1016/j.annals.2012.02.007

Da Costa, M. T. G., & Carvalho, L. M. C. (2011). The Sustainability of Tourism Supply Chain: A Case Study Research. *Tourismos*, *6*(2), 393–404.

Dahanayake, S. N. S., Biyiri, E. W., & Dassanayake, D. M. C. (2019). Tourism and hospitality undergraduates' internship experience, their satisfaction and impact on future career intention. *Journal of Management Matters*, *6*(1), 33–44.

Daniel, A. D., Costa, R. A., Pita, M., & Costa, C. (2017). Tourism Education: What about entrepreneurial skills? *Journal of Hospitality and Tourism Management*, *30*, 65–72. doi:10.1016/j.jhtm.2017.01.002

Das, A. (2015). Skills Development for SMEs: Mapping of Key Initiatives in India. *Institutions and Economies*, *7*(2), 120–143.

Davydova, O. Yu., Pisarevsky, I. M., & Ladyzhenskaya, R. S. (2012). *Quality management of products and services in the hotel and restaurant industry*. Tutorial.

Debpriya, De. (2019). Issues and challenges in implementing the skill India movement: Training partner perspective. *Worldwide Hospitality and Tourism Themes*.

Del Vecchio, P., Mele, G., Ndou, V., & Secundo, G. (2018). Creating value from social big data: Implications for smart tourism destinations. *Information Processing & Management, 54*(5), 847–860. doi:10.1016/j.ipm.2017.10.006

Dellova, R. I. (2019). Student Workplace Competency: Industry Outcomes-Based Assessment in Selected Higher Education Institutions Offering Tourism and Hospitality Courses. *APCoRE Journal of Proceedings.*

DHNS. (2010). *Michelle spends $25 on Channapatna toys.* Deccan Herald. https://www.deccanherald.com/content/111225/michelle-spends-25-channapatna-toys.html

Diochon, M., Gasse, Y., Menzies, T., & Garand, D. (2002). Attitudes and entrepreneurial action: exploring the link. *Administrative Sciences of Canada 2002, Conference Proceedings, 23*(21), 1–11.

Dixit, S. K., & Mawroh, H. (2019). Vocational education and training for hospitality and tourism industry in India. *Tourism Education and Asia*, 35-48.

Dragomir, C. C., & Panzaru, S. (2015). The relationship between education and entrepreneurship in EU Member States. *Review of General Management, 22*(2), 55–65.

Echtner, C. (1995). Entrepreneurial training in developing countries. *Annals of Tourism Research, 22*(1), 119–134. doi:10.1016/0160-7383(94)00065-Z

Economic Survey of Karnataka 2020-21. (2021). *Planning, Programme Monitoring and Statistics Department.* https://des.karnataka.gov.in/storage/pdf-files/CIS/Economic%20Survey%202020-21_Eng_Final_R.pdf

Educational Council. (2016). *Technical and Vocational Education in the Sultanate of Oman.* Diwan of Royal Court, D.G of Telecommunication and Information System. www.educouncil.gov.om

Ennis, C. A. (2015). Between trend and necessity: Top-down entrepreneurship promotion in Oman and Qatar. *The Muslim World, 105*(1), 116–138. doi:10.1111/muwo.12083

Epler Wood, M., Milstein, M., & Ahamed-Broadhurst, K. (2019). *Destinations at risk: the invisible burden of tourism.* The Travel Foundation.

Esfandiar, K., Sharifi-Tehrani, M., Pratt, S., & Altinay, L. (2019). Understanding entrepreneurial intentions: A developed integrated structural model approach. *Journal of Business Research, 94*, 172–182. doi:10.1016/j.jbusres.2017.10.045

Explanatory Cambridge Dictionary. (2022). https://dictionary.cambridge.org/ru/%D1%81%D0%BB%D0%BE%D0%B2%D0%B0%D1%80%D1%8C/%D0%B0%D0%BD%D0%B3%D0%BB%D0%B8%D0%B9%D1%81%D0%BA%D0%B8%D0%B9/entrepreneurship

Farmaki, A. (2018). Tourism and hospitality internships: A prologue to career intentions? *Journal of Hospitality, Leisure, Sport and Tourism Education, 23*, 50–58. doi:10.1016/j.jhlste.2018.06.002

Fatoki, O., & Oni, O. (2014). Students' perception of the effectiveness of entrepreneurship education at a South African University. *Mediterranean Journal of Social Sciences*, *5*(20), 585–585. doi:10.5901/mjss.2014.v5n20p585

Fayolle, A. (2009). Entrepreneurship Education in Europe: Trends and Challenges. *OECD LEED Programme. Universities, Innovation and Entrepreneurship: Good Practice Workshop*. Retrieved from: https: www.oecd.org/datao

Fedosova, K. S. (2010). Modern control automation systems in the hotel and restaurant business of Ukraine. *Economics of the Food Industry*, *2*, 41-50.

Fedosova, K. S. (2021). Training of specialists in the field of restaurant consulting with the use of information and communication technologies on the basis of the department of hotel and restaurant business. *Odessa National Academy of Food Technologies Collection of materials of the III All-Ukrainian scientific-methodical conference "Ensuring the quality of higher education: improving the efficiency of information technology in the educational process"*, 325-326.

Fitzsimmons, J., & Douglas, E. (2011). Interaction between feasibility and desirability in the formation of entrepreneurial intentions. *Journal of Business Venturing*, *26*(4), 431–440. doi:10.1016/j.jbusvent.2010.01.001

Fomenko, N. A. (2012). *Theoretical and methodical bases of formation of standards of education in the field of tourism* [Doctoral dissertation]. Kyiv University of Tourism, Economics and Law, Kyiv, Ukraine.

Fong, V., Wong, I., & Hong, J. (2018). Developing institutional logics in the tourism industry through coopetition. *Tourism Management*, *66*, 244–262. doi:10.1016/j.tourman.2017.12.005

Forgacs, G., & Dimanche, F. (2016). Revenue challenges for hotels in the sharing economy: Facing the Airbnb menace. *Journal of Revenue and Pricing Management*, *15*(6), 509–515. doi:10.105741272-016-0071-z

Francis, K., Wamathai, A., Wandaka, J. K., & Jilo, N. (2020). Analysis of the skills gap in the tourism and hospitality industry in Kenya. *Journal of Tourism Management Research*, *7*(1), 42–51. doi:10.18488/journal.31.2020.71.42.51

Franklin, A. (2014). Tourist studies. In *The routledge handbook of mobilities* (pp. 94–104). Routledge.

Frey, L.V., & Solovjova, O.V. (2018). Current problems of staff training for the hospitality industry. *Current trends and strategies of development of tourist and hotel and restaurant business*, 237.

Fuchs, K. (2021). Advances in tourism education: A qualitative inquiry about emergency remote teaching in higher education. *Journal of Environmental Management and Tourism*, *12*(02 (50)), 538–543. doi:10.14505//jemt.v12.2(50).23

Fu, H., Okumus, F., Wu, K., & Köseoglu, M. A. (2019). The entrepreneurship research in hospitality and tourism. *International Journal of Hospitality Management*, *78*, 1–12. doi:10.1016/j.ijhm.2018.10.005

Gamage, A. (2003). Small and medium enterprise development in Sri Lanka: A review. *Masuki Ronso, 3*(4), 133–150.

Gaur, A. D., & Padiya, J. (2017). A Conceptual Study of "Skill India" Mission Bridge to "Make in India" Program. Editorial Advisory Board, 52.

Gautam, M. K., & Singh, S. K. (2015). Entrepreneurship Education: Concept, Characteristics and Implications for Teacher Education. *Shaikshik Parisamvad, 5*(1), 21–35.

Genesis Analytics. (2021). *The contribution of Airbnb to inclusive growth in South Africa.* Retrieved from: https://www.genesis-analytics.com

George, R. (2020). *Marketing Tourism in South Africa* (6th ed.). Oxford University Press.

Getz, D., & Carlsen, J. (2005). Family business in tourism. *Annals of Tourism Research, 32*(1), 237–258. doi:10.1016/j.annals.2004.07.006

Ghani, E. K., & Muhammad, K. (2019). Industry 4.0: Employers' Expectations of Accounting Graduates and Its Implications on Teaching and Learning Practices. *International Journal of Education and Practice, 7*(1), 19–29. doi:10.18488/journal.61.2019.71.19.29

Ghouse, S., McElwee, G., Meaton, J., & Durrah, O. (2017). Barriers to Rural Women Entrepreneurs in Oman. *International Journal of Entrepreneurial Behaviour & Research, 23*(6), 998–1016. doi:10.1108/IJEBR-02-2017-0070

Gibb, A. (2003). In Pursuit of a New 'Enterprise' and 'Entrepreneurship' Paradigm for Learning: Creative Destruction, New Values, New Ways of Doing Things and New Combinations of Knowledge. *International Journal of Management Reviews, 4*(3), 233–269. Advance online publication. doi:10.1111/1468-2370.00086

Goga, S. (2020). *The Impact of Digital Platforms on Competition in the South African Tourism Industry*. Industrial Development Think Thank.

Goldin, C., & Katz, L. F. (2009). The Race Between Education and Technology. *The Journal of American History, 96*(1), 246. Advance online publication. doi:10.2307/27694819

Gostrik, A. M., Nikitina, N. A., & Kalashnikov, E. A. (2017). *Features of teaching specialized subjects to English-speaking students*. https://repo.odmu.edu.ua/xmlui/bitstream/handle/123456789/9596/Nikitina.pdf?sequence=1&isAllowed=y

Govt of Karnataka. (2022). *Tourists Foot Falls Karnataka*. https://karnataka.data.gov.in/catalog/tourists-footfalls-karnataka 3#web_catalog_tabs_block_10

Gray, E. G. (2004). *Doing research in the real world*. Sage Publications Inc.

Griffin, W. C. (2020). Hospitality faculty: Are we meeting the demands of industry? *Journal of Teaching in Travel & Tourism, 20*(4), 1–22. doi:10.1080/15313220.2020.1746225

Griggio, C., & Oxemswardh, A. (2021). Human capital and sustainability challenges for Airbnb Bed and Breakfast lifestyle entrepreneur. *Scandinavian Journal of Hospitality and Tourism*, *21*(3), 286–312. doi:10.1080/15022250.2021.1927828

Guerrero, M., Rialp, J., & Urbano, D. (2006). The impact of desirability and feasibility on entrepreneurial intentions: A structural equation model. *The International Entrepreneurship and Management Journal*, *4*(1), 35–50. doi:10.100711365-006-0032-x

Gupta, V. (2016). Indian reality tourism-a critical perspective. *Tourism and Hospitality Management*, *22*(2), 111–133. doi:10.20867/thm.22.2.6

Gurel, E., Altinay, L., & Daniele, R. (2010). Tourism students' entrepreneurial intentions. *Annals of Tourism Research*, *37*(3), 646–669. doi:10.1016/j.annals.2009.12.003

Halibas, A. S., Sibayan, R. O., & Maata, R. L. R. (2017). The Penta helix Model of Innovation in Oman: An HEI Perspective. *Interdisciplinary Journal of Information, Knowledge & Management*, *12*, 159-172. Retrieved from https://www.informingscience.org/Publications/373

Handayani, B., Seraphin, H., Korstanje, M., & Pilato, M. (2019). Street food as a special interest and sustainable form of tourism for Southeast Asia destinations. In *Special interest tourism in Southeast Asia: Emerging research and opportunities* (pp. 81–104). IGI Global. doi:10.4018/978-1-5225-7393-7.ch005

Hanieh, A. (2021). Thinking about Capital and Class in the Arab Gulf Arab States. *Marx in the Field, 3*(1), 77-88.

Haque, A., & Patnaik, A. K. (2016). Contribution of Tourism sector to Oman's GDP. *International Journal of Economics, Commerce and Management*, 185-195.

Henama, U.S. (2017a). International Migration and National Tourism Industry Development: The Case of South Africa. *The EurAseans: Journal of Global Socio-Economic Dynamic, 2*(3), 72-82.

Henama, U.S. (2021). eCommerce within the Tourism Industry in the Global South: The case of sharing economy in South Africa. *Advances in Digital Marketing and eCommerce*, 280-290.

Henama, U. S. (2017b). Marikana: Opportunities for Heritage Tourism. *African Journal of Hospitality, Tourism and Leisure*, *6*(4), 1–16.

Henama, U. S. (2018). Disruptive entrepreneurship using Airbnb: The South African experience. *African Journal of Hospitality, Tourism and Leisure*, *7*(1), 1–16.

Henama, U. S. (2019a). *The Sharing Economy in South Africa's Tourism Industry: The Case of Uber-Hailing Taxi Services. Oncioiu, I. Improving Business Performance through Innovation in the Digital Economy*. IGI Global.

Henama, U. S. (2019b). *Tourism as Neoliberal Messiah: The Case of South Africa. Nadda, V., Azam, M. & Mulindwa, D. Neoliberalism in the Tourism and Hospitality Sector*. IGI Global.

Henama, U. S., & Apleni, L. (2020). *Religious Tourism in Africa's Global South: Indigenous African Traditional Spirituality. In Global Development of Religious Tourism*. IGI Global.

Herrington, M., & Kew, P. (2018). *Global Entrepreneurship Monitor*. Retrieved from: www.seda.gov.za/

Heuchemer, S., Martins, E., & Szczyrba, B. (2020). Problem-Based Learning at a "Learning University": A View from the Field. *The Interdisciplinary Journal of Problem-Based Learning*, *14*(2). doi:10.14434/ijpbl.v14i2.28791

Hilal, N. (2020). Tourism in the gulf cooperation council countries as a priority for economic prospects and diversification. *Journal of Tourism & Hospitality (Los Angeles, Calif.)*, *9*(451), 2167–2269.

Hisrich, R. D. (1990). Entrepreneurship/intrapreneurship. *The American Psychologist*, *45*(2), 209–222. doi:10.1037/0003-066X.45.2.209

Hisrich, R. D., Peters, M. P., & Shepherd, D. A. (2013). *Entrepreneurship* (9th ed.). McGraw-Hill Education.

Holmgren, C., & From, J. (2005). Taylorism of the Mind: Entrepreneurship Education from a Perspective of Educational Research. *European Educational Research Journal*, *4*(4), 382–390. doi:10.2304/eerj.2005.4.4.4

Hsu, C. H. (2018). Tourism education on and beyond the horizon. *Tourism Management Perspectives*, *25*, 181–183. doi:10.1016/j.tmp.2017.11.022

Hsu, C., Xiao, H., & Chen, N. (2017). Hospitality and tourism education research from 2005 to 2014. *International Journal of Contemporary Hospitality Management*, *29*(1), 141–160. doi:10.1108/IJCHM-09-2015-0450

Husar, U. E. (2020). Curriculum in the discipline "Project Management in the hotel and restaurant business" for students majoring in 241 "Hotel and restaurant business". Academic Press.

Husar, U. E. (2020). Project management in the hotel and restaurant business: the program of the discipline of master's degree in the field of knowledge 24 "Service area", specialty 241 "Hotel and restaurant business". Academic Press.

Hutchins, G. (2019). *Regenerative leadership*. eBook Partnership.

Hvidt, M. (2013). *Economic diversification in GCC countries: Past record and future trends*. https://www.lse.ac.uk/LSEKP

Ibrahim, O. A., Devesh, S., & Ubaidullah, V. (2017). Implication of attitude of graduate students in Oman towards entrepreneurship: An empirical study. *Journal of Global Entrepreneurship Research*, *7*(1), 1–17. doi:10.118640497-017-0066-2

Ikeja. (2022). *Welcome to Ikeja*. Retrieved from: https://www.ikeja.co.za

Ilyas, I. P., & Semiawan, T. (2017). Industrial-Based Learning (IBL): Promoting Excellent on Polytechnics and Vocational Higher Education. Academic Press.

Inui, Y., Wheeler, D., & Lankford, S. (2006). Rethinking tourism education: What should schools teach. *Journal of Hospitality, Leisure, Sport and Tourism Education*, *5*(2), 25–35. doi:10.3794/johlste.52.122

IOL. (2017). *Airbnb and Ikhaya le Langa partner to help entrepreneurs thrive*. Retrieved from: https://www.iol.co.za/travel/africa

IOL. (2021). *Airbnb contributes more than $550 million to SA economy*. Retrieved from: web.sabc.co.za/sabc/home/channelafrica/details?id=c79a6d87-6bd6-46a8-bb14-e8b053a922a5&title=Airbnbcontributes

Irvine Partners. (2021). *Hosts on Airbnb awarded funds to help see them through the COVID crisis*. Retrieved from: https://irvinepartners.co.za/hosts

Isaacs, E., Visser, K., Friendrich, C., & Brijlal, P. (2007). Entrepreneurship education and training at the Further Education and Training (FET) level in South Africa. *South African Journal of Education*, *27*, 613–629.

ITB. (2016). *World Travel Trends Report 2016–2017*. Berlin: Messe Berlin.

Ivanchenkova, L. V., & Sklyar, V. Y. (2021). The importance of teaching the discipline "Business Planning in Hospitality" for masters of "Hotel and Restaurant Business". *The III All-Ukrainian Scientific and Methodological Conference "Quality Assurance in Higher Education: Improving the efficiency of information technology in the educational process"*, 407-408.

Ivkov, M., Simon, V., Tepavčević, J., & Stojković, I. (2020). Expectations and satisfaction of hospitality students with employment in hospitality industry. *Turizam*, *24*(2), 57–67. doi:10.5937/turizam24-24810

Iyengar, V., & Mishra, D. K. (2017). Skilling for inclusive growth: SOAR analysis of 'Skill India 'Mission. *International Journal of Applied Business and Economic Research*, *15*(16), 209–221.

Jafari, J., & Ritchie, J. B. (1981). Toward a framework for tourism education: Problems and prospects. *Annals of Tourism Research*, *8*(1), 13–34. doi:10.1016/0160-7383(81)90065-7

Jagadisha, T. (2016). Opportunities and Challenges of Skill Development Programmes in India: An Analysis. Skill India and Development: Emerging Debates, 170.

Jamal, T., & Mandal, K. (2013). Skill development mission in vocational areas–mapping government initiatives. *Current Science*, 590–595.

Jamal, T., Taillon, J., & Dredge, D. (2011). Sustainable tourism pedagogy and academic-community collaboration: A progressive service-learning approach. *Tourism and Hospitality Research*, *11*(2), 133–147. doi:10.1057/thr.2011.3

Kabii, F., Wamathai, A., John, K. M., & Jilo, N. (2019). Analysis of the Skills Gap in Tourism and Hospitality Industry in Kenya. *Asean Journal on Hospitality and Tourism*, *17*(2), 95–105. doi:10.5614/ajht.2019.17.2.3

Kannadhasan, S. (2020). Women Empowerment and Economic Development Schemes through Skill India. Skill India: A Catalyst to Nation Building, 72.

Karolop, O. O. (2020). Pedagogical conditions of formation of readyness for professional activity of bachelors of hotel and restaurant business. *Pedagogical Education: Theory and Practice*, *29*, 276-285.

Kavita, K. M., & Sharma, P. (2011). Gap analysis of skills provided in hotel management education with respect to skills required in the hospitality industry: The indian scenario. *International Journal of Hospitality and Tourism Systems*, *4*(1), 31.

Kearsley, G., & Shneiderman, B. (1998). Engagement Theory: A Framework for Technology-Based Teaching and Learning. *Journal of Educational Technology, 38*, 20-23.

Keat, O. Y., Selvarajah, C., & Meyer, D. (2011). Inclination towards entrepreneurship among university students: An empirical study of Malaysian university students. *International Journal of Business and Social Science*, *2*(4).

Khan, F. R., & Krishnamurthy, J. (2016). Future proofing of tourism entrepreneurship in Oman: Challenges and prospects. *Journal of Work-Applied Management*, *8*(1), 79–94. doi:10.1108/JWAM-06-2016-0008

Khan, M. I., & Pal, M. (2016). Foreign Direct Investment and Labour Process in India: The Role of 'Make in India 'and 'Skill India" Programmes. *International Journal of Multidisciplinary Research and Development*, *3*(8), 396–403.

Kherson Regional Council. (2019). Development strategy of Kherson region for the period of 2021-2027. Author.

Kihima, B.O. (2015). Community and Tourism Entrepreneurship: Toward a Viable Community Based Tourism Initiatives in Kenya. *The East African Journal of Hospitality, Leisure and Tourism*.

Kihima, B. O. (2014). Unlocking the Kenyan tourism potential through park branding exercise. *Tourism Recreation Research*, *39*(1), 51–64. doi:10.1080/02508281.2014.11081326

Kim, D., & Kim, S. (2017). The role of mobile technology in tourism: Patents, articles, news, and mobile tour app reviews. *Sustainability*, *9*(11), 2082. doi:10.3390u9112082

King, K. (2012). The geopolitics and meanings of India's massive skills development ambitions. *International Journal of Educational Development*, *32*(5), 665–673. doi:10.1016/j.ijedudev.2012.02.001

Kirby, D. A. (2005). Entrepreneurship education: Can business schools meet the challenge. *Proceedings of the 2005 San Francisco-Silicon Valley Global Entrepreneurship Research Conference*, 173–193.

Kiswani, A. E. (2013). *Entrepreneurship Education in the Arab States A joint project between UNESCO and StratREAL Foundation, UK Component II: Regional Synthesis Report*. UNESCO. https://unesdoc.unesco.org/ark:/48223/pf0000220305_eng

Kitchenko, E. N., Chemeris, A.V. (2017). Use of marketing tools in the restaurant business. *Technological Audit and Production Reserves, 1*(4), 8-13.

Klapchuk, V. M. (2013a). The program of professional entrance examination for enrollment in the EQL "Master" in the specialty 8.14010102 "Resort Business". Academic Press.

Klapchuk, V. M. (2017b). Hotel and restaurant business (independent work of students): Educational and methodical manual. Faculty of Tourism, Vasyl Stefanyk Precarpathian National University. Ivano-Frankivsk: "Foliant".

Klapchuk, V. M. (2020c). Hotel and restaurant business (independent work of students). Academic Press.

Koh, E., & King, B. (2017). Accommodating the sharing revolution: A qualitative evaluation of the impact of Airbnb on Singapore's budget hotels. *Tourism Recreation Research, 41*(4), 409–421. doi:10.1080/02508281.2017.1314413

Kolvereid, L. (1996). Organizational Employment versus Self-Employment: Reasons for Career Choice Intentions. *Entrepreneurship Theory and Practice, 20*(3), 23–31. doi:10.1177/104225879602000302

Korkuna, O. (2020). Pricing in the hotel and restaurant business: the procedure for assessing learning outcomes in the discipline of higher education "bachelor" specialty 241 "Hotel and restaurant business" full-time and part-time education. Academic Press.

Korniyaka, A. A., & Golikova, T. P. (2013). Ways to improve the education system in the field of hospitality. *Scientific Bulletin Poltava University of Economy & Trade: Economic Sciences, 4*(60), 34–38.

Korstanje, M. (2008). Education Issues in Tourism, an analysis of Students expectatives in Argentina. *Tourism Today (Nicosia), 8*, 154–166.

Korstanje, M. E. (2011). The importance of social sciences in the curricula of tourism students. *Journal of Tourism, 12*(1), 1–15.

Korstanje, M., & George, B. (2021). *The Nature and future of tourism: a post COVID-19 context*. Apple Academic Press.

Koul, M. (2013). Skill development through government initiatives: Anything for women? *Current Science, 105*(2), 146.

Kozik, K. I. (2017). Information technologies of hotel management. Modern information technologies and systems in management: Coll. materials and All-Ukrainian. scientific-practical conf. young scientists, graduate students and students; April 6-7. Kyiv: KNEU.

Krueger, N. (1993). The Impact of Prior Entrepreneurial Exposure on Perceptions of New Venture Feasibility and Desirability. *Entrepreneurship Theory and Practice, 18*(1), 5–21. doi:10.1177/104225879301800101

Krueger, N. Jr, & Brazeal, D. (1994). Entrepreneurial Potential and Potential Entrepreneurs. *Entrepreneurship Theory and Practice, 18*(3), 91–104. doi:10.1177/104225879401800307

Krueger, N. Jr, Reilly, M., & Carsrud, A. (2000). Competing models of entrepreneurial intentions. *Journal of Business Venturing, 15*(5-6), 411–432. doi:10.1016/S0883-9026(98)00033-0

Kumar, A. (2019). Skill India: Bridging the Gap in Skills of Hospitality Sector Manpower. *Emerging Trends in Indian Tourism and Hospitality: Transformation and Innovation, 140.*

Kumar, P., & Chansoria, M. (2021). Assessment of Hospitality education in terms of Lacking Skill Development in Meeting the demand of Industry: An Integrative review. *Revista de turism-studii si cercetari in turism,* (31).

Kuratko, D. F., Hornsby, J. S., & Naffziger, D. W. (1997). 'An examination of owners' goals in sustaining entrepreneurship. *Journal of Small Business Management, 35*(1), 24–33.

Lackeus, M. (2015). *Entrepreneurship in Education: What, Why, When, How.* Retrieved from: https: www.oecd.org/datao

Lakshitha, H. D. T., & Biyiri, E. W. (2021). *A Study on Tourism and Hospitality Undergraduates' Entrepreneurial Intention. 4th National Research Symposium on Management,* Mihintale, Sri Lanka.

Law of Ukraine. (2017). *On Education.* https://zakon.rada.gov.ua/laws/show/2145-19#Text

Law of Ukraine. (2019). *On Higher Education.* https://zakon.rada.gov.ua/laws/show/1556-18#Text

Law of Ukraine. (2020). *On Tourism.* https://zakon.rada.gov.ua/laws/show/324/95-%D0%B2%D1%80#Text

Lebedenko, T. E., Solonitskaya, I. V., & Novichkova, T. P. (2021). Modern requirements for the training of specialists for the hospitality industry. National Academy of Food Technologies.

Lepp, A. (2008). Tourism and dependency: An analysis of Bigondi village, Uganda. *Tourism Management, 29*(6), 1206–1214. doi:10.1016/j.tourman.2008.03.004

Letsebe, K. (2018). *Airbnb makes good on $1m Africa investment.* Retrieved from: https://www.itweb.co.za/content/GxwQDM1AWJpM1PVo

Lew, A. A. (2014). Scale, change and resilience in community tourism planning. *Tourism Geographies, 16*(1), 14–22. doi:10.1080/14616688.2013.864325

Lew, A. A., Hall, C. M., & Williams, A. M. (2008). *A companion to tourism.* John Wiley & Sons.

Lewis, A., & Tribe, J. (2002). Critical issues in the globalisation of tourism education. *Tourism Recreation Research, 27*(1), 13–20. doi:10.1080/02508281.2002.11081352

Liñán, F. (2004). Intention-based models of entrepreneurship education. *PiccollaImpresa/Small Business*, *3*, 11-35.

Liñán, F., & Chen, Y. (2009). Development and Cross–Cultural Application of a Specific Instrument to Measure Entrepreneurial Intentions. *Entrepreneurship Theory and Practice*, *33*(3), 593–617. doi:10.1111/j.1540-6520.2009.00318.x

Li, W.LI. (2007). Ethnic Entrepreneurship: Studying Chinese and Indian Students in the United States. *Journal of Developmental Entrepreneurship*, *12*(04), 449–466. doi:10.1142/S1084946707000769

Liyanage, V. (2020). *Daily News e paper*. Retrieved from Education for entrepreneurship: https://www.dailynews.lk/2020/01/07/features/207687/education-entrepreneurship

Li, Z., Chen, H., & Huang, X. (2020). Airbnb or Hotel?:A Comparative Study on the Sentiment of Airbnb Guests in Sydney–Text Analysis Based on Big Data. *International Journal of Tourism and Hospitality Management in the Digital Age*, *4*(2), 1–10. doi:10.4018/IJTHMDA.2020070101

Lu, W. (2019, September). Exploration on the problems and deepening ways of International Exchange and Cooperation in Colleges and Universities. In *2019 3rd International Seminar on Education, Management and Social Sciences (ISEMSS 2019)*. Atlantis Press. 10.2991/isemss-19.2019.71

Lukianets, H., & Yevstafiev, V. (2019). Training systems for staff in hotel industry. *VIII All-Ukrainian scientific-practical conference, dedicated to the 135th anniversary of the National University of Food Technology "Innovative technologies in the hotel and restaurant business", March 19 – 20.* Kyiv: NUHT.

Lukyanova, L., Babushko, S., & Banit, O. (2018). Coaching as an innovative technology for personal and professional development of staff. *Rocenka Ukrajinsko-Slovenska*, *2018*, 154–166.

Luong, A., & Lee, C. (2021). The Influence of Entrepreneurial Desires and Self-Efficacy on the Entrepreneurial Intentions of New Zealand Tourism and Hospitality Students. *Journal of Hospitality & Tourism Education*, 1–18. doi:10.1080/10963758.2021.1963751

Lu, W., Wang, W., & Millington, J. (2010). Comparison of entrepreneurial intention among college students in the USA and China. *International Journal Of Pluralism And Economics Education*, *1*(4), 327. doi:10.1504/IJPEE.2010.037974

Maclean, R., & Pavlova, M. (2013). Vocationalization of secondary and higher education: pathways to the world of work. *Revisiting global trends in TVET: Reflections on theory and practice*, 40-85.

Magd, H. A., & McCoy, M. P. (2014). Entrepreneurship in Oman: Paving the way for a sustainable future. *Procedia Economics and Finance*, *15*, 1632–1640. doi:10.1016/S2212-5671(14)00634-0

Makumbirofa, S., & Saayman, A. (2018). Forecasting demand for qualified labour in the South African hotel industry. *Journal of Economic and Financial Sciences*, *11*(1). Advance online publication. doi:10.4102/jef.v11i1.189

Malik, A., & Gupta, S. (2017). Bridging the skill gap: An overview of skill India campaign. *Asian Journal of Research in Social Sciences and Humanities*, *7*(7), 271–283. doi:10.5958/2249-7315.2017.00385.9

Malyuk, L. P. (2016). Professional ethics and etiquette in the hotel and restaurant business. Kharkiv: KhDUHT.

Malyuk, L. P., & Varipaeva, L. M. (2018). Professional ethics and etiquette in the hotel and restaurant business. Methodical instructions for independent study of discipline by students of a specialty 241 "Hotel and restaurant business". Academic Press.

Mani, M. (2015). Entrepreneurship Education: A Students' Perspective. *International Journal of E-Entrepreneurship and Innovation*, *5*(1), 1–14. doi:10.4018/ijeei.2015010101

Manoj, A. S. (2013). A Study on the Efficiency of Training in Hospitality–A Kerala Tourism Development Corporation (KTDC) Experience, Trivandrum, Karela. *International Journal of Advanced Research in Management and Social Sciences, 9*.

Mansour, S., Al-Awhadi, T., & Al-Hatrushi, S. (2020). Geospatial based multi-criteria analysis for ecotourism land suitability using GIS & AHP: A case study of Masirah Island, Oman. *Journal of Ecotourism*, *19*(2), 148–167. doi:10.1080/14724049.2019.1663202

Marchant, B., & Mottiar, Z. (2011). Understanding Lifestyle Entrepreneurs and Digging Beneath the Issues of Profits: Profiling Surf Tourism Lifestyle Entrepreneurs in Ireland. *Tourism Planning & Development*, *8*(2), 171–183. doi:10.1080/21568316.2011.573917

Marshall, S. (2005). Making Money with Memories: The Fusion of Heritage, Tourism and Identify Formations in South Africa. *Historia (Wiesbaden, Germany)*, *50*(1), 103–121.

Martin, B. C., Mcnally, J. J., & Kay, M. J. (2013). Examining the formation of human capital in entrepreneurship: A metaanalysis of entrepreneurship education outcomes. *Journal of Business Venturing*, *28*(2), 211–224. doi:10.1016/j.jbusvent.2012.03.002

Matsuka, V. N. (2009). *The system of professional training of specialists in the field of tourism in Ukraine*. http://91.250.23.215:8080/jspui/bitstream/123456789/600/1/sistema_prof_podgotovki.pdf

Mayaka, M. A., & Prasad, H. (2012). Tourism in Kenya: An analysis of strategic issues and challenges. *Tourism Management Perspectives*, *1*, 48–56. doi:10.1016/j.tmp.2011.12.008

Medinskaya, S. I. (2019). Competence approach to training specialists in the field of tourism and hospitality industry to increase their competitiveness in national and international markets. *Bulletin of Alfred Nobel University. Pedagogy and Psychology, 2*(18), 208-214.

Mehrotra, S., Raman, R., Kumra, N., & Röß, D. (2014). *Vocational Education and Training Reform in India: Business Needs in India and Lessons to be Learned from Germany*. Working paper.

Mhlanga, O. (2019). Peer-to-peer travel: Is Airbnb a friend or foe to hotels. *International Journal of Culture, Tourism and Hospitality Research*, *13*(4), 443–457. doi:10.1108/IJCTHR-05-2019-0087

Ministry of Commerce and Investment. (2022). *License simulator*. Invest Easy Portal. www.business.gov.om/

Ministry of Higher Education. (2010). Colleges of Applied Sciences Bylaw. Ministerial Decision No. 13/2010, Ministry of Higher Education.

Ministry of Higher Education. (2013). Workshop Introducing a Module for Entrepreneurship and Students Activities in Higher Education Institutions in Oman. Ministry of Higher Education (MOHE).

Ministry of Higher Education. (2021). *Student Guide for Joining Higher Education Institutions for the academic year 2020/2021*. Ministry of Higher Education, Research and Innovation.

Ministry of Manpower. (2004). Colleges of Technology Bylaws. Ministerial Decision No. 72/2004.

Ministry of Manpower. (2011). *Bylaws and Regulations of Private Vocational Training Institutes and Centers*. Ministry of Manpower.

Ministry of Manpower. (2011). *Overview of Vocational Training*. Ministry of Manpower.

Ministry of Manpower. (2012). Amendments of Colleges of Technology Bylaws. Ministerial Decision No. 17/2012.

Ministry of Manpower. (2019). *Vocational Education and Training Pathways*. Ministry of Manpower, General Directorate for Vocational Training. www.manpower.gov.om/

Ministry of MSME. (2016). *District Industrial Profile of Ramanagara*. https://msmedibangalore.gov.in/files/Ramanagar.pdf

Ministry of Tourism. (2015). *Oman Tourism Alternative*. Vision of Ministry of Tourism. Available at: www.alternativer.co/omantourism.gov.om/sites-like-omantourism

Mirza, J. (2017, September 20). *Why Sri Lanka needs more entrepreneurs*. Retrieved April 27, 2022, from https://www.ft.lk/Columnists/Why-Sri-Lanka-needs-more-entrepreneurs/14-639925#:%7E:text=For%20the%20past%20two%20decades,towards%20business%20amongst%20younger%20generation

Mody, M., & Gomez, M. (2018). Airbnb and the Hotel Industry: The Past, Present and Future of Sales, Marketing, Branding and Revenue Management. *Boston Hospitality Review*. Retrieved from: https: www.bu.edu/bhr

Mokhalles, M. M. (2018). Skill Gap Analysis: A Review of Hospitality Sector in Assam. *Journal of Rural and Industrial Development*, *6*(1), 49.

Molefe, L. P., Tauoatsoala, P., Sifolo, P. P. S., Manavhela, P., & Henama, U. S. (2018). The effects of tourism supply chain management on practices on tourism operations in Pretoria, South Africa. *African Journal of Hospitality, Tourism and Leisure*, *7*(1), 1–16.

Moneyweb. (2017). *Namibia tells Airbnb hosts to register or face jail*. Retrieved from: https://www.moneyweb.co.za/news-fast-news

Morellato, M. (2014). Digital competence in tourism education: Cooperative-experiential learning. *Journal of Teaching in Travel & Tourism, 14*(2), 184–209. doi:10.1080/15313220.2014.907959

Moremong-Nganunu, T., Rametse, N., Al-Muharrami, S., & Sharma, S. K. (2018). Perceptions towards entrepreneurship and intention to become entrepreneurs: the case of Sultan Qaboos university female undergraduate students. In *Entrepreneurship education and research in the Middle East and North Africa (MENA)* (pp. 215–238). Springer. doi:10.1007/978-3-319-90394-1_12

Morozov, M., & Morozova, N. (2020, January). Innovative Staff Training Strategies for the Tourism and Hospitality Industry. In *5th International Conference on Economics, Management, Law and Education (EMLE 2019)* (pp. 393-396). Atlantis Press.

Morrison, A. (2006). A contextualization of entrepreneurship. *International Journal of Entrepreneurial Behaviour & Research, 12*(4), 192–209. doi:10.1108/13552550610679159

Morrison, A., & Johnston, B. (2003). Personal creativity for entrepreneurship: Teaching and learning strategies. *Active Learning in Higher Education, 4*(2), 145–158. doi:10.1177/1469787403004002003

Muge, C. C., Sempele, C., & Kiplagat, H. (2019). The Impact of Curriculum Content on the Quality of Food and Beverage Training in Selected Technical and Vocational Education and Training Institutions in the Western Region, Kenya. *East African Journal of Education Studies, 1*(1), 28–32.

Munar, A. M., & Gyimóthy, S. (2013). Critical digital tourism studies. In *Tourism social media: Transformations in identity, community and culture* (pp. 245–262). Emerald Group Publishing Limited. doi:10.1108/S1571-5043(2013)0000018016

Mussi, G. A. (2017). *When consuming becomes collaborative: Airbnb Case Study*. ISCTE Business School.

MyBroadband. (2021). *Airbnb launches fee WI-FI in South African townships*. Retrieved from: https://mybroadband.co.za/news/wireless/415762

Najar, A. H., & Bukhari, S. A. M. (2017). Gap Analysis in Hospitality Education and Industrial Requirements. *International Journal of Engineering and Management Research, 7*(4), 170–173.

Naseer, T. (2020, May 8). *Channapatna toy makers have been hit badly by the lockdown*. The Hindu. https://www.thehindu.com/society/talk-of-the-toy-town-the-channapatna-artisans-are-in-dire-straits/article31533199.ece

Nawaratne, S. (2012). Shifting Paradigms of Higher Education in Sri Lanka. In R. Senaratne & S. Sivasegaram (Eds.), Re-creating and Re-positioning of Sri Lankan Universities to meet Emerging Opportunities and Challenges in a Globalized Environment (pp. 75–95). Academic Press.

NCSI. (2022, Jan.). *Monthly Statistical Bulletin*. https://ncsi.gov.om /Elibrary/Pages/Library ContentDetails.aspx?ItemID=Vs6NFz%2B2xQSbfUBfw5b4ng%3D%3D

Ndiuini, A., & Baum, T. (2020). Underemployment and lived experiences of migrant workers in the hotel industry: Policy and industry implications. *Journal of Policy Research in Tourism, Leisure & Events*, 1–23.

Ndofirepi, T. M. (2020). Relationship between entrepreneurship education and entrepreneurial goal intentions: Psychological traits as mediators. *Journal of Innovation and Entrepreneurship*, *9*(2), 1–20. doi:10.118613731-020-0115-x

Ndou, V., Mele, G., & Del Vecchio, P. (2019). Entrepreneurship education in tourism: An investigation among European Universities. *Journal of Hospitality, Leisure, Sport and Tourism Education*, *25*, 100175. doi:10.1016/j.jhlste.2018.10.003

NERA Economic Consulting. (2017). *Airbnb's Global Support to Local Economies: Output and Employment: Prepared for Airbnb.* Retrieved from: https://www.nera.com

Neuhofer, B., Buhalis, D., & Ladkin, A. (2014). A typology of technology-enhanced tourism experiences. *International Journal of Tourism Research*, *16*(4), 340–350. doi:10.1002/jtr.1958

Niselow, T. Y. (2019). *The location and the nature of Airbnb listings in Johannesburg and their impact on property prices and the availability of long term rental stock* [Masters Thesis]. University of Witwatersrand.

O'Keefe, T. (2014). *Epicureanism.* Routledge. doi:10.4324/9781315711645

Observer, O. (2017). *Tapping-the-entrepreneurial-potential-of-omans-tourism-resources.* Available at: https://www.Omanobserver.om/article/82049/Features/tapping–the–entrepreneurial–potential–of-omans-tourism-resources

OECD Publishing. (2016). OECD Tourism Trends and Policies 2016. OECD Publishing.

OECD. (2018). *Organisation for Economic Co-operation and Development (OECD). Tourism Trends and Policies*. OECD.

Oleynyk, V. D. (2016). Problems of service of business travelers in Ukraine. Strategic prospects of tourist and hotel-restaurant industry in Ukraine: theory, practice and innovations of development: materials All-Ukrainian. scientific-practical Internet conference, Uman, October 31. University of Horticulture.

Oman National Centre for Statistics and Information. (2018). *Statistical Year Book. Statistical Year Book.* National Centre of Statistics and Information.

Omanuna, The Official Oman eGovernment Service Protal. (n.d.). *SAS Entrepreneurship program.* https://www.oman.om/wps/portal/index/bz/ManagingBusiness/SASEP/!ut/p/a1/hc9Nb4JAEAbgX8OVmd1

On approval of the Standard of higher education in the specialty 242 "Tourism" for the first (bachelor's) level of higher education: the order of the Ministry of Education and Science of Ukraine from 04. 10. 2018 N° 1068. Kyiv.

Onuoha, G. (2007). Entrepreneurship. *AIST International Journal, 10*, 20–32.

Orlova, M. L., & Shekera, S. S. (2021). Show respect for individual and cultural diversity: the importance of the program result and the peculiarities of its achievement by students majoring in 242 “Tourism”. *Odessa National Academy of Food Technologies Collection of materials of the III All-Ukrainian scientific-methodical conference “Ensuring the quality of higher education: improving the efficiency of information technology in the educational process”,* 414-416.

Ospina, S., & Parry, K. (2004). Qualitative research. In G. Goethals, G. Sorenson, & J. Burns (Eds.), *Encyclopedia of leadership* (pp. 1280–1285). SAGE Publications.

Owen, C. (2007). *Regenerative tourism: a case study of the resort town Yulara.* Open House International.

Ozturk, H. M. (2021). Technological Developments: Industry 4.0 and Its Effect on the Tourism Sector. In *Research Anthology on Cross-Industry Challenges of Industry 4.0, 1464-1487.* IGI Global. doi:10.4018/978-1-7998-8548-1.ch073

Pandow, B. A., & Omar, A. S. (2019). Evaluating Inclination of Youth to Start Enterprise: A Study in Oman. In *Creative Business and Social Innovations for a Sustainable Future* (pp. 133–142). Springer. doi:10.1007/978-3-030-01662-3_15

Parambi, R. (2014). *The case of the missing middle.* Available at: www.muscatdaily.com/ Archive/ Business/SME-Development-in-Oman-2y7u

Paris, C. M. (2011). Social constructivism and tourism education. *Journal of Hospitality, Leisure, Sports and Tourism Education, 10*(2), 103.

Paryshkura, Yu. V. (2020) Perspektyvy ta praktyky industriy fitnesu [Perspectives and practices of the fitness industry]. In Scientific-Practical Conf. Kyiv: KNUTD.

Pasichnyuk, V. B. (2020). *Economic and labor law.* http://ep3.nuwm.edu.ua/19288/1/od_gospodarske_i_trudove_pravo%20%2812%29.pdf

Paska, M. Z. (2020). The syllabus of the course of engineering in the hotel and restaurant industry. Educational degree: master Branch of knowledge: 24 Sphere of service Specialty: 241 Hotel and restaurant business. Component of the educational program: free choice of the student.

Paska, M. Z. (2021). *Engineering in the hotel and restaurant industry: syllabus of the course, educational degree: master, field of knowledge: 24 Sphere of service, specialty: 241 Hotel and restaurant business. Academic Press.*

Peterman, N., & Kennedy, J. (2003). Enterprise Education: Influencing Students’ Perceptions of Entrepreneurship. *Entrepreneurship Theory and Practice, 28*(2), 129–144. doi:10.1046/j.1540-6520.2003.00035.x

Peters, M., Frehse, J., & Buhalis, D. (2009). The importance of lifestyle entrepreneurship: A conceptual study of the tourism industry. *PASOP, 7*(2), 393–405. doi:10.25145/j.pasos.2009.07.028

Phuc, P. T., Vinh, N. Q., & Do, Q. H. (2020). Factors affecting entrepreneurial intention among tourism undergraduate students in Vietnam. *Management Science Letters*, 3675–3682. doi:10.5267/j.msl.2020.6.026

Pittaway, L., & Edwards, C. (2012). Assessment: Examining practice in entrepreneurship education. *Education and Training, 54*(8/9). doi:10.1108/00400911211274882

Pittaway, L., & Cope, J. (2007). Entrepreneurship Education a Systematic Review of the Evidence. *International Small Business Journal, 25*(5), 479–510. doi:10.1177/0266242607080656

Polchaninova, I. L. (2016). *Metodychni vkazivky do vykonannia kontrolnoi roboty z dystsypliny «Upravlinnia yakistiu produktsii ta posluh v hotelno-restorannomu hospodarstvi» (dlia studentiv 5 kursu zaochnoi formy navchannia napriamu pidhotovky 6.140101 – Hotelno-restoranna sprava)* [Methodical instructions for performance of control work on discipline "Management of quality of production and services in hotel and restaurant economy" (for students of 5th course of a correspondence form of training of a direction of preparation 6.140101 – Hotel and restaurant business)]. Kharkiv: KhNUMH im. O. M. Beketova.

Pollock, A. (2019). Flourishing beyond sustainability. *ETC Workshop in Krakow.*

Pranila & Irin. (2010). *Technical and Vocational Education and Training in Ethiopia.* International Growth Center.

Presenza, A., Yucelen, M., & Camillo, A. (2015). Passion before profits in hospitality ventures: Some thoughts on Lifestyle Entrepreneur and the case of "Albergo Diffuso". *Sinergie, 34*, 221–239.

Qiu, H., Li, Q., & Li, C. (2021). How technology facilitates tourism education in COVID-19: Case study of Nankai University. *Journal of Hospitality, Leisure, Sport and Tourism Education, 29*, 100288. doi:10.1016/j.jhlste.2020.100288 PMID:34720752

Qiu, S., Dooley, L. M., & Xie, L. (2020). How servant leadership and self-efficacy interact to affect service quality in the hospitality industry: A polynomial regression with response surface analysis. *Tourism Management, 78*, 104051. doi:10.1016/j.tourman.2019.104051

Räisänen, J. (2018). *Changing perceptions of tourism as a respectable career choice for Omani women.* Academic Press.

Ramdzan, A. S., Arasinah, K., & Zuraidah, Z. (2020). Entrepreneurship education: Unemployment issues, people's wellbeing, and entrepreneurial intentions among TVET graduates in Malaysia. *International Journal of Psychosocial Rehabilitation, 23*(4), 953–965.

Ranasinghe, R. (2019). Antecedents of Job Performance of Tourism Graduates: Evidence from State University-Graduated Employees in Sri Lanka. *Journal of Tourism and Services, 10*(18), 16–34. doi:10.29036/jots.v10i18.83

Rani, P., & Agrawal, R. (2020). Women Empowerment Through Skill India to Achieve Gender Equality–A Review. Skill India: A Catalyst to Nation Building, 140.

Ratten, V. (2019). Tourism entrepreneurship research: a perspective article. *Tourism Review*. https://www.researchgate.net/publication/338038696_Tourism_entrepreneurship_research_a_perspective_article

Ratten, V. (2020). Coronavirus (Covid-19) and the entrepreneurship education community. Journal of Enterprising Communities: People and Places in the Global Economy. *Journal of Enterprising Communities: People and Places in the Global Economy*, *14*(5), 753–764. doi:10.1108/JEC-06-2020-0121

Rauch, A., & Rijsdijk, S. (2013). The Effects of General and Specific Human Capital on Long–Term Growth and Failure of Newly Founded Businesses. *Entrepreneurship Theory and Practice*, *37*(4), 923–941. doi:10.1111/j.1540-6520.2011.00487.x

Ravenelle, A. J. (2020). Digitalization and the hybridization of markets and circuits in Airbnb. *Consumption Markets & Culture*, *23*(2), 154–173. doi:10.1080/10253866.2019.1661244

Regenerative Travel. (2020). *Taking Regenerative Tourism to Scale - Everyone has a Role to Play*. https://www.regenerativetravel.com/impact/taking-regenerative-tourism-to-scale-everyone-has-a-role-to-play

Reihana, F., Sisley, M., & Modlik, H. (2007). Maori entrepreneurial activity in Aotearoa New Zealand. *International Journal of Entrepreneurship and Small Business*, *4*(5), 636–653. doi:10.1504/IJESB.2007.014394

Reitan, B. (1997, June). Where do we learn that entrepreneurship is feasible, desirable, and/or profitable. In *ICSB World Conference* (pp. 21-24). Academic Press.

Rentalscaleup. (2022). *How Airbnb wants to unlock the next generation of Hosts*. Retrieved from: https:www://www.rentalscaleup.com/airbnb-unlock-the-next-generation-of-hosts

Rogerson, C. M., & Rogerson, J. M. (2019). How African is the African Journal of Hospitality Tourism and Leisure? An analysis of publishing trends for the period 2011-2018. *African Journal of Hospitality, Tourism and Leisure*, *8*(2), 1–17.

Rohwerder, B. (2020). *Inclusion Works Kenya Situational Analysis June 2020 update*. Academic Press.

Royal Decree. (2007). Organizing Colleges of Applied Sciences. Royal Decree 62/2007.

Royal Decree. (2020a). *Amending the Name of the Ministry of Higher Education to the Ministry of Higher Education, Research, and Innovation, Determining Its Competences, and Adopting Its Organizational Structure*. Royal Decree 98/2020.

Royal Decree. (2020b). *Establishing the Ministry of Labor and Determining Its Competences and Adopting Its Organizational Structure*. Royal Decree 89/2020.

Royal Decree. (2020c). *Establishing the University of Technology and Applied Sciences*. Royal Decree 76/2020.

Rozemond, M. (1998). *Descartes's dualism*. Harvard University Press. doi:10.4159/9780674042926

Rybchynska, A. A. (2015). *E-learning as an innovative tool for training and development of hotel and restaurant business staff*. http://dspace.nuft.edu.ua/bitstream/123456789/20049/1/136.pdf

Saadin, M. N., & Daskin, M. (2015). Perceived desirability, feasibility, and social norms as antecedents on hospitality students' entrepreneurial intention in Malaysia: Does gender make a difference? *International Journal of Entrepreneurship and Small Business*, *456*(4), 456. Advance online publication. doi:10.1504/IJESB.2015.070218

Sadgopal, A. (2016). 'Skill India 'or Deskilling India: An Agenda of Exclusion. *Economic and Political Weekly*, 33–37.

Saleh, M. S., & Alalouch, C. (2015). Towards sustainable construction in Oman: Challenges & opportunities. *Procedia Engineering*, *118*, 177–184. doi:10.1016/j.proeng.2015.08.416

Samarathunga, W., & Dissanayake, D. (2018). School Students' Attitude Towards the Career Intention in the Tourism Industry: The Case of North Central Province, Sri Lanka. *Journal of Management Matters*, *5*(2), 1–16.

Sarantakos, S. (2013). *Social research* (4th ed.). Palgrave Macmillan. doi:10.1007/978-1-137-29247-6

Sazegar, M., Forouharfar, A., Hill, V., & Faghih, N. (2018). The innovation-based competitive advantage in Oman's transition to a knowledge-based economy: dynamics of innovation for promotion of entrepreneurship. In *Entrepreneurship Ecosystem in the Middle East and North Africa, 491-518*. Springer. doi:10.1007/978-3-319-75913-5_18

Scarpetta, S., Sonnet, A., Livanos, I., Núñez, I., Craig Riddell, W., Song, X., & Maselli, I. (2012). Challenges facing European labour markets: Is a skill upgrade the appropriate instrument? *Inter Economics*, *47*(1), 4–30. doi:10.100710272-012-0402-2

Schumpeter, J. A. (1965). Economic Theory and Entrepreneurial History. *Explorations in Enterprise*, 45–64. doi:10.4159/harvard.9780674594470.c5

Scott, M., & Twomey, D. (1988). Long-term supply of entrepreneurs: Student career aspirations in relation to entrepreneurship. *Journal of Small Business Management*, *26*(4), 5–13.

Segal, G., Borgia, D., & Schoenfeld, J. (2002). Using Social Cognitive Career Theory to Predict Self-Employment Goals. *New England Journal Of Entrepreneurship*, *5*(2), 47–56. doi:10.1108/NEJE-05-02-2002-B007

Séraphin, H., Ambaye, M., Capatina, A., & Dosquet, F. (2018). DRA Model and Visual Online Learning Material in Tourism. *International Journal of Hospitality and Tourism Systems*, *11*(1).

Serrano, L., Sianes, A., & Ariza-Montes, A. (2020). Understanding the Implementation of Airbnb in Urban Context: Towards a Categorization of European Cities. *Land (Basel)*, *9*(12), 1–32. doi:10.3390/land9120522

Seryogina, I. Y. (2020). Modeling of hotel service "Parkour and workout in the hotel" in the study of the discipline "Industrial training of hotel and restaurant business". *Integration of education, science and business in the modern environment: winter disputes: theses add. I International Scientific and Practical Conference, February 6-7, 3,* 165-167.

Set, K., Yaakop, A. Y., Hussin, N. Z. I., & Mohd, B. (2015). Understanding Motivation Factors of Tourism Entrepreneurs in Tasik Kenyir. *International Academic Research Journal of Social Science, 1*(2), 248–254.

Shapero, A. (1982). The social dimension of entrepreneurship. In C. A. Kent, D. L. Sexton, & K. H. Vesper (Eds.), *The Encyclopaedia of Entrepreneurship* (pp. 72–90). Prentice-Hall.

Sharma, S., & Mishra, P. (2019). Hotel employees' perceptions about CSR initiatives and there potential to support the skill India initiative. *Worldwide Hospitality and Tourism Themes, 11*(1), 78–86. doi:10.1108/WHATT-10-2018-0064

Sharma, S., & Sharma, R. (2019). Culinary skills: the spine of the Indian hospitality industry: Is the available labour being skilled appropriately to be employable? *Worldwide Hospitality and Tourism Themes, 11*(1), 25–36. doi:10.1108/WHATT-10-2018-0061

Sheldon, P. J., & Daniele, R. (2017). *Social Entrepreneurship and Tourism.* Cham: Springer International Publishing. https://www. lusem. lu. se/library

Sheldon, P. J., Fesenmaier, D. R., & Tribe, J. (2011). The tourism education futures initiative (TEFI): Activating change in tourism education. *Journal of Teaching in Travel & Tourism, 11*(1), 2–23. doi:10.1080/15313220.2011.548728

Sheldon, P. J., Pollock, A., & Daniele, R. (2017). Social entrepreneurship and tourism: Setting the stage. In *Social Entrepreneurship and Tourism* (pp. 1–18). Springer. doi:10.1007/978-3-319-46518-0_1

Shepel, M., & Tretiak, V. (2021). *Future tourism industry professionals' cross-cultural communicatiive competence development at foreign language tutorials. Academic Press.*

Shereni, N. C. (2019). The tourism sharing economy and sustainability in developing countries: Contribution to SDGs in the hospitality sector. *African Journal of Hospitality, Tourism and Leisure, 8*(5), 110.

Shikalepo, E. E. (2019). Sustainability of entrepreneurship and innovation among TVET graduates in Namibia. *International Journal for Innovation Education and Research, 7*(5), 133–145. doi:10.31686/ijier.vol7.iss5.1484

SiddiquiD. M.SiddiquiA. (2016). *Integrating the NSDC Agenda in the Higher Education Institutions: A New Model for Employability Skill Development.* Available at SSRN 2744609. doi:10.2139/ssrn.2744609

Sifolo, P. P. S. (2020). Tourism supply chain management: A catalyst to development in Africa. The Gaze. *Journal of Tourism & Hospitality (Los Angeles, Calif.), 11*(1), 126–139.

Sigala, M. (2020). Tourism and COVID-19: Impacts and implications for advancing and resetting industry and research. *Journal of Business Research, 117*, 312–321. doi:10.1016/j.jbusres.2020.06.015 PMID:32546875

Singh, I., Prasad, T., & Raut, D. (2012). Entrepreneurial intent: a review of literature. In *Ninth AIMS International Conference on Management* (pp. 201-207). Academic Press.

Sisson, L., & Adams, A. (2013). Essential Hospitality Management Competencies: The Importance of Soft Skills. *Journal of Hospitality & Tourism Education, 25*(3), 131–145. doi:10.1080/10963758.2013.826975

Skill Development and Training. (n.d.). *NITI Aayog*. Retrieved October 20, 2021, Ch (5) from https://niti.gov.in/planningcommission.gov.in

Sokhalingam, C. P., Manimekalai, N., & Sudhahar, C. (2013). Entrepreneurial approach to tourism development in Oman. *International Journal of Management, 4*(3), 48–60.

Solvoll, S., Alsos, G. A., & Bulanova, O. (2015). Tourism Entrepreneurship – Review and Future Directions. *Scandinavian Journal of Hospitality and Tourism, 15*(sup1), 120–137. doi:10.1080/15022250.2015.1065592

Sotiriadis, M., & Apostolakis, A. (2015). Marketing challenges in travel, tourism and hospitality industries of the European and Mediterranean regions. *EuroMed Journal of Business, 10*(3), 107–120. doi:10.1108/EMJB-07-2015-0035

Srivastava, A. I., & Hasan, A. (2016). Bridging the Skill Gap in India: Challenges and Solutions. JIMS8M. *The Journal of Indian Management & Strategy, 21*(1), 45–54. doi:10.5958/0973-9343.2016.00007.7

Stadnytsky, Y. I., Dzyana, O.S., Koropetskaya, T. O. (2013). Features of formation of professional competence of managerial staff of hotel and restaurant economy. *Economic Strategy and Prospects for the Development of Trade and Services, 2*(1), 222-230.

Stahl, T. V., & Kozub, V. O. (2018). Features of the formation of the country's international competitiveness. *Development of food production, restaurant and hotel farms and trade: Problems, prospects, efficiency. International Scientific-Practical Conference,* (2), 105-106.

Stipanović, C., Rudan, E., & Zubović, V. (2021). *The entrepreneurial intentions of tourism and hospitality students in the face of the covid-19 pandemic*. Tourism in Southern and Eastern Europe. doi:10.20867/tosee.06.48

Strategy for the development of tourism and resorts for the period up to 2026. (2017). https://zakon.rada.gov.ua/laws/show/168-2017-%D1%80#Text

Su, Y. (2014). Lifelong learning in tourism education. The Routledge Handbook of Tourism and Hospitality Education, 322.

Tapper, R. & Font, X. (2008). Tourism Supply Chains: Report of Desk Research Project for the Travel Foundation. *Environment Business and Development Group,* 1-23.

Tarkenton, F. (2012). *Culture of entitlement threatens entrepreneurship.* Newsmax. Available at: www.newsmax.com/FranTarkenton/culture-entrepreneurs-America-entitlements/2012/09/07/id/451109/

The Global Entrepreneurship and Development Institute. (2018). *Global Entrepreneurship Index.* The Global Entrepreneurship and Development Institute.

The Presidency. (2021). *The South African Economic Reconstruction and Recovery Plan.* Retrieved from: https://www.gov.za/sites/default/files/gcis_document/202010/south-african-economic-reconstruction-and-recovery-plan.pdf

Times of Oman. (2014). Oman has tourism challenges to tackle. *Times of Oman.* Available at: www.timesofoman.com/news/37615/Article-Oman-has-tourism-challengesto-tackle

Tiwari, S., & Munjal, S. (2019). What are the key challenges that the Indian hospitality industry is facing in search of skilled labour? *Worldwide Hospitality and Tourism Themes, 11*(1), 99–102. doi:10.1108/WHATT-10-2018-0063

Tkachenko, O. V., Sokolenko, V. M., & Medved, L. M. (2019). *Individualization of education as one of the priority directions of modern pedagogy taking into account individual-typological features of personality.* Retrived from: http://elibumsa.pl.ua/bitstream/umsa/15050/1/Individualization%20_of%20_education.pdf

Tkachev, A., & Kolvereid, L. (1999). Self-employment intentions among Russian students. *Entrepreneurship and Regional Development, 11*(3), 269–280. doi:10.1080/089856299283209

Tomalya, T. S., & Shchipanova, Y. I. (2014). Quality management in the hotel and restaurant business. *Economy. Management. Innovation,* 2.

Tribe, J. (2002a). Research trends and imperatives in tourism education. *Acta Turistica,* 61-81.

Tribe, J. (2002b). The philosophic practitioner. *Annals of Tourism Research, 29*(2), 338–357. doi:10.1016/S0160-7383(01)00038-X

UNESCO. (2014). *Technical and Vocational Teachers and Trainers in the Arab Region: A Review of Policies and Practices on Continuous Professional Development.* The United Nations Educational, Scientific and Cultural Organization.

UNESCO. (2015). *Technical Vocational Education and Training.* Retrieved from http://www.unesco.org/new/en/newdelhi/areas-of-action/education/technical-vocational-education-and-training-tvet/

UNESCO. (2019). *Reviewing Work-Based Learning Programmes for Young People in the Arab Region: A Comparative and Longitudinal Analysis.* The UNESCO Regional Bureau for Education in the Arab States.

UNESCO. (2020). *UNESCO Recommendation concerning Technical and Vocational Education and Training (2015).* The United Nations Educational, Scientific and Cultural Organization.

UNESCO-ILO. (2020). *Decent Work Country Programme Sultanate of Oman*. International Labor Organization, Regional Office for the Arab States. www.ilo.org/

UNESCO-UNEVOC. (2013). *World TVET Database Oman*. UNESCO-UNEVOC International Centre for Technical and Vocational Education and Training. www.unevoc.unesco.org/

UNESCO-UNEVOC. (2019). *Innovation in TVET*. The UNESCO-UNEVOC International Centre for Technical and Vocational Education and Training. www.unevoc.unesco.org/

United Nations Conference on Trade and Development (UNCTAD). (2011). *Bilateral Investment Treaties: Kenya's Total number of Bilateral Investment Treaties 143. Concluded by 1 June 2011*. Retrieved 22.01.2011 from: http://archive.unctad.org/sections/dite_pcbb/docs/bits_kenya.pdf

UNWTO. (2011). *Tourism toward 2030, Global overview*. UNWTO.

UNWTO. (2020). *International Tourism Highlights, 2020 edition*. UNWTO.

Urbančič, J., Kuralt, V., Ratkajec, H., Straus, M., Vavroš, A., Mokorel, S., & Ilijaš, T. (2020). Expansion of Technology Utilization Through Tourism 4.0 in Slovenia. In *Handbook of Research on Smart Technology Applications in the Tourism Industry* (pp. 229–253). IGI Global. doi:10.4018/978-1-7998-1989-9.ch011

UTAS. (2022). *Tourism and Hospitality Management program audit*. University of Technology and Applied Sciences. www.cas.edu.om/

Valerio, A., Parton, B., & Robb, A. (2014). *Entrepreneurship Education and Training Programs around the World: Dimensions for Success*. World Bank Publications. doi:10.1596/978-1-4648-0202-7

Van Burg, E., Romme, A. G. L., Gilsing, V. A., & Reymen, I. M. M. J. (2008). Creating university spin-offs: A science-based design perspective'. *Journal of Product Innovation Management*, *25*(2), 114–128. doi:10.1111/j.1540-5885.2008.00291.x

Van Pletzen, D. (2019). *Improving Tax Compliance in the Sharing Economy: A focus on Airbnb in South Africa* [Masters Thesis]. University of Johannesburg.

Van Raatle, D., Parsons, S., & Hendrickse, K. (2018). Recommendations for Improving Tax Compliance by South African Airbnb Hosts. *2018 South African Accounting Association. Natioonal Teaching and Learning and Regional Conference Proceedings*, 255-271.

Vanevenhoven, J., & Liguori, E. (2013). The Impact of entrepreneurship education: Introducing the entrepreneurship education project. *Journal of Small Business Management*, *51*(3), 315–328. doi:10.1111/jsbm.12026

Veciana, J., Aponte, M., & Urbano, D. (2005). University Students' Attitudes Towards Entrepreneurship: A Two Countries Comparison. *The International Entrepreneurship and Management Journal*, *1*(2), 165–182. doi:10.100711365-005-1127-5

Venkatapathy, R., & Pretheeba, P. (2014). Gender, family business background and entrepreneurial intentions in an emerging economy. *International Journal Of Business And Emerging Markets*, *6*(3), 217. doi:10.1504/IJBEM.2014.063890

Venkateshwarlu, N., Sharma, R., & Agarwal, A. (2016). Skill Development Training Programme: A Case Study of IGNOU. *Global Journal of Enterprise Information System*, *8*(4), 66–70. doi:10.18311/gjeis/2016/15775

Verheul, I., Wennekers, S., Audretsch, D., & Thurik, R. (2001). An eclectic theory of entrepreneurship. *Tinbergen Institute Discussion Papers*.

Vidal, B. (2019). *The new technology and travel revolution*. Retrieved November, 30, 2020. https://www.wearemarketing.com/blog/tourism-and-technology-how-tech-is-revolutionizing-travel.html

Vinduk, A. V. (2017). Features of practice-oriented content of professional training of future specialists in tourism in higher education institutions. *Bulletin of Zaporizhzhia National University. Pedagogical Sciences*, (2), 98–103.

Visser, G., Erasmus, I., & Miller, M. (2017). Airbnb: The emergence of a new accommodation type in Cape Town, South Africa. *Tourism Review International*, *21*(2), 151–168. doi:10.3727/154427217X14912408849458

Volgger, M., Pforr, C., Stawinoga, A. E., Taplin, R., & Matthews, S. (2018). Who adopts the Airbnb innovation? An analysis of international visitors to Western Australia. *Tourism Recreation Research*, *43*(3), 305–320. doi:10.1080/02508281.2018.1443052

Walker, A. (2019). *Airbnb believes it has a R10 billion impact on South Africa's economy.* Retrieved from: https://memeburn.com/2019/07/

Wallace, L. K. (2020). *The Cultural Influence on Sharing Economy Services: The Case of Airbnb* [Honours Thesis]. The University of Southern Mississippi. Retrieved from: https:Aquila.usm.edu/honors_theses/

Wang, C. K., & Wong, P. K. (2004). Entrepreneurial interest of university students in Singapore. *Technovation*, *24*(2), 163–172. doi:10.1016/S0166-4972(02)00016-0

Wang, J., Ayres, H., & Huyton, J. (2010). Is tourism education meeting the needs of the tourism industry? An Australian case study. *Journal of Hospitality & Tourism Education*, *22*(1), 8–14. doi:10.1080/10963758.2010.10696964

Wang, S., Hung, K., & Huang, W. J. (2019). Motivations for entrepreneurship in tourism and hospitality sector: A social cognitive theory perspective. *International Journal of Hospitality Management*, *78*, 78–98. doi:10.1016/j.ijhm.2018.11.018

Wanjiku, C. P. (2020). *Effects of Employee Behavioral Factors on HACCP System Practices in Four and Five Star Rated Hotels in Nairobi County, Kenya* (Unpublished Dissertation).

Weber, M. R., Lee, J., & Crawford, A. (2020). A suggested best practices for enhancing performance of soft skills with entry-level hospitality managers. *Anatolia*, *31*(1), 76–87. doi:10.1080/13032917.2019.1703770

Weeratunge, N. (2010). Developing Youth Entrepreneurs: A Viable Youth Employment Strategy in Sri Lanka. [E-book] In R. Gunatlilaka, M. Mayer, & M. Vodopivec (Eds.), *The Challenge of Youth Employment in Sri Lanka* (pp. 167–198). World Bank Publications.

Wickramasinghe, V., & Perera, L. (2010). Graduates, University lecturers and employers' perceptions towards employability skills. *Education + Training*, *52*(3), 226–244. doi:10.1108/00400911011037355

Wijesundara, W. (2015). An Evaluation of Graduates' Perception on Employment in Tourism and Hospitality Industry. *7th Tourism Outlook Conference/Tropical Tourism Outlook Conference*.

Williams, P., & Hobson, J. P. (1995). Virtual reality and tourism: Fact or fantasy? *Tourism Management*, *16*(6), 423–427. doi:10.1016/0261-5177(95)00050-X

Williams, W., Knight, H., & Rutter, R. (2015). A Study of the Convergence between Entrepreneurship, Government Policy and Higher Education in the Sultanate of Oman. *60th Annual ICSB World Conference, Entrepreneurship at a Global Crossroads*, 6-9.

World Bank Group. (2010). *Kenya's tourism: polishing the jewel, Finance and Private Sector Development, Africa Region Summary Report, 2010*. Author.

World Bank. (2017). *World Development Report, Governance and the Law*. World Bank Group.

World Bank. (2018). *Jobs and Inequality*. Retrieved from: https://thedocs.worldbank.org/en/doc/798731523331698204-0010022018/original/SouthAfricaEconomicUpdateApril2018.pdf/

World Travel and Tourism Council (WTTC). (2020). *Travel and Tourism, Global Economic Impact and Trends 2020*. WTTC.

WTTC (World Travel and Tourism Council). (2016). *Global Talent Trends and Issues for the Travel and Tourism Sector*. WTTC.

Yakimenko-Tereshchenko, N. V., Zhadan, T. A., Mardus, N. Yu., Melen, O. V., & Poberezhna, N. M. (2019). Hotel and restaurant business. Academic Press.

Yakubenko, V. M., Yakubenko, V. N., Zakharchuk, M. Ya. Ye., Zakharchuk, M. E., Arabskaya, K. L., & Arabskaya, E. L. (2015). Organization, goals and socio-cultural features of foreign language teaching in the system of postgraduate adult education. *Science and Education*, *8*, 223–228.

Yanchuk, T. V., Lubinchak, K. R., & Vovkolup, A. Yu. (2020). The effectiveness of the introduction of marketing technologies in the hotel and restaurant business. *Scientific Bulletin of Uzhhorod National University*, (29), 176–179.

Yang, J. (2012). Identifying the attributes of blue ocean strategies in hospitality. *International Journal of Contemporary Hospitality Management*, *24*(5), 13–27. doi:10.1108/09596111211237255

Yarahmadi, F., & Magd, H. A. (2016). Entrepreneurship infrastructure and education in Oman. *Procedia: Social and Behavioral Sciences*, *219*, 792–797. doi:10.1016/j.sbspro.2016.05.079

Yuksel, S. (2014). Roadmap Of Recovery Amid Challenges Facing Oman Tourism. *Omani Journal of Applied Sciences*, *5*(1), 1–28.

Yusof, M. F. M., Wong, A., Ahmad, G., Aziz, R. C., & Hussain, K. (2020). Enhancing hospitality and tourism graduate employability through the 2u2i program. *Worldwide Hospitality and Tourism Themes*.

Zavidna, L. D. (2017). Hotel business: development strategies. Academic Press.

Zehrer, A., & Mössenlechner, C. (2008). Industry relations and curricula design in Austrian tourism master programs: A comparative analysis. *Journal of Teaching in Travel & Tourism*, *8*(1), 73–95. doi:10.1080/15313220802441992

Zhang, S., Li, Y., Liu, C., & Ruan, W. (2020). Critical factors identification and prediction of tourism and hospitality students' entrepreneurial intention. *Journal of Hospitality, Leisure, Sport and Tourism Education*, *26*, 100234. doi:10.1016/j.jhlste.2019.100234

Zhao, W., Ritchie, J. B., & Echtner, C. M. (2011). Social capital and tourism entrepreneurship. *Annals of Tourism Research*, *38*(4), 1570–1593. doi:10.1016/j.annals.2011.02.006

Zinkova, I. I. (2020). *Pedagogical conditions for the formation of entrepreneurial culture of future specialists in the field of services and tourism* [PhD dissertation, Vasyl Stefanyk Precarpathian National University", Ivano-Frankivsk]. ProQuest Dissertations and Theses database.

Zubar, N. M. (2016). Formation of competence of teachers of professional training in hotel and restaurant business. *Problems of Methods of Physical-Mathematical and Technological Education*, *1*(7).

Zuccoli, A., Seraphin, H., & Korstanje, M. (2021). *Nuevas Discusiones Alrededor de la Educacuón en Turismo: el Método Pancoe, Laboratorio del Disfrute, Universidad de Palermo*. Revista Latino-Americana de Turismologia.

Related References

To continue our tradition of advancing information science and technology research, we have compiled a list of recommended IGI Global readings. These references will provide additional information and guidance to further enrich your knowledge and assist you with your own research and future publications.

Abdul Razak, R., & Mansor, N. A. (2021). Instagram Influencers in Social Media-Induced Tourism: Rethinking Tourist Trust Towards Tourism Destination. In M. Dinis, L. Bonixe, S. Lamy, & Z. Breda (Eds.), *Impact of New Media in Tourism* (pp. 135-144). IGI Global. https://doi.org/10.4018/978-1-7998-7095-1.ch009

Abir, T., & Khan, M. Y. (2022). Importance of ICT Advancement and Culture of Adaptation in the Tourism and Hospitality Industry for Developing Countries. In C. Ramos, S. Quinteiro, & A. Gonçalves (Eds.), *ICT as Innovator Between Tourism and Culture* (pp. 30–41). IGI Global. https://doi.org/10.4018/978-1-7998-8165-0.ch003

Abtahi, M. S., Behboudi, L., & Hasanabad, H. M. (2017). Factors Affecting Internet Advertising Adoption in Ad Agencies. *International Journal of Innovation in the Digital Economy*, *8*(4), 18–29. doi:10.4018/IJIDE.2017100102

Afenyo-Agbe, E., & Mensah, I. (2022). Principles, Benefits, and Barriers to Community-Based Tourism: Implications for Management. In I. Mensah & E. Afenyo-Agbe (Eds.), *Prospects and Challenges of Community-Based Tourism and Changing Demographics* (pp. 1–29). IGI Global. doi:10.4018/978-1-7998-7335-8.ch001

Agbo, V. M. (2022). Distributive Justice Issues in Community-Based Tourism. In I. Mensah & E. Afenyo-Agbe (Eds.), *Prospects and Challenges of Community-Based Tourism and Changing Demographics* (pp. 107–129). IGI Global. https://doi.org/10.4018/978-1-7998-7335-8.ch005

Agrawal, S. (2017). The Impact of Emerging Technologies and Social Media on Different Business(es): Marketing and Management. In O. Rishi & A. Sharma (Eds.), *Maximizing Business Performance and Efficiency Through Intelligent Systems* (pp. 37–49). Hershey, PA: IGI Global. doi:10.4018/978-1-5225-2234-8.ch002

Ahmad, A., & Johari, S. (2022). Georgetown as a Gastronomy Tourism Destination: Visitor Awareness Towards Revisit Intention of Nasi Kandar Restaurant. In M. Valeri (Ed.), *New Governance and Management in Touristic Destinations* (pp. 71–83). IGI Global. https://doi.org/10.4018/978-1-6684-3889-3.ch005

Alkhatib, G., & Bayouq, S. T. (2021). A TAM-Based Model of Technological Factors Affecting Use of E-Tourism. *International Journal of Tourism and Hospitality Management in the Digital Age*, *5*(2), 50–67. https://doi.org/10.4018/IJTHMDA.20210701.oa1

Altinay Ozdemir, M. (2021). Virtual Reality (VR) and Augmented Reality (AR) Technologies for Accessibility and Marketing in the Tourism Industry. In C. Eusébio, L. Teixeira, & M. Carneiro (Eds.), *ICT Tools and Applications for Accessible Tourism* (pp. 277-301). IGI Global. https://doi.org/10.4018/978-1-7998-6428-8.ch013

Anantharaman, R. N., Rajeswari, K. S., Angusamy, A., & Kuppusamy, J. (2017). Role of Self-Efficacy and Collective Efficacy as Moderators of Occupational Stress Among Software Development Professionals. *International Journal of Human Capital and Information Technology Professionals*, *8*(2), 45–58. doi:10.4018/IJHCITP.2017040103

Aninze, F., El-Gohary, H., & Hussain, J. (2018). The Role of Microfinance to Empower Women: The Case of Developing Countries. *International Journal of Customer Relationship Marketing and Management*, *9*(1), 54–78. doi:10.4018/IJCRMM.2018010104

Antosova, G., Sabogal-Salamanca, M., & Krizova, E. (2021). Human Capital in Tourism: A Practical Model of Endogenous and Exogenous Territorial Tourism Planning in Bahía Solano, Colombia. In V. Costa, A. Moura, & M. Mira (Eds.), *Handbook of Research on Human Capital and People Management in the Tourism Industry* (pp. 282–302). IGI Global. https://doi.org/10.4018/978-1-7998-4318-4.ch014

Arsenijević, O. M., Orčić, D., & Kastratović, E. (2017). Development of an Optimization Tool for Intangibles in SMEs: A Case Study from Serbia with a Pilot Research in the Prestige by Milka Company. In M. Vemić (Ed.), *Optimal Management Strategies in Small and Medium Enterprises* (pp. 320–347). Hershey, PA: IGI Global. doi:10.4018/978-1-5225-1949-2.ch015

Aryanto, V. D., Wismantoro, Y., & Widyatmoko, K. (2018). Implementing Eco-Innovation by Utilizing the Internet to Enhance Firm's Marketing Performance: Study of Green Batik Small and Medium Enterprises in Indonesia. *International Journal of E-Business Research, 14*(1), 21–36. doi:10.4018/IJEBR.2018010102

Asero, V., & Billi, S. (2022). New Perspective of Networking in the DMO Model. In M. Valeri (Ed.), *New Governance and Management in Touristic Destinations* (pp. 105–118). IGI Global. https://doi.org/10.4018/978-1-6684-3889-3.ch007

Atiku, S. O., & Fields, Z. (2017). Multicultural Orientations for 21st Century Global Leadership. In N. Baporikar (Ed.), *Management Education for Global Leadership* (pp. 28–51). Hershey, PA: IGI Global. doi:10.4018/978-1-5225-1013-0.ch002

Atiku, S. O., & Fields, Z. (2018). Organisational Learning Dimensions and Talent Retention Strategies for the Service Industries. In N. Baporikar (Ed.), *Global Practices in Knowledge Management for Societal and Organizational Development* (pp. 358–381). Hershey, PA: IGI Global. doi:10.4018/978-1-5225-3009-1.ch017

Atsa'am, D. D., & Kuset Bodur, E. (2021). Pattern Mining on How Organizational Tenure Affects the Psychological Capital of Employees Within the Hospitality and Tourism Industry: Linking Employees' Organizational Tenure With PsyCap. *International Journal of Tourism and Hospitality Management in the Digital Age, 5*(2), 17–28. https://doi.org/10.4018/IJTHMDA.2021070102

Ávila, L., & Teixeira, L. (2018). The Main Concepts Behind the Dematerialization of Business Processes. In M. Khosrow-Pour, D.B.A. (Ed.), Encyclopedia of Information Science and Technology, Fourth Edition (pp. 888-898). Hershey, PA: IGI Global. https://doi.org/ doi:10.4018/978-1-5225-2255-3.ch076

Ayorekire, J., Mugizi, F., Obua, J., & Ampaire, G. (2022). Community-Based Tourism and Local People's Perceptions Towards Conservation: The Case of Queen Elizabeth Conservation Area, Uganda. In I. Mensah & E. Afenyo-Agbe (Eds.), *Prospects and Challenges of Community-Based Tourism and Changing Demographics* (pp. 56–82). IGI Global. https://doi.org/10.4018/978-1-7998-7335-8.ch003

Baleiro, R. (2022). Tourist Literature and the Architecture of Travel in Olga Tokarczuk and Patti Smith. In R. Baleiro & R. Pereira (Eds.), *Global Perspectives on Literary Tourism and Film-Induced Tourism* (pp. 202-216). IGI Global. https://doi.org/10.4018/978-1-7998-8262-6.ch011

Barat, S. (2021). Looking at the Future of Medical Tourism in Asia. *International Journal of Tourism and Hospitality Management in the Digital Age, 5*(1), 19–33. https://doi.org/10.4018/IJTHMDA.2021010102

Barbosa, C. A., Magalhães, M., & Nunes, M. R. (2021). Travel Instagramability: A Way of Choosing a Destination? In M. Dinis, L. Bonixe, S. Lamy, & Z. Breda (Eds.), *Impact of New Media in Tourism* (pp. 173-190). IGI Global. https://doi.org/10.4018/978-1-7998-7095-1.ch011

Bari, M. W., & Khan, Q. (2021). Pakistan as a Destination of Religious Tourism. In E. Alaverdov & M. Bari (Eds.), *Global Development of Religious Tourism* (pp. 1-10). IGI Global. https://doi.org/10.4018/978-1-7998-5792-1.ch001

Bartens, Y., Chunpir, H. I., Schulte, F., & Voß, S. (2017). Business/IT Alignment in Two-Sided Markets: A COBIT 5 Analysis for Media Streaming Business Models. In S. De Haes & W. Van Grembergen (Eds.), *Strategic IT Governance and Alignment in Business Settings* (pp. 82–111). Hershey, PA: IGI Global. doi:10.4018/978-1-5225-0861-8.ch004

Bashayreh, A. M. (2018). Organizational Culture and Organizational Performance. In W. Lee & F. Sabetzadeh (Eds.), *Contemporary Knowledge and Systems Science* (pp. 50–69). Hershey, PA: IGI Global. doi:10.4018/978-1-5225-5655-8.ch003

Bechthold, L., Lude, M., & Prügl, R. (2021). Crisis Favors the Prepared Firm: How Organizational Ambidexterity Relates to Perceptions of Organizational Resilience. In A. Zehrer, G. Glowka, K. Schwaiger, & V. Ranacher-Lackner (Eds.), *Resiliency Models and Addressing Future Risks for Family Firms in the Tourism Industry* (pp. 178–205). IGI Global. https://doi.org/10.4018/978-1-7998-7352-5.ch008

Bedford, D. A. (2018). Sustainable Knowledge Management Strategies: Aligning Business Capabilities and Knowledge Management Goals. In N. Baporikar (Ed.), *Global Practices in Knowledge Management for Societal and Organizational Development* (pp. 46–73). Hershey, PA: IGI Global. doi:10.4018/978-1-5225-3009-1.ch003

Bekjanov, D., & Matyusupov, B. (2021). Influence of Innovative Processes in the Competitiveness of Tourist Destination. In J. Soares (Ed.), *Innovation and Entrepreneurial Opportunities in Community Tourism* (pp. 243–263). IGI Global. https://doi.org/10.4018/978-1-7998-4855-4.ch014

Bharwani, S., & Musunuri, D. (2018). Reflection as a Process From Theory to Practice. In M. Khosrow-Pour, D.B.A. (Ed.), Encyclopedia of Information Science and Technology, Fourth Edition (pp. 1529-1539). Hershey, PA: IGI Global. doi:10.4018/978-1-5225-2255-3.ch132

Bhatt, G. D., Wang, Z., & Rodger, J. A. (2017). Information Systems Capabilities and Their Effects on Competitive Advantages: A Study of Chinese Companies. *Information Resources Management Journal*, *30*(3), 41–57. doi:10.4018/IRMJ.2017070103

Bhushan, M., & Yadav, A. (2017). Concept of Cloud Computing in ESB. In R. Bhadoria, N. Chaudhari, G. Tomar, & S. Singh (Eds.), *Exploring Enterprise Service Bus in the Service-Oriented Architecture Paradigm* (pp. 116–127). Hershey, PA: IGI Global. doi:10.4018/978-1-5225-2157-0.ch008

Bhushan, S. (2017). System Dynamics Base-Model of Humanitarian Supply Chain (HSCM) in Disaster Prone Eco-Communities of India: A Discussion on Simulation and Scenario Results. *International Journal of System Dynamics Applications, 6*(3), 20–37. doi:10.4018/IJSDA.2017070102

Binder, D., & Miller, J. W. (2021). A Generations' Perspective on Employer Branding in Tourism. In V. Costa, A. Moura, & M. Mira (Eds.), *Handbook of Research on Human Capital and People Management in the Tourism Industry* (pp. 152–174). IGI Global. https://doi.org/10.4018/978-1-7998-4318-4.ch008

Birch Freeman, A. A., Mensah, I., & Antwi, K. B. (2022). Smiling vs. Frowning Faces: Community Participation for Sustainable Tourism in Ghanaian Communities. In I. Mensah & E. Afenyo-Agbe (Eds.), *Prospects and Challenges of Community-Based Tourism and Changing Demographics* (pp. 83–106). IGI Global. https://doi.org/10.4018/978-1-7998-7335-8.ch004

Biswas, A., & De, A. K. (2017). On Development of a Fuzzy Stochastic Programming Model with Its Application to Business Management. In S. Trivedi, S. Dey, A. Kumar, & T. Panda (Eds.), *Handbook of Research on Advanced Data Mining Techniques and Applications for Business Intelligence* (pp. 353–378). Hershey, PA: IGI Global. doi:10.4018/978-1-5225-2031-3.ch021

Boragnio, A., & Faracce Macia, C. (2021). "Taking Care of Yourself at Home": Use of E-Commerce About Food and Care During the COVID-19 Pandemic in the City of Buenos Aires. In M. Korstanje (Ed.), *Socio-Economic Effects and Recovery Efforts for the Rental Industry: Post-COVID-19 Strategies* (pp. 45–71). IGI Global. https://doi.org/10.4018/978-1-7998-7287-0.ch003

Borges, V. D. (2021). Happiness: The Basis for Public Policy in Tourism. In A. Perinotto, V. Mayer, & J. Soares (Eds.), *Rebuilding and Restructuring the Tourism Industry: Infusion of Happiness and Quality of Life* (pp. 1–25). IGI Global. https://doi.org/10.4018/978-1-7998-7239-9.ch001

Bücker, J., & Ernste, K. (2018). Use of Brand Heroes in Strategic Reputation Management: The Case of Bacardi, Adidas, and Daimler. In A. Erdemir (Ed.), *Reputation Management Techniques in Public Relations* (pp. 126–150). Hershey, PA: IGI Global. doi:10.4018/978-1-5225-3619-2.ch007

Buluk Eşitti, B. (2021). COVID-19 and Alternative Tourism: New Destinations and New Tourism Products. In M. Demir, A. Dalgıç, & F. Ergen (Eds.), *Handbook of Research on the Impacts and Implications of COVID-19 on the Tourism Industry* (pp. 786–805). IGI Global. https://doi.org/10.4018/978-1-7998-8231-2.ch038

Bureš, V. (2018). Industry 4.0 From the Systems Engineering Perspective: Alternative Holistic Framework Development. In R. Brunet-Thornton & F. Martinez (Eds.), *Analyzing the Impacts of Industry 4.0 in Modern Business Environments* (pp. 199–223). Hershey, PA: IGI Global. doi:10.4018/978-1-5225-3468-6.ch011

Buzady, Z. (2017). Resolving the Magic Cube of Effective Case Teaching: Benchmarking Case Teaching Practices in Emerging Markets – Insights from the Central European University Business School, Hungary. In D. Latusek (Ed.), *Case Studies as a Teaching Tool in Management Education* (pp. 79–103). Hershey, PA: IGI Global. doi:10.4018/978-1-5225-0770-3.ch005

Camillo, A. (2021). *Legal Matters, Risk Management, and Risk Prevention: From Forming a Business to Legal Representation*. IGI Global. doi:10.4018/978-1-7998-4342-9.ch004

Căpusneanu, S., & Topor, D. I. (2018). Business Ethics and Cost Management in SMEs: Theories of Business Ethics and Cost Management Ethos. In I. Oncioiu (Ed.), *Ethics and Decision-Making for Sustainable Business Practices* (pp. 109–127). Hershey, PA: IGI Global. doi:10.4018/978-1-5225-3773-1.ch007

Chan, R. L., Mo, P. L., & Moon, K. K. (2018). Strategic and Tactical Measures in Managing Enterprise Risks: A Study of the Textile and Apparel Industry. In K. Strang, M. Korstanje, & N. Vajjhala (Eds.), *Research, Practices, and Innovations in Global Risk and Contingency Management* (pp. 1–19). Hershey, PA: IGI Global. doi:10.4018/978-1-5225-4754-9.ch001

Charlier, S. D., Burke-Smalley, L. A., & Fisher, S. L. (2018). Undergraduate Programs in the U.S: A Contextual and Content-Based Analysis. In J. Mendy (Ed.), *Teaching Human Resources and Organizational Behavior at the College Level* (pp. 26–57). Hershey, PA: IGI Global. doi:10.4018/978-1-5225-2820-3.ch002

Chumillas, J., Güell, M., & Quer, P. (2022). The Use of ICT in Tourist and Educational Literary Routes: The Role of the Guide. In C. Ramos, S. Quinteiro, & A. Gonçalves (Eds.), *ICT as Innovator Between Tourism and Culture* (pp. 15–29). IGI Global. https://doi.org/10.4018/978-1-7998-8165-0.ch002

Dahlberg, T., Kivijärvi, H., & Saarinen, T. (2017). IT Investment Consistency and Other Factors Influencing the Success of IT Performance. In S. De Haes & W. Van Grembergen (Eds.), *Strategic IT Governance and Alignment in Business Settings* (pp. 176–208). Hershey, PA: IGI Global. doi:10.4018/978-1-5225-0861-8.ch007

Damnjanović, A. M. (2017). Knowledge Management Optimization through IT and E-Business Utilization: A Qualitative Study on Serbian SMEs. In M. Vemić (Ed.), *Optimal Management Strategies in Small and Medium Enterprises* (pp. 249–267). Hershey, PA: IGI Global. doi:10.4018/978-1-5225-1949-2.ch012

Daneshpour, H. (2017). Integrating Sustainable Development into Project Portfolio Management through Application of Open Innovation. In M. Vemić (Ed.), *Optimal Management Strategies in Small and Medium Enterprises* (pp. 370–387). Hershey, PA: IGI Global. doi:10.4018/978-1-5225-1949-2.ch017

Daniel, A. D., & Reis de Castro, V. (2018). Entrepreneurship Education: How to Measure the Impact on Nascent Entrepreneurs. In A. Carrizo Moreira, J. Guilherme Leitão Dantas, & F. Manuel Valente (Eds.), *Nascent Entrepreneurship and Successful New Venture Creation* (pp. 85–110). Hershey, PA: IGI Global. doi:10.4018/978-1-5225-2936-1.ch004

David, R., Swami, B. N., & Tangirala, S. (2018). Ethics Impact on Knowledge Management in Organizational Development: A Case Study. In N. Baporikar (Ed.), *Global Practices in Knowledge Management for Societal and Organizational Development* (pp. 19–45). Hershey, PA: IGI Global. doi:10.4018/978-1-5225-3009-1.ch002

De Uña-Álvarez, E., & Villarino-Pérez, M. (2022). Fostering Ecocultural Resources, Identity, and Tourism in Inland Territories (Galicia, NW Spain). In G. Fernandes (Ed.), *Challenges and New Opportunities for Tourism in Inland Territories: Ecocultural Resources and Sustainable Initiatives* (pp. 1-16). IGI Global. https://doi.org/10.4018/978-1-7998-7339-6.ch001

Delias, P., & Lakiotaki, K. (2018). Discovering Process Horizontal Boundaries to Facilitate Process Comprehension. *International Journal of Operations Research and Information Systems*, *9*(2), 1–31. doi:10.4018/IJORIS.2018040101

Denholm, J., & Lee-Davies, L. (2018). Success Factors for Games in Business and Project Management. In *Enhancing Education and Training Initiatives Through Serious Games* (pp. 34–68). Hershey, PA: IGI Global. doi:10.4018/978-1-5225-3689-5.ch002

Deshpande, M. (2017). Best Practices in Management Institutions for Global Leadership: Policy Aspects. In N. Baporikar (Ed.), *Management Education for Global Leadership* (pp. 1–27). Hershey, PA: IGI Global. doi:10.4018/978-1-5225-1013-0.ch001

Deshpande, M. (2018). Policy Perspectives for SMEs Knowledge Management. In N. Baporikar (Ed.), *Knowledge Integration Strategies for Entrepreneurship and Sustainability* (pp. 23–46). Hershey, PA: IGI Global. doi:10.4018/978-1-5225-5115-7.ch002

Dezdar, S. (2017). ERP Implementation Projects in Asian Countries: A Comparative Study on Iran and China. *International Journal of Information Technology Project Management*, *8*(3), 52–68. doi:10.4018/IJITPM.2017070104

Domingos, D., Respício, A., & Martinho, R. (2017). Reliability of IoT-Aware BPMN Healthcare Processes. In C. Reis & M. Maximiano (Eds.), *Internet of Things and Advanced Application in Healthcare* (pp. 214–248). Hershey, PA: IGI Global. doi:10.4018/978-1-5225-1820-4.ch008

Dosumu, O., Hussain, J., & El-Gohary, H. (2017). An Exploratory Study of the Impact of Government Policies on the Development of Small and Medium Enterprises in Developing Countries: The Case of Nigeria. *International Journal of Customer Relationship Marketing and Management*, *8*(4), 51–62. doi:10.4018/IJCRMM.2017100104

Durst, S., Bruns, G., & Edvardsson, I. R. (2017). Retaining Knowledge in Smaller Building and Construction Firms. *International Journal of Knowledge and Systems Science*, *8*(3), 1–12. doi:10.4018/IJKSS.2017070101

Edvardsson, I. R., & Durst, S. (2017). Outsourcing, Knowledge, and Learning: A Critical Review. *International Journal of Knowledge-Based Organizations*, *7*(2), 13–26. doi:10.4018/IJKBO.2017040102

Edwards, J. S. (2018). Integrating Knowledge Management and Business Processes. In M. Khosrow-Pour, D.B.A. (Ed.), Encyclopedia of Information Science and Technology, Fourth Edition (pp. 5046-5055). Hershey, PA: IGI Global. doi:10.4018/978-1-5225-2255-3.ch437

Eichelberger, S., & Peters, M. (2021). Family Firm Management in Turbulent Times: Opportunities for Responsible Tourism. In A. Zehrer, G. Glowka, K. Schwaiger, & V. Ranacher-Lackner (Eds.), *Resiliency Models and Addressing Future Risks for Family Firms in the Tourism Industry* (pp. 103–124). IGI Global. https://doi.org/10.4018/978-1-7998-7352-5.ch005

Eide, D., Hjalager, A., & Hansen, M. (2022). Innovative Certifications in Adventure Tourism: Attributes and Diffusion. In R. Augusto Costa, F. Brandão, Z. Breda, & C. Costa (Eds.), *Planning and Managing the Experience Economy in Tourism* (pp. 161-175). IGI Global. https://doi.org/10.4018/978-1-7998-8775-1.ch009

Ejiogu, A. O. (2018). Economics of Farm Management. In *Agricultural Finance and Opportunities for Investment and Expansion* (pp. 56–72). Hershey, PA: IGI Global. doi:10.4018/978-1-5225-3059-6.ch003

Ekanem, I., & Abiade, G. E. (2018). Factors Influencing the Use of E-Commerce by Small Enterprises in Nigeria. *International Journal of ICT Research in Africa and the Middle East*, *7*(1), 37–53. doi:10.4018/IJICTRAME.2018010103

Ekanem, I., & Alrossais, L. A. (2017). Succession Challenges Facing Family Businesses in Saudi Arabia. In P. Zgheib (Ed.), *Entrepreneurship and Business Innovation in the Middle East* (pp. 122–146). Hershey, PA: IGI Global. doi:10.4018/978-1-5225-2066-5.ch007

El Faquih, L., & Fredj, M. (2017). Ontology-Based Framework for Quality in Configurable Process Models. *Journal of Electronic Commerce in Organizations*, *15*(2), 48–60. doi:10.4018/JECO.2017040104

Faisal, M. N., & Talib, F. (2017). Building Ambidextrous Supply Chains in SMEs: How to Tackle the Barriers? *International Journal of Information Systems and Supply Chain Management*, *10*(4), 80–100. doi:10.4018/IJISSCM.2017100105

Fernandes, T. M., Gomes, J., & Romão, M. (2017). Investments in E-Government: A Benefit Management Case Study. *International Journal of Electronic Government Research*, *13*(3), 1–17. doi:10.4018/IJEGR.2017070101

Figueira, L. M., Honrado, G. R., & Dionísio, M. S. (2021). Human Capital Management in the Tourism Industry in Portugal. In V. Costa, A. Moura, & M. Mira (Eds.), *Handbook of Research on Human Capital and People Management in the Tourism Industry* (pp. 1–19). IGI Global. doi:10.4018/978-1-7998-4318-4.ch001

Gao, S. S., Oreal, S., & Zhang, J. (2018). Contemporary Financial Risk Management Perceptions and Practices of Small-Sized Chinese Businesses. In I. Management Association (Ed.), Global Business Expansion: Concepts, Methodologies, Tools, and Applications (pp. 917-931). Hershey, PA: IGI Global. doi:10.4018/978-1-5225-5481-3.ch041

Garg, R., & Berning, S. C. (2017). Indigenous Chinese Management Philosophies: Key Concepts and Relevance for Modern Chinese Firms. In B. Christiansen & G. Koc (Eds.), *Transcontinental Strategies for Industrial Development and Economic Growth* (pp. 43–57). Hershey, PA: IGI Global. doi:10.4018/978-1-5225-2160-0.ch003

Gencer, Y. G. (2017). Supply Chain Management in Retailing Business. In U. Akkucuk (Ed.), *Ethics and Sustainability in Global Supply Chain Management* (pp. 197–210). Hershey, PA: IGI Global. doi:10.4018/978-1-5225-2036-8.ch011

Gera, R., Arora, S., & Malik, S. (2021). Emotional Labor in the Tourism Industry: Strategies, Antecedents, and Outcomes. In V. Costa, A. Moura, & M. Mira (Eds.), *Handbook of Research on Human Capital and People Management in the Tourism Industry* (pp. 73–91). IGI Global. https://doi.org/10.4018/978-1-7998-4318-4.ch004

Giacosa, E. (2018). The Increasing of the Regional Development Thanks to the Luxury Business Innovation. In L. Carvalho (Ed.), *Handbook of Research on Entrepreneurial Ecosystems and Social Dynamics in a Globalized World* (pp. 260–273). Hershey, PA: IGI Global. doi:10.4018/978-1-5225-3525-6.ch011

Glowka, G., Tusch, M., & Zehrer, A. (2021). The Risk Perception of Family Business Owner-Manager in the Tourism Industry: A Qualitative Comparison of the Intra-Firm Senior and Junior Generation. In A. Zehrer, G. Glowka, K. Schwaiger, & V. Ranacher-Lackner (Eds.), *Resiliency Models and Addressing Future Risks for Family Firms in the Tourism Industry* (pp. 126–153). IGI Global. https://doi.org/10.4018/978-1-7998-7352-5.ch006

Glykas, M., & George, J. (2017). Quality and Process Management Systems in the UAE Maritime Industry. *International Journal of Productivity Management and Assessment Technologies*, *5*(1), 20–39. doi:10.4018/IJPMAT.2017010102

Glykas, M., Valiris, G., Kokkinaki, A., & Koutsoukou, Z. (2018). Banking Business Process Management Implementation. *International Journal of Productivity Management and Assessment Technologies*, *6*(1), 50–69. doi:10.4018/IJPMAT.2018010104

Gomes, J., & Romão, M. (2017). The Balanced Scorecard: Keeping Updated and Aligned with Today's Business Trends. *International Journal of Productivity Management and Assessment Technologies*, *5*(2), 1–15. doi:10.4018/IJPMAT.2017070101

Gomes, J., & Romão, M. (2017). Aligning Information Systems and Technology with Benefit Management and Balanced Scorecard. In S. De Haes & W. Van Grembergen (Eds.), *Strategic IT Governance and Alignment in Business Settings* (pp. 112–131). Hershey, PA: IGI Global. doi:10.4018/978-1-5225-0861-8.ch005

Goyal, A. (2021). Communicating and Building Destination Brands With New Media. In M. Dinis, L. Bonixe, S. Lamy, & Z. Breda (Eds.), *Impact of New Media in Tourism* (pp. 1-20). IGI Global. https://doi.org/10.4018/978-1-7998-7095-1.ch001

Grefen, P., & Turetken, O. (2017). Advanced Business Process Management in Networked E-Business Scenarios. *International Journal of E-Business Research, 13*(4), 70–104. doi:10.4018/IJEBR.2017100105

Guasca, M., Van Broeck, A. M., & Vanneste, D. (2021). Tourism and the Social Reintegration of Colombian Ex-Combatants. In J. da Silva, Z. Breda, & F. Carbone (Eds.), *Role and Impact of Tourism in Peacebuilding and Conflict Transformation* (pp. 66-86). IGI Global. https://doi.org/10.4018/978-1-7998-5053-3.ch005

Haider, A., & Saetang, S. (2017). Strategic IT Alignment in Service Sector. In S. Rozenes & Y. Cohen (Eds.), *Handbook of Research on Strategic Alliances and Value Co-Creation in the Service Industry* (pp. 231–258). Hershey, PA: IGI Global. doi:10.4018/978-1-5225-2084-9.ch012

Hajilari, A. B., Ghadaksaz, M., & Fasghandis, G. S. (2017). Assessing Organizational Readiness for Implementing ERP System Using Fuzzy Expert System Approach. *International Journal of Enterprise Information Systems, 13*(1), 67–85. doi:10.4018/IJEIS.2017010105

Haldorai, A., Ramu, A., & Murugan, S. (2018). Social Aware Cognitive Radio Networks: Effectiveness of Social Networks as a Strategic Tool for Organizational Business Management. In H. Bansal, G. Shrivastava, G. Nguyen, & L. Stanciu (Eds.), *Social Network Analytics for Contemporary Business Organizations* (pp. 188–202). Hershey, PA: IGI Global. doi:10.4018/978-1-5225-5097-6.ch010

Hall, O. P. Jr. (2017). Social Media Driven Management Education. *International Journal of Knowledge-Based Organizations, 7*(2), 43–59. doi:10.4018/IJKBO.2017040104

Hanifah, H., Halim, H. A., Ahmad, N. H., & Vafaei-Zadeh, A. (2017). Innovation Culture as a Mediator Between Specific Human Capital and Innovation Performance Among Bumiputera SMEs in Malaysia. In N. Ahmad, T. Ramayah, H. Halim, & S. Rahman (Eds.), *Handbook of Research on Small and Medium Enterprises in Developing Countries* (pp. 261–279). Hershey, PA: IGI Global. doi:10.4018/978-1-5225-2165-5.ch012

Hartlieb, S., & Silvius, G. (2017). Handling Uncertainty in Project Management and Business Development: Similarities and Differences. In Y. Raydugin (Ed.), *Handbook of Research on Leveraging Risk and Uncertainties for Effective Project Management* (pp. 337–362). Hershey, PA: IGI Global. doi:10.4018/978-1-5225-1790-0.ch016

Hass, K. B. (2017). Living on the Edge: Managing Project Complexity. In Y. Raydugin (Ed.), *Handbook of Research on Leveraging Risk and Uncertainties for Effective Project Management* (pp. 177–201). Hershey, PA: IGI Global. doi:10.4018/978-1-5225-1790-0.ch009

Hawking, P., & Carmine Sellitto, C. (2017). Developing an Effective Strategy for Organizational Business Intelligence. In M. Tavana (Ed.), *Enterprise Information Systems and the Digitalization of Business Functions* (pp. 222–237). Hershey, PA: IGI Global. doi:10.4018/978-1-5225-2382-6.ch010

Hawking, P., & Sellitto, C. (2017). A Fast-Moving Consumer Goods Company and Business Intelligence Strategy Development. *International Journal of Enterprise Information Systems*, *13*(2), 22–33. doi:10.4018/IJEIS.2017040102

Hawking, P., & Sellitto, C. (2017). Business Intelligence Strategy: Two Case Studies. *International Journal of Business Intelligence Research*, *8*(2), 17–30. doi:10.4018/IJBIR.2017070102

Hee, W. J., Jalleh, G., Lai, H., & Lin, C. (2017). E-Commerce and IT Projects: Evaluation and Management Issues in Australian and Taiwanese Hospitals. *International Journal of Public Health Management and Ethics*, *2*(1), 69–90. doi:10.4018/IJPHME.2017010104

Hernandez, A. A. (2018). Exploring the Factors to Green IT Adoption of SMEs in the Philippines. *Journal of Cases on Information Technology*, *20*(2), 49–66. doi:10.4018/JCIT.2018040104

Hollman, A., Bickford, S., & Hollman, T. (2017). Cyber InSecurity: A Post-Mortem Attempt to Assess Cyber Problems from IT and Business Management Perspectives. *Journal of Cases on Information Technology*, *19*(3), 42–70. doi:10.4018/JCIT.2017070104

Ibrahim, F., & Zainin, N. M. (2021). Exploring the Technological Impacts: The Case of Museums in Brunei Darussalam. *International Journal of Tourism and Hospitality Management in the Digital Age*, *5*(1), 1–18. https://doi.org/10.4018/IJTHMDA.2021010101

Igbinakhase, I. (2017). Responsible and Sustainable Management Practices in Developing and Developed Business Environments. In Z. Fields (Ed.), *Collective Creativity for Responsible and Sustainable Business Practice* (pp. 180–207). Hershey, PA: IGI Global. doi:10.4018/978-1-5225-1823-5.ch010

Iwata, J. J., & Hoskins, R. G. (2017). Managing Indigenous Knowledge in Tanzania: A Business Perspective. In P. Jain & N. Mnjama (Eds.), *Managing Knowledge Resources and Records in Modern Organizations* (pp. 198–214). Hershey, PA: IGI Global. doi:10.4018/978-1-5225-1965-2.ch012

Jain, P. (2017). Ethical and Legal Issues in Knowledge Management Life-Cycle in Business. In P. Jain & N. Mnjama (Eds.), *Managing Knowledge Resources and Records in Modern Organizations* (pp. 82–101). Hershey, PA: IGI Global. doi:10.4018/978-1-5225-1965-2.ch006

James, S., & Hauli, E. (2017). Holistic Management Education at Tanzanian Rural Development Planning Institute. In N. Baporikar (Ed.), *Management Education for Global Leadership* (pp. 112–136). Hershey, PA: IGI Global. doi:10.4018/978-1-5225-1013-0.ch006

Janošková, M., Csikósová, A., & Čulková, K. (2018). Measurement of Company Performance as Part of Its Strategic Management. In R. Leon (Ed.), *Managerial Strategies for Business Sustainability During Turbulent Times* (pp. 309–335). Hershey, PA: IGI Global. doi:10.4018/978-1-5225-2716-9.ch017

Jean-Vasile, A., & Alecu, A. (2017). Theoretical and Practical Approaches in Understanding the Influences of Cost-Productivity-Profit Trinomial in Contemporary Enterprises. In A. Jean Vasile & D. Nicolò (Eds.), *Sustainable Entrepreneurship and Investments in the Green Economy* (pp. 28–62). Hershey, PA: IGI Global. doi:10.4018/978-1-5225-2075-7.ch002

Joia, L. A., & Correia, J. C. (2018). CIO Competencies From the IT Professional Perspective: Insights From Brazil. *Journal of Global Information Management, 26*(2), 74–103. doi:10.4018/JGIM.2018040104

Juma, A., & Mzera, N. (2017). Knowledge Management and Records Management and Competitive Advantage in Business. In P. Jain & N. Mnjama (Eds.), *Managing Knowledge Resources and Records in Modern Organizations* (pp. 15–28). Hershey, PA: IGI Global. doi:10.4018/978-1-5225-1965-2.ch002

K., I., & A, V. (2018). Monitoring and Auditing in the Cloud. In K. Munir (Ed.), *Cloud Computing Technologies for Green Enterprises* (pp. 318-350). Hershey, PA: IGI Global. https://doi.org/ doi:10.4018/978-1-5225-3038-1.ch013

Kabra, G., Ghosh, V., & Ramesh, A. (2018). Enterprise Integrated Business Process Management and Business Intelligence Framework for Business Process Sustainability. In A. Paul, D. Bhattacharyya, & S. Anand (Eds.), *Green Initiatives for Business Sustainability and Value Creation* (pp. 228–238). Hershey, PA: IGI Global. doi:10.4018/978-1-5225-2662-9.ch010

Kaoud, M. (2017). Investigation of Customer Knowledge Management: A Case Study Research. *International Journal of Service Science, Management, Engineering, and Technology*, *8*(2), 12–22. doi:10.4018/IJSSMET.2017040102

Katuu, S. (2018). A Comparative Assessment of Enterprise Content Management Maturity Models. In N. Gwangwava & M. Mutingi (Eds.), *E-Manufacturing and E-Service Strategies in Contemporary Organizations* (pp. 93–118). Hershey, PA: IGI Global. doi:10.4018/978-1-5225-3628-4.ch005

Khan, M. Y., & Abir, T. (2022). The Role of Social Media Marketing in the Tourism and Hospitality Industry: A Conceptual Study on Bangladesh. In C. Ramos, S. Quinteiro, & A. Gonçalves (Eds.), *ICT as Innovator Between Tourism and Culture* (pp. 213–229). IGI Global. https://doi.org/10.4018/978-1-7998-8165-0.ch013

Kinnunen, S., Ylä-Kujala, A., Marttonen-Arola, S., Kärri, T., & Baglee, D. (2018). Internet of Things in Asset Management: Insights from Industrial Professionals and Academia. *International Journal of Service Science, Management, Engineering, and Technology*, *9*(2), 104–119. doi:10.4018/IJSSMET.2018040105

Klein, A. Z., Sabino de Freitas, A., Machado, L., Freitas, J. C. Jr, Graziola, P. G. Jr, & Schlemmer, E. (2017). Virtual Worlds Applications for Management Education. In L. Tomei (Ed.), *Exploring the New Era of Technology-Infused Education* (pp. 279–299). Hershey, PA: IGI Global. doi:10.4018/978-1-5225-1709-2.ch017

Kővári, E., Saleh, M., & Steinbachné Hajmásy, G. (2022). The Impact of Corporate Digital Responsibility (CDR) on Internal Stakeholders' Satisfaction in Hungarian Upscale Hotels. In M. Valeri (Ed.), *New Governance and Management in Touristic Destinations* (pp. 35–51). IGI Global. https://doi.org/10.4018/978-1-6684-3889-3.ch003

Kożuch, B., & Jabłoński, A. (2017). Adopting the Concept of Business Models in Public Management. In M. Lewandowski & B. Kożuch (Eds.), *Public Sector Entrepreneurship and the Integration of Innovative Business Models* (pp. 10–46). Hershey, PA: IGI Global. doi:10.4018/978-1-5225-2215-7.ch002

Kumar, J., Adhikary, A., & Jha, A. (2017). Small Active Investors' Perceptions and Preferences Towards Tax Saving Mutual Fund Schemes in Eastern India: An Empirical Note. *International Journal of Asian Business and Information Management*, *8*(2), 35–45. doi:10.4018/IJABIM.2017040103

Latusi, S., & Fissore, M. (2021). Pilgrimage Routes to Happiness: Comparing the Camino de Santiago and Via Francigena. In A. Perinotto, V. Mayer, & J. Soares (Eds.), *Rebuilding and Restructuring the Tourism Industry: Infusion of Happiness and Quality of Life* (pp. 157–182). IGI Global. https://doi.org/10.4018/978-1-7998-7239-9.ch008

Lavassani, K. M., & Movahedi, B. (2017). Applications Driven Information Systems: Beyond Networks toward Business Ecosystems. *International Journal of Innovation in the Digital Economy*, *8*(1), 61–75. doi:10.4018/IJIDE.2017010104

Lazzareschi, V. H., & Brito, M. S. (2017). Strategic Information Management: Proposal of Business Project Model. In G. Jamil, A. Soares, & C. Pessoa (Eds.), *Handbook of Research on Information Management for Effective Logistics and Supply Chains* (pp. 59–88). Hershey, PA: IGI Global. doi:10.4018/978-1-5225-0973-8.ch004

Lechuga Sancho, M. P., & Martín Navarro, A. (2022). Evolution of the Literature on Social Responsibility in the Tourism Sector: A Systematic Literature Review. In G. Fernandes (Ed.), *Challenges and New Opportunities for Tourism in Inland Territories: Ecocultural Resources and Sustainable Initiatives* (pp. 169–186). IGI Global. https://doi.org/10.4018/978-1-7998-7339-6.ch010

Lederer, M., Kurz, M., & Lazarov, P. (2017). Usage and Suitability of Methods for Strategic Business Process Initiatives: A Multi Case Study Research. *International Journal of Productivity Management and Assessment Technologies*, *5*(1), 40–51. doi:10.4018/IJPMAT.2017010103

Lee, I. (2017). A Social Enterprise Business Model and a Case Study of Pacific Community Ventures (PCV). In V. Potocan, M. Üngan, & Z. Nedelko (Eds.), *Handbook of Research on Managerial Solutions in Non-Profit Organizations* (pp. 182–204). Hershey, PA: IGI Global. doi:10.4018/978-1-5225-0731-4.ch009

Leon, L. A., Seal, K. C., Przasnyski, Z. H., & Wiedenman, I. (2017). Skills and Competencies Required for Jobs in Business Analytics: A Content Analysis of Job Advertisements Using Text Mining. *International Journal of Business Intelligence Research*, *8*(1), 1–25. doi:10.4018/IJBIR.2017010101

Levy, C. L., & Elias, N. I. (2017). SOHO Users' Perceptions of Reliability and Continuity of Cloud-Based Services. In M. Moore (Ed.), *Cybersecurity Breaches and Issues Surrounding Online Threat Protection* (pp. 248–287). Hershey, PA: IGI Global. doi:10.4018/978-1-5225-1941-6.ch011

Levy, M. (2018). Change Management Serving Knowledge Management and Organizational Development: Reflections and Review. In N. Baporikar (Ed.), *Global Practices in Knowledge Management for Societal and Organizational Development* (pp. 256–270). Hershey, PA: IGI Global. doi:10.4018/978-1-5225-3009-1.ch012

Lewandowski, M. (2017). Public Organizations and Business Model Innovation: The Role of Public Service Design. In M. Lewandowski & B. Kożuch (Eds.), *Public Sector Entrepreneurship and the Integration of Innovative Business Models* (pp. 47–72). Hershey, PA: IGI Global. doi:10.4018/978-1-5225-2215-7.ch003

Lhannaoui, H., Kabbaj, M. I., & Bakkoury, Z. (2017). A Survey of Risk-Aware Business Process Modelling. *International Journal of Risk and Contingency Management, 6*(3), 14–26. doi:10.4018/IJRCM.2017070102

Li, J., Sun, W., Jiang, W., Yang, H., & Zhang, L. (2017). How the Nature of Exogenous Shocks and Crises Impact Company Performance?: The Effects of Industry Characteristics. *International Journal of Risk and Contingency Management, 6*(4), 40–55. doi:10.4018/IJRCM.2017100103

Lopez-Fernandez, M., Perez-Perez, M., Serrano-Bedia, A., & Cobo-Gonzalez, A. (2021). Small and Medium Tourism Enterprise Survival in Times of Crisis: "El Capricho de Gaudí. In D. Toubes & N. Araújo-Vila (Eds.), *Risk, Crisis, and Disaster Management in Small and Medium-Sized Tourism Enterprises* (pp. 103–129). IGI Global. doi:10.4018/978-1-7998-6996-2.ch005

Mahajan, A., Maidullah, S., & Hossain, M. R. (2022). Experience Toward Smart Tour Guide Apps in Travelling: An Analysis of Users' Reviews on Audio Odigos and Trip My Way. In R. Augusto Costa, F. Brandão, Z. Breda, & C. Costa (Eds.), *Planning and Managing the Experience Economy in Tourism* (pp. 255-273). IGI Global. https://doi.org/10.4018/978-1-7998-8775-1.ch014

Malega, P. (2017). Small and Medium Enterprises in the Slovak Republic: Status and Competitiveness of SMEs in the Global Markets and Possibilities of Optimization. In M. Vemić (Ed.), *Optimal Management Strategies in Small and Medium Enterprises* (pp. 102–124). Hershey, PA: IGI Global. doi:10.4018/978-1-5225-1949-2.ch006

Malewska, K. M. (2017). Intuition in Decision-Making on the Example of a Non-Profit Organization. In V. Potocan, M. Ünğan, & Z. Nedelko (Eds.), *Handbook of Research on Managerial Solutions in Non-Profit Organizations* (pp. 378–399). Hershey, PA: IGI Global. doi:10.4018/978-1-5225-0731-4.ch018

Maroofi, F. (2017). Entrepreneurial Orientation and Organizational Learning Ability Analysis for Innovation and Firm Performance. In N. Baporikar (Ed.), *Innovation and Shifting Perspectives in Management Education* (pp. 144–165). Hershey, PA: IGI Global. doi:10.4018/978-1-5225-1019-2.ch007

Marques, M., Moleiro, D., Brito, T. M., & Marques, T. (2021). Customer Relationship Management as an Important Relationship Marketing Tool: The Case of the Hospitality Industry in Estoril Coast. In M. Dinis, L. Bonixe, S. Lamy, & Z. Breda (Eds.), Impact of New Media in Tourism (pp. 39-56). IGI Global. https://doi.org/doi:10.4018/978-1-7998-7095-1.ch003

Martins, P. V., & Zacarias, M. (2017). A Web-based Tool for Business Process Improvement. *International Journal of Web Portals*, *9*(2), 68–84. doi:10.4018/IJWP.2017070104

Matthies, B., & Coners, A. (2017). Exploring the Conceptual Nature of e-Business Projects. *Journal of Electronic Commerce in Organizations*, *15*(3), 33–63. doi:10.4018/JECO.2017070103

Mayer, V. F., Fraga, C. C., & Silva, L. C. (2021). Contributions of Neurosciences to Studies of Well-Being in Tourism. In A. Perinotto, V. Mayer, & J. Soares (Eds.), *Rebuilding and Restructuring the Tourism Industry: Infusion of Happiness and Quality of Life* (pp. 108–128). IGI Global. https://doi.org/10.4018/978-1-7998-7239-9.ch006

McKee, J. (2018). Architecture as a Tool to Solve Business Planning Problems. In M. Khosrow-Pour, D.B.A. (Ed.), Encyclopedia of Information Science and Technology, Fourth Edition (pp. 573-586). Hershey, PA: IGI Global. doi:10.4018/978-1-5225-2255-3.ch050

McMurray, A. J., Cross, J., & Caponecchia, C. (2018). The Risk Management Profession in Australia: Business Continuity Plan Practices. In N. Bajgoric (Ed.), *Always-On Enterprise Information Systems for Modern Organizations* (pp. 112–129). Hershey, PA: IGI Global. doi:10.4018/978-1-5225-3704-5.ch006

Meddah, I. H., & Belkadi, K. (2018). Mining Patterns Using Business Process Management. In R. Hamou (Ed.), *Handbook of Research on Biomimicry in Information Retrieval and Knowledge Management* (pp. 78–89). Hershey, PA: IGI Global. doi:10.4018/978-1-5225-3004-6.ch005

Melian, A. G., & Camprubí, R. (2021). The Accessibility of Museum Websites: The Case of Barcelona. In C. Eusébio, L. Teixeira, & M. Carneiro (Eds.), *ICT Tools and Applications for Accessible Tourism* (pp. 234–255). IGI Global. https://doi.org/10.4018/978-1-7998-6428-8.ch011

Mendes, L. (2017). TQM and Knowledge Management: An Integrated Approach Towards Tacit Knowledge Management. In D. Jaziri-Bouagina & G. Jamil (Eds.), *Handbook of Research on Tacit Knowledge Management for Organizational Success* (pp. 236–263). Hershey, PA: IGI Global. doi:10.4018/978-1-5225-2394-9.ch009

Menezes, V. D., & Cavagnaro, E. (2021). Communicating Sustainable Initiatives in the Hotel Industry: The Case of the Hotel Jakarta Amsterdam. In F. Brandão, Z. Breda, R. Costa, & C. Costa (Eds.), *Handbook of Research on the Role of Tourism in Achieving Sustainable Development Goals* (pp. 224-234). IGI Global. https://doi.org/10.4018/978-1-7998-5691-7.ch013

Menezes, V. D., & Cavagnaro, E. (2021). Communicating Sustainable Initiatives in the Hotel Industry: The Case of the Hotel Jakarta Amsterdam. In F. Brandão, Z. Breda, R. Costa, & C. Costa (Eds.), *Handbook of Research on the Role of Tourism in Achieving Sustainable Development Goals* (pp. 224-234). IGI Global. https://doi.org/10.4018/978-1-7998-5691-7.ch013

Mitas, O., Bastiaansen, M., & Boode, W. (2022). If You're Happy, I'm Happy: Emotion Contagion at a Tourist Information Center. In R. Augusto Costa, F. Brandão, Z. Breda, & C. Costa (Eds.), *Planning and Managing the Experience Economy in Tourism* (pp. 122-140). IGI Global. https://doi.org/10.4018/978-1-7998-8775-1.ch007

Mnjama, N. M. (2017). Preservation of Recorded Information in Public and Private Sector Organizations. In P. Jain & N. Mnjama (Eds.), *Managing Knowledge Resources and Records in Modern Organizations* (pp. 149–167). Hershey, PA: IGI Global. doi:10.4018/978-1-5225-1965-2.ch009

Mokoqama, M., & Fields, Z. (2017). Principles of Responsible Management Education (PRME): Call for Responsible Management Education. In Z. Fields (Ed.), *Collective Creativity for Responsible and Sustainable Business Practice* (pp. 229–241). Hershey, PA: IGI Global. doi:10.4018/978-1-5225-1823-5.ch012

Monteiro, A., Lopes, S., & Carbone, F. (2021). Academic Mobility: Bridging Tourism and Peace Education. In J. da Silva, Z. Breda, & F. Carbone (Eds.), *Role and Impact of Tourism in Peacebuilding and Conflict Transformation* (pp. 275-301). IGI Global. https://doi.org/10.4018/978-1-7998-5053-3.ch016

Muniapan, B. (2017). Philosophy and Management: The Relevance of Vedanta in Management. In P. Ordóñez de Pablos (Ed.), *Managerial Strategies and Solutions for Business Success in Asia* (pp. 124–139). Hershey, PA: IGI Global. doi:10.4018/978-1-5225-1886-0.ch007

Murad, S. E., & Dowaji, S. (2017). Using Value-Based Approach for Managing Cloud-Based Services. In A. Turuk, B. Sahoo, & S. Addya (Eds.), *Resource Management and Efficiency in Cloud Computing Environments* (pp. 33–60). Hershey, PA: IGI Global. doi:10.4018/978-1-5225-1721-4.ch002

Mutahar, A. M., Daud, N. M., Thurasamy, R., Isaac, O., & Abdulsalam, R. (2018). The Mediating of Perceived Usefulness and Perceived Ease of Use: The Case of Mobile Banking in Yemen. *International Journal of Technology Diffusion*, *9*(2), 21–40. doi:10.4018/IJTD.2018040102

Naidoo, V. (2017). E-Learning and Management Education at African Universities. In N. Baporikar (Ed.), *Management Education for Global Leadership* (pp. 181–201). Hershey, PA: IGI Global. doi:10.4018/978-1-5225-1013-0.ch009

Naidoo, V., & Igbinakhase, I. (2018). Opportunities and Challenges of Knowledge Retention in SMEs. In N. Baporikar (Ed.), *Knowledge Integration Strategies for Entrepreneurship and Sustainability* (pp. 70–94). Hershey, PA: IGI Global. doi:10.4018/978-1-5225-5115-7.ch004

Naumov, N., & Costandachi, G. (2021). Creativity and Entrepreneurship: Gastronomic Tourism in Mexico. In J. Soares (Ed.), *Innovation and Entrepreneurial Opportunities in Community Tourism* (pp. 90–108). IGI Global. https://doi.org/10.4018/978-1-7998-4855-4.ch006

Nayak, S., & Prabhu, N. (2017). Paradigm Shift in Management Education: Need for a Cross Functional Perspective. In N. Baporikar (Ed.), *Management Education for Global Leadership* (pp. 241–255). Hershey, PA: IGI Global. doi:10.4018/978-1-5225-1013-0.ch012

Nedelko, Z., & Potocan, V. (2017). Management Solutions in Non-Profit Organizations: Case of Slovenia. In V. Potocan, M. Üngan, & Z. Nedelko (Eds.), *Handbook of Research on Managerial Solutions in Non-Profit Organizations* (pp. 1–22). Hershey, PA: IGI Global. doi:10.4018/978-1-5225-0731-4.ch001

Nedelko, Z., & Potocan, V. (2017). Priority of Management Tools Utilization among Managers: International Comparison. In V. Wang (Ed.), *Encyclopedia of Strategic Leadership and Management* (pp. 1083–1094). Hershey, PA: IGI Global. doi:10.4018/978-1-5225-1049-9.ch075

Nedelko, Z., Raudeliūnienė, J., & Črešnar, R. (2018). Knowledge Dynamics in Supply Chain Management. In N. Baporikar (Ed.), *Knowledge Integration Strategies for Entrepreneurship and Sustainability* (pp. 150–166). Hershey, PA: IGI Global. doi:10.4018/978-1-5225-5115-7.ch008

Nguyen, H. T., & Hipsher, S. A. (2018). Innovation and Creativity Used by Private Sector Firms in a Resources-Constrained Environment. In S. Hipsher (Ed.), *Examining the Private Sector's Role in Wealth Creation and Poverty Reduction* (pp. 219–238). Hershey, PA: IGI Global. doi:10.4018/978-1-5225-3117-3.ch010

Obicci, P. A. (2017). Risk Sharing in a Partnership. In *Risk Management Strategies in Public-Private Partnerships* (pp. 115–152). Hershey, PA: IGI Global. doi:10.4018/978-1-5225-2503-5.ch004

Obidallah, W. J., & Raahemi, B. (2017). Managing Changes in Service Oriented Virtual Organizations: A Structural and Procedural Framework to Facilitate the Process of Change. *Journal of Electronic Commerce in Organizations*, *15*(1), 59–83. doi:10.4018/JECO.2017010104

Ojo, O. (2017). Impact of Innovation on the Entrepreneurial Success in Selected Business Enterprises in South-West Nigeria. *International Journal of Innovation in the Digital Economy*, *8*(2), 29–38. doi:10.4018/IJIDE.2017040103

Okdinawati, L., Simatupang, T. M., & Sunitiyoso, Y. (2017). Multi-Agent Reinforcement Learning for Value Co-Creation of Collaborative Transportation Management (CTM). *International Journal of Information Systems and Supply Chain Management*, *10*(3), 84–95. doi:10.4018/IJISSCM.2017070105

Olivera, V. A., & Carrillo, I. M. (2021). Organizational Culture: A Key Element for the Development of Mexican Micro and Small Tourist Companies. In J. Soares (Ed.), *Innovation and Entrepreneurial Opportunities in Community Tourism* (pp. 227–242). IGI Global. doi:10.4018/978-1-7998-4855-4.ch013

Ossorio, M. (2022). Corporate Museum Experiences in Enogastronomic Tourism. In R. Augusto Costa, F. Brandão, Z. Breda, & C. Costa (Eds.), Planning and Managing the Experience Economy in Tourism (pp. 107-121). IGI Global. https://doi.org/doi:10.4018/978-1-7998-8775-1.ch006

Ossorio, M. (2022). Enogastronomic Tourism in Times of Pandemic. In G. Fernandes (Ed.), *Challenges and New Opportunities for Tourism in Inland Territories: Ecocultural Resources and Sustainable Initiatives* (pp. 241–255). IGI Global. https://doi.org/10.4018/978-1-7998-7339-6.ch014

Özekici, Y. K. (2022). ICT as an Acculturative Agent and Its Role in the Tourism Context: Introduction, Acculturation Theory, Progress of the Acculturation Theory in Extant Literature. In C. Ramos, S. Quinteiro, & A. Gonçalves (Eds.), *ICT as Innovator Between Tourism and Culture* (pp. 42–66). IGI Global. https://doi.org/10.4018/978-1-7998-8165-0.ch004

Pal, K. (2018). Building High Quality Big Data-Based Applications in Supply Chains. In A. Kumar & S. Saurav (Eds.), *Supply Chain Management Strategies and Risk Assessment in Retail Environments* (pp. 1–24). Hershey, PA: IGI Global. doi:10.4018/978-1-5225-3056-5.ch001

Palos-Sanchez, P. R., & Correia, M. B. (2018). Perspectives of the Adoption of Cloud Computing in the Tourism Sector. In J. Rodrigues, C. Ramos, P. Cardoso, & C. Henriques (Eds.), *Handbook of Research on Technological Developments for Cultural Heritage and eTourism Applications* (pp. 377–400). Hershey, PA: IGI Global. doi:10.4018/978-1-5225-2927-9.ch018

Papadopoulou, G. (2021). Promoting Gender Equality and Women Empowerment in the Tourism Sector. In F. Brandão, Z. Breda, R. Costa, & C. Costa (Eds.), Handbook of Research on the Role of Tourism in Achieving Sustainable Development Goals (pp. 152-174). IGI Global. https://doi.org/ doi:10.4018/978-1-7998-5691-7.ch009

Papp-Váry, Á. F., & Tóth, T. Z. (2022). Analysis of Budapest as a Film Tourism Destination. In R. Baleiro & R. Pereira (Eds.), *Global Perspectives on Literary Tourism and Film-Induced Tourism* (pp. 257-279). IGI Global. https://doi.org/10.4018/978-1-7998-8262-6.ch014

Patiño, B. E. (2017). New Generation Management by Convergence and Individual Identity: A Systemic and Human-Oriented Approach. In N. Baporikar (Ed.), *Innovation and Shifting Perspectives in Management Education* (pp. 119–143). Hershey, PA: IGI Global. doi:10.4018/978-1-5225-1019-2.ch006

Patro, C. S. (2021). Digital Tourism: Influence of E-Marketing Technology. In M. Dinis, L. Bonixe, S. Lamy, & Z. Breda (Eds.), *Impact of New Media in Tourism* (pp. 234-254). IGI Global. https://doi.org/10.4018/978-1-7998-7095-1.ch014

Pawliczek, A., & Rössler, M. (2017). Knowledge of Management Tools and Systems in SMEs: Knowledge Transfer in Management. In A. Bencsik (Ed.), *Knowledge Management Initiatives and Strategies in Small and Medium Enterprises* (pp. 180–203). Hershey, PA: IGI Global. doi:10.4018/978-1-5225-1642-2.ch009

Pejic-Bach, M., Omazic, M. A., Aleksic, A., & Zoroja, J. (2018). Knowledge-Based Decision Making: A Multi-Case Analysis. In R. Leon (Ed.), *Managerial Strategies for Business Sustainability During Turbulent Times* (pp. 160–184). Hershey, PA: IGI Global. doi:10.4018/978-1-5225-2716-9.ch009

Perano, M., Hysa, X., & Calabrese, M. (2018). Strategic Planning, Cultural Context, and Business Continuity Management: Business Cases in the City of Shkoder. In A. Presenza & L. Sheehan (Eds.), *Geopolitics and Strategic Management in the Global Economy* (pp. 57–77). Hershey, PA: IGI Global. doi:10.4018/978-1-5225-2673-5.ch004

Pereira, R., Mira da Silva, M., & Lapão, L. V. (2017). IT Governance Maturity Patterns in Portuguese Healthcare. In S. De Haes & W. Van Grembergen (Eds.), *Strategic IT Governance and Alignment in Business Settings* (pp. 24–52). Hershey, PA: IGI Global. doi:10.4018/978-1-5225-0861-8.ch002

Pérez-Uribe, R. I., Torres, D. A., Jurado, S. P., & Prada, D. M. (2018). Cloud Tools for the Development of Project Management in SMEs. In R. Perez-Uribe, C. Salcedo-Perez, & D. Ocampo-Guzman (Eds.), *Handbook of Research on Intrapreneurship and Organizational Sustainability in SMEs* (pp. 95–120). Hershey, PA: IGI Global. doi:10.4018/978-1-5225-3543-0.ch005

Petrisor, I., & Cozmiuc, D. (2017). Global Supply Chain Management Organization at Siemens in the Advent of Industry 4.0. In L. Saglietto & C. Cezanne (Eds.), *Global Intermediation and Logistics Service Providers* (pp. 123–142). Hershey, PA: IGI Global. doi:10.4018/978-1-5225-2133-4.ch007

Pierce, J. M., Velliaris, D. M., & Edwards, J. (2017). A Living Case Study: A Journey Not a Destination. In N. Silton (Ed.), *Exploring the Benefits of Creativity in Education, Media, and the Arts* (pp. 158–178). Hershey, PA: IGI Global. doi:10.4018/978-1-5225-0504-4.ch008

Pipia, S., & Pipia, S. (2021). Challenges of Religious Tourism in the Conflict Region: An Example of Jerusalem. In E. Alaverdov & M. Bari (Eds.), *Global Development of Religious Tourism* (pp. 135-148). IGI Global. https://doi.org/10.4018/978-1-7998-5792-1.ch009

Poulaki, P., Kritikos, A., Vasilakis, N., & Valeri, M. (2022). The Contribution of Female Creativity to the Development of Gastronomic Tourism in Greece: The Case of the Island of Naxos in the South Aegean Region. In M. Valeri (Ed.), *New Governance and Management in Touristic Destinations* (pp. 246–258). IGI Global. https://doi.org/10.4018/978-1-6684-3889-3.ch015

Radosavljevic, M., & Andjelkovic, A. (2017). Multi-Criteria Decision Making Approach for Choosing Business Process for the Improvement: Upgrading of the Six Sigma Methodology. In J. Stanković, P. Delias, S. Marinković, & S. Rochhia (Eds.), *Tools and Techniques for Economic Decision Analysis* (pp. 225–247). Hershey, PA: IGI Global. doi:10.4018/978-1-5225-0959-2.ch011

Radovic, V. M. (2017). Corporate Sustainability and Responsibility and Disaster Risk Reduction: A Serbian Overview. In M. Camilleri (Ed.), *CSR 2.0 and the New Era of Corporate Citizenship* (pp. 147–164). Hershey, PA: IGI Global. doi:10.4018/978-1-5225-1842-6.ch008

Raghunath, K. M., Devi, S. L., & Patro, C. S. (2018). Impact of Risk Assessment Models on Risk Factors: A Holistic Outlook. In K. Strang, M. Korstanje, & N. Vajjhala (Eds.), *Research, Practices, and Innovations in Global Risk and Contingency Management* (pp. 134–153). Hershey, PA: IGI Global. doi:10.4018/978-1-5225-4754-9.ch008

Raman, A., & Goyal, D. P. (2017). Extending IMPLEMENT Framework for Enterprise Information Systems Implementation to Information System Innovation. In M. Tavana (Ed.), *Enterprise Information Systems and the Digitalization of Business Functions* (pp. 137–177). Hershey, PA: IGI Global. doi:10.4018/978-1-5225-2382-6.ch007

Rao, Y., & Zhang, Y. (2017). The Construction and Development of Academic Library Digital Special Subject Databases. In L. Ruan, Q. Zhu, & Y. Ye (Eds.), *Academic Library Development and Administration in China* (pp. 163–183). Hershey, PA: IGI Global. doi:10.4018/978-1-5225-0550-1.ch010

Ravasan, A. Z., Mohammadi, M. M., & Hamidi, H. (2018). An Investigation Into the Critical Success Factors of Implementing Information Technology Service Management Frameworks. In K. Jakobs (Ed.), *Corporate and Global Standardization Initiatives in Contemporary Society* (pp. 200–218). Hershey, PA: IGI Global. doi:10.4018/978-1-5225-5320-5.ch009

Rezaie, S., Mirabedini, S. J., & Abtahi, A. (2018). Designing a Model for Implementation of Business Intelligence in the Banking Industry. *International Journal of Enterprise Information Systems*, *14*(1), 77–103. doi:10.4018/IJEIS.2018010105

Richards, V., Matthews, N., Williams, O. J., & Khan, Z. (2021). The Challenges of Accessible Tourism Information Systems for Tourists With Vision Impairment: Sensory Communications Beyond the Screen. In C. Eusébio, L. Teixeira, & M. Carneiro (Eds.), *ICT Tools and Applications for Accessible Tourism* (pp. 26–54). IGI Global. https://doi.org/10.4018/978-1-7998-6428-8.ch002

Rodrigues de Souza Neto, V., & Marques, O. (2021). Rural Tourism Fostering Welfare Through Sustainable Development: A Conceptual Approach. In A. Perinotto, V. Mayer, & J. Soares (Eds.), *Rebuilding and Restructuring the Tourism Industry: Infusion of Happiness and Quality of Life* (pp. 38–57). IGI Global. https://doi.org/10.4018/978-1-7998-7239-9.ch003

Romano, L., Grimaldi, R., & Colasuonno, F. S. (2017). Demand Management as a Success Factor in Project Portfolio Management. In L. Romano (Ed.), *Project Portfolio Management Strategies for Effective Organizational Operations* (pp. 202–219). Hershey, PA: IGI Global. doi:10.4018/978-1-5225-2151-8.ch008

Rubio-Escuderos, L., & García-Andreu, H. (2021). Competitiveness Factors of Accessible Tourism E-Travel Agencies. In C. Eusébio, L. Teixeira, & M. Carneiro (Eds.), *ICT Tools and Applications for Accessible Tourism* (pp. 196–217). IGI Global. https://doi.org/10.4018/978-1-7998-6428-8.ch009

Rucci, A. C., Porto, N., Darcy, S., & Becka, L. (2021). Smart and Accessible Cities?: Not Always – The Case for Accessible Tourism Initiatives in Buenos Aries and Sydney. In C. Eusébio, L. Teixeira, & M. Carneiro (Eds.), *ICT Tools and Applications for Accessible Tourism* (pp. 115–145). IGI Global. https://doi.org/10.4018/978-1-7998-6428-8.ch006

Ruhi, U. (2018). Towards an Interdisciplinary Socio-Technical Definition of Virtual Communities. In M. Khosrow-Pour, D.B.A. (Ed.), Encyclopedia of Information Science and Technology, Fourth Edition (pp. 4278-4295). Hershey, PA: IGI Global. doi:10.4018/978-1-5225-2255-3.ch371

Ryan, L., Catena, M., Ros, P., & Stephens, S. (2021). Designing Entrepreneurial Ecosystems to Support Resource Management in the Tourism Industry. In V. Costa, A. Moura, & M. Mira (Eds.), *Handbook of Research on Human Capital and People Management in the Tourism Industry* (pp. 265–281). IGI Global. https://doi.org/10.4018/978-1-7998-4318-4.ch013

Sabuncu, I. (2021). Understanding Tourist Perceptions and Expectations During Pandemic Through Social Media Big Data. In M. Demir, A. Dalgıç, & F. Ergen (Eds.), *Handbook of Research on the Impacts and Implications of COVID-19 on the Tourism Industry* (pp. 330–350). IGI Global. https://doi.org/10.4018/978-1-7998-8231-2.ch016

Safari, M. R., & Jiang, Q. (2018). The Theory and Practice of IT Governance Maturity and Strategies Alignment: Evidence From Banking Industry. *Journal of Global Information Management, 26*(2), 127–146. doi:10.4018/JGIM.2018040106

Sahoo, J., Pati, B., & Mohanty, B. (2017). Knowledge Management as an Academic Discipline: An Assessment. In B. Gunjal (Ed.), *Managing Knowledge and Scholarly Assets in Academic Libraries* (pp. 99–126). Hershey, PA: IGI Global. doi:10.4018/978-1-5225-1741-2.ch005

Saini, D. (2017). Relevance of Teaching Values and Ethics in Management Education. In N. Baporikar (Ed.), *Management Education for Global Leadership* (pp. 90–111). Hershey, PA: IGI Global. doi:10.4018/978-1-5225-1013-0.ch005

Sambhanthan, A. (2017). Assessing and Benchmarking Sustainability in Organisations: An Integrated Conceptual Model. *International Journal of Systems and Service-Oriented Engineering*, *7*(4), 22–43. doi:10.4018/IJSSOE.2017100102

Sambhanthan, A., & Potdar, V. (2017). A Study of the Parameters Impacting Sustainability in Information Technology Organizations. *International Journal of Knowledge-Based Organizations*, *7*(3), 27–39. doi:10.4018/IJKBO.2017070103

Sánchez-Fernández, M. D., & Manríquez, M. R. (2018). The Entrepreneurial Spirit Based on Social Values: The Digital Generation. In P. Isaias & L. Carvalho (Eds.), *User Innovation and the Entrepreneurship Phenomenon in the Digital Economy* (pp. 173–193). Hershey, PA: IGI Global. doi:10.4018/978-1-5225-2826-5.ch009

Sanchez-Ruiz, L., & Blanco, B. (2017). Process Management for SMEs: Barriers, Enablers, and Benefits. In M. Vemić (Ed.), *Optimal Management Strategies in Small and Medium Enterprises* (pp. 293–319). Hershey, PA: IGI Global. doi:10.4018/978-1-5225-1949-2.ch014

Sanz, L. F., Gómez-Pérez, J., & Castillo-Martinez, A. (2018). Analysis of the European ICT Competence Frameworks. In V. Ahuja & S. Rathore (Eds.), *Multidisciplinary Perspectives on Human Capital and Information Technology Professionals* (pp. 225–245). Hershey, PA: IGI Global. doi:10.4018/978-1-5225-5297-0.ch012

Sarvepalli, A., & Godin, J. (2017). Business Process Management in the Classroom. *Journal of Cases on Information Technology*, *19*(2), 17–28. doi:10.4018/JCIT.2017040102

Saxena, G. G., & Saxena, A. (2021). Host Community Role in Medical Tourism Development. In M. Singh & S. Kumaran (Eds.), *Growth of the Medical Tourism Industry and Its Impact on Society: Emerging Research and Opportunities* (pp. 105–127). IGI Global. https://doi.org/10.4018/978-1-7998-3427-4.ch006

Saygili, E. E., Ozturkoglu, Y., & Kocakulah, M. C. (2017). End Users' Perceptions of Critical Success Factors in ERP Applications. *International Journal of Enterprise Information Systems*, *13*(4), 58–75. doi:10.4018/IJEIS.2017100104

Saygili, E. E., & Saygili, A. T. (2017). Contemporary Issues in Enterprise Information Systems: A Critical Review of CSFs in ERP Implementations. In M. Tavana (Ed.), *Enterprise Information Systems and the Digitalization of Business Functions* (pp. 120–136). Hershey, PA: IGI Global. doi:10.4018/978-1-5225-2382-6.ch006

Schwaiger, K. M., & Zehrer, A. (2021). The COVID-19 Pandemic and Organizational Resilience in Hospitality Family Firms: A Qualitative Approach. In A. Zehrer, G. Glowka, K. Schwaiger, & V. Ranacher-Lackner (Eds.), *Resiliency Models and Addressing Future Risks for Family Firms in the Tourism Industry* (pp. 32–49). IGI Global. https://doi.org/10.4018/978-1-7998-7352-5.ch002

Scott, N., & Campos, A. C. (2022). Cognitive Science of Tourism Experiences. In R. Augusto Costa, F. Brandão, Z. Breda, & C. Costa (Eds.), Planning and Managing the Experience Economy in Tourism (pp. 1-21). IGI Global. https://doi.org/ doi:10.4018/978-1-7998-8775-1.ch001

Seidenstricker, S., & Antonino, A. (2018). Business Model Innovation-Oriented Technology Management for Emergent Technologies. In M. Khosrow-Pour, D.B.A. (Ed.), Encyclopedia of Information Science and Technology, Fourth Edition (pp. 4560-4569). Hershey, PA: IGI Global. doi:10.4018/978-1-5225-2255-3.ch396

Selvi, M. S. (2021). Changes in Tourism Sales and Marketing Post COVID-19. In M. Demir, A. Dalgıç, & F. Ergen (Eds.), *Handbook of Research on the Impacts and Implications of COVID-19 on the Tourism Industry* (pp. 437–460). IGI Global. doi:10.4018/978-1-7998-8231-2.ch021

Senaratne, S., & Gunarathne, A. D. (2017). Excellence Perspective for Management Education from a Global Accountants' Hub in Asia. In N. Baporikar (Ed.), *Management Education for Global Leadership* (pp. 158–180). Hershey, PA: IGI Global. doi:10.4018/978-1-5225-1013-0.ch008

Sensuse, D. I., & Cahyaningsih, E. (2018). Knowledge Management Models: A Summative Review. *International Journal of Information Systems in the Service Sector, 10*(1), 71–100. doi:10.4018/IJISSS.2018010105

Seth, M., Goyal, D., & Kiran, R. (2017). Diminution of Impediments in Implementation of Supply Chain Management Information System for Enhancing its Effectiveness in Indian Automobile Industry. *Journal of Global Information Management, 25*(3), 1–20. doi:10.4018/JGIM.2017070101

Seyal, A. H., & Rahman, M. N. (2017). Investigating Impact of Inter-Organizational Factors in Measuring ERP Systems Success: Bruneian Perspectives. In M. Tavana (Ed.), *Enterprise Information Systems and the Digitalization of Business Functions* (pp. 178–204). Hershey, PA: IGI Global. doi:10.4018/978-1-5225-2382-6.ch008

Shaqrah, A. A. (2018). Analyzing Business Intelligence Systems Based on 7s Model of McKinsey. *International Journal of Business Intelligence Research, 9*(1), 53–63. doi:10.4018/IJBIR.2018010104

Sharma, A. J. (2017). Enhancing Sustainability through Experiential Learning in Management Education. In N. Baporikar (Ed.), *Management Education for Global Leadership* (pp. 256–274). Hershey, PA: IGI Global. doi:10.4018/978-1-5225-1013-0.ch013

Shetty, K. P. (2017). Responsible Global Leadership: Ethical Challenges in Management Education. In N. Baporikar (Ed.), *Innovation and Shifting Perspectives in Management Education* (pp. 194–223). Hershey, PA: IGI Global. doi:10.4018/978-1-5225-1019-2.ch009

Sinthupundaja, J., & Kohda, Y. (2017). Effects of Corporate Social Responsibility and Creating Shared Value on Sustainability. *International Journal of Sustainable Entrepreneurship and Corporate Social Responsibility*, *2*(1), 27–38. doi:10.4018/IJSECSR.2017010103

Škarica, I., & Hrgović, A. V. (2018). Implementation of Total Quality Management Principles in Public Health Institutes in the Republic of Croatia. *International Journal of Productivity Management and Assessment Technologies*, *6*(1), 1–16. doi:10.4018/IJPMAT.2018010101

Skokic, V. (2021). How Small Hotel Owners Practice Resilience: Longitudinal Study Among Small Family Hotels in Croatia. In A. Zehrer, G. Glowka, K. Schwaiger, & V. Ranacher-Lackner (Eds.), *Resiliency Models and Addressing Future Risks for Family Firms in the Tourism Industry* (pp. 50–73). IGI Global. doi:10.4018/978-1-7998-7352-5.ch003

Smuts, H., Kotzé, P., Van der Merwe, A., & Loock, M. (2017). Framework for Managing Shared Knowledge in an Information Systems Outsourcing Context. *International Journal of Knowledge Management*, *13*(4), 1–30. doi:10.4018/IJKM.2017100101

Sousa, M. J., Cruz, R., Dias, I., & Caracol, C. (2017). Information Management Systems in the Supply Chain. In G. Jamil, A. Soares, & C. Pessoa (Eds.), *Handbook of Research on Information Management for Effective Logistics and Supply Chains* (pp. 469–485). Hershey, PA: IGI Global. doi:10.4018/978-1-5225-0973-8.ch025

Spremic, M., Turulja, L., & Bajgoric, N. (2018). Two Approaches in Assessing Business Continuity Management Attitudes in the Organizational Context. In N. Bajgoric (Ed.), *Always-On Enterprise Information Systems for Modern Organizations* (pp. 159–183). Hershey, PA: IGI Global. doi:10.4018/978-1-5225-3704-5.ch008

Steenkamp, A. L. (2018). Some Insights in Computer Science and Information Technology. In *Examining the Changing Role of Supervision in Doctoral Research Projects: Emerging Research and Opportunities* (pp. 113–133). Hershey, PA: IGI Global. doi:10.4018/978-1-5225-2610-0.ch005

Stipanović, C., Rudan, E., & Zubović, V. (2022). Reaching the New Tourist Through Creativity: Sustainable Development Challenges in Croatian Coastal Towns. In M. Valeri (Ed.), *New Governance and Management in Touristic Destinations* (pp. 231–245). IGI Global. https://doi.org/10.4018/978-1-6684-3889-3.ch014

Tabach, A., & Croteau, A. (2017). Configurations of Information Technology Governance Practices and Business Unit Performance. *International Journal of IT/Business Alignment and Governance*, *8*(2), 1–27. doi:10.4018/IJITBAG.2017070101

Talaue, G. M., & Iqbal, T. (2017). Assessment of e-Business Mode of Selected Private Universities in the Philippines and Pakistan. *International Journal of Online Marketing*, *7*(4), 63–77. doi:10.4018/IJOM.2017100105

Tam, G. C. (2017). Project Manager Sustainability Competence. In *Managerial Strategies and Green Solutions for Project Sustainability* (pp. 178–207). Hershey, PA: IGI Global. doi:10.4018/978-1-5225-2371-0.ch008

Tambo, T. (2018). Fashion Retail Innovation: About Context, Antecedents, and Outcome in Technological Change Projects. In I. Management Association (Ed.), Fashion and Textiles: Breakthroughs in Research and Practice (pp. 233-260). Hershey, PA: IGI Global. https://doi.org/ doi:10.4018/978-1-5225-3432-7.ch010

Tantau, A. D., & Frăţilă, L. C. (2018). Information and Management System for Renewable Energy Business. In *Entrepreneurship and Business Development in the Renewable Energy Sector* (pp. 200–244). Hershey, PA: IGI Global. doi:10.4018/978-1-5225-3625-3.ch006

Teixeira, N., Pardal, P. N., & Rafael, B. G. (2018). Internationalization, Financial Performance, and Organizational Challenges: A Success Case in Portugal. In L. Carvalho (Ed.), *Handbook of Research on Entrepreneurial Ecosystems and Social Dynamics in a Globalized World* (pp. 379–423). Hershey, PA: IGI Global. doi:10.4018/978-1-5225-3525-6.ch017

Teixeira, P., Teixeira, L., Eusébio, C., Silva, S., & Teixeira, A. (2021). The Impact of ICTs on Accessible Tourism: Evidence Based on a Systematic Literature Review. In C. Eusébio, L. Teixeira, & M. Carneiro (Eds.), *ICT Tools and Applications for Accessible Tourism* (pp. 1–25). IGI Global. doi:10.4018/978-1-7998-6428-8.ch001

Trad, A., & Kalpić, D. (2018). The Business Transformation Framework, Agile Project and Change Management. In M. Khosrow-Pour, D.B.A. (Ed.), Encyclopedia of Information Science and Technology, Fourth Edition (pp. 620-635). Hershey, PA: IGI Global. https://doi.org/ doi:10.4018/978-1-5225-2255-3.ch054

Trad, A., & Kalpić, D. (2018). The Business Transformation and Enterprise Architecture Framework: The Financial Engineering E-Risk Management and E-Law Integration. In B. Sergi, F. Fidanoski, M. Ziolo, & V. Naumovski (Eds.), *Regaining Global Stability After the Financial Crisis* (pp. 46–65). Hershey, PA: IGI Global. doi:10.4018/978-1-5225-4026-7.ch003

Trengereid, V. (2022). Conditions of Network Engagement: The Quest for a Common Good. In R. Augusto Costa, F. Brandão, Z. Breda, & C. Costa (Eds.), *Planning and Managing the Experience Economy in Tourism* (pp. 69-84). IGI Global. https://doi.org/10.4018/978-1-7998-8775-1.ch004

Turulja, L., & Bajgoric, N. (2018). Business Continuity and Information Systems: A Systematic Literature Review. In N. Bajgoric (Ed.), *Always-On Enterprise Information Systems for Modern Organizations* (pp. 60–87). Hershey, PA: IGI Global. doi:10.4018/978-1-5225-3704-5.ch004

Vargas-Hernández, J. G. (2017). Professional Integrity in Business Management Education. In N. Baporikar (Ed.), *Management Education for Global Leadership* (pp. 70–89). Hershey, PA: IGI Global. doi:10.4018/978-1-5225-1013-0.ch004

Varnacı Uzun, F. (2021). The Destination Preferences of Foreign Tourists During the COVID-19 Pandemic and Attitudes Towards: Marmaris, Turkey. In M. Demir, A. Dalgıç, & F. Ergen (Eds.), *Handbook of Research on the Impacts and Implications of COVID-19 on the Tourism Industry* (pp. 285–306). IGI Global. https://doi.org/10.4018/978-1-7998-8231-2.ch014

Vasista, T. G., & AlAbdullatif, A. M. (2017). Role of Electronic Customer Relationship Management in Demand Chain Management: A Predictive Analytic Approach. *International Journal of Information Systems and Supply Chain Management, 10*(1), 53–67. doi:10.4018/IJISSCM.2017010104

Vieru, D., & Bourdeau, S. (2017). Survival in the Digital Era: A Digital Competence-Based Multi-Case Study in the Canadian SME Clothing Industry. *International Journal of Social and Organizational Dynamics in IT, 6*(1), 17–34. doi:10.4018/IJSODIT.2017010102

Vijayan, G., & Kamarulzaman, N. H. (2017). An Introduction to Sustainable Supply Chain Management and Business Implications. In M. Khan, M. Hussain, & M. Ajmal (Eds.), *Green Supply Chain Management for Sustainable Business Practice* (pp. 27–50). Hershey, PA: IGI Global. doi:10.4018/978-1-5225-0635-5.ch002

Vlachvei, A., & Notta, O. (2017). Firm Competitiveness: Theories, Evidence, and Measurement. In A. Vlachvei, O. Notta, K. Karantininis, & N. Tsounis (Eds.), *Factors Affecting Firm Competitiveness and Performance in the Modern Business World* (pp. 1–42). Hershey, PA: IGI Global. doi:10.4018/978-1-5225-0843-4.ch001

Wang, C., Schofield, M., Li, X., & Ou, X. (2017). Do Chinese Students in Public and Private Higher Education Institutes Perform at Different Level in One of the Leadership Skills: Critical Thinking?: An Exploratory Comparison. In V. Wang (Ed.), *Encyclopedia of Strategic Leadership and Management* (pp. 160–181). Hershey, PA: IGI Global. doi:10.4018/978-1-5225-1049-9.ch013

Wang, J. (2017). Multi-Agent based Production Management Decision System Modelling for the Textile Enterprise. *Journal of Global Information Management, 25*(4), 1–15. doi:10.4018/JGIM.2017100101

Wiedemann, A., & Gewald, H. (2017). Examining Cross-Domain Alignment: The Correlation of Business Strategy, IT Management, and IT Business Value. *International Journal of IT/Business Alignment and Governance, 8*(1), 17–31. doi:10.4018/IJITBAG.2017010102

Wolf, R., & Thiel, M. (2018). Advancing Global Business Ethics in China: Reducing Poverty Through Human and Social Welfare. In S. Hipsher (Ed.), *Examining the Private Sector's Role in Wealth Creation and Poverty Reduction* (pp. 67–84). Hershey, PA: IGI Global. doi:10.4018/978-1-5225-3117-3.ch004

Yablonsky, S. (2018). Innovation Platforms: Data and Analytics Platforms. In *Multi-Sided Platforms (MSPs) and Sharing Strategies in the Digital Economy: Emerging Research and Opportunities* (pp. 72–95). Hershey, PA: IGI Global. doi:10.4018/978-1-5225-5457-8.ch003

Yaşar, B. (2021). The Impact of COVID-19 on Volatility of Tourism Stocks: Evidence From BIST Tourism Index. In M. Demir, A. Dalgıç, & F. Ergen (Eds.), *Handbook of Research on the Impacts and Implications of COVID-19 on the Tourism Industry* (pp. 23–44). IGI Global. https://doi.org/10.4018/978-1-7998-8231-2.ch002

Yusoff, A., Ahmad, N. H., & Halim, H. A. (2017). Agropreneurship among Gen Y in Malaysia: The Role of Academic Institutions. In N. Ahmad, T. Ramayah, H. Halim, & S. Rahman (Eds.), *Handbook of Research on Small and Medium Enterprises in Developing Countries* (pp. 23–47). Hershey, PA: IGI Global. doi:10.4018/978-1-5225-2165-5.ch002

Zacher, D., & Pechlaner, H. (2021). Resilience as an Opportunity Approach: Challenges and Perspectives for Private Sector Participation on a Community Level. In A. Zehrer, G. Glowka, K. Schwaiger, & V. Ranacher-Lackner (Eds.), *Resiliency Models and Addressing Future Risks for Family Firms in the Tourism Industry* (pp. 75–102). IGI Global. https://doi.org/10.4018/978-1-7998-7352-5.ch004

Zanin, F., Comuzzi, E., & Costantini, A. (2018). The Effect of Business Strategy and Stock Market Listing on the Use of Risk Assessment Tools. In *Management Control Systems in Complex Settings: Emerging Research and Opportunities* (pp. 145–168). Hershey, PA: IGI Global. doi:10.4018/978-1-5225-3987-2.ch007

Zgheib, P. W. (2017). Corporate Innovation and Intrapreneurship in the Middle East. In P. Zgheib (Ed.), *Entrepreneurship and Business Innovation in the Middle East* (pp. 37–56). Hershey, PA: IGI Global. doi:10.4018/978-1-5225-2066-5.ch003

About the Contributors

Satish Chandra Bagri was working as Professor of Tourism Management at HNB Garhwal Central University, Uttarakhand till August 2021 and presently associated with Centre for Tourism and Hospitality Training and Research Dehradun as a Professor. Prof Bagri carries a 41 years of teaching and research experience in tourism and has published more than 60 research papers and 8 books besides his recent publication on " Global Opportunities and Challenges for Rural and Mountain Tourism, published by IGI Global, New York. He was the Editor in Chief of a biannual research Journal of Tourism and had also worked with Indian Institute of Tourism and Travel Management Gwalior as professor from 1995-98 running under the Ministry of Tourism, Govt. of India and Vice Chancellor of Himgiri Zee University, Dehradun from 2012 to 2015.He had also held the position of consultant of United Nations World Tourism Organization (UNWTO), Madrid for a year duration and was one of the members UNWTO team designed the Tourism Master plans of Punjab as well as the Coastal Tourism Development Plan of West Bengal state of India in 2007-08. Dr Bagri was also the team leader of a research project on "Off Beat Tourism Destinations for Ecotourism promotion in Uttarakhand State of India " sponsored by GTZ Germany. He was given the responsibility to act as a Coordinator of the Cost Effective and Eco - friendly Tourism in the Himalayan States, which was one of the themes of ." A Study of Indian Himalayan Region (IHR) research project undertaken by the consortium of the Central Universities of Indian Himalayan States (IHCUC)Under the supervision of the NITI Aayog, Govt of India in 2020. In this project Prof S.C. Bagri supervised a team of 25 tourism faculty members of 11 central Universities of the Himalayan states. He is also Honorary Member of the Indian National Commission for Cooperation with UNESCO from 2020 to 2024.

R. K. Dhodi is an Associate Professor at the Centre for Mountain Tourism and Hospitality Studies, HNB Garhwal Central University. He is also an Associate Editor of UGC Approved Journal (Journal of Tourism, ISSN: 0972-7310). He has over 25 years of teaching and research experience in tourism and management. His research interests and field studies focus on responsible tourism, community-based tourism and social entrepreneurship in Uttarakhand, especially in rural villages of the Uttarkashi region relying on tourism and hospitality activities for livelihood. He has authored several research papers in peer-reviewed indexed journals and is currently working on an international Edited Book titled `Entrepreneurship Education in Tourism and Hospitality Management' published by IGI Global, Pennsylvania, USA. He has been invited as an expert to many international and national level conferences, workshops and seminars. Moreover, he has guided many eminent scholars, management professionals and social leaders.

K. C. Junaid is a sociocultural anthropologist, and Junior Research Fellow at the Center for Mountain Tourism and Hospitality Studies, HNB Garhwal Central University. He holds a Master's degree in both Tourism Management and Anthropology from Pondicherry University. His research interests focus on Social Entrepreneurship in tourism, Community-driven tourism planning and HRD in the Tourism sector. Specialized in ethnography, netnographic techniques and currently focused on 'Tourism and Education/HRD in the Malabar region of Kerala'. He has authored several research papers in peer-reviewed journals and presented research results in international and national level conferences and seminars.

* * *

Suresh Babu Anbalagan works as assistant professor of tourism in Government Arts College, Ooty, The Nilgris Tamil Nadu for the past 11 years, involved in teaching and research. Dr. Babu started teaching as Guest Faculty at Centre for Mountain Tourism and Hospitality Studies (CMTHS), HNB Garhwal University, Srinagar Garhwal Uttrakhand India before taking up the present assignment. He has completed his doctoral program from HNB Garhwal Central University (HNBGU), Uttarakhand and also holds UGC-NET. He served as project assistant at CMTHS-HNBGU and involved in various research projects under the guidance of Prof. S.C.Bagri. He has successfully completed couple of minor projects funded by Tamil Nadu state Council for Higher Education (TANSCHE) and has 15 research papers in both domestic and international journal to his credit. He has actively served as a guest editor of Journal of Tourism for 3 issues and continue to be the managing editor of Journal of Tourism. His areas of interest include Mountain Tourism, Hospitality and Destination Planning.

Aarti Dangwal is a PhD holder in Management. She is working as an Assistant Professor with the University School of Business, Department of Commerce, Chandigarh University, Gharuan, Punjab. Her research areas are Tourism, Finance and Business, etc.

M. R. Dileep is a noted tourism academic, author, and columnist. He is working as a Vice-Principal at Pazhassiraja College, University of Calicut, Kerala, India. In addition to having a number of research publications and conference presentations, his latest books ('Tourism, Transport, and Travel Management' and 'Air Transport and Tourism: Interrelationship, Operations and Strategies') are published by Routledge (Taylor & Francis). Furthermore, he was one of the contributors in the 'Encyclopedia of Tourism' published by Springer, New York.

Maheshika Dissanayake is a Senior Lecturer attached to the Department of Tourism and Hospitality Management, Faculty of Management Studies, Rajarata University of Sri Lanka Specialised in Hospitality Management, Events Management, And Tourism and Hospitality Marketing.

Unathi Sonwabile Henama is a specialist in disruptive technology and teaches marketing in tourism at the Central University of Technology, Free State. He has published extensively and presented paper at local and international conferences.

Agnes Historia holds an MBA and Tourism Degree from PUP and EARIST, Philippines. She was a former Tourism Lecturer at Gondar University and Adama Science and Technology University, Ethiopia. She facilitates with the Ethiopian Aviation Academy on Sabre Orientation and Mock Tour Guiding as part of Tourism Simulation. She was a TVET Capacitator for Tourism Education and Industry in Ethiopia. She had been teaching in the higher education for 21 years. Currently, she was a Tourism Instructor at Cavite State University, Silang, Philippines.

Bonface O. Kihima holds a PhD and Msc. in Tourism Management from the University of Lyon 2 in France. His areas of research interest include Ecotourism, Community Based Tourism, Beach Tourism, Destination Management, Marketing and Tourism Education. He is a member of the Eco-rating committee of the Ecotourism Kenya as well as the Tourism Professional Association in Kenya. He has 15 years of University teaching and supervision of post graduate students in the area of Tourism. He has published widely in the area of tourism and is actively involved in tourism consultancy. Currently, he is an Associate Professor of Tourism and Travel Management, the Academic Team Leader and Chair Hospitality and Leisure Studies of the Technical University of Kenya.

Maximiliano E. Korstanje is editor in chief of International Journal of Safety and Security in Tourism (UP Argentina) and Editor in Chief Emeritus of International Journal of Cyber Warfare and Terrorism (IGI-Global US). Korstanje is Senior Researchers in the Department of Economics at University of Palermo, Argentina. In 2015 he was awarded as Visiting Research Fellow at School of Sociology and Social Policy, University of Leeds, UK and the University of La Habana Cuba. In 2017 is elected as Foreign Faculty Member of AMIT, Mexican Academy in the study of Tourism, which is the most prominent institutions dedicated to tourism research in Mexico. He had a vast experience in editorial projects working as advisory member of Elsevier, Routledge, Springer, IGI global and Cambridge Scholar publishing. Korstanje had visited and given seminars in many important universities worldwide. He has also recently been selected to take part of the 2018 Albert Nelson Marquis Lifetime Achievement Award. a great distinction given by Marquis Who´s Who in the world.

Mohit Kukreti holds a PhD in HRD and MTA in Tourism Management from the HNBGU India. He is the former Head of Tourism Department, Gondar University, Ethiopia; Program Director with the DG Colleges of Applied Sciences, Ministry of Higher Education, Oman. He has 23 years of university teaching experience and presently, associated with the University of Technology and Applied Sciences, Oman.

Nadezhda Anatolievna Lebedeva is a Doctor of Philosophy in the field of Cultural Studies, professor of the International Personnel Academy (Kyiv, Ukraine), works at the Kherson State Agrarian and Economic University, full member of the Eurasian Academy of Television and Radio. She is the author of more than 100 scientific articles. The focus of her research is the cultural and social aspects of regional development. She graduated from the Kherson State Pedagogical Institute in 1996. After graduating from the postgraduate course at the Kherson State University, became a lecturer at the History of World Culture and Literature Department of the Kherson State University. In June 2008 was enrolled in the doctoral program of the Interregional Academy of Personnel Management in Kyiv, specializing in Cultural Studies. She was awarded the medal "For Civil Courage" of the Afghan Veterans' Ukrainian Union for the book "My Afghan" by Nikolay Vishnyak". Participation in the creation of documentary films and scientific articles are marked by membership in the Eurasian Academy of Television and Radio (November 2012). The monograph "Cultural Aspect of Alexander Elagin'sCreativeness" was awarded by the 1-st place in scientific direction "Cultural Studies" in 2017 and became the winner of the competition for educational projects "Interclover - 2017" in the nomination – "Research Project".

Lebogang Matholwane Mathole is a tourism management, business management and marketing lecturer at the Tshwane University of Technology, South Africa. She holds a Master's Degree which specializes in Digital Marketing. Lebogang is currently pursuing an inter-disciplinary doctoral research which focuses on entrepreneurship, consumer psychology and local economic development (LED). She has presented papers at several conferences and is growing as a researcher by publishing in journals and book chapters.

Ananya Mitra, PhD, MSc, MATM, PGD-HRM, is a dynamic, well disciplined, highly motivated teaching professional with 13 years of achievements and success, demonstrated in the field of teaching Postgraduate, Graduate, Diploma, Certificate and Vocational courses. A Authored a book for Cambridge Scholars Publishing; UK ISBN 978-1-5275-1379-2 A Co-authored 5 Books (with ISBN numbers) for various publications A Authored and co-authored research papers for various national & international journals. A Participated and presented paper in 2 International Level & 13 National Level Seminars. A Successfully completed editorial and translation work of five books in a span of six months, acting as an efficient Subject head in a publishing house. A Member of Advisory Committee to the 2nd International Conference on Contemporary Development in Business- 2016 organized by Academic Research in Science, Engineering, Art & Management (ARSEAM) Foundation on 28th May 2016. A Served as exclusive Member of BOS (Board of Studies) for- Jyoti Nivas College (Autonomous)and BOE (Board of Examiners) for- Jyoti Nivas College, Bangalore University, NSOU and Mysore University; One of the youngest to be invited for question paper set up at university level. A Participated and Presented paper in the young scholar award, during the prestigious 31st IIG Meet and International Conference On: Environment, Agriculture and Food Security, Feb-2010. Won lots of accolades from the participating delegates and dignitaries. A Holds 3rd Rank in Bangalore University for M.Sc. (Geography).

Mohammed Ali Ahmed Obaid is an Associate Professor in Tourism Studies, Faculty of Tourism and Hotels, Fayoum University, Egypt. He is currently working as an Assistant Professor at the Department of Business Administration, University of Technology and Applied Sciences (UTAS), Nizwa Branch, Sultanate of Oman.

María Alejandra Zuccoli is Professor of the University of Palermo, Argentina and the University of Salvador, Argentina. Zuccoli is the director of the Joy Labs at the University of Palermo, Argentina. Besides, she was distinguished as innovator of method ALTAX to improve human hospitality applying neuromarketing to education.

Index

K

L

M

N

O

P

Q

R

S

T

U

V